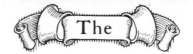

The

RED BOOK of FRUIT JARS

№ 3

AN ILLUSTRATED PRICE GUIDE LISTING OVER 3100 JARS

Printed by IMAGE GRAPHICS, Paducah, Kentucky

Introduction

10
YEARS OF SERVICE

1967   1977

With the publication of our new books, 1977 marks the 10th year we have been involved in the writing of fruit jar books. This seems a good occasion to look back and very briefly reminisce on the fruit jar collecting hobby, and how it has grown during the past ten years.

In 1966, the hobby was still in its infancy. Undoubtedly there were collectors who had been collecting jars for years prior to this, but the hobby was not widely known, and for the majority of today's collectors, interest in the hobby seems to date within the last ten or twelve year period.

In 1967, we listed about 400 jars with the most valued being, the R. M. Dalbey's Fruit Jar, the profile Lafayette, the Gilberds, and the Van Vliet Jar of 1881. In 1969, our first price guide, the Cresrod Blue Book, listed 1035 jars, with the highest priced jar listed being the Van Vliet jar, valued at $75-100. By 1973, the Red Book of Fruit Jars No. 2, listed 1654 jars. The Van Vliet (in aqua) was still a popular jar and now priced at $250 and up, but many rare jars had been reported and the Van Vliet was no longer the highest priced jar listed. Among the aqua jars, the Wm. Pogue jar now held the spotlight with the value listed at $500. The Pogue jar was followed closely by such jars as the Ramsay, the Ravenna Glass Works barrel, and the J. J. Squire jars. Nearly all of the older jars had advanced in value. The jars in rare colors such as the black jars, the cobalt blue Millville, and the amber Van Vliet, were all priced at $500.

By April 1977, the cutoff date for entries in "Fruit Jars" and "The Red Book of Fruit Jars No. 3", the number of jars reported to us had grown to over 3100 (over 4100 if we were to count colors separately). Of course, this includes jars which are variations, but also includes a large number of jars which are one of a kind, or of which only a very few are known. The number of known jars had increased nearly double in 4 years! This would indicate that there are still rare jars waiting to be discovered, and that the hobby is indeed, very much alive and flourishing.

As the number of jars grows, the task of listing a value on these jars, becomes an increasingly difficult one. How, for instance, can one place a value on a one-of-a-kind jar? With the help of the owners, we have attempted to place a value on some, but on jars such as these, we feel the price is really best determined between the buyer and seller. Such jars are rarely offered for sale, and in most cases, the owner has turned down offers much higher than a price which could be listed in a price guide.

We owe a debt of gratitude to the knowledgeable collectors in various parts of the country who responded to our plea for help in determining prices for this book which would truly reflect today's jar prices. This made a seemingly impossible task, much easier to accomplish. To these people, we say a big thank you!

While jar prices and ideas of value, do vary from one area of the country to another, and it would be impossible to list prices with which everyone would completely agree, there are definite trends. The dramatic increases have been in the rarer jars, and because of the old law of supply and demand, these jars are certain to continue to rapidly increase in value. Prices on the intermediate jars have increased but at a slower pace, and prices on the more common, and very common jars, have stayed much the same. We feel there are some fairly scarce jars among the $25 and under group, but the demand has not been great enough to drive up the prices to any great extent.

Almost two years ago, when we began to condense our information into manuscript form for Red Book No. 3, it was our hope to bring you a price guide, which was not only fully illustrated, but which would also include all of the research information we have gathered over the past twelve years. By the time the manuscript had been completed, with more than double the jars listed in Red Book No. 2, we realized this would result in too costly a book for a price guide. Therefore, in order to bring you all of the information, we will be publishing two books. The first is Red Book of Fruit Jars No. 3, which you are now reading. This is printed in the same concise, easy to read style which has made the Red Books so popular over the years, and for those of you who were looking forward to the jar illustrations, we have included as many as possible...over 650.

The second book which is now in progress (publishing date not yet available), will be a hard cover book. This book will include a complete and detailed description of each jar along with an illustration, as well as the patent and maker information, and other historical data. The jars will be numbered the same in both books for easy reference. The number of books published will be limited.

For all collectors, beginners and advanced, we hope these books will be a source of knowledge and enjoyment.

Alice Creswick

Acknowledgments

This book has been made possible by the contributions of jar material, by many collectors, over a span of years. Some no longer collect jars. Some have passed away. But each have left their mark in our memories and in our books.

Our special thanks to Junne & Norman Barnett, Roy & Barbara Brown Don Burkett, William Dudley, Alex Kerr, George McConnell, Betty & Ed Schwennesen, and Richard VanderLaan for all of their help. And to Vivian Kath, Jerry McCann, William Brantley & Eleanor Towne.
Also to Maynard Kendall, Anne Mashey, & Robert McAfee, whose contributions will appear in "Fruit Jars".

In appreciation to Frank Thrine, the talented gentleman from Indiana, who has made such accurate reproductions of those hard to find jar closures.

To my husband, Howard, who almost neve_____
illustrate all these jars. And to our childr_____
Steven, Norma, and Nathan who encourage _____

To these, and to each and every one of yo_____
and knowledge so that we all might learn an_____

RAVENNA GLASS WORKS OHIO

Lafayette

THE VAN VLIET JAR OF 1881

THE BEST

JUL. 27 1982

[

☞ General

Information

PRICES SHOWN IN THIS GUIDE ARE RETAIL PRICES, FOR QUART SIZED JARS, IN MINT CONDITION AND COMPLETE WITH THE CORRECT CLOSURES. PINTS AND 1/2 GALLONS ARE VALUED SLIGHTLY HIGHER.

SEPARATE PRICES ARE SHOWN FOR THE 1/2 PINTS, 1/4 PINTS, 1/3 PINTS, THE SMALL MOUTH PINTS, (KNOWN AS MIDGET PINTS), & THE EXTRA LARGE SIZES SUCH AS THE GALLON, 3 GALLON, 4 GALLON, AND 5 GALLON. PRICES ARE ALSO SHOWN FOR THE UNUSUAL COLORS.

VALUES ARE BASED ON AGE, RARITY, AND SPECIAL FEATURES SUCH AS AN INTERESTING CLOSURE. CLOSURES ARE AN IMPORTANT CONSIDERATION WHEN PRICING A JAR. ON COMMON JARS FOR WHICH CLOSURES ARE EASILY FOUND, IT MAKES VERY LITTLE DIFFERENCE PRICE WISE BETWEEN A COMPLETE AND AN INCOMPLETE JAR. HOWEVER, WHEN THE CLOSURE IS UNUSUAL AND THE JAR IS DIFFICULT TO FIND COMPLETE, THE DIFFERENCE IN PRICE CAN BE ALMOST ONE-HALF.

WAX SEALERS ARE USUALLY OFFERED WITHOUT THE LIDS. THESE JARS USE A SIMPLE TIN CAP. A FEW WAX SEALERS DO HAVE THEIR OWN SPECIAL LIDS, AND THESE ARE DESCRIBED WHEN KNOWN.

AS WITH ANY PRICE GUIDE, THIS CAN SERVE ONLY AS A GUIDE.... YOU, THE COLLECTOR, HAVE THE FINAL SAY IN HOW MUCH YOU WISH TO PAY FOR ANY GIVEN JAR.

SUCH TERMS AS "MASON SHOULDER SEAL", "MASON BEADED NECK SEAL", OR "OLD STYLE LIGHTNING SEAL" ARE USED THROUGHOUT THE BOOK TO DESCRIBE TYPES OF SEAL. WE HAVE SHOWN BELOW SIX OF THE MOST COMMON TYPE OF JAR SEALS. "S" INDICATES SEALING POINTS.

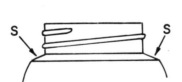

Mason shoulder seal.

Glass lid & screw band top seal.

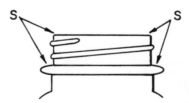

Mason beaded neck seal.

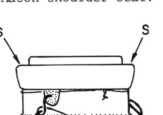

Old style Lightning seal.

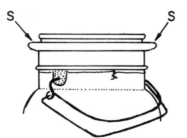

Lightning beaded neck seal.

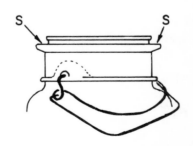

Lightning dimple neck seal.

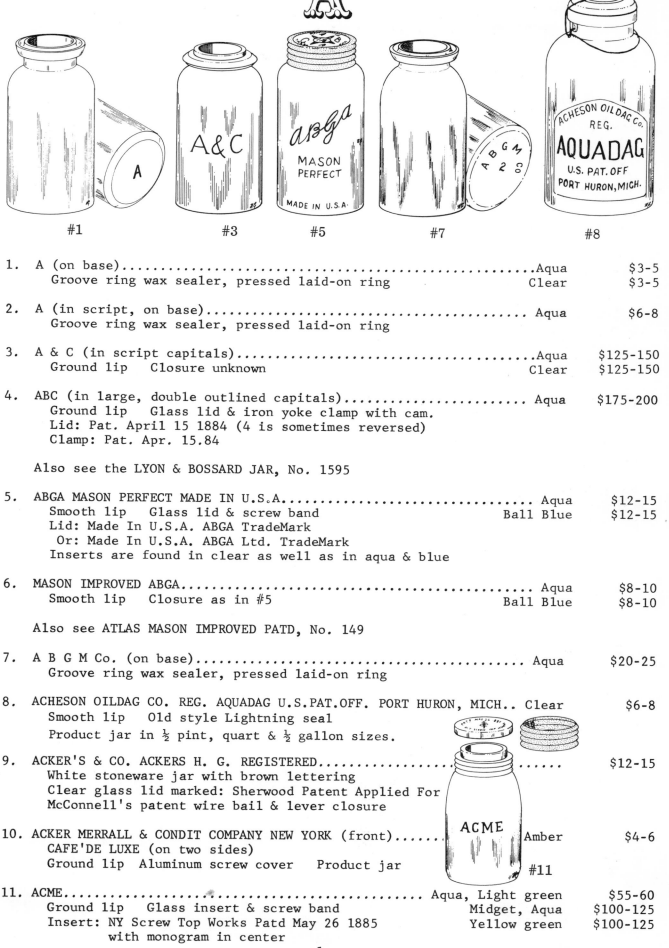

#1	#3	#5	#7	#8

1. A (on base)..Aqua $3-5
    Groove ring wax sealer, pressed laid-on ring   Clear $3-5

2. A (in script, on base).. Aqua $6-8
    Groove ring wax sealer, pressed laid-on ring

3. A & C (in script capitals)...................................Aqua $125-150
    Ground lip   Closure unknown   Clear $125-150

4. ABC (in large, double outlined capitals)...................... Aqua $175-200
    Ground lip   Glass lid & iron yoke clamp with cam.
    Lid: Pat. April 15 1884 (4 is sometimes reversed)
    Clamp: Pat. Apr. 15.84

    Also see the LYON & BOSSARD JAR, No. 1595

5. ABGA MASON PERFECT MADE IN U.S.A................................. Aqua $12-15
    Smooth lip   Glass lid & screw band   Ball Blue $12-15
    Lid: Made In U.S.A. ABGA TradeMark
    Or: Made In U.S.A. ABGA Ltd. TradeMark
    Inserts are found in clear as well as in aqua & blue

6. MASON IMPROVED ABGA.. Aqua $8-10
    Smooth lip   Closure as in #5   Ball Blue $8-10

    Also see ATLAS MASON IMPROVED PATD, No. 149

7. A B G M Co. (on base).. Aqua $20-25
    Groove ring wax sealer, pressed laid-on ring

8. ACHESON OILDAG CO. REG. AQUADAG U.S.PAT.OFF. PORT HURON, MICH.. Clear $6-8
    Smooth lip   Old style Lightning seal
    Product jar in ½ pint, quart & ½ gallon sizes.

9. ACKER'S & CO. ACKERS H. G. REGISTERED..................... ...... $12-15
    White stoneware jar with brown lettering
    Clear glass lid marked: Sherwood Patent Applied For
    McConnell's patent wire bail & lever closure

10. ACKER MERRALL & CONDIT COMPANY NEW YORK (front)....... Amber $4-6
    CAFE'DE LUXE (on two sides)
    Ground lip Aluminum screw cover   Product jar   #11

11. ACME... Aqua, Light green $55-60
    Ground lip   Glass insert & screw band   Midget, Aqua $100-125
    Insert: NY Screw Top Works Patd May 26 1885   Yellow green $100-125
            with monogram in center

12. ACME (on shield with stars & stripes)......................... Clear $2-3
    Smooth lip   Lightning beaded neck seal   ½ pint, Clear $4-6
    Square shape

13. ACME BUTTER SCOTCH SUNDAE (within stippled panel).. ... Clear $4-6
    Smooth lip   Old style Lightning seal
    ½ gallon product jar

14. ACME (L.G.Co. surrounding a star) TRADEMARK 1893.. .. Aqua $100-125
    Reverse: MASON'S PATENT NOV 30th 1858
    Ground lip   Mason shoulder seal

15. ACME (L.G.Co. surrounding a star) TRADEMARK 1893.. .. Aqua $125-130
    Reverse: MASON'S PATENT NOV 30th 1858
    The N in Nov is incomplete
    Ground lip   Mason shoulder seal
    Found in pint size   #14

16. ACME SEAL (in script)... Clear $20-25
    Smooth lip   Glass insert & screw band   Midget, Clear $50-75

17. ADAMS & CO MANUFACTURERS PITTSBURGH, Pa....................... Aqua $200-225
    Pressed laid-on ring, stopper neck finish for glass stopper
    Vertical serrations on lower inside of the stopper well
    Stopper: Bennett's Patent Feb. 6th 1866
         Or: Bennett's Patent Feb. 6th 1866
             A. Kline Oct. 21 8163 (error)
             This stopper is found in aqua & clear

18. BENNETT'S No. 1 (superimposed over erased ADAMS & CO
    MANUFACTURERS PITTSBURGH, Pa. (all on front).................... Aqua $150-200
    Pressed laid-on ring, stopper neck finish for glass stopper
    Vertical serrations on lower inside of the stopper well
    Stopper: Bennett's Patent Feb. 6th 1866

    Also see BENNETT jars, Nos. 443 thru 446

19. ADLAM PATENT PAIL (on lid).................................. Clear $15-18
    Base: Pat. Glass Pail Boston Mass.   Yellow Amber $20-25
    Ground lip   2 pc. metal cover with wire carrying bail
    Candy jar

20. ADLAM PATENT PAIL (on lid).................................. Clear $20-25
    Base: Pat. Glass Pail June 24, 84 Boston Mass.   Yellow Amber $25-30
    Ground lip   2 pc. metal cover with wire carrying bail
    Candy jar

21. ADLAM'S PATENT (on base).................................... Aqua $35-40
    Ground lip   Metal screw cover with attached
                  handle & wooden liner
    Approximately 3 quart size, candy jar

22. ADLAM PATENT BOSTON MASS. (on base).............. .. Aqua $20-25
    Ground lip   Metal screw cover with attached
                  handle & cork liner
    Approximately pint size, candy jar

23. PPC CO (monogram, on front)........................ .. Clear $35-40
    Reverse: has ounce measurements
    Base: Adlam's Patent
    Ground lip   Metal screw cover with attached
                  handle & wooden liner
    Approximately quart size, candy jar
                                                      #23

-2-

#27   #28   #29   #30   #31   #33

24. LICORICE YS (monogram) LOZENGES (on front)...................... Aqua $35-40
    Base: Adlam's Patent
    Ground lip   Metal screw cover with attached handle, &
                  wooden liner
    Approximately 3 quart size, candy jar

25. ADLER CONSERVENGLAS (on lid)....................................Clear   -$1
    Smooth lip   Glass lid, hinged wire clamp
    A fairly modern German jar

26. ADLER PROGRESS DRP 261889 (on base)............................Clear   -$1
    Smooth lip   Glass lid, hinged wire clamp
    Modern German jar

27. TRADEMARK ADVANCE (overlaid on JW monogram) PAT APL'D FOR........ Aqua $85-95
    Ground lip   Glass lid & wire clamp with coil in center   Pint, Aqua   Unpriced
    Lid, inside: Trademark Advance (overlaid on JW)
    Alice Moulton has reported this jar in pint size,
      with inside mouth diameter of 1 3/4 inches.

28. TRADEMARK ADVANCE (overlaid on JW monogram) PAT SEPT. 18,1883.... Aqua $85-100
    Ground lip   Glass lid & wire clamp with coil in center   Pint, Aqua   Unpriced
    Lid, inside: Trademark Advance (overlaid on JW)
    Lid & clamp variations: Wire clamp is depressed in the
                            center but does not have a coil
        Lid 1: No marking, depressed in center
        Lid 2: Advance Fruit Jar* Patent Sep 18,1883* (inside)
              Lid is depressed in center
    This jar has also been reported in pint size, with
      inside mouth diameter of 1 3/4 inches.

29. AGEE... Clear $2-4
    Rolled lip   Closure unknown   Australian jar   Amber $3-5

30. AGEE LIGHTNING SEAL.. Clear $8-10
    Smooth lip   Old style Lightning seal   Australian jar

31. AGEE MASON JAR..Aqua $10-15
    Base: A.G.M. (for Australian Glass Manufacturers)   Clear $10-15
    Smooth lip   Mason shoulder seal   Australian jar

32. AGEE MASON JAR... Clear $10-12
    Base: A.G.M.
    Smooth lip   Mason beaded neck seal   Australian jar

33. MASON'S..Aqua $10-15
    Smooth lip   Mason shoulder seal   Australian jar   Clear $10-15

34. MASON'S (same embossing design as in #33).......................... Clear $10-12
    Smooth lip Mason beaded neck seal   Australian jar

35. AGEE QUEEN... Clear $8-10
    Base: Made In N. Z. A. G. M.   or   AGM trademark
    Smooth lip Glass lid & twin wire side clamps
    Lid: Agee Queen   Australian jar

36. AGEE SPECIAL.. Clear $4-6
    Base: Made In N.Z.A.G.M. The bottom of the jar has a groove.
    Smooth lip   Mason beaded neck seal, wide mouth
    Australian jar

37. AGEE SPECIAL... Clear $4-6
    Base: A.G.M. N.Z. (no groove)   Amber $20-25
    Smooth lip Mason beaded neck seal, wide mouth
    Australian jar

38. AGEE UTILITY JAR (within oval)........................... Clear $1-3
    Smooth lip   Mason beaded neck seal
    Modern 2 pc. metal closure with insert
    marked: Agee Dome Seal   Australian jar

#38

39. IMPROVED AGEE UTILITY.. Clear $4-6
    Base: AGM trademark
    Smooth lip   Mason beaded neck seal, wide mouth
    Zinc lid marked: Agee   Australian jar

40. AGEE VICTORY.. .Light green $4-6
    Base: 1947 (date of manufacture)
    Smooth lip   Mason beaded neck seal
    Zinc lid marked: Agee   Australian jar

41. AGEE VICTORY (within circle)................... ....Clear $8-10
    Base: AGM Smooth lip Glass lid & twin wire
                  clamps
    Lid: Agee Victory   Australian jar

42. AGEE VICTORY (block letters, no circle)........ ....Clear $8-10
    Base: AGM Smooth lip Glass lid & twin wire
                  clamps
    Lid: Agee Victory   Australian jar

#42

43. AGNEW & CO. PITTSBURG PAT APL FOR 1887...........................Clear $60-70
44. AGNEW & CO. PITTSBURG PATd APL FOR 1887...........................Clear $60-70
45. AGNEW & CO. PITTSBURG PAT APLd FOR 1887...........................Clear $60-70
    All are marked on the base only and have been reported with
    various mold numbers such as 1,2,3,4,5, & 6.
    Blown wax sealer with a ground lip. The wide shoulder was
    pressed down while still on the blowpipe to form the groove.

46. AGNEW & SON PITTSBURGH PA. (on base).............................. Aqua $30-35
    Groove ring wax sealer, pressed laid-on ring

47. JOHN AGNEW & SON PITTSBURGH PA. (on base)........................Aqua $30-35
    Groove ring wax sealer, pressed laid-on ring   Clear $30-35

48. A G W L PITTS. PA. (on base)...................................... Aqua $20-25
    Groove ring wax sealer, pressed laid-on ring

49. A. H. T. CO PHILADA USA (on base)...............................Amber $75-85
    Groove ring wax sealer, pressed laid-on ring

50. AIRTIGHT...Clear $45-55
    Smooth lip   Old style Lightning seal

51. AIRTIGHT FRUIT JAR.. Aqua $350-400
      Barrel shaped, blown wax sealer, with bare iron pontil   Amber Unpriced
      scar on base. The groove was formed by collapsing the
      neck while hot and worked upward to form the groove.
      Only two amber jars are presently known..1 quart, and 1
      half-gallon. On jars such as these, we feel the value
      is best determined by the buyer and seller, but would
      be valued over $3000.

52. THE AIRTIGHT JAR PATENTED MARCH 8th 1892........................ Clear $250-300
      Ground lip Attached metal collar to form a channel for
                wax, tin cover
      Only 3 jars are presently known, all quarts.

53. AJAX BAKING POWDER (on lid).................................... Clear $12-15
      Base: Erie
      Ground lip Glass insert & screw band
      Canadian product jar

54. THE AKRON (front) MASONS PATENT 1858 (reverse)...................Clear $125-150
      Smooth lip Mason shoulder seal, with sloping shoulders
      Only 1 jar is presently known.

55. M.J.B. Co's. ALADDIN COFFEE......................................Clear $1-3
      Smooth lip   Mason beaded neck seal   Product jar

56. ALBANY ANILINE & CHEMICAL WORKS RUMPFF & LUTZ
    NEW YORK SOLE AGENTS (all on front).....................Midget, Aqua $100-125
      Base: Mason's Patent Nov 30th 1858
      Ground lip   Mason shoulder seal

57. ALLEN'S PAT. JUNE 1871 (on base)................................ Aqua $75-100
      Ground lip Glass lid & metal band clamp, unmarked
      A very squarish jar, with slightly beveled corners, as called
      for in the patent.

58. ALL RIGHT (front) PATd JAN 25th 1868 (reverse)................. Aqua $100-125
      Base: Pat. Nov. 26 1867   Cornflower blue $150 & up
      Ground lip Metal dome shaped lid & wire clamp
      Lid: Patented Nov. 4 1862 & Feb. 11th 1868

59. ALL RIGHT (front) PATd JAN 26th 1868 (reverse)...................Aqua $100-125
60. ALL RIGHT (front) PATd JAN 27th 1868 (reverse)...................Aqua $100-125
61. ALL RIGHT (front) PATd JAN 28th 1868 (reverse)...................Aqua $100-125
62. ALL RIGHT (front) PAID JAN 28th 1868 (reverse, error)...........Aqua $125-135
      Base: Pat. Nov. 26 1867
      Ground lip Metal dome shaped lid & wire clamp as in #58
      Note: Prices given are for jars complete with the original
      closure. Those with repro lids are being offered for
      about $70 to $75.

AIR TIGHT FRUIT JAR

MASONS PATENT 1858

The Akron

ALLEN'S PAT. JUNE 1871.

PATd JAN 28TH 1868

ALL RIGHT

#51   #54   #57   #61

63. ALMY.. Aqua $75-85
64. ALMY JAR.. Aqua $85-95
    Base: Patented * Dec. 25 1877 *
    Ground lip Mason shoulder seal with glass screw lid
    Found with matching mold letters on the lid & base

65. THE ALSTON (front) BAIL HERE (on shoulder)............. .Clear $75-85
    Base: Patd April 1900 Dec 1901
    Smooth lip Metal lid & wire bail
    Dimples on sides of the neck for bail
    A woodpulp disk, soaked with paraffine, was placed
      under the lid.

66. PATENTED APRIL 3rd 1900 DEC. 31st 1901 (on base)..... .Clear $50-75
    Smooth lip Metal lid & wire bail. The neck is
      bulbous and has dimples which have metal sockets
      to help prevent breakage of the glass by the
      wire bail. A woodpulp disk, soaked with paraffine,
      was placed under the lid.

#65

67. J.S. ALSTON MFG. CO. PLEASANTVILLE, N.J. PAT.FEB. 3 1903 (lid)...Clear $50-75
    Smooth lip Jar has a bulbous neck with metal lined
      dimples in the neck for the ends of the wire bail.
      The metal lid is permanently attached to the bail
      by a wire staple. The jar itself is not embossed.

68. "Just taste that flavor" IT'S ALTA COFFEE........................Clear   — $1-3
    Smooth lip   Mason beaded neck seal Product jar

69. AMAZON SWIFT SEAL (within circle)...........................Ball blue $3-5
    Smooth lip   Lightning beaded neck seal

70. AMAZON SWIFT SEAL (within circle) PATd JULY 14,1908.........Ball blue $3-5
    Smooth lip   Lightning beaded neck seal

71. AMERICAN CAN COMPANY (within star)(embossed on lid of tin can)........ $3-5
    Base: embossed star   Circa 1913

72. AMERICAN CONDENSED MILK CO. AMERICAN BRAND
    SAN FRANCISCO PAT. MAY 15 1894...................................Clear $6-8
    Ground lip Glass lid & metal screw band closure. A   Amber $15-18
      diaphram of waxed, oiled, or greased paper was first
      placed over the mouth of the jar, followed by the cover
      & screw band. Product jar

73. AMERICAN (eagle & flag) FRUIT JAR........ ....Light green $100-125
    Ground lip Old style Lightning seal
    Wide mouth   Australian jar

74. AMERICAN IMPROVED PRESERVE CAN (front).. . .. Aqua $250-300
    Reverse: EARLE'S PATENT FEB.2d 1864
           (around a star, encircled
            by 13 smaller stars.)
    Ground lip Unmarked glass lid & iron
      yoke clamp with tension spring.

    Also see IMPROVED MERCANTILE, No. 1306,
    NATIONAL PRESERVE CAN, No. 2237 &
    NATIONAL BUTTER CAN, No. 2236

75. THE AMERICAN (NAGCo.) PORCELAIN LINED.. .... Aqua $20-25
    Ground lip Mason shoulder seal   #74   Midget, Aqua $100-125
                                                     Midget, Clear $100-125
76. AMERICAN SODA FOUNTAIN CO. (vertically on jar)................. Clear $6-8
    Smooth lip   Old style Lightning seal ½ gal. Product jar

-6-

77. Anchor emblem, slanted over ANCHOR (block letters).............. Clear $25-30
    Smooth lip   Glass insert & screw band   Midget, clear $75-100

78. Anchor emblem, vertically over ANCHOR (script)................. Clear $30-35
    Smooth lip   Glass insert & screw band   Midget, clear $100-150

79. Anchor emblem, small, vertically over ANCHOR (script).......... Clear $40-50
    Smooth lip   Glass insert & screw band   Midget, clear $150-175
    Of the three Canadian Anchor jars listed here, this
    one is the hardest to find. #77 is the most common.

80. H (superimposed over anchor) LIGHTNING.......................... Clear $3-5
    Smooth lip   Lightning dimple neck seal

#79   #80   #81   #83   #85   #86

81. ANCHOR HOCKING (H superimposed over anchor) MASON................Clear   -$1
    Smooth lip   Mason beaded neck seal
    2 pc. gold lacquered lid, with insert marked: Anchor Flex-lid

82. ANCHOR HOCKING (H superimposed over anchor) MASON (front)........Clear   -$1
    Reverse: (H superimposed over anchor) MASON
    Smooth lip   Mason beaded neck seal   Closure as in #81

83. (H superimposed over anchor) MASON...............................Clear   -$1
    Smooth lip   Mason beaded neck seal   Closure as in #81

84. (H superimposed over anchor) MASON (front).......................Clear   -$1
    Reverse: ANCHOR HOCKING GLASS CORPORATION
    Smooth lip   Mason beaded neck seal   Closure as in #81

85. ANCHOR MASON'S PATENT ("roped" letters)..........................Clear $4-6
    Smooth lip   Mason shoulder seal

86. ANCHOR MASON'S PATENT...Clear $4-6
    Smooth lip   Mason shoulder seal

87. ANCHOR MASON'S PATENT...Clear $4-6
    Smooth lip   Mason beaded neck seal   Cornflower blue $18-20

88. FROM T. ANDERSON   ANDERSON'S LANDING W. VA............................ $50-55
    Tan stoneware jar with blue stenciling
    Wax seal groove

89. ANDERSON PRESERVING CO. CAMDEN N.J. (base)......................Clear $1-3
    Smooth lip   Mason beaded neck seal   Product jar

90. THE APOLLO (in script, on lid)..................................Clear $1-3
    Base: F. H. Roberts Co. Boston, Mass.
    Smooth lip   Metal screw cap   Paneled (12 panels) Product jar

91. AQUA QUALITY PRODUCTS SOLLENZNER CORP. BUFFALO, N.Y.............. Aqua $1-3
    Smooth lip   Metal screw cap   Product jar

92. ARMOUR & COMPANY (on base)..Clear $2-3
    Ground lip Glass lid & metal band clamp Product jar

93. ARMOUR & CO. PACKERS CHICAGO (front)........................Milkglass $3-5
    Rolled lip Closure unknown Approx. pint, Product jar

94. ARS (in fancy script capitals)................................. Aqua $50-55
    Stopper neck finish for glass or metal stopple
    Glass stopper: A. Kline Patd. Oct. 27 1863 or
    Metal stopple: J. D. Willoughby Pat'd Jan 4 1859
    The letters stand for A. R. Samuels

95. MANUFACTURED BY ARTHUR BURNHAM & GILROY PHILADELPHIA (front).... Aqua $500 & up
    Reverse: R. ARTHURS PATENT JANY 2nd 1855   Clear $500 & up
    Blown wax sealer with a ground lip. The shoulder was
    pressed down while still on the blowpipe to form the groove.

96. ARTHUR BURNHAM & GILROY 10th & GEO. STS. PHILADELPHIA (front)... Aqua $500 & up
    Reverse: R. ARTHUR'S PATENT JANY 2nd 1855
    Blown wax sealer as in #95

97. ARTHUR BURNHAM & GILROY 10th & GEO. STS. PHILADELPHIA   Aqua $500 & up
    Reverse: R. ARTHUR'S PATENT JANY 2nd 1855
    Blown wax sealer with a ground lip as in
    Nos. 95 & 96. Although the embossing is the
    same, the shape is entirely different.

#97

98. ROBERT ARTHUR'S PATENT 2nd JANUARY 1855
    ARTHUR BURNHAM & GILROY, PHILADELPHIA (base)........   Unpriced
    Yellow-ware (pottery) Wax seal groove
    Found with ribbed sides or plain
    See "Fruit Jars" by Greswick for illustrations of all Arthur jars.

99. "AS YOU LIKE IT" HORSERADISH..................................... $12-15
    ½ Pint stoneware jar, with blue lettering
    Lid: Weir Patent 92 Weir patent wire & metal clamp
    Body of jar is white, shoulders, neck & lid are brown

#99

100. "AS YOU LIKE IT" TRADEMARK HORSE RADISH.............. $12-15
     Same as #99 except for added word Trademark
     This jar in the author's collection, has a
       paper label on the backside, showing it was
       used for horse radish, packed by the U. S.
     Horse Radish Company, Saginaw, Michigan.

#100

101. ½ pint stoneware jar, unmarked, paper label only... $6-8
     Lid: Weir Pat. 92 Weir patent wire & metal clamp
     White body, brown shoulders, neck & lid

102. AS YOU LIKE IT BRAND ....Clear   -$1
     Base: Naar Food Co. Inc. Brooklyn, N. Y.
     Tumbler shaped, product jar

103. ATHERHOLT, FISHER & CO PHILADA................................. Aqua $150-175
     Tapered neck finish for stopper or cork
     Usually found with a glass stopper marked: Kline's Patent
                                       Oct. 27 63

104. ATLAS.. Clear   -$1
     Smooth lip Mason beaded neck seal Tumbler shaped jar

105. ATLAS... ½ Pint, Clear $1-3
     Smooth lip Mason beaded neck seal   Soft-square shape

106. ATLAS CAN OR FREEZE................................Clear   -$1
     Smooth lip Mason beaded neck seal
     ½ Pint, pint & quart sizes

107. ATLAS E Z SEAL (within circle)............ .... Aqua $8-10
     Smooth lip Old style Lightning seal   Light blue $8-10
     Lid: Made By Hazel Atlas Glass Co.

108. ATLAS E Z SEAL (without hyphen)......... .... Aqua $1-2
     Base: "Atlas" E-Z Seal Trademark Reg.   Light blue $2-3
     Smooth lip   Old style Lightning seal

109. ATLAS E-Z SEAL .... Aqua, Clear $1-2
     Base: "Atlas" E-Z Seal Trademark Reg.   Citron $12-15
     Or: Mold numbers only   Cornflower blue $18-20
     Smooth lip   Old style Lightning seal   Light green $1-2
                                                      Olive green $18-20
                                                   ½ Pint clear $1-3

#107

110. "ATLAS" E-Z SEAL TRADEMARK REG. (base)....................... Aqua $1-2
     Smooth lip   Old style Lightning seal   Cornflower blue $12-15

111. ATLAS E-Z SEAL.................................... Aqua $1-2
     Base: A B C
     Smooth lip   Old style Lightning seal

112. ATLAS E-Z SEAL............................ .... Clear   -$1
     Base: HA trademark   or   Unmarked   ½ Pint clear $2-3
     Smooth lip Lightning dimple neck seal

113. ATLAS E-Z SEAL............................ .... Citron $12-15
     Smooth lip Lightning beaded neck seal   Cornflower blue $18-20
                                                    Light green $1-2

114. ATLAS E-Z SEAL............................ .... Amber $25-30
     Base: 24-K-342
     Smooth lip Lightning beaded neck seal.
     The correct lid for this jar is a matching amber lid. The
     milkglass lid sometime's attributed to this jar goes on an
     unembossed product jar. See jar No. 3066

#114

115. ATLAS E-Z SEAL............................ .... Clear   -$1
     Base: HA trademark or unmarked   ½ Pint Clear $2-3
     Smooth lip Lightning beaded neck seal

116. "ATLAS E-Z SEAL"........................... .... Aqua, Clear $1-2
     Base: "Atlas" E-Z Seal Trademark Reg.
     Smooth lip   Old style Lightning seal

117. "ATLAS" E-Z SEAL........................... ... Aqua, Clear $1-2
     Base: "Atlas" E-Z Seal Trademark Reg.   Light green $1-2
     Smooth lip Old style Lightning seal   Sky blue $12-15
                                                  ½ Pint, Aqua $3-5
                                                  ½ Pint, Clear $2-3
                                       Squatty shaped pint Aqua, clear $2-3

#117

118. "ATLAS" E-Z SEAE (error).. Aqua $3-4
     Base: "Atlas" E-Z Seal Trademark Reg.
     Smooth lip   Old style Lightning seal

119. "ATLAS" E-Z SEAL................................... Light blue $2-3
     Base: "Atlas" E-Z Seae Trademark Reg. (error)
     Smooth lip   Old style Lightning seal

120. ATLAS E-Z SEAL..................................½ Pint, Aqua $3-5
     Smooth lip Old style Lightning seal

121. -ATLAS- E-Z SEAL.. ½ Pint, Aqua $3-5
     Base: "Atlas" E-Z Seal Trademark Reg.   ½ Pint, Clear $2-3
     Smooth lip Old style Lightning seal

122. -ATLAS- E-Z SEAL .... 3/4 Pint, Aqua $2-3
     Base: "Atlas" Trademark Reg.
     Smooth lip   Lightning beaded neck seal

123. ATLAS E-Z SEAL.. . Pint, Clear   -$1
     Base: HA trademark
     Smooth lip   Lightning beaded neck seal

124. "ATLAS E-Z SEAL" 48-OZ.......................... .... Aqua $6-8
125. "ATLAS E-Z SEAL" 52-OZ.......................... .... Aqua $6-8
126. "ATLAS E-Z SEAL" 58-OZ.......................... .... Aqua $6-8
     Base: "Atlas" E-Z Seal Trademark Reg.
     Smooth lip Old style Lightning seal

"ATLAS E-Z SEAL" 58-OZ #126

127. E-Z SEAL (without word Atlas)............................ Light green $8-10
     Base: "Atlas" E-Z Seal Trademark Reg.
      Or: E-Z Seal Trademark Reg.
     Smooth lip   Old style Lightning seal

128. ATLAS (4 leaf clover) GOOD LUCK........... .... Clear $2-4
     Base: HA trademark
     Smooth lip   Lightning beaded neck seal

129. ATLAS (4 leaf clover) GOOD LUCK........... .... Clear $2-4
     Smooth lip   Old style Lightning seal   Light green $4-6

ATLAS GOOD-LUCK #128

130. ATLAS (4 leaf clover) GOOD LUCK........... .... Clear $2-4
     Smooth lip   Lightning dimple neck seal

131. ATLAS GOOD LUCK (no clover)........................½ Pint, Clear $4-6
     Smooth lip   Old style Lightning seal Or   ¼ Pint, Clear $4-6
                   Lightning dimple neck seal   1/3 Pint, Clear $4-6
     This jar (without the clover) has also been
      reported in pint, quart & ½ gallon sizes, tho we
      have not seen them.

132. ATLAS HA E-Z SEAL.................................... Clear $3-5
     Smooth lip   Old style Lightning seal

133. ATLAS HA MASON...................................... Clear   -$1
     Smooth lip   Mason beaded neck seal

134. ATLAS (HA in stippled circle) MASON................. Clear   -$1
135. ATLAS (HA in unstippled circle) MASON............. Clear   -$1
     Smooth lip   Mason beaded neck seal   #132
     Closure: Zinc lid marked Atlas
          Or: Glass insert & screw band Insert: HA or HA Atlas
     These jars were also made in miniature size, with a bank
      slot lid, or with a 2 pc. lid without bank slot.

136. ATLAS HA MASON....................................7 oz., Clear $1-3
     Smooth lip   Mason beaded neck seal   8 oz., Clear $1-3

137. ATLAS HA PRESERVE JAR................................. Clear $2-4
     Smooth lip   Old style Lightning seal

138. -ATLAS- IMPROVED MASON............................... Light green $2-4
     Smooth lip   Glass insert & screw band   Aqua $2-4
     Wide mouth jar

-10-

139. ATLAS JUNIOR MASON................................... 1/2 Pint, Clear $2-4
     Smooth lip Mason beaded neck seal   2/3 Pint, Clear $2-4
     The mouth is smaller than regular size, to use
        the Atlas Seal-All 63 Arc lid.

140. ATLAS MASON...Aqua $1-2
     Smooth lip Mason beaded neck seal

141. ATLAS MASON.............................1/2 Pint, Clear $1-3
     Base: HA trademark   1/2 Pint, Aqua $3-5
     Smooth lip Mason beaded neck seal

142. -ATLAS- MASON FRUIT JAR.................... Aqua $4-6
     Smooth lip Mason shoulder seal

143. ATLAS (erased) MASON FRUIT JAR.......... Aqua $4-6
     Smooth lip Mason shoulder seal

                                                    #144

144. ATLAS (erased) MASON FRUIT JAR (superimposed over erased
     WHITNEY PAT'd 1858)... Aqua $6-8
     Ground lip Mason shoulder seal

145. ATLAS MASON IMPROVED PAT'D.................................Aqua, Clear $6-8
     Smooth lip Glass lid & screw band   Light blue $6-8
                                                Cornflower blue $18-20
                                                     Light green $6-8
                                                     Olive green $18-20
146. ATLAS (erased) MASON IMPROVED PAT'D............................ Aqua $6-8
     Smooth lip Glass lid & screw band   Clear $6-8
                                                Cornflower blue $18-20

147. ATLAS (erased) MASON IMPROVED (Pat'd erased)................... Aqua $6-8
     Smooth lip Glass lid & screw band

148. MASON IMPROVED PAT'D (word Pat'd erased, no word Atlas)........ Aqua $6-8
     Smooth lip Glass lid & screw band   Clear $6-8

149. MASON IMPROVED A.B.G.A. (erased words Atlas & Pat'd)........... Aqua $8-10
     Smooth lip Glass lid & screw band

     Also see MASON IMPROVED ABGA, No. 6

150. -ATLAS- MASON'S PATENT.....................   .... Aqua, Clear $2-4
     Smooth lip Mason shoulder seal   Cornflower blue $18-20
     This jar has been reported in various   Light blue $4-6
        shades of green.   Olive green $18-20

151. ATLAS MASON'S PATENT (without hyphens)....   .... Aqua $2-4
     Smooth lip Mason shoulder seal

152. ATLAS. MASON'S PATENT (period after Atlas)   .... Aqua $2-4
     Smooth lip Mason shoulder seal

                                                    #152

153. ATLAS MASON'S PATENT (front)................................... Aqua $6-8
     Reverse: erased JAR SALT DETROIT SALT CO. MASON'S PAT.
     Smooth lip Mason shoulder seal
     Some of these jars have only JAR SALT or AR SALT in ghost.

     Also see JAR SALT DETROIT SALT CO., No. 1323

154. -ATLAS- MASON'S PATENT NOV 30th 1858................... Aqua, Clear $3-5
     Smooth lip Mason shoulder seal   Cornflower Blue $18-20
                                                     Olive green $18-20
                                                Light olive green $12-15

155. -ATLAS- MASON'S PATENT NOV 30th 1858.................Med. Olive green $20-25
     Error jar with missing crossbars on A's in Atlas
      & Mason's.
     Smooth lip Mason shoulder seal

156. -ATLAS- MASON'S PATENT NOV 30th 1858.................Med. Olive green $20-25
     Error jar with missing crossbars on all A's
     Smooth lip Mason shoulder seal

157. ATLAS SPECIAL.. Pint, Aqua $3-5
     Smooth lip Mason shoulder seal, wide mouth   Lime green $4-6
     Zinc lid: Atlas Special Mason's Patent   Med. Olive green $15-18
      Or: Atlas Special Mason's Patent   Cornflower blue $15-18
        Made In USA

158. ATLAS SPECIAL MASON.................................... Aqua $3-5
     Smooth lip Mason shoulder seal, wide mouth
     Closure as in #157

159. -ATLAS- SPECIAL MASON................................... Aqua $3-5
     Smooth lip Mason shoulder seal, wide mouth
     Closure as in #157

#157

160. ATLAS SPECIAL MASON.................................... Clear   -$1
     Smooth lip Mason beaded neck seal, wide mouth, square

161. -ATLAS- STRONG SHOULDER MASON........................... Aqua   -$1
     Smooth lip Mason beaded neck seal   Light blue $6-8
        Light Olive green $12-15

162. ATLAS STRONG SHOULDER MASON...........................Clear   -$1
     Base: HA trademark
     Smooth lip Mason beaded neck seal
     Also made in miniature size, with or without bank slot lid.

163. ATLAS STRONG SHOULDER MASON............................ Aqua $1-2
     Base: A B C
     Smooth lip Mason beaded neck seal

164. ATLAS STRONG SHOULDER MASON............................ Aqua $1-2
     Base: Mold numbers   Cornflower Blue $18-20
     Smooth lip Mason beaded neck seal   Light green $1-3
        Deep Olive green $20-25

165. ATLA STRONG SHOULDER MASON (error)...................... Aqua $2-3
     Smooth lip Mason beaded neck seal

166. ATLAS STRONG SHOULDER MASON............................ Aqua $2-3
     (Error, no crossbar on A in Mason)
     Smooth lip Mason beaded neck seal

167. ATLAS STRONG SHUOLDER MASON (error)................... Clear $2-3
     Smooth lip Mason beaded neck seal

168. ATLAS STOONG SHOULDER MASON (error)................... Clear $2-3
     Smooth lip Mason beaded neck seal

#169

169. HA ATLAS STRONG SHOULDER MASON HA................... Clear $6-8
     Base: HA 10-K-338
     Smooth lip Mason beaded neck seal
     The large HAs form 8 "ribs" around
      the jar. The purpose may have been
      to form "gripper" ribs on the jar, similiar to those used by
     Brockway on their Brockway Sur-Grip Masons.
     Only 1 of these jars has been reported thus far.

170. ATLAS WHOLEFRUIT JAR... Clear $1-2
    Smooth lip Lightning dimple neck seal, wide mouth. Pint, Lt. green $3-5

171. ATLAS WHOLEFRUIT JAR... Clear $1-2
    Smooth lip Lightning beaded neck seal, wide mouth

172. ATMORE & SON MINCEMEAT PHILADELPHIA (base)................... Aqua $1-3
    Smooth lip Glass insert & screw band Product jar

173. ATTERBURY... Aqua $325-350
    Ground lip. Metal closure, described in the patent as   Clear $325-350
    consisting of a metallic ring, constructed with a cir-
    cular shoulder, a vertical screw and a vertical slotted
    lug, in combination with a shouldered and lipped cover,
    a rubber gasket, and a clamping nut.

174. ATTERBURY'S PATENT JUNE 30 1863................................ Clear $375-400
    Ground lip. This rare jar from the George McConnell
    collection was not complete when found. The June 1863
    patent calls for a glass cover with a beveled edge, and
    raised center, and an India-rubber gasket. See "Fruit
    Jars" by Creswick for patent illustration.

175. AUNT SALLY'S BRAND NET WEIGHT 16 OZ. PASADENA, CALIF.......... Clear $2-3
    (Within stippled diamond, on front)
    Smooth lip Mason beaded neck seal Product jar

176. AUNTYS TRADEMARK REGISTERED US PAT. OFF. PRODUCTS
DENNYSVILLE, MAINE, USA (all on front)......................... Clear $1-3
    Smooth lip Closure unknown Product jar

177. THE AUTOMATIC SEALER.. Aqua $90-100
    Base: Clayton Bottle Works Clayton, N.J.
    Ground lip Dome shaped glass lid, with wire bail with coil
    for tension, & neck tie wire.
    Lid: Pat'd Sept. 15 1885 or Pat. Apld For
        Lid has an arrow which points to a matching arrow on neck.

178. THE AUTOMATIC SEALER.. Aqua $100-125
    Base: Clayton Bottle Works Clayton, N.J.
    Ground lip. Dome shaped glass lid. Lid has a center depression
    with a raised projection like a marble, in the center. The
    wire clamp has a double loop which straddles the glass pro-
    jection. Lid: Pat. App. For or Unmarked

179. AYLMER CANNING CO.. Clear $6-8
    Smooth lip Screw cover Canadian product jar, ½ pint

#170   #173   #174   #175   #177   #179

180. B (on base).. Aqua $3-5
    Groove ring wax sealer, pressed laid-on ring

181. B & B (in script capitals, on base)............................Amber $2-3
    Smooth lip   Glass lid & wire clamp   Product jar

182. B & C (in fancy script capitals, on front)..................... Aqua $20-25
    Ground lip   Closure unknown   Approximately ½ pint

183. BAGLEY & CO. LTD. KNOTTINGLEY & LONDON (on lid)..........Light green $8-10
    Stopper neck finish for glass stopper, cork gasket
    English jar

184. B & CO. Ld. (on base)....................................Light green $8-10
    Stopper neck finish for glass stopper, cork gasket
    English jar   8 sided   Known in 3 sizes.

185. B. & A. C. CO. (on base).. Aqua $6-8
    Stopper neck finish for cork, rolled lip
    Product jar (Baker & Adamson Chemical Co.)

186. BAKER BROS. & CO. BALTIMORE MD (on base)............... ... Aqua $30-35
    Groove ring wax sealer, pressed laid-on ring

187. CROWN JAR J.C. BAKER'S PAT. AUG. 14 1860 (lid)... ... .. Aqua $75-85
    Jar is unmarked
    Ground lip   Glass lid & heavy tin yoke clamp

188. J.C. BAKER'S PATENT AUG 14 1860 (front)........... ... . Aqua $125-150
    Ground lip   Tin lid & heavy tin yoke clamp
    Or: with glass lid marked: J. C. Baker's
       Patent August 14 1860
    Or: with glass lid marked: Crown Jar
       J.C. Baker's Patent August 14 1860

#188

189. BALL (in script)... Clear   -$1
    Small jar about two inches tall. These were made in the 1950's
    for a child's jelly making set, and used a two piece metal
    closure with the No. 63 insert.

190. BALL (script, 3-L loop)....................................Clear   Unpriced
    Smooth lip   One piece tin plated lid
    The neck of the jar has four equally spaced lugs or
    interrupted screw threads, and it is believed to be a
    test jar, circa 1909.

191. BALL (script, 3-L loop)...................................... Aqua   -$1
    Smooth lip   Mason shoulder seal   Zinc lid: Ball   Clear $1-2
                                                    Amber $30-35
           Honey amber with streaks of dark amber $30-35
                   Green with amber streaks $20-25
                               Olive green $25-30

192. BALL (script, front) Measure scale on reverse................. Clear   -$1
    Smooth lip   Mason beaded neck seal, wide mouth   1½ cup size

193. BALL (script, front) Reverse: MASON'S PATENT 1858 .... Aqua $4-6
    Smooth lip   Mason shoulder seal

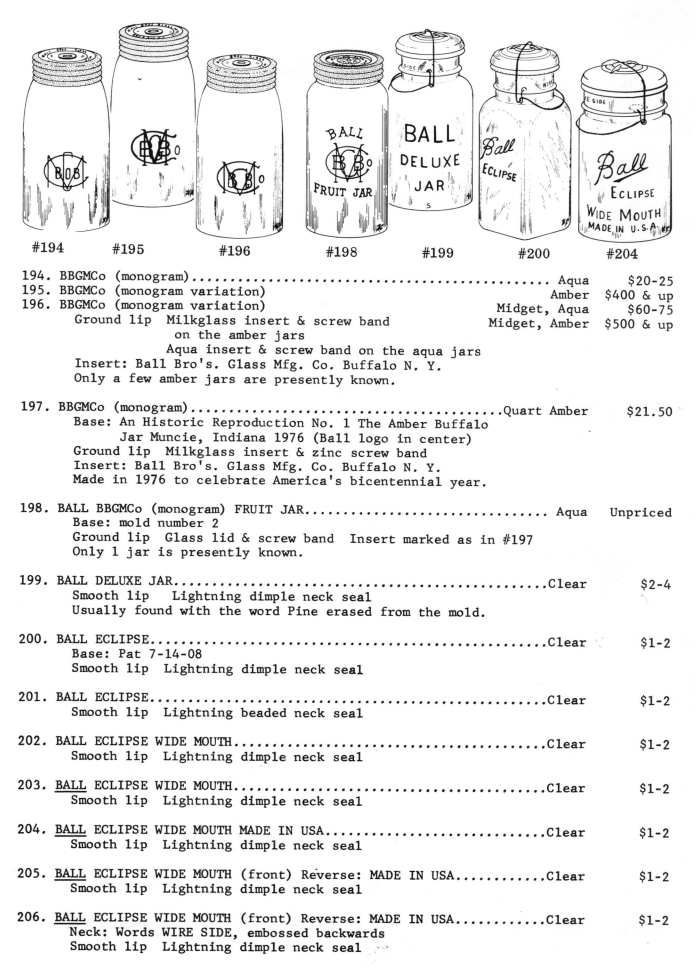

#194   #195   #196   #198   #199   #200   #204

194. BBGMCo (monogram).. Aqua $20-25
195. BBGMCo (monogram variation)   Amber $400 & up
196. BBGMCo (monogram variation)   Midget, Aqua $60-75
     Ground lip Milkglass insert & screw band   Midget, Amber $500 & up
                 on the amber jars
                 Aqua insert & screw band on the aqua jars
       Insert: Ball Bro's. Glass Mfg. Co. Buffalo N. Y.
       Only a few amber jars are presently known.

197. BBGMCo (monogram)...Quart Amber $21.50
       Base: An Historic Reproduction No. 1 The Amber Buffalo
            Jar Muncie, Indiana 1976 (Ball logo in center)
       Ground lip Milkglass insert & zinc screw band
       Insert: Ball Bro's. Glass Mfg. Co. Buffalo N. Y.
       Made in 1976 to celebrate America's bicentennial year.

198. BALL BBGMCo (monogram) FRUIT JAR............................... Aqua   Unpriced
       Base: mold number 2
       Ground lip Glass lid & screw band Insert marked as in #197
       Only 1 jar is presently known.

199. BALL DELUXE JAR...Clear $2-4
       Smooth lip   Lightning dimple neck seal
       Usually found with the word Pine erased from the mold.

200. BALL ECLIPSE...Clear $1-2
       Base: Pat 7-14-08
       Smooth lip Lightning dimple neck seal

201. BALL ECLIPSE...Clear $1-2
       Smooth lip Lightning beaded neck seal

202. BALL ECLIPSE WIDE MOUTH..Clear $1-2
       Smooth lip Lightning dimple neck seal

203. BALL ECLIPSE WIDE MOUTH..Clear $1-2
       Smooth lip Lightning dimple neck seal

204. BALL ECLIPSE WIDE MOUTH MADE IN USA..................................Clear $1-2
       Smooth lip Lightning dimple neck seal

205. BALL ECLIPSE WIDE MOUTH (front) Reverse: MADE IN USA............Clear $1-2
       Smooth lip Lightning dimple neck seal

206. BALL ECLIPSE WIDE MOUTH (front) Reverse: MADE IN USA............Clear $1-2
       Neck: Words WIRE SIDE, embossed backwards
       Smooth lip Lightning dimple neck seal

207. BALL ECLIPSE WIDE MOUTH (front) Reverse: MADE IN USA...........Clear $1-2
        Neck: Words WIRE SIDE, embossed backwards except for the R
        Smooth lip Lightning dimple neck seal

208. BALL IDEAL...Clear $1-2
        Base: B within circle   1/3 Pint, clear $2-3
        Smooth lip Lightning beaded neck
        Known in quart & 1/3 pint sizes   #208

209. BALL IDEAL..................................... Ball blue $1-2
        Smooth lip Lightning dimple neck seal Square shape

210. BALL IDEAL..................................... Ball blue $1-2
        Smooth lip Lightning dimple neck seal

211. BALL IDEAL MADE IN USA........................ Ball blue $1-2
        Smooth lip Lightning dimple neck seal

212. BALL IDEAL (front) MADE IN USA (reverse)....... Ball blue $1-2
        Smooth lip Lightning dimple neck seal

213. BALL IDEAL (front) MADE IN USA (reverse)...... Ball blue $1-2
        Neck: words WIRE SIDE, embossed backwards
              except for the R
        Smooth lip Lightning dimple neck seal

214. BALL IDEAL..................................... Clear   -$1
        Smooth lip Lightning beaded neck seal
                                              #211

215. BALL IDEAL (front) MADE IN USA (reverse)............ 1/3 Pint, Clear $2-3
        Smooth lip Lightning dimple neck seal

216. BALL IDEAL.....................................Ball blue   -$1
        Smooth lip Lightning beaded neck seal Round   Clear   -$1
                                                         Light green $1-2
                                                      ½ Pint, clear $2-3

217. BALL IDEAL.....................................Ball blue   -$1
        Smooth lip Lightning beaded neck seal Round   Clear   -$1
                                                         Light green $1-2
                                                       ½ Pint, blue $10-12

218. BALL IDEAL PAT'D JULY 14, 1908.........................Clear   -$1
        Smooth lip Lightning beaded neck seal

219. BALL IDEAL PAT'D JULY 14, 1908........................Ball blue $1-2
        Smooth lip Lightning dimple neck seal Square

220. BALL IDEAL PAT'D JULY 14, 1908...........................Ball blue   -$1
        Neck: WIRE SIDE   Clear   -$1
        Smooth lip Lightning dimple neck seal   Light green $1-2
                                                        Yellow green $3-5

221. BALL IDEAL PAT'D JULY 14, 1908..................... ....Ball blue $1-2
        Neck: BAIL HERE
        Smooth lip Lightning dimple neck seal

222. BALL IDEAL PAT'D JULY 14, 1908........... .....Ball blue $1-2
        Neck: BALE HERE
        Smooth lip Lightning dimple neck seal

223. BALL IDEAL PAT'D JULY 14, 1908........... .....Ball blue $1-2
        Neck: No marking
        Smooth lip Lightning dimple neck seal
                                              #220

224. BALL IDEAL (front) PAT'D JULY 14 1908 (reverse)...........Ball blue $1-2
        Neck: WIRE SIDE
        Smooth lip Lightning dimple neck seal

225. BALL IDEAL (front) PAT'D JULY 14, 1908 (reverse).............. Clear   -$1
     Neck: BAIL HERE   Ball blue $1-2
     Smooth lip Lightning dimple neck seal

226. BALL IDEAL PAT'D JULY 14, 1908........................Ball blue $1-2
     Neck: Unmarked
     Smooth lip Lightning dimple neck seal

227. BALL IDEAL PAT'D JULY 14, 1908.......................... Clear   -$1
     Neck: WIRE SIDE   Ball blue $1-2
     Smooth lip Lightning dimple neck seal

228. BALL IDEAL PAT'D JULY 14, 1908............................Ball blue $1-2
     Neck: BAIL HERE
     Smooth lip Lightning dimple neck seal

229. BALL IDEAL (front) PAT'D JULY 14, 1908 (reverse)............. Clear   -$1
     Neck: WIRE SIDE   ½ pint, Clear $2-3
     Smooth lip Lightning dimple neck seal   ½ Pint light green $4-6

230. BALL IDEAL (front) PAT'D JULY 14, 1908 (reverse)............. Clear   -$1
     Neck: BAIL HERE   Ball blue $1-2
     Smooth lip Lightning dimple neck seal

231. BALL IDEAL... Clear   -$1
     Smooth lip Lightning dimple neck seal
     Later, round-square shape

232. BALL IDEAL PAT'D JULY 14, 1908................................ Clear   -$1
     Smooth lip Lightning beaded neck seal Square

233. BALL IDEAL PAT'D JULY 14, 1988 (date error).................Ball blue $2-3
     Smooth lip Lightning dimple neck seal   Light green $2-3
     Found in pint size

234. BALL IDEAL PAT'D JULY 14, 1908 (reversed 9)..... .Ball blue $2-3
     Smooth lip Lightning dimple neck seal

235. BALL IDEAL PAT'D JULY 14, 1909 (date error).....Ball Blue $2-3
     Smooth lip Lightning dimple neck seal

236. BALL IDEAL PAT'D JUIY 14, 1908 (spelling error) Ball blue $2-3
     Smooth lip Lightning dimple neck seal

237. BALL IDEAL PAT'D JULY 14, 1808 (date error).... ....Clear $2-3
     Smooth lip Lightning dimple neck seal   #235

238. BALL IDEA (missing L) Reverse: PAT'D JULY 14, 189 (error)...Ball blue $2-3
     Smooth lip Lightning dimple neck seal

239. BALL IDEAL (date is faded out) No crossbar in A in Ideal)...Ball blue $2-3
     Smooth lip Lightning dimple neck seal

240. BALL IDEAL.. Clear $1-2
     Smooth lip Glass bosses or "trunnions" on neck for
                 the wire bail.

241. BALL IDEAL (front)....................................... Clear   Unpriced
     Reverse: Bicentennial Celebration medallion MADE IN U.S.A. Opaque   Unpriced
     Base: 75 A1   Ball blue $2-3
     Smooth lip Lightning dimple neck seal Quart size only
     Made for the bicentennial year. A second run of jars was
      made..these can be distinguished from the original run
      by the small R on the lid and just below the Ball name
      on the jar.

242. <u>BALL</u> IDEAL (front) ....Ball blue   Unpriced
       Reverse: Bicentennial Celebration medallion with the
             signature of Edmund F. Ball across the face
             of the medallion.
       Base: 75 A1
       Smooth lip Lightning dimple neck seal Quarts only

243. <u>BALL</u> IDEAL (front)... Clear   Unpriced
       Reverse: Bicentennial Celebration medallion   Ball blue $2-3
             MADE IN U.S.A.
       Base: 76 A19
       Smooth lip Lightning dimple neck seal
       Lid: Ball   Made in pint size only

244. <u>BALL</u> IDEAL MADE IN U.S.A. (front)..........   Ball blue   Unpriced
       Reverse: Embossed design showing new Ball
             Company Offices in 1976
       Smooth lip Lightning dimple neck seal
       Lid: Ball   Made in pint size only
       For more detailed information on the Ball
        bicentennial jars, see "Fruit Jars" by
        Creswick.

#244

245. <u>BALL</u> IDEAL (front).. Clear $20-25
       Reverse: PROPERTY OF SOUTHERN METHODIST ORPHANS HOME
             WACO, TEXAS
       Smooth lip Lightning dimple neck seal ½ gallon only

246. BALL IMPROVED (3 L loop)...............................Clear $1-2
       Smooth lip Glass lid & screw band   Round shape   Ball blue $1-3
                                               Emerald Green $15-18

247. BALL IMPROVED (3 L loop)...............................Ball blue $1-3
       Smooth lip Glass lid & screw band   Square shape

248. BALL IMPROVED (3 L loop)..........................Aqua $1-3
       Smooth lip Mason shoulder seal

249. BALL IMPROVED (in dual line lettering).........   Aqua $2-3
       Smooth lip Glass insert & screw band

250. <u>BALL</u> IMPROVED....................................   Clear $1-3
       Smooth lip Glass insert & screw band   Ball blue $1-3
       Shoulders are very tapered   Light green $1-3

251. <u>BALL</u> IMPROVED (word Improved in rectangle).....   Ball blue $1-3
       Smooth lip Glass insert & screw band
       Shoulders are very tapered   #249

252. <u>BALL</u> IMPROVED.......................................Ball blue $1-3
       Smooth lip Glass insert & screw band
       Shoulders are very tapered

253. <u>BALL</u> IMPROVED (word Mason in ghost)...........   Ball blue $1-3
       Smooth lip Glass insert & screw band Pint

254. BALL MPROVED (missing letter).................   Ball blue $2-4
       Smooth lip Glass insert & screw band

255. BALL IMPROVED MASON.........................   Aqua $1-3
       Smooth lip Mason shoulder seal

256. BALL IMPROVED MASON.........................   Aqua $1-3
       Smooth lip Glass insert & screw band

#254

257. BALL IMPROVED MASON (3 L loop)......................... Aqua $1-3
     The end of the underline does not go thru
     the I in Improved.
     Smooth lip Mason shoulder seal

258. BALL IMPROVED MASON............................... Clear $1-2
     Smooth lip Glass insert & screw band   Ball blue $1-3

259. BALL IMPROVED MASON'S PATENT 1858 (on four lines.... Aqua $2-4
     Smooth lip Mason shoulder seal Pint

260. BALL IMPROVED MASON'S PATENT 1858 (on five lines.... Aqua $2-4
     Smooth lip Mason shoulder seal

261. BALL IMPPOVED MASON'S PATENT 1858 (error)...................... Aqua $4-6
     Smooth lip Mason shoulder seal

262. BALL IMPPOVED MASON PATENT 1858 (error & no S after Mason)...... Aqua $4-6
     Smooth lip Mason shoulder seal

263. BALL IMPROVED MASON'S PATENT 1858 (on four lines)... . Aqua $2-4
     (Different from #259)
     Smooth lip Mason shoulder seal

264. BALL IMPPOVED MASON'S PATENT 1858 (error)........... . Aqua $4-6
     (Different from #261)
     Smooth lip Mason shoulder seal

#257

#260

265. BALL IMPROVED MASON'S PAT' 1858................................... Aqua $1-2
     Words Ball and Mason in heavy embossing, rest light.
     Smooth lip Mason shoulder seal

266. BALL IMPROVED MASONS PATENT 1858................................ Aqua $1-2
     Words Ball and Mason in heavy embossing, rest light.
     Smooth lip Mason shoulder seal

267. BALL IMPROVED MASON'S PATENT 1858 (all embossing light)......... Aqua $1-2
     Smooth lip Mason shoulder seal

268. BALL IMPROVED MASON'S PATENT 1858............................... Aqua $1-2
     All embossing is light except for Masons Patent 1858.
     Due to the spacing of the letters, it appears to be
     Mason Spatent.
     Smooth lip Mason shoulder seal

269. THE BALL JAR MASON'S PATENT 1858 (all block letters)........... Aqua $4-6
     Ground lip Mason shoulder seal

270. THE BALL JAR MASON'S PATENT 1858 (block letters, front)........ Aqua $8-10
     Reverse: IMPROVED
     Ground lip Glass insert & screw band

271. THE BALL JAR MASON'S PATENT NOV 30th 1858 (all block letters)... Aqua $4-6
     Ground lip Mason shoulder seal

272. THE BALL (script) JAR MASON'S PATENT NOV 30th 1858.............. Aqua $4-6
     Ground lip Mason shoulder seal

273. THE BALL JAR MASON'S N PATENT NOV 30th 1858 (all block letters). Aqua $8-10
     Ground lip Mason shoulder seal

274. BALL MASON...Clear   -25¢
     Measurements on left side, vertical ribs on right & back
     Base: Ball Made In U S A
     Smooth lip Mason beaded neck seal Circa late 1950's

275. <u>BALL</u> MASON.. Clear   -25¢
     Measurements on right side, vertical ribs on left & back
     Base: Unmarked
     Smooth lip Mason beaded neck seal Circa late 1950's

276. <u>BALL</u> MASON (front) Fruit Medallion (reverse)................. Clear   -25¢
     Measurements & ribs on sides
     Base: Genuine Ball Sculptured Glass Mason Jar Circa 1960's

277. <u>BALL</u> MASON (front) Fruit Medallion (reverse)................. Clear   -25¢
     Standard measurements, left. Metric measurements, right.
     Base: Genuine Ball Sculptured Glass Mason Jar
     Smooth lip Mason beaded neck seal   Circa 1974 and later

278. <u>BAL</u> MASON (error, front) Fruit Medallion (reverse)............ Clear   -$1
     Description as in #277   Pint only, circa 1975

279. <u>BALL</u> MASON.. Ball blue $1-2
     Smooth lip Mason beaded neck seal   Light green $1-2
     Round shoulders similiar to the Boyd Mason jars. Med. olive green $15-18
                                 Light olive green $12-15

280. BALL MASON (3 L loop)... Aqua   -$1
     Smooth lip Mason shoulder seal   Clear   -$1
                                   Amber $25-30
                        Med. olive green $15-18
                  Green, amber streaks $20-25

281. BALL MASON (3 L loop)... Aqua   -$1
     Smooth lip Mason beaded neck seal

282. BALL MASON (front) BALL MASON (reverse)...................... Aqua $15-20
     Apparently two front molds were used.
     Smooth lip Mason shoulder seal

283. BALL MASON (front).. Aqua $15-20
     Reverse: MASON'S PATENT NOV 30th 1858
     Apparently two front molds were used.
     Smooth lip Mason shoulder seal

284. BALL MASON (word Ball very light)...   .... Aqua   -$1
     Smooth lip Mason shoulder seal

285. BALL MASON..........................   .... Aqua $20-25
     Base: Hahne & Co. Newark, N. J.
     Smooth lip Mason shoulder seal

286. BALL MA (error, missing letters)....   .... Aqua $2-3
     Smooth lip Mason shoulder seal

287. BALL MASO (error, missing letters)..   .. Aqua $2-3
     Smooth lip Mason shoulder seal

#286

288. BALL MA ON (error, missing letters).............   .. Aqua $2-3
     Smooth lip Mason shoulder seal

289. BALL SON (error, missing letters)......   .. Aqua $2-3
     Smooth lip Mason shoulder seal

290. BALL MASON (no crossbar on A in Mason)..   .. Aqua $2-3
     Smooth lip Mason shoulder seal

#290

291. BALL MASON (a in Ball is incomplete)..   .... Aqua $2-3
     Smooth lip Mason shoulder seal
     Pint size   #291

292. BALL MASON (a in Ball is incomplete)................... Aqua $2-3
     Smooth lip Mason shoulder seal Pint

293. BALL MASON (reversed S)............................... Aqua $2-3
     Smooth lip Mason shoulder seal

294. BALL MASON (the B looks like an R)................... Aqua $2-3
     Smooth lip Mason shoulder seal

                                                      #292

295. BALL MASON (word Ball is superimposed over erased ROOT)...... ...Green $2-3
     Smooth lip Mason shoulder seal   Yellow green $12-15

296. BALL MASON (the S is uneven)........................... Aqua $1-2
     Smooth lip Mason shoulder seal

297. BALL MASON (3 L Loop) (Upside down on jar)............. Aqua, Clear $20-25
     Smooth lip Mason shoulder seal Pint size
     Believed to be dispenser jars, rather than an error.

298. BALL MASON IMPROVED...Aqua, Clear $1-2
     Smooth lip Mason shoulder seal

299. BALL MASON IMPROVED...Aqua, Clear $1-2
     Smooth lip Glass Lid & screw band

300. BALL MASON'S (keystone) PATENT NOV 30th 1858..................... Aqua $8-10
     Smooth lip Mason shoulder seal

301. BALL MASON'S (keystone, within circle) PATENT NOV 30th 1858...... Aqua $8-10
     Smooth lip Mason shoulder seal

302. BALL MASON'S N PATENT NOV 30th 1858.............................. Aqua $6-8
     Smooth lip Mason shoulder seal

303. BALL MASON'S PATENT...Clear $2-4
     Smooth lip Mason beaded neck seal

304. BALL MASON'S PATENT.. Aqua $1-2
     Smooth lip Mason shoulder seal

305. BALL MASON'S PATENT.................................... .... Aqua $3-5
     Ground lip Mason shoulder seal

306. BALL MASON'S PATENT 1858............................. ... Aqua $2-4
     Smooth lip Mason shoulder seal

307. BALL MASON PATENT 1858 (no S after Mason)......... ... Aqua $2-4
     Smooth lip Mason shoulder seal

308. BALL MASONS PATENT 1858 (T's incomplete)......... ... Aqua $4-6
     Note shape of a in Ball
     Smooth lip Mason shoulder seal   #308

309. BALL MASONS PATENT 1858 (final T incomplete)................... Aqua $4-6
     Smooth lip Mason shoulder seal

310. BALL MASON'S PATENT NOV 30th 1858.............................. Aqua $3-5
     Ground lip Mason shoulder seal

311. BALL MASON'S PATENT NOV 30th 1858.............................. Aqua $3-5
     Ground lip Glass lid & screw band

312. BALL MASON'S PATENT NOV. 80th 1858 (date error & incomplete M)... Aqua $6-8
     Ground lip Mason shoulder seal

313. BALL MASON'S PATENT NOV 80th 1858 (date error)................... Aqua $6-8
     Ground lip Mason shoulder seal

314. BALL MASON'S PATENT NOV 30th 1858 .... Aqua $6-8
     Word Ball is very light, incomplete M in Masons, no
       crossbars on A in Patent or Mason, and no middle bar
       on E in Patent.
     Ground lip Mason shoulder seal

315. BALL MASON'S PATENT NOV 30th 1858............................... Aqua $3-5
     Ground lip Mason shoulder seal All block letters

316. THE BALL MASON'S PATENT NOV 30th 1858 (all block letters)....... Aqua $3-5
     Ground lip Mason shoulder seal

317. THE BALL MASON'S PATENT NOV 30th 1858 (no crossbars on A's)..... Aqua $6-8
     Ground lip Mason shoulder seal

318. THE BALL MASON'S PATENT NOV 30th 1858 .... Aqua $6-8
     Incomplete M in Mason & E in Patent
     Ground lip Mason shoulder seal

319. THE BALL MASON'S N PATENT NOV 30th 1858.....   .... Aqua $8-10
     Ground lip Mason shoulder seal

320. BALL The MASON..............................   .... Aqua $3-5
     Smooth lip Mason shoulder seal   Apple green $6-8

     Also see The MASON, No. 1651

                                              #320

321. THE BALL (script) MASON'S PATENT 1858 ....Aqua $3-5
     Ground lip Mason shoulder seal

322. THE BALL (script) MASON'S PATENT 1858 (front)...................Aqua $10-12
     Reverse: IMPROVED
     Ground lip Glass lid & screw band

323. THE BALL (script) MASON'S IMPROVED PATENT 1858..................Aqua $8-10
     Ground lip Glass lid & screw band

324. THE BALL MASON'S IMPROVED PATENT 1858...........   ...Aqua $10-12
     Ghost PAT. APLD. FOR between Mason's & Improved
     Ground lip Glass lid & screw band

325. THE BALL MASON'S PATENT 1858...................   ...Aqua $10-12
     Ghost PAT. APLD. FOR between Mason's & Patent
     Ground lip Mason shoulder seal

326. THE BALL MASON'S PATENT 1858...................   ...Aqua $10-12
     Ghost PAT. APLD FOR between Mason's & Patent
     Reverse: IMPROVED
     Ground lip Glass lid & screw band   #327

327. THE BALL PAT. APL'D. FOR.......................   ....Aqua $50-75
     Ground lip Old style Lightning seal, with tin plated lid   Amber $500 & up
     Lid: Ball Jar Pat Apld For
     Circa about 1899 and made for only one year. 1 Amber jar
       known.

328. THE BALL PAT. APL'D FOR..Aqua $45-50
     Ground lip Mason shoulder seal

329. BALL PERFECTION.. Clear $12-15
    Base: Pat. Apr. 10, 1900 Apr. 26, 1907   Ball blue $12-15
    Smooth lip Glass lid & screw band   ½ Pint Clear $15-18
    Lid (blue) marked: Ball Perfection Pat. Apr 10. 1900 ½ Pint blue $15-18
                Muncie, Ind.
    Lid (blue or milkglass) marked: Pat. Apr. 10. 1900
    Lid (clear) marked: Pat. Apr. 10. 1900

330. BALL PERFECTION (superimposed over ghost Perfect Mason).....Ball blue $12-15
    Smooth lip Glass lid & screw band
    Closure as in #329

331. BALL PERFECTION PAT. APR. 10. 1900 APR. 26. 1907 ....Ball blue $12-15
    Smooth lip Glass lid & screw band
    Closure as in #329

332. BALL PERFECT MASON.......................... .... Aqua $2-3
    Smooth lip Mason beaded neck seal   Light green $2-3
    For illustrations of this and all
      other Ball jars, see "Fruit Jars"
      by Creswick.

333. BALL PERFECT MASON.......................... .... Aqua $2-3
    (Different than #332)   Light green $2-3
    Smooth lip Mason beaded neck seal

334. BALL PERFECT MASON (long L).............. .... Aqua $2-3
    Smooth lip Mason beaded neck seal

335. BALL PERFECT MASON (erased BOYD beneath Ball). .... Aqua $2-3
    Smooth lip Mason beaded neck seal   Light green $2-3

336. BALL PERFECT MASON (erased DREY beneath Ball) .... Clear $2-3
    Smooth lip Mason beaded neck seal

337. BALL PERFECT MASON (in dual line letters).. . Clear $2-3
    Smooth lip Mason beaded neck seal

338. BALL PERFECT MASON (debossed into jar)..... Clear Unpriced
    Base: Ball (debossed, in circle)
    Smooth lip Mason beaded neck seal
    Closure: 1 piece tin plated lid
    With it's markings debossed, rather than embossed, this is
      an unusual jar. Only 2 are presently known.

339. BALL PERFECT MASON...................... ....Ball blue -$1
    Smooth lip Mason beaded neck seal   Clear -25¢
                          Cornflower blue $18-20
                          Brown Amber $30-35
                   Dark Yellow Amber $30-35
                       Straw yellow $1-3
                       Olive green $25-30
                   ½ Pint, Blue $8-10
                   ½ Pint Clear $1-3

340. BALL PERFECT MASON................... ....Ball blue -$1
    Round, ribbed sides   Clear -25¢
    Smooth lip Mason beaded neck seal

341. BALL PERFECT MASON....................................Ball blue -$1
    Smooth lip Mason beaded neck seal Square shape

342. BALL PERFECT MASON (Ball not underlined)....................Ball blue -$1
    Smooth lip Mason beaded neck seal Round shape   Clear -25¢
                         ½ Pint, Clear $1-3

#334

#338

#339

343. <u>BALL</u> PERFECT MASON (word Mason to left)........................ Clear   -$1
      Smooth lip Mason beaded neck seal Round shape   Ball blue   -$1

344. <u>BALL</u> PERFECT MASON.. Clear   -$1
      Smooth lip Mason beaded neck seal Square shape   Ball blue   -$1
                                              ½ Pint clear $1-3

345. <u>BALL</u> PERFECT MASON..½ Gal. amber $20-25
      Vertical ribs and measurements on sides   Pint amber $30-35
      Smooth lip Mason beaded neck seal
      The ½ gallon was also used as a thermos jug liner.

346. <u>BALL</u> PERFECT MASON MADE IN U.S.A............................... Clear   -25¢
      Vertical ribs on sides and reverse
      Smooth lip Mason beaded neck seal Square shape

347. <u>BALL</u> PERFECT MASON (without Made In USA)...................... Clear   -25¢
      Vertical ribs on sides and reverse
      Smooth lip Mason beaded neck seal Square shape

348. <u>BALL</u> PERFECT MASON (front) MADE IN U.S.A. (reverse).......... Clear   -25¢
      Vertical ribs on sides and reverse
      Smooth lip Mason beaded neck seal Square shape

349. <u>BALL</u> PERFECT MASON (front) MADE IN U.S.A. (reverse).......... Clear   -25¢
      Measurements on right side, vertical ribs on left
      Smooth lip Mason beaded neck seal Square shape

350. <u>BALL</u> PERFECT MASON MADE IN U.S.A............................... Clear   -25¢
      Measurements on right side, vertical ribs on left
      Smooth lip Mason beaded neck seal Square shape

351. <u>BALL</u> PERFECT MASON...Ball blue $3-4
      Smooth lip Mason beaded neck seal
      42 oz. size or "Short 1/2 gallon"
      Other known sizes are 56 oz., 58 oz., and 66 oz.
      The Ball Perfect Mason was also made in miniature size,
       round & square with perforated lids for salt & pepper.
      Also made with the lid not perforated as a salesman's sample.

352. <u>BALL</u> PERFFCT MASON (error)..................................Ball blue $2-3
      Smooth lip Mason beaded neck seal Pint

353. <u>BALL</u> PEPFECT MASON (error)..................................Ball blue $2-3
      Smooth lip Mason beaded neck seal Pint

354. <u>BALL</u> PEREFCT MASON (error)..................................Ball blue $2-3
      Smooth lip Mason beaded neck seal Pint & Quart

355. <u>BALL</u> PFRFECT MASON (error)....................... ...Ball blue $2-3
      Smooth lip Mason beaded neck seal Quart

356. <u>BALL</u> PEREECT MASON (error)....................... ...Ball blue $2-3
      Smooth lip Mason beaded neck seal Quart

357. <u>BALL</u> PERFEOT MASON (error)....................... ...Ball blue $2-3
      Smooth lip Mason beaded neck seal Quart

#354

Ball PEREFCT MASON

358. <u>BALL</u> PERFECT MASON (no crossbar on A) ....Ball blue $2-3
      Smooth lip Mason beaded neck seal Quart

359. <u>BALL</u> PERFECT MASON (no crossbars in E's or F)..............Ball blue $2-3
      Smooth lip Mason beaded neck seal Quart

360. BALL PERFECT MASON (incomplete R)............................ Ball blue $2-3
     Smooth lip Mason beaded neck seal Quart

361. BALL PERFECT ASO (missing letters).......................... Ball blue $2-3
     Smooth lip Mason beaded neck seal Quart

362. BALL PERFECT MASON (letter N faint)........................ Ball blue $2-3
     Smooth lip Mason beaded neck seal 48 oz. size

363. BALL PERFECT MASON (word Ball superimposed over ghost Drey)..... Clear $2-3
     Smooth lip Mason beaded neck seal

364. BALL REFRIGERATOR AND FREEZER JAR................................. Clear   -25¢
     Smooth lip 2 pc. gold lacquered lid with No. 63 insert.
     An 8 oz. jar, made in the early 1960's.

365. GARDEN WALK ALL PURPOSE JAR BY BALL MADE IN U.S.A. (on base).... Clear   -$1
     Fruit and vegetable designs enameled, front & reverse
     Smooth lip Mason beaded neck seal Circa 1965

366. BALL MASON (front)... Clear   -$1.25
     Base: Genuine Ball Sculptured Glass Mason Jar
     Vertical ribs, cup & oz. measurements on left side
     Vertical ribs, metric measurements on right side
     Reverse: 1 of six different designs, all with 1776-1976 dates
        Williamsburg Capitol   Mount Vernon   Fort Ticonderoga
        Independence Hall   Valley Forge   Old North Bridge
     Made in 1976 for America's bicentennial.

367. BALL SANITARY SURE SEAL...................................... Ball blue $2-4
     Base: Patd July 14 08 or Patd July 14 1908
     Smooth lip Lightning beaded neck seal

368. BALL SANITARY SURE SEAL...................................... Ball blue $2-4
     Smooth lip Lightning dimple neck seal, full round dimple.

369. BALL SANITARY SURE SEAL .... Ball blue $2-4
     Smooth lip Lightning dimple neck seal, large round dimple.

370. BALL SANITARY SURE SEAL...................................... Ball blue $2-4
     Smooth lip Lightning dimple neck seal, with a bead
                 connecting the dimples.

371. BALL SANITARY SURE SEAL PAT'D JULY 14, 1908. .... Ball blue $2-4
     Smooth lip Lightning beaded neck seal   Clear $2-4

372. BALL SPECIAL (a wide mouth jar)............. ... Ball blue $2-4
     Smooth lip Mason beaded neck seal   ½ Pint blue $8-10

373. BALL SPECIAL (a wide mouth jar)........... ... Ball blue $2-4
     Smooth lip Mason shoulder seal   Clear $2-4

374. BALL SPECIAL MADE IN U.S.A................ .... Clear   -25¢
     Smooth lip Mason beaded neck seal

#376

375. BALL SPECIAL MADE IN U.S.A................................... Clear   -25¢
     Smooth lip Mason beaded neck seal Gripper ribs sides & back

376. BALL SPECIAL WIDE MOUTH MADE IN U.S.A....................... Clear   -25¢
     Smooth lip Mason beaded neck seal Gripper ribs sides & back

377. BALL SPECIAL WIDE MOUTH (front) MADE IN U.S.A. (reverse)........ Clear   -25¢
     Smooth lip Mason beaded neck seal Gripper ribs sides & back

378. BALL SPECIAL WIDE MOUTH MADE IN U.S.A.......................... Clear   -25¢
     Vertical ribs on one side, Cup measurements on other side.
     Smooth lip Mason beaded neck seal

379. BALL WIDE MOUTH MADE IN U.S.A................................. Clear   -25¢
     Smooth lip Mason beaded neck seal Vertical gripper ribs

380. BALL WIDE MOUTH (front) MADE IN U.S.A. (reverse).............. Clear   -25¢
     Gripper ribs on one side, Cup measurements on other side.
     Smooth lip Mason beaded neck seal

381. BALL SQUARE MASON... Clear $2-3
     With carpenter's square design
     Smooth lip Mason beaded neck seal

382. BALL SQUARE MASON (with carpenter's square design)........... Clear $2-4
     Word Ball superimposed over ghost Drey
     Smooth lip Mason beaded neck seal

383. BALL SQUARE MASON (without carpenter's square design)........ Clear $3-5
     Smooth lip Mason beaded neck seal Pint size

384. BALL STANDARD (3 L loop)..................................... Aqua $10-15
     Groove ring wax sealer, pressed laid-on ring
     The shoulders on this variation are somewhat squarish.

385. BALL STANDARD... Aqua $2-3
     Groove ring wax sealer, pressed laid-on ring   Clear $2-4
                                              Brown Amber   Unpriced
                                         Deep olive green $150 & up
                              Olive green with amber swirls $150 & up

386. BALL STANDARD (3 L loop)..................................... Aqua $2-3
     Groove ring wax sealer, pressed laid-on ring

387. BALL STANDAPD (3 L loop) (error) .... Aqua $4-6
     Groove ring wax sealer, pressed laid-on ring

388. BALL STANDARD (3 L loop) Incomplete A in Ball.............. Aqua $4-6
     Groove ring wax sealer, pressed laid-on ring

389. BALL SURE SEAL...Clear $2-4
     Smooth lip Lightning beaded neck seal   Ball blue $2-4
                                               ½ Pint Ball blue $10-12

390. BALL SURE SEAL (word Sanitary erased)..... ......Ball blue $2-4
     Smooth lip Lightning beaded neck seal

391. BALL SURE SEAL PAT'D JULY 14, 1908....... .....Ball blue $2-4
     Smooth lip Lightning beaded neck seal   Clear $2-4

392. BALL SURE SEAL PAT'D JULY 14, 1988 (error .....Ball blue $3-5
     Smooth lip Lightning beaded neck seal

393. BALL SURE SEAL............................. .... Aqua $3-5
     Smooth lip Old style Lightning seal   Clear $3-5
     Reported in ½ pint, pint, quart & ½ gallon sizes. ½ Pint Clear $6-8

394. BALL SURE SEAL...Ball blue $4-6
     Base: Pat'd July 14 08
     Smooth lip Lightning dimple neck seal
     A tall, slender jar, and likely a product jar.
     Same shape as #395.

SURE SEAL #390

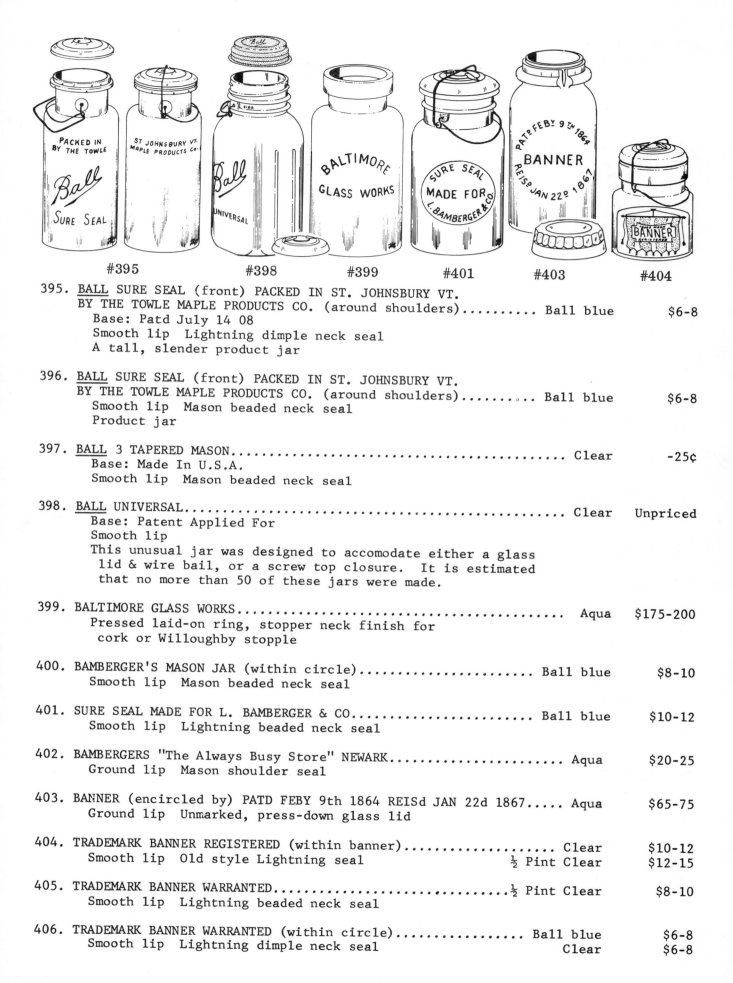

#395	#398	#399	#401	#403	#404

395. BALL SURE SEAL (front) PACKED IN ST. JOHNSBURY VT.
BY THE TOWLE MAPLE PRODUCTS CO. (around shoulders).......... Ball blue $6-8
   Base: Patd July 14 08
   Smooth lip Lightning dimple neck seal
   A tall, slender product jar

396. BALL SURE SEAL (front) PACKED IN ST. JOHNSBURY VT.
BY THE TOWLE MAPLE PRODUCTS CO. (around shoulders).......... Ball blue $6-8
   Smooth lip Mason beaded neck seal
   Product jar

397. BALL 3 TAPERED MASON... Clear -25¢
   Base: Made In U.S.A.
   Smooth lip Mason beaded neck seal

398. BALL UNIVERSAL.. Clear Unpriced
   Base: Patent Applied For
   Smooth lip
   This unusual jar was designed to accomodate either a glass
    lid & wire bail, or a screw top closure. It is estimated
    that no more than 50 of these jars were made.

399. BALTIMORE GLASS WORKS.. Aqua $175-200
   Pressed laid-on ring, stopper neck finish for
   cork or Willoughby stopple

400. BAMBERGER'S MASON JAR (within circle)........................ Ball blue $8-10
   Smooth lip Mason beaded neck seal

401. SURE SEAL MADE FOR L. BAMBERGER & CO........................ Ball blue $10-12
   Smooth lip Lightning beaded neck seal

402. BAMBERGERS "The Always Busy Store" NEWARK...................... Aqua $20-25
   Ground lip Mason shoulder seal

403. BANNER (encircled by) PATD FEBY 9th 1864 REISd JAN 22d 1867..... Aqua $65-75
   Ground lip Unmarked, press-down glass lid

404. TRADEMARK BANNER REGISTERED (within banner)................... Clear $10-12
   Smooth lip Old style Lightning seal   ½ Pint Clear $12-15

405. TRADEMARK BANNER WARRANTED..................................½ Pint Clear $8-10
   Smooth lip Lightning beaded neck seal

406. TRADEMARK BANNER WARRANTED (within circle)................. Ball blue $6-8
   Smooth lip Lightning dimple neck seal   Clear $6-8

407. TRADEMARK BANNER WARRANTED (within circle).......... .... Aqua $8-10
     Smooth lip Old style Lightning seal

408. TRADEMARK BANNER W M WARRANTED (no circle)..... Ball blue $6-8
     Smooth lip Lightning beaded neck seal
     W M stands for wide mouth

409. TRADEMARK BANNER W M WARRANTED (within circle). Ball blue $6-8
     Base: Mold number
     Smooth lip Lightning beaded neck seal

410. TRADEMARK BANNER W M WARRANTED (within circle). ..... Aqua $8-10
     Base: Reg. T.M. No. 43,288
     Ground lip Old style Lightning seal

#408

411. TRADEMARK BANNER WIDEMOUTH.................................. Ball blue $6-8
     Smooth lip Lightning dimple neck seal

412. TRADEMARK BANNER WIDE MOUTH (front)...................... Ball blue $8-10
     Reverse: PAT'D JULY 14 1908
     Smooth lip Lightning dimple neck seal

413. TRADEMARK BANNER WIDE MOUTH REG.U.S.PAT.OFF.
     PAT'D JULY 14, 1908 (all on front)........................ Ball blue $8-10
     Smooth lip Lightning dimple neck seal

414. TRADEMARK BANNER REG. U.S. PAT. OFF. WIDEMOUTH............ Ball blue $8-10
     Smooth lip Lightning dimple neck seal

415. TRADEMARK BANNER REG. U.S. PAT. OFF. WIDEMOUTH (front)..... Ball blue $8-10
     Reverse: PAT'D JULY 14 1908
     Smooth lip Lightning dimple neck seal

416. TRADEMARK BANNER WIDE MOUTH............................. ½ Pint Clear $6-8
     Smooth lip Lightning dimple neck seal
     Found in both round & square shape

417. THE BANNER JELLY (Shield with stars & stripes in center)
     Embossed on the tin lid of a glass jelly tumbler .. .... Clear $8-10
     Smooth lip

418. BARREL SYRUP CORP. OAKLAND, CAL. (on base)......... Clear $1-3
     Smooth lip Mason beaded neck seal
     Barrel shaped product jar

419. WILLIAMS & BATTERSON FAMILY JAR (front)............. . Aqua $600 & up
     Reverse: T. E. BATTERSON PATENTED MAY. 5th 1868
              ROCHESTER N.Y.
     Ground lip Glass lid & wire clamp
     Lid: Pat. May 5th 1868 or Patented May 5th 68
     It is difficult to place a value on this jar as
        only two are presently known.

420. BEACH & CLARRIDGE CO. (front shoulder)............. Clear $10-12
     Reverse shoulder: BOSTON, MASS.   green $10-12
     Ground lip Glass lid & screw band.Product jar.

#419

421. BEACH & CLARRIDGE CO. (front shoulder)........................ Clear $10-12
     Reverse: BOSTON, MASS. MASON'S IMPROVED   green $10-12
     Ground lip Glass lid & screw band.
     Found in clear & pale green, these are
        product jars, made for Beach & Clarridge,
        who were makers of flavorings & extracts.
     Circa 1886-1908.

422. F. R. BEAR CORPORATION LIMITED 24 FL OZS........................Clear $1-3
       Base: C within triangle
       Smooth lip Mason beaded neck seal Canadian product jar

423. BEAVER (no animal, just name)..........................Midget, Clear $50-60
       Ground lip Glass insert & screw band
       Note: On some of these jars there is just a trace
      of the animal..on others there is no trace at all.

424. BEAVER (embossed beaver, chewing log, over word Beaver)......... Aqua $18-20
       Ground lip Glass insert & screw band   Clear $18-20
       The inserts are unmarked and have been found   Amber $350-400
      in clear, aqua, amber & cobalt blue.   Midget, Clear $50-75
       The beaver is facing right, the way most   Midget, Aqua $50-75
      commonly found, and the tail is stippled.   Midget, Amber $1000 & up
       Some jars have a matching mold number just
      below the beaver & on the base.

425. BEAVER (an embossed beaver, chewing log, over word Beaver)..... Clear $18-20
       Ground lip Glass insert & screw band   Aqua $18-20
       The beaver is facing right, and the tail has
      cross hatch markings.

426. BEAVER (embossed beaver, chewing log, over word Beaver)........ Aqua $250 & up
       Ground lip Glass insert & screw band   Clear $250 & up
       The Beaver is facing left, and these are   Midget, Clear $300 & up
      the rarest Beaver jars.   Midget, Aqua $300 & up
                                         Midget, Amber $1200 & up

427. BEAVER (embossed beaver, chewing log, over word Beaver)........ Aqua $18-20
       Ground lip Glass insert & screw band
       The Beaver is facing right. Two lines just below
      the beaver in place of a mold number.
       All of the Beaver jars are Canadian and were made in
       the following sizes: Small mouth midget pint, Imperial
       Pint, Quart, Imperial Quart, ½ Gallon & Imperial ½ Gallon.

428. D. P. BEDELL 118 BANK ST. CLEVELAND, O. (front)............. Aqua $200-225
       Reverse: L & W
       Pressed laid-on ring, stopper neck finish for Kline stopper.

429. BEE.. Aqua $75-100
       Ground lip Glass lid & screw band
       Lid marking, if any, is not known.

430. PATENTED IN U.S. OCT. 23 1900 BEECH NUT TRADEMARK.............. Clear $2-3
       Ground lip Metal press-down lid   Aqua $2-3
       Lid: Unmarked or Pat. July 11 93 Product jar

#423   #424   #425   #426   #427   #428   #429

431. BEECH NUT TRADEMARK (nut & leaf design)......................... Clear $2-3
     Base: Patented July 11th 1893 I.P.C.
     Ground lip Metal press-down lid: Pat. July 11 93
     Product jar

432. BEECHNUT TRADEMARK (nut & leaf design)......................... Clear $2-3
     Base: Beech Nut Packing Company No. 1 Sealed under
          U. S. Patent No. 633660, Dec. 19, 1899,
          Canajoharie, N. Y.
     Ground lip Metal press-down lid: Pat. July 11 93
     Product jar

433. TRADE (nut & leaf) MARK... Clear $2-3
     Base: Patented July 11 1893 I.P.G.
     Ground lip Metal press-down lid: Pat. July 11 93
     Product jar

434. TRADE MARK BEE HIVE (with embossed bees & hive)............... Aqua $85-100
     Smooth lip Glass lid & screw band   Clear $85-100
     Canadian   Midget, clear $200 & up
                                           Midget, Aqua $200 & up

435. BEE KISSED HONEY RIVERSIDE HONEY LOS ANGELES...................Clear $2-3
     Base: PC
     Smooth lip Screw cover   Product jar

436. BEICH'S CHICAGO BLOOMINGTON (on base)........................Clear $2-4
     Smooth lip Old style Lightning seal
     Jar is paneled (14 panels)   Confectionary jar

437. WM. BELL $30-40
     Incised on shoulder of gray stoneware jar   Closure unknown

438. BELLE (front shoulder) PAT. DEC. 14th 1869 (reverse shoulder)... Aqua $375-400+
     Base: has 3 "feet"
     Ground lip Dome shaped glass lid. Wire bail with ends
                 fitting into a metal band around neck of jar.
     Note: Amber has been listed, but we have not been able to
           verify it.

439. BELLE (front shoulder) PAT. DEC. 14th 1869 (reverse shoulder)... Aqua $400 & up
     Base: Not footed
     Reported in ½ gallon size

440. BELLERJEAU'S SIMPLICITY FRUIT JAR PATd MAR 31st 1868...   Light green $250-300
     Ground lip Closure unknown The patent calls for a
                 glass lid & two or more metal clamps to
                 catch under the jar
                 rim.

#431   #432   #434   #436   #438   #440

441. THE BENDICO FRUIT GROWERS COOPERATIVE SOCIETY LTD.
(around) DIGGER BRAND (around) An embossed worker
handling fruits.. Clear $20-25
    Smooth lip Glass insert & screw band Australian jar

442. JAS. BENJAMIN STONEWARE DEPOT CINCINNATI, O........................ $40-50
    Gray stoneware jar with blue stenciling
    Wax seal groove   Jar has a finger handle on side

443. E. BENNETT'S PATENT FEB 6th 1866............................. Aqua $250-300
    Pressed laid-on ring, stopper neck finish for glass stopper.
    Vertical serrations on lower inside of the stopper well.
    Stopper: Bennett's Patent Feb 6 1866
         Or: Bennett's Patent Feb 6 1866
             A. Kline Oct. 21 8163 (error)
    The stoppers are found in aqua and clear.

444. BENNETT'S NO. 1.. Aqua $150-200
    Pressed laid-on ring, stopper neck finish for glass stopper.
    Vertical serrations on lower inside of the stopper well.
    Stopper: Bennett's Patent Feb 6 1866

445. BENNETT'S NO. 1 (superimposed over erased ADAMS & CO.
    MANUFACTURERS PITTSBURGH, PA.).............................. Aqua $150-200
    Pressed laid-on ring, stopper neck finish for glass stopper.
    Vertical serrations on lower inside of the stopper well.
    Stopper: Bennett's Patent Feb 6 1866

    Also see ADAMS & CO. jars, Nos. 17 & 18

446. BENNETT'S NO. 2 (2 is reversed)............................... Aqua $375-400
    Base: has 7 "feet"
    Pressed laid-on ring, stopper neck finish for glass stopper.
    Vertical serrations on lower inside of the stopper well.
    Stopper: Bennett's Patent Feb 6 1866

447. UNION MADE BENN HUBB PEANUT BUTTER
    NET WT. 1 LBS. CHATTANOOGA, TENN. (all on front)............. Clear $1-3
    Reverse: "MADE WITH PEANUTS AND SALT"
    Smooth lip Mason beaded neck seal   Product jar

448. UNION MADE BENN HUBB PEANUT BUTTER
    NET WT. 1/2 LBS. CHATTANOOGA, TENN. (all on front).... Clear $1-3
    Reverse: "MADE WITH PEANUTS AND SALT"
    Smooth lip Mason beaded neck seal   Product jar

449. BENTON MYERS & CO. CLEVELAND, OHIO (on base)........   Clear $6-8
    Smooth lip Glass lid & metal "Safety Valve" clamp
    Product jar   Reported in 1/2 gallon size

450. BENTON MYERS & CO. CLEVELAND, OHIO (on base)........   Clear $2-3
    Smooth lip Old style Lightning seal
    Product jar   Reported in 1/2 gallon size
                                          #451

451. BERNARDIN MASON... Clear $1-3
    Base: Manufactured By Latchford Marble Glass Company
    Smooth lip Mason beaded neck seal. 2 pc. gold lacquered lid
    Lid insert: Bernardin Mason The Ideal Vacuum Seal
              (shows the Good Housekeeping seal)

452. BERNARDIN MASON (front) EXCELLENT FOR JELLY (on reverse)........ Clear
    Base: Manufactured By Latchford Marble Glass Company   1/2 pint $2-4
    Smooth lip Mason beaded neck seal.
    Lid as in #451

453. BEST.. Aqua $20-25
         Ground lip Glass lid & screw band   Clear $20-25
         Wide mouth Canadian sealer   Amber $250 & up

454. BEST..Clear $15-18
         "Rayed" base and lid insert   Light green $15-18
         Smooth lip Glass lid & screw band
         Wide mouth Canadian sealer

455. BEST..Clear $12-15
         With plain base & lid insert   Light green $12-15
         Smooth lip Glass lid & screw band
         Wide mouth Canadian sealer

456. BEST (D within diamond) on lid................ ...... Clear $2-3
         Smooth lip Glass lid & screw band
         Wide mouth Canadian sealer

457. BEST WIDE MOUTH MADE IN CANADA.............. ..... Clear $1-2
         Base: D within diamond
         Smooth lip Glass lid & screw band
         Insert: Best Wide Mouth Made In Canada

458. THE BEST................................ ...... Clear $250-300
         Ground lip Glass stopper with glass   Pale green $250-300
         extensions for internal thread in jar neck.
         Stopper: The Best Patented August 18th 1868

459. THE BEST (on shoulder)......................... ..Aqua $250-275
         Base: S.L.L (for Samuel L. Loomis, patentee)
         Ground lip Glass lid, metal band clamp
         Lid: Pat.May 26 1885 Lid has a groove on top
         for wooden wedges as shown on the patent.

460. "THE BEST" FRUIT KEEPER........................... ..Aqua $30-35
         Ground lip Glass lid & wire clamp
         Lid: Pat. May 5 1896

461. "THE BEST" FRUIT KEEPEP (error)................... ..Aqua $35-40
         Ground lip Closure as in #460

462. PAT. MAY 5 1896 (on lid)................... ..Aqua $20-25
         Jar is unmarked
         Ground lip Glass lid & wire clamp
         Reported in ½ gallon size

463. THE BEST JAR PAT PEND (on glass stopper). ....Aqua $150-175
         Stopper neck finish
         Stopper has a groove for rubber gasket

464. BEST QUALITY.................................. .....Pale green $3-5
         Smooth lip Mason beaded neck seal
         Gripper ribs on sides

465. B. G. CO. (on base)............................... Aqua $10-12
         Groove ring wax sealer, pressed laid-on ring   Amber $85-100
                                                      Cornflower blue $65-70

466. BISHOPS (with eagle, shield & bear)........................... Aqua $12-15
         Metal press-down lid   Product jar

467. PAT. JAN. 12. 1886 (on lid)................................ Aqua $90-100
         Ground lip Glass lid & 4 pc. metal clamp, consisting
                     of tie wire & bail, pressure bar & locking
                     lever.

#458

#459

#460

468. BLOESER JAR.. Aqua $90-100
    Ground lip Glass lid Wire & metal clamp,   Citron $125-135
        neck tie wire
    Lid: Pat. Sept. 27 1887

469. BLUE RIBBON (within ribbon)...................... ....Clear $6-8
    Base: Smalley, Kivlan & Onthank, Boston,
        Mass. Patent Applied For
    Smooth lip Glass lid & metal side clamps

470. BLUE RIBBON GOODS ALWAYS RELIABLE............ ....Clear $12-15
    Ground lip Glass insert & screw band
    Canadian product jar

471. BLUE RIBBON VACUUM PACKED COFFEE............. ...Clear $2-3
    Smooth lip Metal screw cover
    Canadian product jar

#469

472. BODINE & BROS. M. HARBSTER MAKER READING Pa
    PATENTED MARCH 26 1861 (all on metal stopple)....... . Aqua $100-125
    Jar is unmarked
    Stopper neck finish for metal stopple

473. F. & J. BODINE MANUFACTURERS PHILADELPHIA Pa....... . Aqua $75-100
    Ground lip Tin lid with soldered wire clamp
    Lid: F. & J. Bodines Patent Feb. 12, 1867

474. F. & J. BODINE PHILADa.................... . Aqua $75-100
    Ground lip Tin lid with soldered wire clamp
    Lid: F. & J. Bodines Patent Feb. 12, 1867

#473

475. N E PLUS ULTRA AIRTIGHT FRUIT JAR MADE BY BODINE & BROS.
    WM'S TOWN N.J. FOR THEIR PATENTED GLASS LID.................... Aqua $400-450
    The embossing encircles the entire jar
    Base: Pushed up, unmarked
    Glass lid: Patented Aug. 3 1858 Wire clamp

476. THE N E PLUS ULTRA AIRTIGHT FRUIT JAR MADE BY BODINE & BROS.
    WM'S TOWN N.J. FOR THEIR PATENTED GLASS LID.................... Aqua $400-450
    The embossing encircles the entire jar
    Base: Pushed up, unmarked
    Lid as in #475

477. N E PLUS ULTRA AIRTIGHT FRUIT JAR MADE BY BODINE & BROS.
    WM'S TOWN N.J. FOR THEIR PATENTED GLASS LID.................... Aqua $500-600
    The embossing encircles the entire jar. Two rows of
     square indentations and one row of round indentations
     also encircle the jar.
    Glass lid: Patented Aug. 3 1858 Wire clamp

478. N E PLUS ULTRA AIRTIGHT FRUIT JAR MADE BY BODINE & BROS.
    WM'S TOWN N.J. FOR THEIR PATENTED GLASS LID.................Pint, Aqua $700 up
    The embossing encircles the entire jar. Two rows of
     square indentations and one row of round indentations
     also encircle the jar.
    Base: Bare iron pontil scar
    Glass lid: Patented Aug. 3 1858 Wire clamp Pint size

479. BOLA ESPECIAL.. Clear $1-3
    Smooth lip Mason beaded neck seal Ribs on sides
    Zinc lid: Bola
    Made in Japan for export to the Philippines.

480. BOLDT MASON JAR....................................... Aqua $18-20
    Smooth lip Mason shoulder seal

481. BOLDT MASOM JAR (error)... Aqua $20-25
    Smooth lip Mason shoulder seal

482. BONAPARTE POTTERY (on base)... $15-18
    Off-white stoneware jar
    Paneled similiar to the Peoria Pottery jars.
    Wax seal groove

483. BOOTS CASH CHEMISTS... Amber $8-10
    Smooth lip Closure unknown Product jar

484. BORDEN'S CONDENSED MILK CO. BABY (on base)..................... Clear $6-8
    Milkglass lid & screw band
    Lid: Borden's Condensed Milk Co. Baby Brand   Product jar

485. BOSCO DOUBLE SEAL.. Clear $4-6
    Base: PC in divided rectangle
    Smooth lip Lightning beaded neck seal

486. BOSTON TRADE MARK DAGGER (dagger) BRAND............ ... Green $75-85
    Ground lip Old style Lightning seal, wide mouth
    An Australian jar

487. THE BOSTWICK PERFECT SEAL (script)............... .. Clear $35-40
    Smooth lip Glass lid & metal clamp

488. BOWERS THREE THISTLES........................ .. Amber $15-18
    Ground lip Glass lid & screw band
    Snuff jar

489. BOWKER'S PYROX (on base)...................... .. Clear $1-3
    Glass lid & metal clamp
    Product jar (insecticide)

#485

490. BOWKER'S PYROX REGISTERED U.S.PAT.OFF. A COMBINED
    INSECTICIDE & FUNGICIDE BOSTON BALTIMORE CINCINNATI................. $12-15
    Stenciled in black, in two circles, on white stoneware jar.
    Clear glass lid marked: Sherwood Patent Applied For
    McConnel patent wire bail & lever clamp

491. BOYD MASON (word Mason in banner)...................... Aqua $4-6
    Base: IPG or Unmarked   Clear $4-6
    Smooth lip Mason beaded neck seal   Light green $4-6
                                          Med. olive green $15-18

492. BOYD MASON (Mason within banner) over erased GENUINE........... Aqua $4-6
    Ground lip Mason shoulder seal
    Reported in both pint & quart sizes.

493. BOYDS (front).. . Aqua $4-6
    Reverse: MASON (underlined with shepherd's crook)
    Smooth lip Mason shoulder seal

494. GENUINE BOYDS MASON (front)......................... Aqua $4-6
    Reverse: MASON (underlined with shepherd's crook)
    Smooth lip Mason shoulder seal

495. GENUINE BOYDS MASON (all printed, front)........... . Aqua $4-6
    Reverse: MASON (underlined with shepherd's crook)
    Smooth lip Mason shoulder seal

#492

496. GENUINE BOYDS MASON................................... Aqua $3-5
    Smooth lip Mason shoulder seal   Light green $3-5

-34-

497. GENUINE BOYDS MASON.. Aqua $3-5
    Base: IGCo. within diamond   Light green $3-5
    Smooth lip   Mason shoulder seal

498. GENUINE BOYDS MASON.. Aqua $3-5
    Base: IPGCo.   Light green $3-5
    Smooth lip   Mason shoulder seal

499. GENUINE BOYDS MASON (front).................................... Aqua $15-18
    Reverse: GENUINE BOYDS MASON
    Smooth lip   Mason shoulder seal
    Jar was made, using two front molds

500. BOYD PERFECT MASON (No s in Boyd)....... .... Aqua $2-4
    Smooth lip   Mason beaded neck seal   Light green $2-4

501. BOYDS PERFECT MASON.................... .... Aqua $2-4
    Smooth lip   Mason beaded neck seal   Light green $2-4

502. BOYDS PEPFECT MASON (error)............. .... Aqua $4-6
    Smooth lip   Mason beaded neck seal   Light green $4-6

BOYDS PEPFECT MASON

#502

503. B. P. & CO. (on base)...................................... Aqua $10-12
    Groove ring wax sealer, pressed laid-on ring

504. BRACKETT'S PERFECTION JAR.................................... Aqua $200-250
    Applied lip Closure unknown, possibly cork.

505. BRAID'S BEST COFFEE VACUUM PACKED BRAID TUCK CO.
    LTD. VANCOUVER B.C. CANADA...................................Clear $1-3
    Smooth lip Glass lid & screw band
    A Canadian product jar

506. B. S. MFG. CO. LTD. BRANTFORD CANADA.................................. $10-12
    White stoneware jar, screw cover

507. BRANWHITE'S PATENT NEW YORK MARCH 18 1856 (on lid)............. Clear $200-250
    Ground lip Mason shoulder seal Zinc or pewter lid
    This rare jar from the Richard Vanderlaan collection,
     has shoulders similiar to the "Crowleytown" Masons,
     and a small mouth. The internally threaded lid, which
     is lined with a rubber gasket, engages on a threaded
     band which is permanently attached to the jar neck.
     Only 1 jar is known.

508. BRAUN SAFETEE MASON.................................... ... Clear $2-4
    Smooth lip Mason beaded neck seal

509. A. E. BRAY (4 leaf clover) FRUIT JAR PAT. PEND'D..... Clear $175-200
    Ground lip Glass lid & screw band   Amber $600 & up
    The jar has a row of squarish projections encircling
     the shoulder. The patent for this jar, issued on
     June 25, 1901, covered the jar as well as a two-
     piece wrench which fit over the projections to aid
     in opening the jar.

510. A. P. BRAYTON & CO. SAN FRANCISCO, CAL............. Aqua Unpriced
    Pressed laid-on ring
    Iron closure: William Haller Patd Aug. 7 1860
    Only 1 jar known

A.P. BRAYTON & CO.
SAN FRANCISCO
CAL.

511. THE BRELLE JAR.................................... Clear $15-20
    Smooth lip Glass lid & wire clamp
    Lid: The Brelle Fruit Jar Mfg. Co.
      San Jose Cal. Pat. Oct. 29 1912   #510

512. BRIGHTON... Clear $50-60
        Ground lip Glass lid & wire clamp
        Lid, inside: Clamp Pat. March 30th 1886
        Note: Amber has been listed but we have
          not been able to verify this.

513. BRISTOL FARM PATENT APPLIED FOR (on base)..................... Clear   -25¢
        Smooth lip Lightning dimple neck seal
        Modern product jar

514. BROCKWAY CLEAR VU MASON.................................... Clear $1-2
        Base: B within circle   Light straw amber $3-5
        Smooth lip Mason beaded neck seal   ½ pint clear $2-4
        Glass insert & screw band. Insert: Clear Vu
        Jars are found in both round & square shape.

515. BROCKWAY SUR-GRIP MASON....................   ...... Clear $1-2
        Base: Design Patent Applied For   ½ pint clear $2-4
        Smooth lip Mason beaded neck seal
        Vertical "gripper" ribs

516. BROCKWAY SUR-GRIP SQUARE MASON..............   ...... Clear $1-2
        Base: Design Patent Applied For
        Smooth lip Mason beaded neck seal
        Vertical "gripper" ribs

                                                    #516

517. E. BROFFIT & CO. LTD。 KNOTTINGLEY & LONDON (on stopper).. Light green $10-12
        Stopper neck finish, glass stopper
        English jar

518. BROMSON'S...   ... Amber   Unpriced
        More information is needed on this rare, early
          barrel shaped wax sealer.

519. BROOKFIELD 55 FULTON St. N。Y.....................   ... Aqua $350 & up
        Ground lip   Glass lid & iron yoke clamp with
                        thumbscrew
        Only 1 jar has been reported.

520. C。 D. BROOKS BOSTON (on shoulder)...............   .. Amber $45-55
        Closure: Metal cap with attached wire
                   side clamps.

521. MADE EXPRESSLY FOR C. D. BROOKS BOSTON...........   ....   Unpriced
        Impressed into shoulder of stoneware jar
        Closure as in #520
        Recently reported by collector Sam Pierce
          in gallon size.   #519

522. D. C. BROSSEAU & CO COFFEE & SPICE MILL MONTREAL...............Clear $20-25
        Ground lip Metal screw lid with carrying bail.
        Row of Greek Key design around shoulder & base.
        A Canadian product jar

523. J.H. BROUGH & CO. LIVERPOOL (front)......................... Green $20-25
        Reverse: TRADE (swan) MARK
        Stopper neck finish for glass stopper
        Stopper: Red Fearn Bros. Liverpool & Barnsley
        English jar

524. CHARLES BROWN FANCY & STAPLES GROCERIES FRESH MEATS
       745 COR. Sth & MARKET WHEELING, W。 VA.................................. $40-50
        Gray stoneware jar, blue stenciling
        Wax seal groove

525. GEO. D. BROWN & CO. (on shoulder)............................... Clear $60-70
      Ground lip Glass lid & 3-position metal clamp
      Lid: Thomas Patent July 12 1892

526. THOMAS PATENT JULY 12 1892 (on lid)........................... Clear $40-50
      Jar is unmarked
      Ground lip Closure as in #525

      Also see IMPERIAL TRADEMARK, No. 1291

527. BUCKEYE
528. BUCKEYE 1 (mold number. Also reported with other numbers)...... Aqua $150-160
      Ground lip Glass lid & iron yoke clamp   Clear $150-160
      Lid: J. Adams Pat'd May 20 1862
        Or: Patd May 20 1862

529. PATENTED BY W.W. BUFFINGTON, MARCH 5th 1867
      MANUFACTURED ONLY BY WM. FRANK, PITTSBURGH, PA. (all on front). Aqua   Unpriced
        Metal lid with band of rubber around it.
        Only 1 jar is known and difficult to place a value on.

530. BULACH (within diamond) on lid......................... Emerald green $10-12
      Glass lid & wire clamp A Swiss jar

531. BULACH UNIVERSAL (on lid).............................. Emerald green $1-2
      Glass lid & wire clamp
      A fairly recent Swiss jar

532. FRUIT JUICES A.H. BULLARD NEW YORK (within circle).............Clear $3-5
      Smooth lip Old style Lightning seal
      ½ gallon product jar

533. BUNTE, CHICAGO...Clear $1-3
      Base: K-G within oval
      Glass lid & metal clamp Product jar

534. BUNTE, CHICAGO...Clear $1-3
      Base: HA trademark
      Glass lid & wire clamp   Product jar

535. BUNTE ESTABLISHED CHICAGO 1876................................Clear $3-5
      Base: Kivlan Onthank Boston
      Glass lid & twin wire clamps
      Lid: Bunte Bros. Bunte, Chicago World Famous Candy

536. BUNTE BROTHERS CHICAGO (in large fancy lettering)............. Clear $10-12
      Pressed laid-on ring Stopper neck finish for glass stopper
      Product jar

537. THE BURLINGTON B.G.CO. R'D 1875..............   .... Clear $50-75
      Ground lip Glass lid & screw band
      Canadian sealer

538. THE BURLINGTON B.G.CO. R'D 1875 .... Clear $50-75
      All lines arched except Burlington
      Ground lip Glass lid & screw band
      Canadian sealer

539. THE BURLINGTON B.C.GO. R'D 1876 (error).....   ...... Clear $45-55
      Ground lip Glass lid & screw band
      Canadian sealer

#539

540. THE BURLINGTON B.G.CO. R'D 1876............................... Clear $40-50
      Ground lip Glass lid & screw band   Midget clear $200-250
      Canadian sealer

541. THE BURLINGTON B.G.CO- R D 1876....................⎱⎱⎱⎱..Clear $40-50
     Ground lip Glass lid & screw band
     Canadian sealer

542. THE BURLINGTON B.G.CO- R D 1876 (word The curved)....⎱..Clear $40-50
     Ground lip Glass lid & screw band
     Canadian sealer

543. BURNETT BOSTON.....................................⎱⎱..Clear $12-15
     Ground lip Glass lid & "Safety Valve" clamp
     Product jar

544. C. BURNHAM & CO. MANUFACTURERS PHILADa............⎱⎱.. Aqua $225-250
     Ground lip Iron lid with gutta percha insert
     Iron lid: Fridley * Cornman's Patented Oct 25th 1859   #544

         Also see FRIDLEY & CORNMAN'S, No. 1038
                 HUYETT & CORNMAN, No. 1277
                 KEYSTONE, No. 1390

545. BURNS (underlined, within rectangle).........................Clear $1-2
     Base: D within diamond
     Smooth lip Mason beaded neck seal
     Canadian product jar

546. BUTTERNUT DELICIOUS...Clear $1-3
     Base: Paxton Gallagher Co., Omaha, Nebraska
     Smooth lip Screw cover Product jar

547. C (on base).. Aqua $3-5
        Groove ring wax sealer, pressed laid-on ring

548. CADIZ JAR.. Aqua $125-150
        Ground lip   Mason shoulder seal/glass lid
        Lid: Cadiz Jar Patd
          Or: Cadiz Jar Patd 1883

        Also see ECLIPSE JAR, No. 885
               HOOSIER No. 1266   #551

549. CALCUTT'S PATENT APR. 11th NOV. 7th 1893 (on lid).............Clear $35-40
        Ground lip   Glass lid with internal lugs, to
                engage on lugs on jar neck.

550. CALCUTT'S PAT'S APR 11th NOV 7th 1893 (on base)...............Clear $35-40
        Ground lip   Closure as in #549

551. CALIFORNIA (S in triangle) MASON........................Clear $18-20
        Base: Ben Schloss Manufactor
              Patent Applied For S.F.Cal.
        Smooth lip   Tin screw lid
        Lid: Golden State Pat. Applied S Mason

552. CANADA 64 FLUID OZS SIZE (within circle)................Clear   2-3
        Smooth lip   Lightning beaded neck seal
        Lid: Made in Canada   Product jar

553. CANADA (Mariner's compass) TRADEMARK...........   Aqua $300 & up
        Ground lip   Mason shoulder seal   Clear $300 & up
        Canadian sealer   Amber   Unpriced

554. CANADA (Mariner's compass) TRADEMARK...........   Aqua $300 & up
        Ground lip   Glass insert & screw band   Clear $300 & up
        Canadian sealer

555. MADE IN CANADA CANADIAN KING (within shield)
     WIDE MOUTH ADJUSTABLE (all on front)...........   ..Clear $20-25
        Smooth lip   Old style Lightning seal
        Canadian sealer   Square shape   #553

     CANADIAN JEWEL see No. 1331

556. CANADIAN MASON JAR MADE IN CANADA.............................Clear $1-2
        Smooth lip   Mason beaded neck seal   2 pc. metal lid
        Lid insert: Canadian Mason Jar C & variations

557. CANADIAN QUEEN TRADEMARK (within shield)
     WIDE MOUTH ADJUSTABLE (all on front).............   .Clear   Unpriced
        Smooth lip   Old style Lightning seal
        Although this is not a real old jar, it
        seems to be scarce, and Canadian collectors
        value it at $75-100.

558. CANADIAN SURE SEAL MADE IN CANADA..................   .Clear $2-3
        Smooth lip   Mason beaded neck seal
        Wide mouth jar

#557

559. CANDY BROS. MFG. CO. St LOUIS 4 LBS. NET (fancy letters).........Clear $10-12
        Glass stopper type lid & wire clamp   Aqua $10-12
        Lid: Candy Bros. St. Louis C. B.
        Product jar

560. CANNINGTON SHAW & CO. LTD. ST. HELENS (on lid)................... Aqua $10-12
        Base: Pontil scar
        Applied lip Glass stopper
        An English jar

561. THE CANTON FRUIT JAR...Clear $100-125
        Ground lip Glass screw lid
        Lid: Pat. Appd For The Canton Jar
         Or: Patd. Nov. 17 1885 The Canton Jar

562. PATd NOV 17 1885 THE CANTON JAR (on lid).........................Clear $75-80
        Ground lip Glass screw lid
        Jar is unmarked

563. THE CANTON FRUIT JAR..............................   ..Clear $50-75
        Ground lip Glass lid with high fin & notch
                    for spring wire bail. Neck tie wire
        Lid: Patent Appd For

564. THE CANTON FRUIT JAR...........................   ..Clear $50-75
        Ground lip Glass lid with high fin & notch
                    for spring wire bail. Bail
                    hooks into dimples in the neck.
        Lid: Patd Dec. 31 1889   #564

565. THE CANTON DOMESTIC FRUIT JAR....................................Clear $50-75
        Ground lip Glass lid with high fin & notch   Cobalt blue $800 & up
                    for spring wire bail. Bail
                    hooks into dimples in the neck.
        There are 11 or 12 known cobalt blue jars.
        Amber has been listed but we have not been
         able to verify.

566. THE CANTON DOMESTIC FRUIT JAR....................................Clear $50-75
        Word Canton within frame
        Ground lip Glass lid with high fin & notch
                    for spring wire bail. Bail
                    hooks into dimples in the neck.
        Lid: Patd. Dec. 31 1889

567. PATD DEC 31 1889 (on lid)..Clear $10-12
        Unmarked jam jar. Closure as in #566
        8 oz. size

568. THE CANTON ELECTRIC FRUIT JAR.................   ..Cobalt blue $700 & up
        Ground lip Glass lid with high fin & notch
                    for spring wire bail. Neck tie
                    wire
        Lid: Patent Appd For
        There are four or five cobalt blue jars
         known, all with clear lids.

569. THE CANTON FRUIT JAR (word Electric erased)..   ...... Clear $50-75
        Ground lip Closure as in #568
                                                      #569

570. CANTON MANUFACTURING CO. BOSTON (on base)....................... Amber $2-4
        Closure unknown
        Product jar

571. CARROLL'S TRUE SEAL (within frame)............................. Clear $8-10
      Smooth lip Old style Lightning seal
      Canadian product jar

572. CARTER'S BUTTER & FRUIT PRESERVING JAR
      PAT. SEP. 28 1897 (all on lid).................................... Clear $100-125
      Base: J.J. Carter's Air Tight Butter Jar   Pale aqua $100-125
      Glass lid   Metal band around neck of jar with
        "ears" to hold a wire bail handle, and a wire
        loosely pivoted at one end in one of the "ears"
        and adapted to extend across the cover to hold
        it in place.
      Made in both round & oblong style to hold from
        one pound to twelve pounds of butter.

573. CASSIDY (front) CMCo monogram (reverse)...................... Clear $150-175
      Ground lip Glass lid with "stepped" fin,
                  & wire bail

574. C B (on base)... Aqua $2-4
      Ground lip Glass insert & screw band   Light olive green $3-5

575. CCC.. Clear $20-25
      Ground lip Glass screw lid: Pat. Oct. 24 1882
      Reported in ½ gallon size. Possibly a product jar.

576. C.C.CO. (vertically on jar).................................. Clear $4-6
      Smooth lip Old style Lightning seal
      ½ gallon, product jar

577. C. CO. 2 MILW (on base)...................................... Aqua $25-30
      Groove ring wax sealer, pressed laid-on ring

578. PAT'D. MARCH 30 58 EXT'D MARCH 30 72 CFJCo. (on lid of tin can)....... Unpriced
      This can from the Norman Barnett collection, has
      a paper label showing it was used for tea. The
      familiar CFJCo monogram stands for the Consolidated
      Fruit Jar Company.

579. CDE (on base)..Light green $4-6
      Groove ring wax sealer, pressed laid-on ring

580. A & D.H. CHAMBERS UNION FRUIT JAR PITTSBURGH, PA. (front)........ Aqua $50-60
      Groove ring wax sealer, pressed laid-on ring   Cornflower blue $90-100
      Tin lid: A. & D. H. Chambers Pittsburgh,Pa.
               star in center of lid

581. A & D.H. CHAMBERS UNION FRUIT JAR PITTSBURGH, PA. (front)........ Aqua $50-60
      Wax sealer as in #580, slightly different shape.

#571   #573   #578   #579   #580   #581

582. A. & D. H. CHAMBERS UNION FRUIT JAR PITTSBURGH, PA (base)....... Aqua $20-25
        Groove ring wax sealer, pressed laid-on ring   Amber $250 & up
        Tin lid: A. & D. H. Chambers Pittsburgh, Pa.   Cornflower blue $65-75
                 star in center

583. THE CHAMPION PAT. AUG 31, 1869...................................Aqua $100-125
        Ground lip Glass lid & iron yoke clamp
        Also see THE KING jar No. 1418

584. CHAMPION SYRUP & REFINING CO. INDIANAPOLIS. ....Aqua $20-25
        Ground lip Mason shoulder seal
        Product jar

585. MRS. CHAPINS MAYONNAISE, BOSTON, MASS.......... ......Clear $2-3
        Smooth lip Lightning seal, glass bosses on
                    sides of neck for wire
        Pint, Product jar

586. MRS. CHAPINS MAYONNAISE, BOSTON, MASS......... ....Clear $2-3
        Smooth lip Lightning beaded neck seal
        Pint, Product jar

587. CHATTANOOGA MASON (below C within circle)..... ....Clear $4-6
        Smooth lip Mason beaded neck seal

588. CHAUNCEY I. FILLEY IMPORTER OF QUEENSWARE
     108 N. MAIN STREET ST. LOUIS (all on front)... .... Aqua $175-200
        Pressed laid-on ring, stopper neck finish
        Glass stopper: A. Kline Pat'd Oct. 27 1863   #588

589. CHEF (in frame) TRADE (chef) MARK BERDAN & CO. TOLEDO, O....... Clear $4-6
        Smooth lip Old style Lightning seal   ½ pint clear $6-8
        Product jar

590. CHEF TRADEMARK THE BERDAN CO. (around chef)
     PAT'D JULY 14 1908 (all on front)..................   Clear $4-6
        Smooth lip Lightning dimple neck seal
        Also found with Lightning beaded neck seal
        Product jar

591. CHEF TRADEMARK THE BERDAN CO. (around chef)...   Clear $4-6
        Reverse: PAT'D JULY 14, 1908
        Smooth lip Lightning beaded neck seal
        Product jar

592. CHICAGO TRADE CFJP (monogram) MARK FRUIT JAR..   Aqua $125-150
        Ground lip Old style Lightning bail, glass
           Immerser marked: Pat. Reg. 1893
        Neck: BE SURE TO FILL TO TOP RING WITH SYRUP
        An Australian jar
        Also see the COLUMBIA jar No. 642 & FRISCO jar
593. THE CHIEF.......................... No. 1040   Aqua $175-200
        Base: Pat'd Nov 29 1870
        Ground lip Tin lid & snap bar closure   #592

594. THE CHIEF (front) Large script K on reverse.................. Aqua $175-200
        Base: Pat'd Nov 29 1870
        Ground lip Tin lid & snap bar closure

595. Chinese characters (within circle)............................ Clear $3-5
        Smooth lip Old style Lightning seal
        Quart, Product jar

596. CHOICE LEAF LARD QUARANTEED STRICTLY PURE (North Star
     Brand TradeMark) NORTH PACKING AND PROVISION CO.
     BOSTON, U. S. A. (all on front)................................. Clear $20-25
          Base: A. G. Smalley & Co. Boston, Mass. Patented
               April 7th 1896 & December 1st 1896
          Ground lip Glass cover & zinc cap with bail handle
          Zinc cap: North Packing & Provision Co. Boston, Mass.
                    North Star Brand Trademark Pure Leaf Lard
                    Pendleton Manufacturing Co. Improved Cover
                    Carbondale, Pa. Pat. Applied For
          Product jar

597. CHRISTO Good For Everybody GINGER ALE CHRISTO
     MANUFACTURING CO. SODA FOUNTAINS & SUPPLIES
     RICHMOND, VA. U.S.A. (all on front)............ .... Clear $8-10
          Smooth lip Old style Lightning seal
          Also found with a paper label, no embossing.
          ½ Gallon, Product jar

598. PATENT JUNE 9 1863 CIN. O. (on lid)........... ....Dark Aqua $250-300
          Ground lip Jar is "ribbed" with 14
                    mellon ribs
          Metal lid with wrench lugs, unlined or with
          a glass insert. Lid is unthreaded but has
          a wire rolled into the bottom edge which
          forms a helix to engage the threads on the
          neck of the jar.

Christo
GINGER ALE CHRISTO
MANUFACTURING CO.
SODA FOUNTAINS
& SUPPLIES
RICHMOND, VA. U.S.A.
#597

599. PATENT APPLIED FOR CIN. O. (on lid)
600. PATENT JUNE 9, 1863 CIN. O. (on lid)................................Aqua $50-60
          Ground lip No embossing on the jar   Green $50-60
          Closure as in #598. The glass inserts
          have been found in aqua & clear.

601. J.M. CLARK & CO. LOUISVILLE, KY. (around shoulder)..............Amber $35-40
          Pressed laid-on ring. Possibly a cork stopper

602. J.M. CLARK & CO. LOUISVILLE, KY. (on base).......................Amber $30-35
          Pressed laid-on ring. Possibly a cork stopper
          Clark & Company was a pickle works.

603. CLARKE FRUIT JAR CO. CLEVELAND, O................................. Aqua $45-55
          Ground lip Glass lid   Metal cam lever, hinged
                              to wire bail. Neck tie wire.
          Clamp marked: Pat. M'CH 17 1885
          A lid (only) has been reported in olive green.

604. PANTRY CLARKS C JAR (on base)....................................Clear   -$1
          Smooth lip Mason beaded neck seal Metal lid
          Canadian product jar

605. CLARK'S PEERLESS... Clear, Aqua $10-12
          Base: Salem or mold number   Light green $10-12
          Ground lip Old style Lightning seal   Emerald green $20-25
                                                     Cornflower blue $20-25

606. CLARK'S PEERLESS (within circle)................................ Aqua $8-10
          Smooth lip Old style Lightning seal, wide mouth

607. CLARKE & WHITE NEW - YORK...............................Green-black Unpriced
          Base: Pontil scar
          Closure: Cork or waxed paper or cloth, tied with a
                   waxed string.
          This jar, dating in the 1830's, appears black un-
          less held to light.

608. CLEVELAND FRUIT JUICE CO. CLEVELAND OHIO (on base)..............Clear $2-3
      Smooth lip Old style Lightning seal
      ½ gallon, Product jar

609. CLEVELAND FRUIT JUICE CO. CLEVELAND OHIO (on base)..............Clear $6-8
      Ground lip Glass lid & "Safety Valve" clamp
      ½ gallon, Product jar

610. TRADEMARK CLIMAX REGISTERED (within circle)....................Clear $3-5
      Smooth lip Lightning beaded neck seal   Ball blue $4-6
                                                          Light green $4-6

611. TRADEMARK CLIMAX REGISTERED (within circle)................. Ball blue $4-6
      Smooth lip Lightning dimple neck seal   Light green $4-6

612. TRADEMARK CLIMAX REGISTERED (no circle)....................... Clear $3-5
      Smooth lip Lightning beaded neck seal

613. TRADEMARK CLIMAX REGISTERED (within circle) PAT'D
      JULY 14 1908... Clear $4-6
      Smooth lip Lightning beaded neck seal   Ball blue $4-6
      The pints may have the date on reverse   Light green $4-6
        instead of on front.

614. TRADEMARK CLIMAX PEGISTERED (in circle) (error) PAT'D
      JULY 14 1908.. Ball blue $6-8
      Smooth lip Lightning beaded neck seal

615. TRADEMARK CLIMAX REGISTERED (within circle).... . Ball blue $20-25
      Smooth lip Lightning beaded neck seal
      The embossing on this pint reported by Velma
        Scott is upside down. A plated mold was used
        and the slug plate was put on upside down.

#615

616. CLIMAX RYLANDS ATLAS TRADEMARKS...................... Light green $8-10
      Base: Ryland Barnsley 2   #615
      Smooth lip Glass lid & copper screw band
      An English jar

617. THE CLIPPER...Aqua $75-85
      Ground lip Mason shoulder seal
      An Australian jar

618. CLIPPER SPECIAL JAR (script)...................... ... Clear $8-10
      Smooth lip Screw top, wide mouth
      An Australian jar

619. THE CLYDE (in script)............................ ... Clear $8-10
      Ground lip Old style Lightning seal
      Lid: Clyde Glass Works, Clyde, N.Y.

620. THE CLYDE (in script, within circle)............ ... Clear $6-8
      Smooth lip Old style Lightning seal
      Lid: Clyde Glass Works, Clyde, N.Y.   #619

621. CLYDE LIGHTNING... Aqua $10-12
      Ground lip Old style Lightning seal

622. CLYDE MASON'S IMPROVED... Clear $10-12
      Ground lip Also smooth lip Glass insert & screw band
      Insert: Clyde Glass Works, Clyde, N.Y.

623. C.M.F.G.C. (on base).. Aqua $10-12
      Pressed laid-on ring   Closure unknown, possibly cork   Clear $10-12
      Possibly a product jar, circa 1872

624. CODDINGTON'S BOSS JAR PATd FEB. 23rd 1886...................... Aqua $250-300
    An example of the lid has not been found. The patent
    calls for a metal lid, used in conjunction with sealing
    wax. See "Fruit Jars" by Creswick for illustration.

625. COHANSEY GLASS MFG. CO. PHILADa MOULD No. 2 (on base)..........Amber $12-15
    Ground lip Glass lid & circular wire clamp
    Lid: Cohansey Glass Manuf. Co. Philada. Pat.
        July 16 1872 Patented January 18 1876
    Product jar

626. COHANSEY GLASS MFG. CO. PHILADa MOULD No. 2 (on base)..........Amber $12-15
    Jar has a round-oval space for paper label on front.
    Ground lip Closure as in #625
    Product jar

627. COHANSEY (front) *ECHO* FARMS (reverse)........................ Aqua $30-40
    Ground lip Glass lid & circular wire clamp   ½ Pint
    Lid marking as in #625
    A product jar, using the Cohansey closure

628. COHANSEY... Aqua $15-20
    Ground lip Glass lid & circular wire clamp   Cobalt blue   Unpriced
    Lid: Cohansey Glass Manuf. Co. Philada. Pa.   ½ Pint Aqua $60-65
        Patented July 16th 1872
      Or: Cohansey Glass Mfg. Co. Philadelphia, Pa.
        Patented January 18, 1876
      Or: Cohansey Glass Manuf. Co. Philada. Pa.
        Patented January 1876 18
      Or: Tin lid with soldered wire clamp. Lid
        stamped Cohansey Glass Mfg. Co. Pat.
        Feb'y 12th 1867
    Lids are found with backward letters & numbers
    and in two different styles..(a) with the wire
    clamp resting on the top outside edge of the
    lid, and (b) with the wire in a groove around
    the outside of the lid. (See "Fruit Jars" by
    Creswick for lid illustrations.)
    Jars are found in ¼ pint, ½ pint, 3/4 pint, pint,
    quart, 1½ quart & ½ gallon sizes.
    Only 1 cobalt blue jar & lid are known.

#628

629. COHANSEY... ¼ Pint Aqua $300 & up
    Ground lip Metal lid & soldered wire clamp
    Lid stamped, inside: Cohansey Glass Mfg. Co.
        Pat. Feb'y 12th 1867

#629

630. COHANSEY GLASS MFG. CO. PAT. FEB. 12 1867 (on base)........Pint Aqua $45-50
    Ground lip Metal lid & soldered wire clamp   Quart Aqua $75-100
    Lid stamped: Cohansey Glass Mfg. Co. Pat.   1½ Quart Aqua $75-100
        Feb'y 12th 1867
    The jars have tapered sides. The pint in the
    author's collection has an original paper label
    which reads: Jelly Collar.

631. COHANSEY GLASS MF'G CO. (on base)................................. Aqua $90-100
    Barrel shaped jar, slightly flared neck, cork closure

632. COHANSEY GLASS MF'G CO. (on base)................................. Aqua $90-100
    Barrel shaped jar   Glass or tin lid   Sky blue $150 & up
    Groove ring wax sealer. The groove was formed
    by collapsing a blown bulge, pinching it to-
    gether and then tooling upward into a groove.

633. COHANSEY GLASS MF'G CO. PAT. MCH 20 77 (on base)............... Aqua $100-125
    Barrel shaped jar Glass or tin lid   Sky blue $150 & up
    Groove ring wax sealer, with groove formed as in #632

634. COLBURN'S FOUNTAIN STOPPLE JAR..................... Aqua $250-300
    Tooled laid-on ring, stopper lip for glass stopper
    Stopple: G.F.J. Colburn's Patent Nov. 1st 1864
               Seal With Wax
    Stopple has a scalloped edge and a juice hole

635. COLLINS & CHAPMAN WHEELING, W. V..................... Aqua $500-600
    Jar has a permanently attached metal rim around
       the neck to form a wax seal channel. Tin lid.
    Two jars are presently known.

#635

636. COLLINS WHOLESALE HARDWARE CO. SEEDS, HARDWARE,
PAINTS & OILS, LYNN & BOSTON (within frame, front)..............Clear $3-5
    Smooth lip Old style Lightning seal   ½ Pint clear $6-8
    Product jar known in ½ pint & quart sizes.

637. PACKED BY COLLINS, WHEATON & LUHRS S.F........ ....Aqua $125-150
    Ground lip Glass lid & zinc screw band
    The neck finish is like the Victory jars
       with a small indentation below the seal-
       ing surface.

638. COLUMBIA (on base)......................... ....Clear $20-25
    Ground lip Glass lid & wire clamp
    Lid: Patented Columbia Dec. 29th 1896

639. PATENTED COLUMBIA DEC 29th 1896 (on lid)... ......Clear $10-12
    Ground lip Glass lid & wire clamp
    A small jar

640. PATENTED COLUMBIA DEC. 29th 1896 (on lid).. ......Amber $10-12
    Smooth lip Glass lid & wire bail
    A small product jar

641. COLUMBIA (front)......................... ......Clear $20-25
    Ground lip Glass lid & wire clamp   Pale green $20-25
    Lid: Patented Columbia Dec. 29th 1896   Amber $50-75
    Or: Columbia Patent Applied For
    Or: Dec. 29 1896

#642

642. "COLUMBIA" Patd Regd IMMERSER (monogram) WIDE
MOUTH FRUIT JAR FOY & GIBSON MELBOURNE............... Aqua $125-150+
    Ground lip Old style Lightning neck & bail
    Glass immerser lid marked: Pat. Reg. 1893
    An unusual Australian jar. Also see the
    Chicago Jar, No. 592 & the FRISCO jar No. 1040

643. COLUMBIA MADE IN CANADA................................ ..Clear $75-100
    Smooth lip Exact closure is not known. The
    neck finish is similiar to Kerr Economy
    jars. A relatively late Canadian sealer,
    but scarce in most parts of Canada.

#644

644. COLUMBIA, MADE IN CANADA......................................Clear $75-100
    As in #643 except words Made In Canada are lower on jar.

645. THE COLUMBIAN... Unpriced
    Although this jar was advertised in ½ pint, pint, quart,
    and 5 or 6 gallon sizes, an actual example has not yet
    been reported.

646. COMMODORE... Aqua $375-450
        Applied lip Metal stopper with thumbscrew
        Stopper: Doane's * Nov. 7 * 1865 Patent

647. COMMODORE... Aqua $375-450
        As in #646, except different shape jar

648. COMMON SENSE JAR (front)... Aqua $500-600
        Reverse: GREGORY'S PATENT AUG. 17th 1869
        Base: Patd Aug 17 1869
        Glass immerser lid & iron yoke clamp with
         thumbscrew
        Immerser: Gregory's Pat. Aug 17th 1869
        The immersers are made in one piece and
        very crudely made.

649. COMMON SENSE... Aqua $100-150
        Ground lip Glass lid & heavy wire bail
        Exact lid not known

#649

650. FRUIT COMMONWEALTH JAR.. Aqua $75-85
        Ground lip Old style Lightning seal Wide mouth
        An Australian jar

651. COMPTON & BATCHELDER CLEVELAND, O................................... Aqua $150-175
        Groove ring wax sealer, pressed laid-on ring

652. CONSERVE JAR...Clear $6-8
        Ground lip Also with smooth lip   ½ Pint clear $10-12
        Old style Lightning seal

653. C (within diamond, on base of tin can)............................. $2-3
        Lid: Names of fruits & vegatables radiating from center

654. Names of fruits & vegatables radiating from center (on lid).......... $2-3
        Tin can

655. CORONA JAR MADE IN CANADA.. Clear $2-3
        Smooth lip Glass insert & screw band
        Insert: Corona Or Corona, Made In Canada

656. IMPROVED CORONA JAR MADE IN CANADA................................... Clear $1-2
        Base: C within triangle Or Corona Trademark Regd.
        Smooth lip Glass insert & screw band
        Insert: Corona, Made In Canada

657. (Crown emblem) CORONET.. Clear $50-75
        Smooth lip Glass insert & screw band

658. (Crown emblem) CORONET.. Clear $50-75
        Smooth lip Glass insert & screw band
        This jar shows traces of a more elaborate
        Crown emblem erased.

659. (Crown Emblem) CORONET.. Clear $50-75
        Smooth lip Glass insert & screw band
        Crown emblem different from above jars

#657

660. C.P. & U. (on milkglass insert)..................................... Aqua $12-15
        Base: H & D or H21   Clear $12-15
        Ground lip Milkglass insert & screw band
        Product jar

#659

661. C.P. & U. (on milkglass lid insert).......................... Clear $12-15
    Base: H & R   Aqua $12-15
    Ground lip Milkglass insert & screw band
    Product jar

662. THE CRANDALL & GODLEY CO. PERFECTO FRUIT JUICES NEW YORK....... Aqua $10-12
    Base: Trademark Lightning Putnam
    Ground lip Old style Lightning seal
    ½ Gallon product jar

663. THE CRANDALL & GODLEY CO. PERFECTO FRUIT JUICES NEW YORK....... Aqua $10-12
    Base: The C & G. Co. N. Y.
    Ground lip Old style Lightning seal
    ½ Gallon product jar

664. THE CRANDALL-PETTEE CO. PERFECTO FRUIT JUICES NEW YORK......... Aqua $10-15
    Base: C. P. Co.
    Ground lip Old style Lightning seal
    ½ Gallon product jar

665. CRESCA MORE THAN A LITTLE BETTER REISS & BRADY
    NEW YORK (all on front, around a ship)....................... Clear $2-3
    Base: Patented June 9 03 June 23 03
    Smooth lip "Economy type" closure
    Oval shaped product jar in pint and ½ pint sizes

666. CRESCA MORE THAN A LITTLE BETTER REISS & BRADY
    NEW YORK (all on front, around a ship)....................... Clear $2-3
    Base: Patented June 23 03
    Smooth lip "Economy type" closure
    Oval shaped product jar in ½ pint size

667. W. A. Cristy WEST McHENRY, ILL. TradeMark PICKLES (on base).... Clear $12-15
    Ground lip Glass lid & screw band
    Product jar

668. CROFT'S SWISS MILK COCOA...................................... Aqua $6-8
    Base: Croft And Allen Co. Patent Applied For Phila. Pa.
    Ground lip 2 pc. metal lid marked: Croft's Swiss Milk Cocoa
    Oval shaped pint, product jar

669. CROFT'S SWISS MILK COCOA...................................... Aqua $30-35
    Base: Croft And Allen Phila. Pa.
    Ground lip "Cohansey type" closure
    Oval shaped pint, product jar

670. CROMWELL.. Clear $12-15
    Smooth lip Mason beaded neck seal Wide mouth
    An Australian jar

671. CROWN CORDIAL & EXTRACT CO. NEW YORK............. Aqua $10-12
    Base: Trademark Lightning or Unmarked   Clear $10-12
    Ground lip Old style Lightning seal
    ½ Gallon product jar   #672

672. (Crown emblem) CROWN................................... Aqua $10-12
    "No-dot" Crown   Midget pint Aqua $250 & up
    Ground lip Glass insert & screw band
    Insert: Crown emblem
    Believed to be the oldest of the Canadian Crown jars

673. (Crown emblem) CROWN................................... Aqua $3-5
    "Heart-shaped Crown, no jewels"
    Smooth lip Glass insert & screw band
    Insert: Crown emblem

-48-

674. Crown emblem only.. Aqua $18-20
     "Heart" shaped Crown
     Smooth lip Glass insert & screw band
     Insert: Crown emblem
     Known in quart & ½ gallon sizes

675. (Crown emblem) CROWN...................................... Aqua $3-5
     "Heart" shaped crown   Midget pint Aqua $10-12
     Ground lip Glass insert & screw band

676. (Crown emblem) CROWN (reversed N in Crown).................... Aqua $6-8
     "Heart" shaped crown
     Smooth lip Glass insert & screw band
     Insert: Crown emblem Reported in ½ gallon size

677. (Crown emblem) CROWN.. Aqua   Unpriced
     "Maple-leaf" Crown, with leaf on base of jar
     Smooth lip Glass insert & screw band
     Believed to be the scarcest of the Crown jars.

678. (Crown emblem) CROWN..................................... Aqua $10-12
     "Bulge" crown   Midget pint Aqua $30-35
     Ground lip Glass insert & screw band
     Insert: Crown emblem

679. (Crown emblem) CROWN......................................Aqua $3-5
     "Bulge" crown   Midget pint Aqua $20-25
     Smooth lip Glass insert & screw band
     Insert: Crown emblem

680. (Crown emblem) CROWN....................................Aqua $10-12
     "Ring" crown   Midget pint Aqua $30-35
     Ground lip Glass insert & screw band
     Insert: Crown emblem

681. Crown emblem only..Aqua $20-25
     "Ring" crown
     Ground lip Glass insert & screw band
     Insert: Crown emblem   #678

682. (Crown emblem) CROWN....................................Aqua $12-15
     "Tall, narrow" crown   Midget pint Aqua $30-35
     Ground lip Glass insert & screw band
     Insert: Crown emblem

683. (Crown emblem) CROWN....................................Aqua $12-15
     "Tall narrow crown with bulge" crown   Midget pint Aqua $30-35
     Ground lip Glass insert & screw band
     Insert: Crown emblem

684. (Crown emblem) CROWN.........................Aqua $12-15
     "Hybrid" crown
     Ground lip Glass insert & screw band
     Insert: Crown emblem

685. (Crown emblem) CROWN........................Aqua $10-12
     "Blend" crown
     Ground lip Glass insert & screw band
     Insert: Crown emblem

686. (Crown emblem) CROWN..........................Aqua $2-3
     Smooth lip Glass insert & screw band   #686   Amber $40-45
     Insert: Crown emblem

-49-

687. (Crown emblem) CROWN.. Aqua $2-3
    Smooth lip Glass insert & screw band   Midget pint aqua $4-6
    Insert: Crown emblem

688. (Crown emblem) CROWN (front)... Aqua $4-6
    Reverse: E within diamond, TORONTO and WINNIPEG   Clear $4-6
    Smooth lip Glass insert & screw band
    Insert: Crown emblem

689. (Crown emblem) CROWN (front)...Aqua $6-8
    Reverse: E within diamond, TORONTO and WINNIPEG
    The N's in Winnipeg are reversed
    Smooth lip Glass insert & screw band
    Insert: Crown emblem

690. (Crown emblem) CROWN (front)...Aqua $3-5
    Reverse: E within diamond, TORONTO and WINNIPEG   Clear $3-5
        (very lightly embossed)
    Smooth lip Glass insert & screw band
    Insert: Crown emblem

691. (Crown emblem) CROWN (front)...Aqua $4-6
    Reverse: THE T. EATON CO. LIMITED   Clear $4-6
        TORONTO and WINNIPEG   Midget pint Aqua $50-75
    Smooth lip Glass insert & screw band   Midget pint clear $50-75
    Insert: Crown emblem

692. (Crown emblem) CROWN..Aqua $2-3
    Smooth lip Glass insert & screw band   Apple green $8-10
    Insert: Crown emblem   Med. olive green $15-18
                     Midget pint aqua $4-6
                     Midget pint clear $4-6

693. (Crown emblem) CROWN (front)...........   ....Aqua $10-12
    Reverse: THE T. EATON CO. LIMITED   Midget pint aqua $65-75
        190 YONGE ST. TORONTO, CAN.
    Smooth lip Glass insert & screw band
    Insert: Crown emblem   #693

694. CROWN (crown emblem) IMPERIAL QT..................................Aqua $3-5
    Smooth lip Glass insert & screw band   Light cornflower blue $8-10
    Insert: Crown emblem   Imperial Midget pint aqua $18-20
    Also Imperial Pt. &   Imperial Midget pint clear $18-20
      Imperial ½ Gallon sizes

695. MADE IN CANADA (crown emblem) CROWN............   ....Clear   -$1
    Smooth lip Glass insert & screw band

696. MADE IN CANADA CROWN (Crown emblem) IMPERIAL QT   ....Clear   -$1
    Smooth lip Glass insert & screw band

697. IMPROVED (crown emblem) CROWN.................   ......Clear $2-3
    Smooth lip Glass insert & screw band   Light amber $12-15

698. MADE IN CANADA IMPROVED (crown emblem) CROWN..   ......Clear   -$1
    Smooth lip Glass insert & screw band

699. IMPROVED (crown emblem) IMPERIAL QT..........   ......Clear $3-5
    Smooth lip Glass insert & screw band   Light green $3-5

700. IMPROVED (crown emblem) CROWN (front)............................. Aqua $40-50
    Reverse: a boldly embossed cross emblem   #700
    Smooth lip Glass insert & screw band

701. (Crown emblem) CROWN (front).. Aqua $40-50
    Reverse: THE T. EATON CO. LIMITED TORONTO
    Ground lip Glass insert & screw band

    This concludes our listing of Canadian Crown
      jars. There are many other variations which
    we have not listed. See "Fruit Jars" by
    Creswick for illustrations of the Crown jars
    listed.

702. (Crown emblem) CROWN.................................... .Clear   -$1
    Base: Wheaton, N. J.
    Smooth lip Lightning dimple neck seal
    A small jar sold filled with bath salts,
      candies, etc.

THE T. EATON Co LIMITED TORONTO #701

703. CROWN MASON...Clear $3-5
    Smooth lip Mason beaded neck seal   ½ pint clear $4-6
    The porcelain liner of the zinc lid is
      marked Crown Mason to match the jar
      embossing. Found in both round &
      square shapes.

704. CROWN MASON.................................... ....Clear $1-2
    Smooth lip Mason beaded neck seal
    Vertical ribs on sides   Soft square shape

705. CRYSTAL.................................... .....Aqua $50-55
    Base: Pat. Nov. 26 67 Pat. Feb. 4 73
    Ground lip Mason shoulder seal/glass lid
    Lid: February 4 1873

CRYSTAL JAR #706

706. CRYSTAL JAR..Clear $25-30
    Ground lip Mason shoulder seal/glass lid   Midget pint clear $40-50
    Lid has internal lugs to engage on threads
      on neck of jar, and is marked: Patented Dec 17 1878

707. CRYSTAL JAR (reversed S)...........................Clear $35-40
    Ground lip Mason shoulder seal/glass lid
    Lid as in #706

708. CRYSTAL JAR C G....................................Clear $25-30
    Ground lip Mason shoulder seal/glass lid   Midget pint clear $40-50
    Lid as in #706

709. PATENTED DEC. 17 1878 (on lid)......................Clear $20-25
    Ground lip Mason shoulder seal/glass lid
    No marking on the jar

710. CRYSTAL MASON.............................Midget pint clear $50-60
    Ground lip Mason shoulder seal/glass lid
    Lid: Patented Dec. 17 1878

711. CRYSTAL MASON......................................Clear $6-8
    Smooth lip Mason beaded neck seal

712. MASON'S CRYSTAL JAR................................Clear $25-30
    Ground lip Mason shoulder seal, zinc lid   Midget pint clear $50-60

713. PATENTED JULY 28, 1874 CRYSTAL (on lid).............Clear $6-8
    Jelly tumbler

714. H & H CRYSTALVAC...................................Clear $1-2
    Base: Crystalvac Container 3 Rivers Or OI trademark   Amber $2-4
    Smooth lip Mason beaded neck seal
    Product jar

715. C S & CO (on base) Paneled, 8 sided jar..................Light green $12-15
716. C S & CO LD 1107 (on base) Round jar.......................Light green $8-10
717. C S & CO LD 5302 (on base) Paneled, 8 sided jar..........Light green $12-15
    All have glass stoppers marked: Cannington-Shaw
    & Co. Ld. St. Helens
    English jars

718. C S & CO Ld 38 (on base)................................Light green $6-8
    Applied band, cork stopper
    English jar

719. THE CUDDAHY PACKING CO. USA PAT.JULY 11th 1893 (on base)........Clear $2-3
    Ground lip Glass lid & screw band
    ½ pint product jar

720. CULINA...Clear $10-12
    Ground lip Glass lid & metal clamp
    Clamp: Culina Brevete SGDG   A French jar

721. CUNNINGHAM & CO. PITTSBURGH (on base)........................ Aqua $150-175
    Bottom pushed up, bare iron pontil scar   Light green $150-175
    Closure: cork stopper   Med. cobalt blue   1000 & up

722. CUNNINGHAM & CO. PITTSBURGH, PA. (on base).................... Aqua $125-150
    Applied lip Cork closure   Deep Kelly green $250-300

723. CUNNINGHAM'S & CO. PITTSBURGH (on base)...................... Aqua $125-150
    Applied lip Cork closure

724. CUNNINGHAMS & CO. PITTSBURGH PA (on base)..................... Aqua $20-25
    Groove ring wax sealer, pressed laid-on ring

725. C & I (on base)... Aqua $20-25
    Groove ring wax sealer, pressed laid-on ring
    Tin lid: C & I

726. CUNNINGHAMS & IHMSEN PITTSBURGH Pa PATd 1868 (on base).......... Aqua $20-25
    Groove ring wax sealer, pressed laid-on ring   Med. cobalt blue $300 & up
    Tin lid: C & I   Light cobalt blue $175 & up
    Also found without an S after Cunningham

727. CUNNINGHAMS & IHMSEN PITTSBURGH, PA. (on base)...................Aqua $20-25
    Groove ring wax sealer, pressed laid-on ring   Light cobalt blue $150 & up
    Tin lid: C & I

728. CUNNINGHAM & IHMSEN PITTSBURGH PA (on base)....................Amber   Unpriced
    Applied lip Cork closure
    3 amber jars are presently known

729. CUNNINGHAMS & IHMSEN PITTSBURGH PA (on base)...   ....Aqua $125-150
    Rolled lip Cork closure

730. CUNNINGHAMS & CO. LIM. PITTSBURGH PA (on base)   .Aqua $20-25
    Groove ring wax sealer, pressed laid-on ring

    C. IHMSEN & SON, see jars No. 1288 & 1289

731. CURTICE BROTHERS ROCHESTER N.Y................   .Aqua $30-40
    Ground lip Glass lid & screw band
    Product jar   #732

732. CURTICE BROTHERS CO. PRESERVERS ROCHESTER N.Y. (on base)........Clear $30-40
    Ground lip Metal band around neck of jar, carrying bail.
    Screw cover. Lid marking, if any, unknown.
    Product jar

733. CURTIS & MOORE TRADE (monogram) MARK BOSTON MASS................. Clear $20-25
  Ground lip Old style Lightning seal   Aqua $20-25
  Tall, slender ½ gallon product jar

734. CURTIS & MOORE CO. TRADE (monogram) MARK BOSTON, MASS........... Clear $15-20
  Base: A. G. Smalley & Co. Boston & New York
     Patented April 7th 1896
  Ground lip Old style Lightning seal
  Lid: A. G. Smalley & Co. Boston & New York
  Square ½ gallon product jar

735. CUTTING. AND. CO. SAN FRANCISCO.................... Aqua $175-200
  Groove ring wax sealer, pressed laid-on ring
  3 jars are presently known

736. CUTTING PACKING CO. SAN FRANCISCO (on lid)........ Clear $8-10
  Ground lip Glass lid & metal clamp
  The center of the glass lid has a Griffin..a
  trademark used by the Cutting Company.
  Product jar

#735

NOTES

737. D (in script, on base).. Aqua $6-8
     Groove ring wax sealer, pressed laid-on ring   Cornflower blue $12-15

738. D (in script, on base)..Deep aqua $3-5
     Groove ring wax sealer, pressed laid-on ring

739. D (on base)... Aqua $3-5
     Groove ring wax sealer, pressed laid-on ring

740. D and a triangle (on base)................................. Aqua $3-5
     Groove ring wax sealer, pressed laid-on ring

741. DAISY...Clear $8-10
     Smooth lip   Old style Lightning seal

742. DAISY (within circle)............................... Aqua $8-10
     Smooth lip   Old style Lightning seal   Clear $8-10

743. THE DAISY   F.E. WARD & CO...................... Aqua $10-12
     Ground lip   Also found with smooth lip
     Old style Lightning seal

#745

744. THE DAISY F. E. WARD & CO. (within circle)..................... Aqua $8-10
     Smooth lip   Old style Lightning seal   Cornflower blue $12-15

745. THE DAISY JAR..Clear $125-150
     Ground lip   Glass lid & metal clamp with cam
     Lid: Pat. Jany 3d 88

746. THE DAISY PATENT APPLIED FOR (on lid)........... $15-18
     White stoneware jar with amber glass lid
     McConnel patent wire clamp and lever

747. R. M. DALBEY'S FRUIT JAR PAT NOV 16 1858....... .... Aqua $500 & up
     Ground lip   Metal lid & collar, with   Clear $500 & up
       thumbscrews & leather ring
     Jar has a groove encircling the neck
       for the leather ring.

748. R. M. DALBEY'S FRUIT JAR PAT NOV 16 1858.......   ....Aqua $500 & up
     Ground lip   Metal lid & collar, with   Clear $500 & up
       thumbscrews
     Jar has 3 equally spaced indentations
       in the neck for pieces of leather

#747

749. DALLAS $30-40
     Incised on shoulder of brown stoneware jar
     Wax seal groove

750. DANAGLAS..Clear $1-2
     Smooth lip   Glass lid & metal clamp
     Made in Denmark

751. TRADEMARK THE DANDY................................Clear $30-35
     Base: Gilberds   Aqua $30-35
     Ground lip   Glass lid & wire bail, neck tie wire   Amber $75-90
     Lid: Pat. Oct. 13th 1885

#752

752. DARBY & CO BALTIMORE MD....................................Clear $12-15
     Ground lip   Mason shoulder seal   Tin lid
     Product jar

753. THE DARLING (below ADM monogram).................................. Aqua $25-30
     Ground lip Glass insert & screw band   Midget pint aqua $100-150
     Canadian sealer

754. THE DARLING IMPERIAL (below ADM monogram)....................... Aqua $30-35
     Ground lip Glass insert & screw band   Midget pint aqua $40-50
     The ADM stands for Adam Darling who operated
     a glass & pottery shop in Montreal, Canada.

755. DAVIDSON FRUIT CO. HOOD RIVER, ORE. (on base).....   ...Clear $2-3
     Ground lip Glass lid & metal band clamp
     Product jar

756. DAYTON PRENTISS & BORDEN NEW YORK................   .. Aqua $100-150
     Base: Pontil scar
     Rolled lip Closure: Waxed cork
     Product jar

757. DEAN'S HIGH GRADE COFFEE (front).................   ..Clear $1-3
     Side: "A TASTE OF THE GOOD OLD SOUTH" 1 LB NET
     Side: "WE FED YOUR GRANDMOTHERS" 1 LB NET
     Smooth lip Metal screw cover Product jar

#756

758. DECKER DEPENDABLE FOOD JACOB E. DECKER & SONS MASON CITY IOWA...Clear $1-3
     Smooth lip Mason beaded neck seal Product jar

759. DECKER'S IOWANA MASON CITY, IOWA (within circle)
     PAT'D JULY 14 1908 (all on front)................................Clear $3-5
     Smooth lip Lightning dimple neck seal Product jar

760. DECKER'S IOWANA MASON CITY, IOWA (within circle, front)........Clear $3-5
     Reverse: PAT'D JULY 14 1908
     Smooth lip Lightning dimple neck seal Product jar

761. DECKER'S IOWANA MASON CITY, IOWA (within circle)...............Clear $3-5
     Smooth lip Lightning dimple neck seal Product jar

762. DECKER'S VICTOR MASON CITY, IOWA (within circle)...............Clear $3-5
     Smooth lip Lightning beaded neck seal Product jar

763. DECKER'S MASON CITY, IOWA...............................   .Clear $1-3
     Smooth lip Mason beaded neck seal Product jar

764. DEERFOOT FARM REGISTERED (front)...................   .Clear $3-5
     Base: Pat. Applied For
     Ground lip Metal screw lid
     Lid: Deerfoot Farm Cream Southborough, Mass.
     Product jar

765. DEERFOOT FARM REGISTERED (front)...............   .Clear $3-5
     Base: Pat Applied For
     Ground lip Metal screw lid
     Lid: TradeMark Deerfoot Farm Southborough, Mass. Registered
     Product jar

#764

766. 1/2 PINT DEERFOOT HEAVY CREAM THIS JAR NOT TO BE SOLD
     PLEASE RETURN (all on front)....................................Clear $6-8
     Reverse: MASS C SEAL REGISTERED
     Ground lip Metal screw lid as in #765
     Product jar

767. DEERFOOT FARM SOUTHBORO, MASS.................................. Aqua $35-40
     Ground lip "Cohansey" lid & circular wire clamp
     Pint product jar

768. DEERFOOT FARM SOUTHBORO, MASS. (front)........................ Aqua $35-40
        Reverse: TO BE WASHED AND RETURNED
        Ground lip "Cohansey" lid & circular wire clamp
        Pint product jar

769. DELICIOUS CRUSHED FRUIT (in script)..............Pale green $35-40
        Base: Habight, Braun & Co. Chicago
        Ground lip Glass lid & wire clamp
        Product jar

770. DENVER STONEWARE CO. DENVER. Colo. (on base).... .... $15-18
        Bluish brown stoneware jar with stoneware lid

771. S. B. DEWEY Jr No 65 BUFFALO St ROCHESTER N.Y..   ..... Aqua $250-300
        Cupped stopper well for Willoughby stopple
        Stopple: J. D. Willoughby Patd Jan 4 1859
        Two jars are presently known

772. DEXTER.. Aqua $25-30
        Ground lip Glass insert & screw band
        Insert: Patd. Aug. 8th 1865

773. DEXTER (encircled by fruits & vegatables).......... ... Aqua $55-60
        Ground lip Glass insert & screw band
        Insert: Patd. Aug. 8th 1865

774. DEXTER (encircled by fruits & vegatables).......... ... Aqua $55-60
        Ground lip Glass insert & screw band
        Insert: Patented Dexter Improved Aug. 8 1865
        The mouth is slightly larger than in #773

775. DEXTER IMPROVED (around circle of fruits)......... .. Aqua $55-60
        Ground lip Glass insert & screw band
        Insert: Patented Dexter Improved Aug. 8 1865
          Or: Dexter Improved Patented Aug. 8 1865
             "Tudor Rose" in center

        Also see FRANKLIN DEXTER, No. 1034 & 1035

776. D G CO (large intertwined monogram)..................... Aqua $35-40
        Ground lip Glass insert & screw band   Clear $35-40
        Insert: DGCo monogram
        The monogram stands for Diamond Glass Co.
        Canadian sealer

777. D G Co (framed within a maple leaf)........ ....Clear   Unpriced
        Ground lip 1 Piece metal screw lid
        One jar known   Canadian sealer

778. DIAMOND FRUIT JAR IMPROVED TRADEMARK (base)   Clear $3-5
        Smooth lip Old style Lightning seal
        Lid: Diamond Fruit Jar Trademark

779. DIAMOND FRUIT JAR TRADEMARK (on base)......   ..Clear $3-5
        Smooth lip Old style Lightning seal
        Lid: Diamond Fruit Jar Trademark

780. THE DIAMOND NOVA SCOTIA................................... Aqua $200-225
        Ground lip Glass insert & screw band   Clear $200-225
        Canadian Sealer   Midget pint Aqua   Unpriced

781. Diamond symbol (on front)...................................Clear $15-18
        Smooth lip Glass or metal insert & screw band
        Canadian sealer   Midget pint clear $40-50

#771

#775

#778

782. THE DICTATOR.. Aqua $70-75
      Base: Wm McCully Pittsburgh
      Groove ring wax sealer, pressed laid-on ring

783. DICTATOR (front)... Aqua $70-75
      Reverse: PATENTED D. I. HOLCOMB DEC 14th 1869
      Base: WM McCully & Co. Pitts-
      Groove ring wax sealer, pressed laid-on ring

784. DICTATOR B (front)... Aqua $75-100
      Reverse: PATENTED D. I. HOLCOMB DEC 14th 1869
      Base: Wm McCully & Co. Pitts-
      Glass or metal lid & wire clamp
      Glass lid is marked: Patd Dec 14 - 69
                           D. I. Holcomb

785. DICTATOR C (front)... Aqua $75-100
      Reverse: PATENTED D. I. HOLCOMB DEC 14th 1869
      Base: Wm McCully & Co. Pitts-
      Glass or metal lid & wire clamp

786. DICTATOR D (front)... Aqua $75-100
      Reverse: PATENTED D. I. HOLCOMB DEC 14th 1869
      Base: Wm McCully & Co. Pitts-
      Glass or metal lid & wire clamp

787. DICTATOR D (front)... Aqua $75-100
      Reverse: PATENTED D. I. HOLCOMB DEC 14th 1869 (incomplete 4)
      Base: Wm McCully & Co. Pitts-
      Glass or metal lid & wire clamp

788. PATENTED D. I. HOLCOMB DEC 14th 1869 (front) .... Aqua $75-100
      Reverse, ghost: DICTATOR FROM HOLLWEG & REESE
                            INDIANAPOLIS, IND.
      Base: W. McCully

789. J E & L R DILLINER * (around jar)..................................... $95-100
      Gray stoneware jar with blue stenciling
      Wax seal groove

790. DILLON G. CO. FAIRMONT, IND. (on base)........................ Aqua $10-12
      Groove ring wax sealer, pressed laid-on ring   Emerald green $100-125

791. DILLON GLASS CO. FAIRMONT, IND. (on base)............. Aqua $10-12
      Groove ring wax sealer, pressed laid-on ring

792. D J (or J D) on base................................. Blue $4-6
      Gro

793. DIXIE JELLY GLASS (picture of Southern Colonel)....   .... $3-5
      Painted on metal lid of jelly glass
      Tumbler is clear and unmarked on front
      Base: Dixie Jelly HA

794. DOANES GREAT AIRTIGHT PRESERVING JAR (encircling jar)........... Aqua $500 & up
      Applied lip Metal stopper with thumbscrew   #794
      Stopper: Doane's * Nov 7 1865 Patent

795. D. O. C. (on base).. Aqua $12-15
      Groove ring wax sealer, pressed laid-on ring   Amber $75-85
                                                    Deep yellow green $70-75

      DOCTOR RAMSAY, see No. 2464 & 2465

                               -57-

796. DODGE SWEENEY & CO'S CALIFORNIA BUTTER........................ Aqua $40-45
       Ground lip Glass insert & screw band   Product jar

797. DOME...Clear $100-125
       Ground lip Glass lid & wire clamp Metal band around
       jar neck for ends of wire clamp.
       Lid, inside: Patented Aug 7 1883

798. DOME (superimposed over erased PERFECTION).......................Clear $100-125
       Ground lip Glass lid & wire clamp Metal band around
       jar neck for ends of wire clamp.
       Lid, inside: Patented Aug 7 1883
       This jar was made using a reworked Perfection mold.
       Collectors have reported these jars found with the
       Perfection closure as well as the Globe closure.

799. DOMINION... Aqua $75-100
       Ground lip Glass insert & screw band   Clear $75-100
       Canadian sealer   Midget pint clear $125-150
                                                Midget pint aqua $125-150

800. DOMINION MASON MADE IN CANADA...Clear   -$1
       Smooth lip Mason beaded neck seal
       2 pc. metal lid. Insert: Dominion D Mason & variations
       Canadian sealer   Square shape

801. DOMINION MASON WIDE MOUTH MADE IN CANADA........................Clear   -$1
       Smooth lip Mason beaded neck seal
       2 pc. metal lid. Insert: D Dominion Wide Mouth & variations
       Canadian sealer   Square shape

802. DOMINION WIDE MOUTH MADE IN CANADA...............................Clear   -$1
       Smooth lip Mason beaded neck seal
       Closure as in #801

803. DOMINION WIDE MOUTH MADE IN THE BRITISH EMPIRE.................. Aqua $6-8
       Smooth lip Mason shoulder seal   Pint, round shape

804. DOMINION SPECIAL..Clear $1-2
       Smooth lip Mason beaded neck seal
       Canadian sealer   Round shape

805. DOMINION WIDE MOUTH SPECIAL........................   .Clear $1-2
       Smooth lip Mason beaded neck seal
       Canadian sealer   Round shape

806. DOMINION WIDE MOUTH SPECIAL MADE IN CANADA..........   .Clear $1-2
       Smooth lip Mason beaded neck seal
       Canadian sealer   Round shape

807. A. P. DONAGHHO PARKERSBURG, W. VA........   ...... $25-30
       Gray stoneware jar with blue stenciling
       Wax seal groove

808. DONAGHHO PARKERSBURG.....................................   ... $25-30
       Dark brown stoneware, letters etched into glaze
       Wax seal groove

809. DOOLITTLE (in block letters).................................... Aqua $30-35
       Smooth lip. Glass lid held on by two wire clips which are
          attached to the ears on the lid & fold back under the jar
          rim. Top of jar & bottom of lid are slotted to match.
       Lid: "Doolittle" Patented Jan 2 & June 12 1900 Match Cover
            And Slots
       Canadian sealer

DOOLITTE

#809

810. DOOLITTLE PATENTED DEC 3 1901 (on lid)........................ Clear $18-20
    Smooth lip Glass lid, fitted with two   Imperial ½ pint clear $25-30
                wire clips on the ears
      Lid variation: Doolittle Jan 2 & June 12 1900
              Dec 24 1901

811. DOOLITTLE (in script, on front)............................... Clear $20-25
    Smooth lip Glass lid, fitted with two
                wire clips on the ears
      Lid: "Doolittle" Patented Jan 2 & June 12 1900

812. DOOLITTLE PATENTED DEC 3 1901 (on lid)........................ Clear $18-20
    Smooth lip Glass lid, fitted with two   Imperial ½ pint clear $25-30
                wire clips on the ears
    Square shaped jar

813. THE DOOLITTLE SELF SEALER............................. Aqua $50-75
    Base: GJCo. (for the Gilchrist Jar Co.)
    Smooth lip Glass lid with ears & wire clips.
    The closure works on the same principle as
    the other Doolittle closures but has a wire
    across the top which acts as a hinge for the
    wires that lock the lid onto the jar.
    Lid: Patented January 2nd 1900

#813

814. DORLON & SHAFFER PICKLED OYSTERS FULTON MARKET NEW YORK........ Aqua $35-40
    Base: Cohansey Glass Mfg. Co. Philada.
    Ground lip "Cohansey" lid & clamp Product jar

815. DOUBLE SAFETY... Clear $3-5
    Base: SKO (for Smalley, Kivlan, Onthank)   ½ pint clear $4-6
    Smooth lip Old style Lightning seal

816. DOUBLE SAFETY... Clear $2-4
    Base: Smalley, Kivlan & Onthank, Boston Mass.
      Pat'd Feb 23 '09
    Smooth lip Glass lid & twin wire clamps
    Lid: KantKrack Pat'd Feb. 23 09

817. DOUBLE SAFETY... Clear $2-3
    Base: Smalley, Kivlan & Onthank, Boston Mass.   ½ pint clear $4-6
    Smooth lip Old style Lightning seal

818. DOUBLE SAFETY... Clear $2-3
    Base: Kivlan & Onthank Boston Pat'd
    Smooth lip Old style Lightning seal

819. DOUBLE SAFETY... Clear $2-4
    Base: Smalley, Kivlan & Onthank, Boston, Mass.
      (N & K in Kivlan are reversed)
    Smooth lip Old style Lightning seal

820. DOUBLE SAFETY... Clear $2-4
    Base: Smalley, Kivlan & Onthank, Boston, Mass.
      (N in Onthank is reversed)
    Smooth lip Old style Lightning seal

#817

821. DOUBLE SAFETY... Clear $2-4
    Base: Smalley, Kivlan & Onthank, Boston, Mass.
      (Most of the letters are reversed or upside down)
    Smooth lip Old style Lightning seal

822. DOUBLE SAFETY... Clear $2-3
    Base: Unmarked
    Smooth lip Old style Lightning seal

823. DOUBLE SAFETY (T is not crossed)..............................Clear $3-5
      Base: Smalley, Kivlan & Onthank Boston, Mass.
      Smooth lip Old style Lightning seal

824. DOUL SAFETY (missing letters)...............................Clear $3-5
      Base: Smalley, Kivlan & Onthank Boston, Mass.
      Smooth lip Old style Lightning seal

825. DOUBLE SAFETY (on neck of jar only, front)....................Clear $2-4
      Reverse, on neck: IMPROVED
      Base: Smalley, Kivlan & Onthank Boston Patd Feb 23 '09
      Smooth lip Glass lid: KantKrack Pat'd Feb 23 '09
      Twin side clamps

826. DOUBLE SEAL...Clear $3-5
      Smooth lip Old style Lightning seal

827. DOUBLE SEAL...Clear $3-5
      Smooth lip Lightning beaded neck seal

828. DOUBLE SEAL MASON...Clear $2-3
      Base: PC in broken rectangle
      Smooth lip Mason beaded neck seal

829. DOVE BRAND (2 doves) PREPARED MUSTARD
      COLORED WITH TUMERIC (all on front).........................Clear $2-3
      Reverse: THE FRANK TEA & SPICE CO. CINTI. OHIO
      Smooth lip Mason beaded neck seal   Product jar

#829

830. DREY EVER SEAL..Clear $1-2
      Smooth lip Old style Lightning seal

831. DREY EVER SEAL..Clear $1-2
      Smooth lip Lightning beaded neck seal

832. DREY EVER SEAL (no crossbar on A)............................Clear $2-3
      Smooth lip Lightning closure with lever wire
                  held by glass bosses on neck of jar.

833. DREY PAT'D EVER SEAL..Clear $1-3
      Smooth lip Lightning closure with lever wire
                  held by glass bosses on neck of jar.

834. DREY PAT'D 1920 IMPROVED EVER SEAL...........................Clear $2-3
      Smooth lip Lightning closure with lever wire
                  held by glass bosses on neck of jar.

835. DREY IMPROVED EVER SEAL.......................................Clear $1-2
      Base: Patd 1920
      Smooth lip. Lightning closure with lever wire
                  held by glass bosses on neck of jar.

#834

836. DREY IMPROVED EVER SEAL (front)...............................Clear $1-3
      Reverse: PAT. SEPT 7 1920
      Smooth lip Lightning closure with lever wire
                  held by glass bosses on neck of jar

837. DREY IMPROVED EVER SEAL.......................................Clear $1-2
      Smooth lip Lightning beaded neck seal

838. DREY IMPROVED EVER SEAL.......................................Clear $1-2
      Smooth lip Lightning beaded neck seal
      (Embossing different than #837)

839. DREY MASON...Clear $1-2
         Smooth lip Mason shoulder seal   Pale green $1-3

840. DREY MASON...Clear $1-2
         Smooth lip Mason beaded neck seal

841. DREY MASON (different style D).......................................Clear $1-2
         Smooth lip Mason shoulder seal

842. DREY PERFECT MASON...Clear $1-2
         Smooth lip Mason beaded neck seal

843. DREY PERFECT MASON (different embossing than #842)............... Aqua $1-2
         Smooth lip Mason beaded neck seal   Clear $1-2
                                                            Light blue $3-5
844. DREY PERFECT MASON...Clear   -$1
         Smooth lip Mason beaded neck seal Gripper ribs on sides

845. DREY PEREECT MASON (error)..Clear $2-3
         Smooth lip Mason beaded neck seal

846. DREY PERFECT MASON (on two lines)...........   ½ Pint Clear $2-4
         Smooth lip Mason beaded neck seal

847. DREY SQUARE MASON (with carpenters square)..   ....Clear $2-3
         Smooth lip Mason beaded neck seal

848. DREY SQUARE MASON (without square)..........   ....Pint Clear $2-4
         Smooth lip Mason beaded neck seal

#847

849. D.S.G.Co. (on base)...................................... Aqua $15-18
         Groove ring wax sealer, pressed laid-on ring   Lime green $15-18
         The aqua & lime green jars were made with 2 pc. mold   Amber $75-85
         and the amber is a turnmold jar (no seams).

850. U. H. DUDLEY NEW YORK.................................... .. Aqua   Unpriced
         Fruit bottle Waxed cork closure
         This jar from the William Dudley collection
         dates circa 1861 to 1877, when Uriah H. Dudley
         was a commercial canner in New Jersey. One jar
         reported.

851. DUERR'S JAMS MANCHESTER (on base)...................   green $8-10
         Ground lip Closure unknown Canadian product jar

852. THE DUNKLEY CELERY CO. KALAMAZOO (on base)...........   Clear $20-25
         Ground lip Glass lid & double cam lever held by
         a wire yoke that hooks into dimples on the sides
         of the neck.
         Lid: Patd Jan 29-95

#850

853. THE DUNKLEY CELERY CO. KALAMAZOO PATD JAN 1895 (base)............Clear $20-25
         Ground lip Closure as in #852

854. THE DUNKLEY PRESERVING CO. KALAMAZOO
         PATD SEPT 20th 1898 APRIL 30th 1901 (all on base)...............Clear $4-6
         Smooth lip Glass lid & metal band clamp
         Lid: Patd Sept. 20th 1898

855. THE DUNKLEY PRESERVING CO. KALAMAZOO PATD SEPT 20th 1898 (base)..Clear $4-6
         Ground lip Glass lid & metal band clamp   ¼ Pint clear $6-8
         Lid: Patd Sept. 20th 1898   ½ Pint clear $6-8

         The Dunkley jars are product jars.

856. DUNKLEY PATD SEPT. 20 98/APR 30 01 (on base)....................Clear $4-6
     Smooth lip Glass lid & metal band clamp
     Lid: Patd. Sept. 20th 1898
     Product jar

857. PATD SEPT. 20th 1898 (on lid)....................................Clear $2-3
     Smooth lip Glass lid & metal band clamp   ½ Pint clear $6-8
     Product jar

858. JAMES VIOLETTE & CO. BORDEAUX JE SUIS COMME JE PAROIS (on lid).. Aqua $10-12
     Ground lip Lid is brass, with a design of violets
                 in center.
     Jar has a threaded pewter band, permanently
      attached to the neck threads.
     A French product jar with paper label

859. BOUCHAGE DE LABAT JEUNE BREVETES G.D.G.A. DURFOUR &
     CO. SEULS CESSIONARES POUR LA PRUNE (all on lid)....   Aqua $10-12
     Base: Pontil scar
     Brass lid & threaded pewter band on jar neck.
     A French product jar with paper label

860. A DUFOUR & CO. BORDAUX (on jar)...............   Aqua $40-50
     Base: Pontil scar   Barrel shaped jar
     Brass lid & threaded pewter band on jar neck.
     Lid: Bouchage DeLabat Jeune Brevetts G.D.C.
        A. Durfour & Co. Seuls Cessionares Pour   #858
        La Prune
     A French product jar

861. DUR FOR (within circle)...Green   -$1
     Glass lid with wire hinge and snap wire bail
     A Modern French jar

862. DURHAM (within circle)... Aqua $12-15
     Smooth lip Old style Lightning seal

863. "DAVID J. DYSON LIMITED" around shoulder.......................Clear $1-3
     Smooth lip Metal screw cover Canadian product jar

864. RED CROSS (cross) PICKLES THE DYSON CO. WINNIPEG...............Clear $15-18
     Closure: Flat glass stopper and metal spring clamp
     Canadian product jar

865. DYSON'S (cross) PURE FOOD PRODUCTS.............................Clear $15-18
     Smooth lip Glass insert & screw band   Pale aqua $15-18
     Canadian product jar

866. DYSON'S (cross) PURE FOOD PRODUCTS (base)......................Amber   -$25
     Smooth lip Screw cover
     Neck tie wire & wire bail with wooden handle
      for carrying. Canadian product jar

867. DYSON'S RED CROSS PRODUCTS ARE RELIABLE (within circle)............ $15-20
     White stoneware jar, black stenciling
     Stoneware lid & "Weir" type clamp
     Canadian product jar

868. E 1 (on base)..Greenish Amber $60-70
        Groove ring wax sealer, pressed laid-on ring

869. E 2 (on base)... Light green $3-5
        Groove ring wax sealer, pressed laid-on ring   Light olive green $20-25

870. E 5 (on base)..Aqua $3-5
        Groove ring wax sealer, pressed laid-on ring   Deep citron green $40-50

871. EAGLE...Aqua $100-150
        Unmarked glass lid Brass wire &
        cast brass clamp, metal band
        around neck of jar

872. EAGLE... ...Aqua $70-75
        Unmarked glass lid Iron yoke
        clamp with thumbscrew

873. EAGLE (encircled by) PATd DEC 28th 1858
        REISD JUNE 16th 1868 (all on front)....   ..Aqua $85-95
        Unmarked glass lid Iron yoke
        clamp with thumbscrew

874. Embossed Eagle within circle of stars
        REGISTERED 1898 FULL MEASURE ONE QUART (front).....   ..Aqua $1-2
        Base: Jar Made In Italy 1965
              Crownford China Co. C.

875. EASI-PAK MASON...Clear   -$1
        Base: M within hexagon
        Smooth lip Mason beaded neck seal

876. EAST INDIA PICKLES (around shoulder)..................... Light green $4-6
        Base: Pat. July 11 1893 & monogram
        Ground lip Glass or metal lid & 3-position wire clamp
        Lid: Pat. July 11 1893
        Product jar

877. FORMERLY EASTON (on lid)..Clear   -$1
        Smooth lip Old style Lightning seal
        Product jar (Kraft Mayonnaise)

878. EASY TRADE VJC CO (monogram) MARK VACUUM JAR.......... Aqua $20-25
        Base: Pat. July 11 1893 VJC Co. monogram   Clear $20-25
        Ground lip Glass or metal lid & 3-position wire clamp
        Metal lid marked: Pat. July 11 1893

879. PAT. JULY 11 1893 VJC Co monogram (on base)..........Clear $15-20
        Ground lip Glass or metal lid &   Light green $15-20
                    3-position wire clamp
        Glass lid, unmarked
        Metal lid: Pat. July 11 1893

880. PATd JULY 11th & VJC CO 1893 (on base).....Clear $15-20
        Ground lip Closure as in #879

881. PAT'D JULY 11th 1893 (on base).............Clear $15-20
        Ground lip Closure as in #879

#871   #873   #878

EAGLE

PATd DEC 28TH 1858
EAGLE
REISd JUNE 16TH 1868

EASY
CO
TRADE   MARK
VACUUM
JAR

PAT. JULY 11
CO
1893

882. E. B. & CO. (on base).. Aqua $4-6
    Hand finished, laid-on ring   Closure unknown
    English jar made by Edgar F. Breffit & Co.

883. ECKELS FRUIT JAR (around embossed eagle)...................Olive green Unpriced
    Base: Pat. Mar 21 54 & a pontil scar
    Glass lid & iron yoke clamp
    Note: The closure would seem to indicate a date of
        manufacture later than the 1854 date.

884. THE ECLIPSE....................................... .Light green $85-95
    Groove ring wax sealer, pressed laid-on ring   Amber $500 & up

885. ECLIPSE JAR....................................... Light green $150-175
    Ground lip Mason shoulder seal/glass lid
    Lid: Patd Sept 12 1882 Jan 3d 1883
        Eclipse Jar (reversed N in Jan)
    Also see CADIZ jar No. 548 & HOOSIER No. 1266

886. ECONOMY (underlined, closed end)............... Clear $2-4
    Base: Kerr Glass Mfg. Co. Portland, Ore. 1
    Smooth lip Metal lid & spring metal clamp
    Lid: Economy Jar Kerr Glass Mfg. Co.
    The Economy jars will turn amethyst.

#885

887. ECONOMY (underlined, closed end)................................. Clear $2-4
    Base: Kerr Glass Mfg. Co. Patented Portland, Ore.
    Closure as in #886

888. ECONOMY (underlined, closed end)................................. Clear $2-4
    Base: Unmarked
    Closure as in #886

889. ECONOMY (underlined, open end)................................. Clear $2-4
    Base: PAT.
    Closure as in #886

890. ECONOMY (underlined, open end)................................. Clear $2-4
    Base: Patented
    Closure as in #886

891. ECONOMY (underlined, open end)............... .... Clear $2-4
    Base: Kerr Glass Mfg. Co. Portland, Ore.
        Pat June 9 & 23 1903
    Closure as in #886

892. ECONOMY (underlined, open end)............ .... Clear $2-4
    Base: Kerr Glass Mfg. Co. Portland, Ore,
        Pat June 9 1903

893. ECONOMY TRADEMARK (underlined, open end)... .... Clear $2-4
    Base: Unmarked
    Closure as in #886

894. ECONOMY TRADEMARK (underlined, 4 lines).... Clear $2-4
    Base: Kerr Glass Mfg. Co. Portland, Ore.
        Pat. June 9 & 23 1903
    Closure as in #886

#895

895. ECONOMY TRADEMARK (underlined, 4 lines)........................ Clear $2-4
    Base: Kerr Glass Mfg. Co. Patented Portland, Ore.
    Closure as in #886

896. ECONOMY TRADEMARK (underlined, 4 lines)........................ Clear $2-4
    Base: Kerr Glass Mfg. Co. Portland, Ore.
    Closure as in #886

897. ECONOMY TRADEMARK (underlined, open end)....................Clear $4-6
        Base: Kerr Glass Mfg. Co. Patent Chicago Ill.
        Smooth lip Metal lid & spring metal clamp
        Lid: Economy Jar Kerr Glass Mfg. Co.

898. ECONOMY TRADEMARK (3 underlines, closed end)..................Clear $2-4
        Base: Kerr Glass Mfg. Co. Pat June 9 1903 Portland, Ore.
        Closure as in #897

899. ECONOMY TRADEMARK (3 underlines, closed end)..................Clear $2-4
        Base: Kerr Glass Mfg. Co. Pat. June 9 & 23 Portland, Ore.
        Closure as in #897

900. ECONOMY TRADEMARK (4 underlines, closed end)..................Clear $2-4
        Base: Pat. June 9 1903
        Closure as in #897

901. ECONOMY TRADEMARK (4 underlines, closed end)..................Clear $2-4
        Base: Kerr Glass Mfg. Co. Portland, Oreg.
        Closure as in #897

902. ECONOMY TRADEMARK (front) Reverse: SAFE (in ghost lettering)...Clear $4-6
        Smooth lip Metal lid & spring band clamp

        Also see the KERR ECONOMY jars under K

903. THE ECONOMY PAT APPLIED FOR.......................   .. Aqua $150-175
        Ground lip Closure unknown
        Neck has a glass projection on each side.
        The base is pushed up, unmarked

904. ECONOMY SEALER PATD SEPT 13th 1858..............   .. Aqua $20-25
        (All lettering faint)
        Groove ring wax sealer, pressed laid-on ring

905. ECONOMY SEALER PATd SEPT 13th 1858.....................   .. Aqua $20-25
        (All lettering readable)   #903
        Groove ring wax sealer, pressed laid-on ring

906. ECONOMY SEALER PATd SEPt 15th 1885..............................Aqua $20-25
        (All lettering faint)
        Groove ring wax sealer, pressed laid-on ring

907. ECONOMY SEALER PATd SEPt 15th 1885.................. .... Aqua $85-100-
        The top of the jar has a slight annular recess.
        The metal lid was constructed of two pieces,
        with a rubber gasket in between. Bent wire
        spring clamp.

908. ECONOMY SEALER PATd SEPt 15th 1885.............. .... Aqua $85-100
        Ground lip Glass or metal lid & wire clamp

909. EDDY & EDDY PURE FOOD PRODUCTS......................... ..Clear $15-20
        Blown glass stopper: Eddy & Eddy Mfg. Co.   #909
        Product jar

910. EDWARDSBURG CROWN (crown) BRAND REGISTERED
        PURE CORN SYRUP PERFECT SEAL JAR (all on front)... ..Clear $12-15
        Smooth lip Lightning beaded neck seal
        Canadian product jar

911. E. H. E. 1 (lower front of jar) .... Aqua $20-25
        Reverse: Erased Western Pride
        Base: N within star
        Groove ring wax sealer, pressed laid-on ring   E.H.E.1   #911
-65-

912. Erased WESTERN PRIDE PATENTED JUNE 22 1875...................... Aqua $20-25
     Base: N within star
     Groove ring wax sealer, pressed laid-on ring

913. E. H. E. Co. 6 (on lower front)................................. Aqua $20-25
     Base: S K & Co. with a star
     Groove ring wax sealer, pressed laid-on ring

914. E. H. E. Co. 7 (on lower front)................................. Aqua $20-25
     Base: S K & Co. with a star
     Groove ring wax sealer, pressed laid-on ring

915. ELECTRIC (in script, within circle)............................ Aqua $10-12
     Ground lip Old style Lightning seal, wide mouth

916. ELECTRIC TRADEMARK... Aqua $8-10
     Smooth lip Old style Lightning seal, wide mouth

917. ELECTRIC TRADEMARK (within circle)............................. Aqua $8-10
     Smooth lip Old style Lightning seal, wide mouth

918. TRADEMARK ELECTRIC.......................   .... Aqua $10-12
     Base: Unmarked
     Ground lip Old style Lightning seal

919. TRADEMARK ELECTRIC.......................   .... Aqua $10-12
     Base: Salem, N. J.
     Ground lip Old style Lightning seal

920. TRADEMARK ELECTRIC.......................   .... Aqua $10-12
     Base: Erased H. W. Pettit
     Ground lip Old style Lightning seal

921. ELECTRIC FRUIT JAR (around world globe)..   .... Aqua $60-70
     Base: Pat Appl For
     Ground lip Glass lid, wire bail & lever
                 action clamp
     Clamp: Pat. M'ch 17 1885

     #918

     Also see CLARKE FRUIT JAR CO. No. 603

922. ELECTRIC FRUIT JAR (around world globe)...........   .... Aqua $60-70
     Base: Pat Appl For
     Ground lip Glass lid with 2 slots, wire clamp

923. ELMA CONFECTION CO. LTD PHILADELPHIA PA
     DRUGGISTS CONFECTIONS (all on front)...........   .Clear $12-15
     Stopper neck finish, glass stopper
     Product jar 2 gallon size

924. EMPIRE..   . Aqua $200-250
     Stopper neck finish Metal stopple
     Stopple: Patented January 10, 1860 King & Co.
              Pittsburgh, Pa. Empire
     The stopple is difficult to find.   #924

925. EMPIRE (within stippled cross, within frame)................Clear $8-10
     Smooth lip Old style Lightning seal, wide mouth   ½ Pint clear $10-12

926. THE EMPIRE...Clear $15-18
     Smooth lip Old style Lightning seal

927. THE EMPIRE.. Aqua $60-70
     Base: Pat Feb 13 1866
     Glass lid Metal yoke clamp with lever action

928. THE EMPIRE (front)... Aqua $65-75
        Reverse: FEB 13th 1866
        Base: Pat. Feb. 13th 1866
        Ground lip Glass lid Metal clamp with
                        lever action

929. THE EMPIRE (front)... Aqua $100-125
        Reverse: F. A. BUNNELL'S PAT. NO. 52.525
                    FEB. 13th 1866 SYRACUSE. N. Y.
        Base: Pat. Feb. 13th 1866
        Ground lip Glass lid Metal clamp with
                        lever action

930. EMPIRE BRAND CRUSHED FRUITS AND FRUIT JUICES
        CRAINE & CO, NEW YORK (all on front).......... .... Clear $10-12
        Base: A. G. Smalley Co. Patented
                April 7th 1896 Boston & New York
        Ground lip Old style Lightning seal
        ½ Gallon product jar, square shape   #931

931. EMPRESS.. Aqua $100-150
        Ground lip Glass insert & screw band
        A rare Canadian sealer

932. EMPRESS (front shoulder).. Aqua $25-35
        Reverse shoulder: PAT. FEB. 25 1879
        Ground mouth, very rough Jar holds 3 Imperial quarts
        This jar is believed to be a kerosene jar which had
        a tin lid with pouring spout, and possibly a tin jacket.

933. EMPRESS MFG. CO. VANCOUVER, B.C. (vertically).................Clear $1-3
        Smooth lip Metal lid: Empress Brands Jams, Jellies &
                            Marmalade Empress Mfg. Co. Ltd.
                            Vancouver, B.D.
        Canadian product jar

934. ENG HUNG CHI BEAN CAKE 12 OZ. NET..................... ..Clear $3-5
        Smooth lip Lightning dimple neck seal Product jar

935. FULL MEASURE 1/2 GAL. ENG-SKELL CO. SAN FRANCISCO..   Clear $2-3
        Smooth lip Glass lid & wire clamp Product jar

936. ESPY PHIL (around shoulder)................   Aqua   Unpriced
        Fruit bottle, applied lip, cork closure
        Base: Kick up, bare iron pontil scar

937. WENDELL & ESPY (around shoulder)...........   Aqua   Unpriced
        Fruit bottle, applied lip, cork closure
        Base: Kick up, bare iron pontil scar
        Early New Jersey fruit bottle
                                                    #936

938. ERIE (on base)...........................   ....Clear $12-15
        Ground lip Glass insert & screw band
        Canadian product jar

939. ERIE (on base)...........................   ....Amber $40-50
        Ground lip Glass insert & screw band
        Canadian sealer

940. ERIE (E within hexagon) FRUIT JAR (front).   .... Aqua $100-125
        Reverse: THE T. EATON CO. LIMITED TORONTO   Clear $100-125
        Ground lip Glass insert & screw band   #940   Midget pint aqua $250-275
        Insert: E within hexagon   Midget pint clear $250-275
        Canadian sealer

941. ERIE (E within hexagon) FRUIT JAR............................... Aqua $75-100
       Base: Erie or Mold number   Clear $75-100
       Ground lip Glass lid & screw band   Midget pint clear $250-275
       Insert: E within hexagon
       Canadian sealer

942. ERIE LIGHTNING.. Pale Aqua $20-25
       Smooth lip Old style Lightning seal   Clear $20-25
       Canadian sealer

943. ERMEBLOK (on lid)...................................Clear $1-3
       Smooth lip Hinged glass lid.
       Fairly modern European jar

944. ESKAY'S PAT JULY 11th 1893 (on base)..................Amber $2-4
       Ground lip Metal press-down lid
       Product jar

945. EUREKA (in script)....................   .... Aqua $10-12
       Base: Eureka Jar Co. Pat Pending   Clear $10-12
             Boston, Mass.   ½ Pint Aqua $12-15
       Smooth lip Glass lid & metal clamp   ½ Pint Clear $12-15
       Neck is threaded to engage clamp
       Lid: Eureka or Unmarked

#945

946. EUREKA (in script)..Aqua $12-15
       Base: Eureka Jar Co. Pat Pending
             Boston, Mass.
       Smooth lip Glass lid with round projection on top
       Clamp with hole in center to fit over projection on lid
       Neck has two wide cam surfaces to engage clamp, rather
         than threads.

947. EUREKA (in script).. Aqua $12-15
       Base: Eureka Jar Co. Pat Pending
             Dunbar, W. Va.
       Smooth lip Glass lid & metal clamp
       Neck is threaded to engage clamp
       Lid: Eureka or Unmarked

948. EUREKA 1 PAT'd DEC. 27th 1864............................... Aqua $75-100
       (Found with various mold numbers below Eureka)   Minus lid Aqua $40-50
       Ground lip Metal push-down cap, rubber gasket
                   with pull tab
       Lid: Unmarked or Patd July 18 1854 May 22nd 1860
                   Reisd Nov 24 1863

949. EUREKA N. O. F. PATd DEC 27th 1864............................ Aqua $100-125
       Ground lip Closure as in #948

950. PATd JULY 18 1854 MAY 22nd 1860 REISd NOV 24 1863 (on lid)....... Aqua $40-50
       No embossing on jar
       Ground lip Metal push-down cap, rubber gasket
                   with pull tab.

951. EVERETT EGCo (monogram)... Unpriced
       Glass lid & metal clamp
       Note: Although this jar has been pictured in advertising,
             an example has not yet been reported.

952. EVERLASTING JAR (word Jar in flag)............................... Aqua $15-20
       Smooth lip Glass lid & double wire clamp
       Lid: Pat. Aug 22 05
        Or: Pat. Nov 29 04

953. EVERLASTING JAR (word Jar in flag).......... .... Aqua $15-20
        Smooth lip Mason shoulder seal

954. IMPROVED EVERLASTING JAR (within oval)...... ....Clear $15-20
        Jar has 14 panels
        Base: Unmarked
          Or: Illinois Pacific Glass Co.
              S. F. Cal. Pat.
        Smooth lip Glass lid & double wire clamp
        Lid: Pat. Aug. 22. 02.

955. IMPROVED EVERLASTING JAR (word Jar in flag).. ....Clear $12-15
        Base: I. P. C. Co. S. F. Cal. (within triangle)
        Smooth lip Glass lid & double wire clamp
        Also found with a metal spring band clamp
        Lid: Pat. Aug. 22. 02.

956. EXCELSIOR.................................... .Clear $90-100
        Ground lip Glass lid & narrow screw band   Aqua $90-100
        Lid: "cupped" shape, marked Patent Aplied For
        Jar is somewhat milkbottle shape

957. EXCELSIOR (front)............................ Aqua $125-150
        Reverse: Embossed basket of fruits
        Ground lip Shape & closure as in #956

958. EXCELSIOR.................................... Aqua $50-55
        Ground lip Glass insert & screw band
        Lid: Patented Aug 3rd 1858 (may not be
              correct lid)

959. EXCELSIOR IMPROVED.......................... Aqua $45-50
        Ground lip Glass insert & screw band

960. EXCELSIOR IMRROVED (error).................. Aqua $50-55
        Ground lip Glass insert & screw band

961. EXCELSIOR IMPROVED 6....................... Aqua $45-50
        Ground lip Glass insert & screw band

962. THE EGCO (monogram) IMPERIAL................ Aqua $18-20
        Ground lip Glass insert & screw band   Midget pint aqua $30-35
        Insert: Excelsior Glass Co. Incorporated 1879
          Or: Excelsior Glass Co. Register'd Apr 1879
        Canadian sealer

963. THE EGCO (monogram within circle) IMPERIAL.................... Aqua $20-25
        Ground lip Closure as in #962

964. EXCELSIOR MUSTARD MILLS NEW YORK (within circle)........ Apple green $4-6
        Paper label on reverse reads French Mustard,
                              Excelsior Mustard Mills
        Applied top Tin cover Product jar

965. EXWACO (on base)...Amber $10-12
        Ground lip Milkglass insert & screw band   Green $10-12
        Product jar made for Exley, Watkins & Co.   Milkglass $12-15

966. Unmarked jar, paper label: Exwaco Brand Prepared Mustard........Green $10-12
        Ground lip Milkglass insert & screw band Product jar

        E-Z SEAL see jar No. 127

-69-

967. F. A. & Co (script, on front)...Aqua $50-75
        Groove ring wax sealer, pressed laid-on ring

968. F A & CO. (on base)...Aqua $125-150
        Pushed up bottom, bare iron pontil scar
        Closure: Waxed cork or Willoughby stopple

969. F A & CO (script, on front).....................................Aqua $40-50
        Closure: Waxed cork or Willoughby stopple

970. FAHNESTOCK ALBREE & CO. (base)..............................Aqua $70-80
        Pushed up bottom, pontil scar
        Closure: waxed cork or Willoughby stopple

971. FAHNESTOCK ALBREE & CO. (base)..............................Aqua $150-160
        Pushed up bottom, bare iron pontil scar
        Waxed cork or Willoughby stopple

#967

972. FAHNESTOCK ALBREE & CO. PITTS. PA. (base)..................Aqua $25-30
        Groove ring wax sealer, pressed laid-on ring   Medium cobalt blue $400 & up

973. B. L. FAHNESTOCK FORTUNE & CO. PITTS. PA. (base).....Aqua $40-50
        Waxed cork or Willoughby stopple

974. B. L. FAHNESTOCK FORTUNE & CO. PITTS. PA. (base).....Aqua $25-30
        Groove ring wax sealer, pressed laid-on ring   Clear $25-30

975. THE FAMILY FRUIT JAR...................................Clear $200-250
        Base: Patd Oct. 18 1887
        Ground lip   Glass lid with glass fin
                Wire bail clamp   Neck tie wire
        Lid: Patd. Oct. 18 1887

#975

976. THE WIDEMOUTH "FAMOUS" JAR (within circle)....................... Aqua $12-15
        Base: B & P or Unmarked
        Smooth lip   Old style Lightning seal, wide mouth

977. MANUFACTURED FOR N. O. FANSLER CLEVELAND OHIO...... Aqua $75-100
        Stopper neck finish for Kline stopper

978. FARLEY CHICAGO...Clear $2-3
        Smooth lip   Old style Lightning seal
        Product jar   Square shape

979. BUCK GLASS CO. FARM FAMILY BALTIMORE, MD. (on lid).....Clear $1-3
        Smooth lip   Lid held on by two metal clips
        Product jar
        Also see Garden Queen jar Nos. 1047 & 1048

980. FARM LAND GLASS CO. (on base).......................... ...... Unpriced
        Groove ring wax sealer, pressed laid-on ring
        More information is needed on this jar.

#982

981. FARRAR'S PATENT SELF SEALING JAR 1893 (lid)........................... Unpriced
        Glazed brown pottery with glass lid & locking wire clamp
        A Canadian pottery jar

982. J. FAU PRUNES DENTE BORDEAUX (within rectangle).............Pale Green $50-60
        Base: Pushed up, pontil scar
        Glass lid: N. M. Alinau. Invante J. R. Bordeux
        The lid on this early French jar, has threads
        and screws into the neck of the jar.

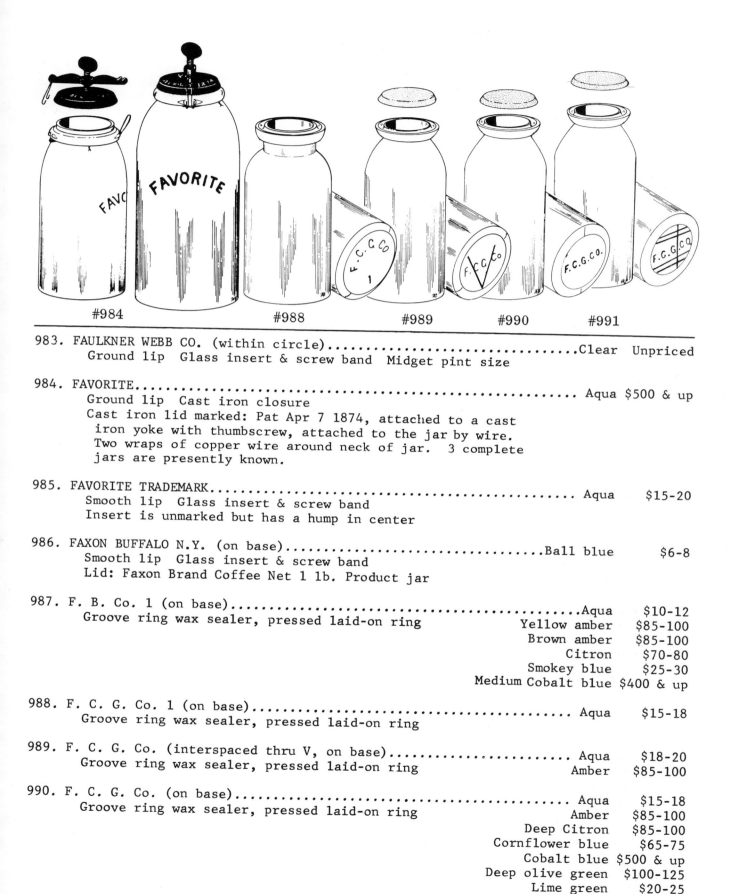

| #984 | #988 | #989 | #990 | #991 |

---

983. FAULKNER WEBB CO. (within circle).....................................Clear Unpriced
    Ground lip Glass insert & screw band Midget pint size

984. FAVORITE.. Aqua $500 & up
    Ground lip Cast iron closure
    Cast iron lid marked: Pat Apr 7 1874, attached to a cast
    iron yoke with thumbscrew, attached to the jar by wire.
    Two wraps of copper wire around neck of jar. 3 complete
    jars are presently known.

985. FAVORITE TRADEMARK... Aqua $15-20
    Smooth lip Glass insert & screw band
    Insert is unmarked but has a hump in center

986. FAXON BUFFALO N.Y. (on base)....................................Ball blue $6-8
    Smooth lip Glass insert & screw band
    Lid: Faxon Brand Coffee Net 1 lb. Product jar

987. F. B. Co. 1 (on base).....................................Aqua $10-12
    Groove ring wax sealer, pressed laid-on ring   Yellow amber $85-100
                                                         Brown amber $85-100
                                                            Citron $70-80
                                                         Smokey blue $25-30
                                            Medium Cobalt blue $400 & up

988. F. C. G. Co. 1 (on base)................................... Aqua $15-18
    Groove ring wax sealer, pressed laid-on ring

989. F. C. G. Co. (interspaced thru V, on base)........................ Aqua $18-20
    Groove ring wax sealer, pressed laid-on ring   Amber $85-100

990. F. C. G. Co. (on base)............................... Aqua $15-18
    Groove ring wax sealer, pressed laid-on ring   Amber $85-100
                                                        Deep Citron $85-100
                                                     Cornflower blue $65-75
                                                        Cobalt blue $500 & up
                                                     Deep olive green $100-125
                                                          Lime green $20-25

991. F. C. G. Co. (with lines, on base)................................... Aqua $15-18
    Groove ring wax sealer, pressed laid-on ring

992. F. C. G. Co. (with lines, on base).................................Aqua $15-18
     Groove ring wax sealer, pressed laid-on ring   Apple green $15-18

993. F. C. G. Co. (interspaced thru W, on base)......................Aqua $18-20
     Groove ring wax sealer, pressed laid-on ring   Amber $85-100
                                                  Yellow amber $85-100
                                               Deep olive green $100-125

994. F. C. O. N. (on base)...Aqua $18-20
     Groove ring wax sealer, pressed laid-on ring

995. FEARMAN'S STAR BRAND MINCEMEAT HAMILTON (within shield)........Clear $15-25
     Smooth lip Old style Lightning seal
     Canadian product jar, square shape

996. FEDERAL (draped flag) FRUIT JAR........................ Light green $75-100
     Ground lip Old style Lightning seal
     Wide mouth, Australian jar

997. FERNDELL BRAND PRESERVES DISTRIBUTED BY
     SPRAGUE, WARNER & COMPANY, CHICAGO, ILL.
     U.S.A. SPICED CANTALOUPLE (all on paper label)..........Clear $2-4
     Smooth lip Glass lid & "Safety Valve" clamp
     Product jar

998. F. H. 6 (on base)............................ .... Aqua $12-15
     Groove ring wax sealer, pressed laid-on ring

999. F. H. (on base)............................. .... Aqua $12-15
     Groove ring wax sealer, pressed laid-on ring

1000. F H G W 1 (on base)............................ .... Aqua $18-20
      Groove ring wax sealer, pressed laid-on ring   Amber $125 & up

1001. F. H. G. W. 3 (on base)............................ Amber $125 & up
      Groove ring wax sealer, pressed laid-on ring   #996   Aqua $18-20
                                                   Clear $18-20
                                     Light olive green $30-35
                                           Med. Citron $50-60

1002. FINK & NASSE ST. LOUIS (within circle)...... .... Aqua $45-50
      Base: Cohansey Glass Co. Philada
      Ground lip Cohansey lid & wire clamp
      Product jar, quart size

1003. FINNEY ISLES & CO. BRISBANE LET US BE
      JUDGED BY OUR ACTIONS (all on front)....... Light green $75-100
      Has a seal (mammal) in the center
      Ground lip Old style Lightning seal
      Wide mouth Australian jar   #1003

1004. PATENTED IN GREAT BRITAIN CANADA USA
      NO. 1842226 (all on base)................................ Clear $2-3
      Smooth lip Glass lid with notch, rubber
                        sealing ring
      This jar is called the FISHER jar because
      a printed sheet accompanying the jar gave
      instructions for using the Fisher Jars.

1005. THE F. W. FITCH CO. LTD. CANADA.............................. Clear $1-2
      Smooth lip Tin screw cover
      Canadian product jar

1006. FLACCUS BROS WHEELING, W. VA. (steers head)............ ....Clear $65-75
        Smooth lip Lightning closure
        Tall, slim product jar

1007. FLACCUS BROS STEERS HEAD FRUIT JAR (steers head). ...Clear $70-75
        Flower & leaf design around jar
        Smooth lip Cupped top for blown glass stopper
        Product jar

                                                    #1008

1008. FLACCUS BROS TABLE DELICACIES WHEELING,
        W. VA. (steers head)..............................Approx. ½ pint Clear $50-60
        Ground lip Unmarked glass screw lid   Pint Clear $75-85
        Square shaped, product jar

1009. FLACCUS BROS. TABLE DELICACIES WHEELING,
        W. VA. (steers head)..............................Approx. ½ pint Clear $50-60
        Ground lip Metal screw cover   Pint Clear $75-85
        Lid: Flaccus Bros TradeMark Preservers
              Wheeling, W. Va. (steers head)
        Product jar

1010. FLACCUS BROS STEERS HEAD TABLE DELICACIES
        WHEELING, W. VA. (steers head)................Approx. ½ pint Clear $50-60
        Closure unknown Product jar   Pint Clear $75-85

1011. FLACCUS BROS MUSTARD FRUIT JAR...................................Clear $125 & up
        Ground lip Insert & screw band closure
        Product jar

1012. FLACCUS BROS STEERS HEAD FRUIT JAR (steers head)..............Clear $65-75
        Flower & leaf design around jar
        Glass lid & Lightning wire bail
        Product jar

1013. FLACCUS BROS STEERS HEAD FRUIT JAR (steers head).....Clear $40-50
        Flower & leaf design around jar   Amber $200-225
        Ground lip Milkglass insert & screw band   Green $300 & up
        Insert: Flaccus Bros TradeMark Preservers   Milkglass $225-250
              Wheeling, W. Va. (steers head)

                                                    #1013

1014. FLACCUS BROS STEERS HEAD FRUIT JAR (steers head).....Clear $40-50
        Flower & leaf design around jar   Amber $200-225
        Ground lip One piece screw lids, matching color Green $500 & up
        Clear lid marked: Simplex   Milkglass $225-250
        Amber lid unmarked or marked: To Remove Cap Press
                          Down Unscrew (on inside)
        Green lid unmarked
        Milkglass lid marked: To Remove Cap Press Down
                          Unscrew (on inside)

1015. FLACOUS BROS STEERS HEAD FRUIT JAR (steers head)......Clear $50-55
        Spelling error
        Ground lip One piece screw lid marked Simplex
        Product jar

1016. E. C. FLACCUS CO. TRADEMARK (stag head)........... ...Clear $40-50
        Flower & leaf design around jar   Amber $200-225
        Ground lip Domed milkglass insert & screw band   Green $300 & up
        Insert: The E. C. Flaccus Co. Trademark #1016   Milkglass $225-250
              Wheeling, W. Va. (stag head)
        Product jar

1017. C. L. FLACCUS PITTSBURGH (on base)..............................Clear $30-35
        Groove ring wax sealer, pressed laid-on ring

1018. W & J. FLETT (sun) LIVERPOOL......................................Green $20-25
      Basketweave pattern around jar
      Glass stopper: Red Fearn Bros. Liverpool & Barnesley
          Or: W. J. Flett Sykes, MacVay & Co.
            Albion Glass Works, Castleford
      English jar

1019. W & J. FLETT (sun) LIVERPOOL......................................Green $20-25
      With mellon-ribs instead of basketweave pattern
      Closure as in #1018   English jar

1020. Unmarked jar, mellon-ribs, flat place for paper label....Green $20-25
      Closure as in #1018   English jar

FLORIDA TROPICAL CANNERS, see jar No. 2819

1021. FLOUR CITY JAR PAT 1868 ROCHESTER N.Y...............   Aqua $600 & up
      Ground lip A closure was not on the jar when
        found but the patent calls for a flat metal
        disk, held on by a wide rubber ring which
        stretched partly over the disk and around the
        neck of the jar. Only 1 jar is known.

FLUID DRY see jar No. 1156

#1021

1022. Chinese characters, within circle...........................Clear $3-5
      Translated: Food Friend
      Smooth lip Old style Lightning seal Product jar

1023. FOREST CITY BAKING POWDER GORMAN ECKERT & CO. LONDON....Aqua $20-25
      Ground lip Glass insert & screw band
      Canadian product jar

1024. THE FORSTER JAR...Clear $6-8
      Base: F. G. C.
      Smooth lip Glass insert & screw band
      Insert: Forster's Glass Co. Ltd.
      English jar

1025. THE FORSTER (ATLAS TYPE) JAR...............................Clear $6-8
      Base: F. G. C. 2 LB.
      Smooth lip Glass insert & screw band
      Insert: Atlas Type Lid Forster Glass Co.
      English jar

#1025

1026. FOSTORIA GLASS CO. TRADE MARK 4 FOLD SEAL FRUIT
     JAR THAT WILL PRESERVE FRUIT MOUNDSVILLE, W. VA. (on lid).......Clear $12-15
      Smooth lip Glass insert & narrow screw band

1027. 4 SEASONS MASON...Clear $2-4
      Smooth lip Mason beaded neck seal

1028. FOWLER'S VACUUM BOTTLE......................................Clear $6-8
      Smooth lip Glass lid & spring metal clamp
      English jar

1029. FRANCIS (on base)...Clear $6-8
      Ground lip Old style Lightning seal
      Lid has fin with ridges for wire bail
      Product jar

#1027

1030. THE FRANCO AMERICAN FOOD CO. JERSEY CITY (on base).............Clear $2-4
      Ground lip Glass lid & Safety Valve clamp
      ½ Pint product jar

1031. Wm. FRANK & SONS PITTs. (on base)...................................... Aqua $20-25
       Groove ring wax sealer, pressed laid-on ring

1032. F. H. FRANKE & CO. THE NORTHSIDE FAIR 285 &
       285½ NORTH AVE. CHICAGO, ILL. (on front)............... Aqua $35-40
       Ground lip Mason shoulder seal

1033. FRANKLIN FRUIT JAR.. Aqua $40-50
       Ground lip Unlined zinc lid, with two   Midget Aqua $70-75
       horizonal prongs on top. Unmarked or
       marked Franklin Fruit Jar, or marked
       Gillinder & Bennett Patd. Aug. 8 1865.
       The jar is often reported with a glass
       insert & screw band with the insert
       marked Patd Aug 8th 1865

1034. FRANKLIN DEXTER FRUIT JAR............................... Aqua $25-30
       Ground lip Glass insert & screw band
       Insert: Patd Aug 8th 1865

1035. FRANKLIN DEXTER NO. 2 FRUIT JAR...................... Aqua $25-30
       Ground lip Closure as in #1034

1036. FRANKLIN J. T. KINNEY TRENTON N.J. FRUIT JAR...... Aqua $125-150
       Ground lip Closure as in #1034

       Also see DEXTER jars, Nos. 772 thru 775
       and J. D. KINNEY jar Nos. 1419 & 1420   #1033

1037. 14 OZ NET FRENCH'S MEDFORD BRAND PREPARED MUSTARD..... Clear $2-3
       Smooth lip. Glass insert & screw band
       or metal screw lid. Product jar.

1038. FRIDLEY & CORNMAN'S PATENT OCT. 25th 1859
       LADIES CHOICE.. Aqua $275-300
       Ground lip Irom rim with gutta percha insert
       Lid: Fridley & Cornman's Patented Oct. 25th 1859
       Or: Fridley & Cornman's Carlisle, Pa.
       Patd Oct. 25 1859

1039. FRIEDLEY & CORNMAN'S PATENT OCT. 25th 1859
       LADIES CHOICE (spelling error)...................... #1039
       Ground lip Closure as in #1038   Aqua $300-325

       Also see BURNHAM jar No. 554, HUYETT & FRIDLEY jar No. 1277
       and KEYSTONE jar No. 1390

1040. FRISCO (crown) A-1 TRADE (monogram) MARK FRUIT JAR.............Green $75-100
       Ground lip Old style Lightning bail, glass
       Immerser marked Pat. Reg. 1893 An Australian jar
       Also see the CHICAGO jar No. 592 & COLUMBIA 642
1041. FRUIT GROWERS TRADE (triangle) MARK CO............. Aqua $45-50
       Applied lip Closure unknown, possibly cork
       Oval shaped product jar

1042. FRUIT KEEPER GCCo.. Aqua $25-30
       Ground lip Glass lid, wire & metal clamp
       Clamp: Pat. Mar 30 86

1043. F & S (within circle).. Aqua $12-15
       Base: H within circle)
       Smooth lip Old style Lightning seal

                          #1042

1044. G & D (on base)..Aqua $12-15
      Ground lip Metal push-down lid
      A product jar, similiar to the Lyman jars

1045. GALLOWAY'S EVERLASTING JAR PAT'd FEB. 8th AND
      PAT APP FOR 1870 (incised on shoulder)............................. $20-25
      Gray stoneware jar & lid

1046. EVERLASTING JAR PATd. FEB. 8th AND PAT APP'D FOR 1870.............. $20-25
      Incised on shoulder of brown stoneware jar
      See "Fruit Jars" by Creswick for illustrations of
        the jars and closures.

1047. GARDEN QUEEN (on lid)... Clear $1-3
      Smooth lip Glass lid & 2 metal clips

1048. BUCK GLASS CO. GARDEN QUEEN BALTIMORE MD. (on lid)............ Clear $1-2
      Smooth lip Glass lid & 2 metal clips

      Also see FARM FAMILY jar No. 979

1049. THE GAYNER GLASS TOP... Clear $4-6
      Reverse: MFG. BY GAYNER GLASS WORKS, SALEM N.J.
      Smooth lip Lightning dimple neck seal

1050. THE GAYNER MASON (front).. Clear $3-5
      Reverse: MFD BY GAYNER GLASS WORKS, SALEM N. J.
      Smooth lip Mason beaded neck seal

1051. G Co X I (on base)...Aqua $8-10
      Groove ring wax sealer, pressed laid-on ring
      This may be IGCo for Illinois Glass Co.

1052. QUALITY GELFANDS PRODUCTS (within circle)....... $12-15
      Stoneware jar, stoneware lid & Weir closure
      Lid: Weir Seal Western Stoneware Co.
      White jar with brown shoulders & lid   #1051

1053. GEM...Aqua $6-8
      Base: Pat. Nov. 26 67   Midget pint Aqua $20-25
      Ground lip Glass insert & screw band
      Insert: Patd Feb 12 56 Dec 17 61 Nov 4 62 Dec 6 64
              June 9 68 Sep 1 68 Dec 22 68 Jan 19 69

1054. GEM...Aqua $6-8
      Base: Pat. Nov. 26 67 Pat. Feb 4 73   Midget pint Aqua $20-25
      Ground lip Glass insert & screw band
      Insert as in #1053

1055. GEM...Aqua $6-8
      Base: Aug 23 70 Feb 7 71 Patd Nov 26 67
            Patd Dec 17 61 Reis Sep 1 68
      Ground lip Glass insert & screw band
      Insert as in #1053

1056. GEM (front) HGW monogram (reverse)...........................Aqua $10-12
      Base: Pat. Nov 26 67 Feb 4 73   Midget pint Aqua $20-25
      Ground lip Glass insert & screw band
      Insert as in #1075

1057. GEM (front) Hourglass emblem (reverse)......................... Aqua $10-12
      Base: Pat. Nov 26 67
      Ground lip Glass insert & screw band
      Insert as in #1053

1058. GEM (front).. Aqua $400-500
      Reverse: MANUFACTURED BY THE HERO GLASS WORKS
              PHILADELPHIA, PA.
      Ground lip Glass insert & screw band
      Insert: Patd Feb 12 56 Dec 17 61 Nov 4 62 Dec 6 64
            June 9 68 Sep 1 68 Sep 8 68 Dec 22 68 Jan 19 69
      4 Gallon size

1059. (Cross) GEM.. Aqua $8-10
      Base: Pat. Nov. 26 67   Clear $8-10
      Ground lip Glass insert & screw band   Light green $8-10
      Insert Pat Feb 12 56 Dec 17 61 Nov 4 62 Dec 6 64   Midget Aqua $20-25
           June 9 68 Sep 1 68 Sep 8 68 Dec 22 68 Jan 19 69
           (cross in center of lid)
      Note: A lid has been found in cobalt blue

1060. THE GEM (two lines).. Aqua $8-10
      Base: Pat. Nov. 26 1867   Midget Aqua $20-25
      Ground lip Glass insert & screw band
      Insert as in #1053

1061. THE GEM (two lines).. Aqua $8-10
      Base: Patd Nov. 26 1867 Sep 1 68 Dec 22 68 Jan 19 69   Yellow Green $20-25
           Patd Feb 12 56 Dec 4 61 Nov 17 Dec 22 68   Midget Aqua $20-25
           Jan 19 69 Sep 8 68
      Ground lip Glass insert & screw band
      Insert as in #1053

1062. THE GEM (one line) with erased THE HERO (two lines)............ Aqua $10-12
      Base: Patd Nov. 26 1867 Patd Dec 17 61 Nov 4 62
           Dec 14 69 Reis's Sep 1 68 June 9 69
      Ground lip Glass insert & screw band
      Insert as in #1053

1063. THE GEM (one line) with erased THE GEM just below.............. Aqua $10-12
      Base: Feb 12 56 Dec 17 61 Nov 4 62 Dec 6 64 June 9 68
           Sep 1 68 Sep 8 68 Dec 22 68 Jan 19 69
      Ground lip Glass insert & screw band
      Insert as in #1053

1064. THE GEM (one line)... Aqua $6-8
      Base: Patd Jat. 26 1867 (error)
      Ground lip Closure as in #1053

1065. THE GEM (one line)... Aqua $6-8
      Base: Jan 26 67 (reversed 6 in 26)
      Ground lip Closure as in #1053

                                            #1059

1066. THE GEM (one line)... Aqua $6-8
      Base: Patd Nov 26 1867   Midget Aqua $20-25
      Ground lip Closure as in #1053

1067. THE GEM (one line)... Aqua $6-8
      Base: Pat. Nov. 26 67 Pat Feb 4 73
      Ground lip Closure as in #1053

                              #1064

1068. THE GEM (one line)... Aqua $6-8
      Base: Pat. Dec 17 61 Reis Sept 1 68 Patd Nov 26 1867
      Ground lip Closure as in #1053
      Also found in 1½ pint size

1069. THE GEM (one line)..Aqua $6-8
      Base: Patd Dec 17 61 Reis Sept 68 & Jan 19 69
         Patd Nov 26 1867
      Ground lip Closure as in #1053

1070. THE GEM (one line)..Aqua $6-8
      Base: Patd Dec 17 61 Reis Sep 1 68 Patd Nov 26 67   Light Green $6-8
         Jan 19 69
      Ground lip Closure as in #1053

1071. THE GEM (one line)..Aqua $250-300
      Base: H. Brooke, Mould Maker, N. Y. Pat'd Nov. 26th 1868
         Patd Dec 17th 1861 Reis' Sep 1st 1868
      Ground lip Glass insert & screw band
      Insert: Patd Feby 12 56 Nov 4 62 Dec 6 64 June 9 68
         Sep 8 68 Jan 19 69 Sep 1 68 Sep 8 68 Dec 22 68
      Gallon size

1072. THE GEM (front) Hourglass emblem (reverse)..................Aqua $10-12
      Base: Patd Nov. 26 1867
      Ground lip Closure as in #1053

1073. THE GEM (front) Hourglass emblem (reverse)..................Aqua $10-12
      Base: Patd Nov. 26 1867 Pat Dec 17 61 Reis Sept 1 68
      Ground lip Closure as in #1053

1074. THE GEM (front) Hourglass emblem (reverse)..................Aqua $10-12
      Base: Patd Jan 26 1867   Midget Aqua $25-30
      Ground lip Closure as in #1053

1075. THE GEM (front) HGW monogram (reverse)......................Aqua $12-15
      Base: Pat Nov 26 67 Pat Feb 4 73
      Ground lip Glass insert & screw band
      Insert: Patd Feb 12 56 Dec 17 61 Nov 4 62 Dec 6 64
         June 9 68 Sep 1 68 Dec 22 68 Jan 19 69
         HGW monogram in center

1076. THE GEM (front) HGW monogram (reverse)....   ....Aqua $12-15
      Base: Patd Nov. 26 1867 Reis Sep 1 68   Midget Aqua $25-30
         Pat Dec 17 61
      Ground lip Closure as in #1075

1077. THE GEM (front) Cross emblem (reverse).. ....Aqua $12-15
      Base: Pat Nov 26 67
      Ground lip Closure as in #1059

1078. THE GEM CFJCo........................... ....Aqua $12-15
      Base: Mold number   Midget Aqua $25-35
      Ground lip Glass insert & screw band

#1078

1079. GEM BUTTER JAR...Aqua $65-75
      Ground lip Glass insert & screw band
      Insert: Patd Feb 12 56 Dec 17 61 Nov 4 62 Dec 6 64
         Jan 19 69 Sept 1 68 Sept 8 68 Dec 22 68

1080. GEM BUTTER JAR 5 LBS....................................Aqua $75-85
      Ground lip Closure as in #1079

1081. GEM RUTHERFORD & CO......................................Aqua $15-18
      Ground lip Glass insert & screw band   Midget Aqua $200-250
      Insert: Rutherford & Co. Hamilton, Ont.
      Canadian sealer

1082. GEM RUTHERFORD & CO.. Aqua $15-18
      Variation in embossing
      Ground lip Glass insert & screw band
      Insert: Rutherford & Co. Hamilton, Ont.

1083. GEM RUTHERFORD & CO... Aqua $15-18
      Variation in embossing
      Ground lip Closure as in #1082
      See "Fruit Jars" by Creswick for illustrations
      of all variations.

1084. THE GEM RUTHERFORD & CO.. Aqua $12-15
      Ground lip Closure as in #1082

1085. THE GEM RUTHERFORD & CO... Aqua $12-15
      Variation in embossing
      Ground lip Closure as in #1082

#1082

1086. GEM (in script)...Clear $4-6
      Smooth lip Glass insert & screw band
      Canadian sealer

1087. 1908 GEM..Clear $4-6
      Smooth lip Glass insert & screw band
      Canadian sealer

1088. NEW GEM...Clear $4-6
      Smooth lip Glass insert & screw band   Amber $45-50
      Canadian sealer

1089. NEW GEM (with erased 1908 under New).................................Clear $4-6
      Smooth lip Glass insert & screw band
      Canadian sealer

#1090

1090. WALLACEBURG GEM...Clear $4-6
      Smooth lip Glass insert & screw band
      Canadian sealer

1091. WALLACEBURG GEM with erased 1908 under Wallaceburg...............Clear $4-6
      Smooth lip Glass insert & screw band
      Canadian sealer

1092. WALLACEBURG GEM IMPERIAL 1/2 GAL......................................Clear $6-8
      Smooth lip Glass insert & screw band
      Canadian sealer

1093. GEM JAR MADE IN CANADA..Clear $2-4
      Smooth lip Glass insert & screw band

1094. IMPROVED GEM MADE IN CANADA..Clear $1-2
      Smooth lip Glass insert & screw band   Amber $45-50
      Insert: Improved Gem Made In Canada

1095. IMPROVED GEM TRADEMARK REG'D...Clear $1-2
      Smooth lip Closure as in #1094

1096. IMPROVED "GEM" TRADEMARK REG'D.......................................Clear $1-2
      Smooth lip Closure as in #1094

1097. IMPROVED "GEM" TRADEMARK REG'D V I...................................Clear $1-2
      Smooth lip Closure as in #1094

#1095

1098. IMPROVED "GEM" TRADEMARK REG'D I V...................................Clear $1-2
      Smooth lip Closure as in #1094

1099. THE GENUINE...Clear $45-50
      Smooth lip   Old style Lightning seal

1100. GENUINE MASON (word Mason in flag)................. Aqua $6-8
      Smooth lip   Mason shoulder seal

1101. GENUINE MASON (word Mason in flag)................. Aqua $6-8
      Smooth lip   Mason beaded neck seal

1102. GENUINE MASON (word Mason in flag, from left)..... Aqua $8-10
      Smooth lip   Mason shoulder seal

                                                          #1100

1103. GENUINE MASON.................................... Aqua $6-8
      Smooth lip   Mason shoulder seal   Light green $6-8
                                                  Olive green $15-20
                                                       Citron $15-20

1104. GERRIX.. Clear $2-4
      Base: Rillenglas Din Gerrix
      Smooth lip   Glass lid & wire clamp
      Lid: Gerrix Din Ges. Geschutzt Rillenglas
      German jar

                                                          #1102

1105. GESSNER'S PATENT.................................Clear $150-175
      Smooth lip
      An original closure has not been reported.
      The patent calls for a cap formed with an
       annular recess, a rubber packing seated
       in the recess, & a disk of parafine closely
       fitting the interior of the cap and covering
       the rubber packing. See "Fruit Jars" by
      Creswick for patent illustration.

1106. ROBERT GIBSON'S TABLETS MANCHESTER ENGLAND MADE
      BY E. C. RICH NEW YORK (all on front)............. Aqua $6-8
      Smooth lip   Glass stopper: E. C. Rich
                                Gibson's New York

      Product jar

1107. GILBERDS (star) JAR.............................. Aqua $140-150
      Ground lip   Glass lid   Wire clamp extending
       vertically around entire jar
      Lid: Jas. Gilberds Patd Jan. 30 1883 Jamestown, NY
      Or: Gilberds Jar Jamestown NY Pat. July 31 83

                                                          #1108

1108. GILBERDS IMPROVED (star) JAR..................... Aqua $90-100
      Ground lip   Glass lid   Wire clamp extending
       vertically around entire jar
      Lid: Gilberds Jar Jamestown NY Pat. July 31 83
      Or: Gilberds Improved Jar Cap Jamestown N. Y.
          Pat. July 31 83
      Or: Gilberds Improved Jar Cap Jamestown, New
          York Pat July 31 83 Oct. 13 1885

1109. GJCo (monogram for Gilchrist Jar Co.)............ Clear $20-25
      Smooth lip   Wide mouth   Aqua $20-25
      Zinc screw lid with inverted dome shaped
       milkglass liner to hold fruit below juice
       line. Illustrated in cut-away view to show
       liner.
      Lid variations:
      (1) Outside: Gilchrist Fruit & Food Jar
             Inside: April 2nd 1895 May 28th 1895
      (continued on next page)   #1109

-80-

Lid variations, continued....
    (2) Outside unmarked
       Inside: Pat. April 2nd & May 28th 1895
    (3) Unlined aluminum lid with center depressed
       to hold fruit below juice line, marked:
       The Keystone Jar The Gilchrist Jar Co. Pure
       Aluminum Patented July 1898.

1110. GJCo (in dual line lettering).......... .... Aqua $25-30
     Smooth lip   Closure as in #1109   Clear $25-30

1111. RAG monogram (for Ruth A. Gilchrist)... .... Aqua $25-30
     Smooth lip   Closure as in #1109

1112. GILLARD & CO. LTD. LONDON (on shoulder) .....Light green $8-10
     Base: S. Y. G. B. Co.
      Or: E. B. & Co. Ld.
     Glass stopper   English jar   #1111

1113. GIMBEL BROTHERS PURE FOOD STORE PHILADELPHIA (within circle).. Clear $20-25
     Ground lip   Old style Lightning seal

1114. GLASSBORO TRADE MARK IMPROVED.................................. Aqua $15-20
     Ground lip   Glass insert & screw band
      Insert: Trademark Glassboro Improved Regis'td
         Jany 9, 1884

1115. GLASSBORO TRADE MARK IMPROVED (TradeMark in slug plate)........ Aqua $18-20
     Ground lip   Closure as in #1114

1116. GLASSBORO TRADE 1 MARK IMPROVED...................... .. Aqua $15-20
     Ground lip   Closure as in #1114

1117. GLASSBORO TRADE 2 MARK IMPROVED...................... . Aqua $15-20
     Ground lip   Closure as in #1114

1118. GLASS BROS. LONDON (on base)..................... ..... $12-15
     Stoneware jar & lid, dark brown glaze
     Wire bail with ends fitting into holes in neck

1119. GLASS BROS & CO. LONDON ONT. PAT'D 1891 (on base) $20-25
     Stoneware jar & lid, dark brown glaze
     Wire bail with ends fitting into holes in neck

1120. W. H. GLENNY SON & CO IMPORTERS OF QUEENSWARE
     NO 162 MAIN STREET BUFFALO N.Y. (all on front)... Aqua $125-150
     Stopper neck finish for Kline stopper

1121. GLEN ROSA PURE PRODUCTS   NORTH ONTARIO PACKING CO.
     LOS ANGELES, CAL. U.S.A...................................Clear $1-3
     Base: I.P.G. Co. (within diamond)   #1120
     Smooth lip   Mason beaded neck seal   Product jar

1122. GLENSHAW G (within square) MASON.................................Clear $3-5
     Base: G within square
     Smooth lip   Mason beaded neck seal
     Glass insert & screw band   Insert: Glenshaw G Mason

1123. GLOBE... Aqua $12-15
     Ground lip   Glass lid   Wire & iron clamp, metal band   Clear $15-18
                  around neck   Amber $30-35
     Lid: Patented May 25 1886   Cornflower blue $30-35
                                 Olive green $35-40
                                 Black $800 & up
                             ½ pint Clear   Unpriced

1124. GLOBE.. Aqua $25-30
      Ground lip Closure as in #1123 Wide mouth variation

1125. GLOBE BRANDS..Clear $1-2
      Smooth lip Mason beaded neck seal Product jar

1126. GLOCKER TRADEMARK SANITARY PAT. 1911 OTHERS PENDING............ Aqua $20-25
      Smooth lip Glass lid & rubber gasket   Clear $20-25
      Lid: Glocker Pat. 1911 Others Pending Sanitary

1127. GLOCKER SANITARY JAR PATENT PENDING................................Clear $15-20
      Smooth lip Glass lid & rubber gasket
      Lid: Glocker Patent

1128. GLOCKER PAT. 1911 OTHERS PENDING SANITARY (on lid)........... Aqua $12-15
      Smooth lip Glass lid & rubber gasket   Clear $12-15
      Jar is unmarked

1129. GOLD BRAND PURE LEAF LARD GEO. C. NAPHEYS &
     SON PHILADELPHIA (all on front)....................Clear $12-15
      Ground lip Tin Screw lid with bail handle
      Lid: Geo. C. Napheys & Son Pure Leaf Gold
          Brand Lard
      Wide mouth product jar

#1127

1130. GOLDEN CROWN (crown) TABLE SYRUP................... Clear $4-6
      Smooth lip Mason beaded neck seal
      Canadian product jar

1131. GOLDEN HARVEST (over a cornucopia with fruit) MASON 6 GC......Clear   -25¢
      Smooth lip Modern 2 pc. closure
      Circa 1976 Pints & Quarts

1132. GOLDEN STATE PAT. DEC. 20th 10 (S in triangle)
     PATENTS PENDING MASON (all on front)........................Clear $12-15
      Base: Ben Schloss Manufactor Patent
          Applied For S. F. Cal.
      Smooth lip Metal screw lid Rubber gasket
             inside of lid
      Lid variations:
       (1) 1 Pc. screw lid with 3 slots on sides
          Design & lettering in red, black & gold
       (2) 1 Pc. screw lid with 3 slots on sides
          Design & lettering in red, black & gold
       (3) 1 Pc. screw lid with 1 slot on side
          Letters are embossed & entire lid is silver
       (4) Screw lid with inner metal liner
          Gold lacquered with green letters No slots
       (5) Screw lid with inner metal liner
          Gold lacquered, no marking, no slots
      See "Fruit Jars" by Creswick for lid illustrations

#1133

1133. GOLDEN STATE TRADE PAT'D DEC 20th 1910 (S in triangle)
     OTHER PATENTS PENDING MARK MASON (all on front).............Clear $12-15
      Base: Ben Schloss Manfr. & Patentee S. F. Cal.
      Smooth lip Closure as in #1132

1134. BEN SCHLOSS MANUFACTOR PATENT APPLIED
     FOR S.F.CAL. (on base)......................................Clear $8-10
      Smooth lip Closure as in #1132
      No marking on jar front   3/4 Pint size jar

1135. IMPROVED GOLDEN STATE TRADE PAT. DEC. 20th 1910
     S (in triangle) PATENTS PENDING MARK MASON (all on front)......Clear $12-15
     Base: Ben Schloss Manfr. & Patentee S. F. Cal.
     Smooth lip 2 pc. unmarked gold lacquered lid

1136. GOLDEN TREE BRAND SYRUP MADE FROM GRANULATED AND
     MAPLE SUGAR COPYRIGHTED (front)...................Clear $6-8
     Reverse, vertically: NEW ENGLAND MAPLE SYRUP
                  CO. BOSTON
     Smooth lip Lightning beaded neck seal
     Tall, slender product jar

1137. GOLDEN TREE BRAND SYRUP MADE FROM GRANULATED AND
     MAPLE SUGAR COPYRIGHTED 1907 (front)..............Clear $6-8
     Reverse, vertically: NEW ENGLAND MAPLE SYRUP
                  CO. BOSTON
     Smooth lip Lightning beaded neck seal
     Tall, slender product jar

1138. GOLDEN TREE BRAND SYRUP MADE FROM GRANULATED AND
     MAPLE SUGAR COPYRIGHTED 1907 (front)..............Clear $6-8
     Reverse, vertically: NEW ENGLAND MAPLE SYRUP
                  CO. BOSTON
     Smooth lip Mason beaded neck seal
     Tall, slender product jar

#1136

1139. FOR CANNING USE MASON CAP (within triangle).........Clear $1-3
     Embossed peanuts over entire jar
     Base: Golden West Peanut Butter
     Smooth lip Mason beaded neck seal
     Product jar intended for reuse as a canning jar

1140. GOLDEN WEST VACUUM PACKET CLOSSET & DEVERS
     PORTLAND, ORE. (front).............................Clear $1-3
     Smooth lip Mason beaded neck seal
     Product jar

1141. GOLDEN WEST VACUUM PACKED COFFEE.................Clear $1-3
     Smooth lip Mason beaded neck seal
     Product jar

#1139

1142. GOOD HOUSE KEEPERS MASON....................................Clear $1-2
     Base: Cupples Co. (J within keystone) St. Louis
     Smooth lip Mason beaded neck seal

1143. GOOD HOUSE KEEPERS MASON JAR (front).....................Clear $1-2
     Reverse: MANUFACTURED BY OWENS ILLINOIS
              PACIFIC COAST COMPANY
     Smooth lip Mason beaded neck seal

1144. GOOD HOUSE KEEPERS R (within circle) REGULAR MASON   Clear $1-2
     Base: Cupples Co. St. Louis (OI trademark)
     Smooth lip Mason beaded neck seal

1145. GOOD HOUSE KEEPERS R (within circle).............   Clear $2-4
     Base: Cupples Co. St. Louis (OI trademark)
     Smooth lip Mason beaded neck seal
     ½ Pint, ¼ Pint, and 1/3 pint sizes

#1144

1146. GOOD HOUSE KEEPERS R (within circle) WIDE MOUTH MASON..........Clear $1-2
     Base: Cupples Co. St. Louis (OI trademark)
     Smooth lip Mason beaded neck seal

1147. GRAHAM & STONE GENERAL MERCHANDISE JACKSON C.H. W. Va.............. $40-50
    Gray stoneware jar with blue stenciling
    Wax seal groove

1148. GRANDMA WHEATON'S OLD FASHIONED RECEIPTS CANNING JAR...........Clear   -$1
    Base: Wheaton N. J.   Light green   -$1
    Smooth lip Lightning dimple neck seal
    Modern product jar

1149. GRAND RIVER GRAVEL CO. MUSKOGEE OKLA. PHONE L.D. 38....Clear $6-8
    Smooth lip Lightning beaded neck seal
    ½ Gallon product jar

1150. THE GREAT EASTERN PHILADA. E.T. WHITEHEAD..........   Aqua $600 & up
    On front with erased A. Stone & Co.
    Jar has neck with internal screw threads
    Threaded glass stopper marked: The Great
      Eastern Philada. E. T. Whitehead
    Two jars are presently known

1151. GREEN MOUNTAIN C. A. Co. (within circle)......Clear $12-15
    Base: C. A. Co.   Aqua $12-15
    Smooth lip Old style Lightning seal, wide mouth
    Product jar

1152. GREEN MOUNTAIN C. A. Co. (within circle) C. A........... Aqua $12-15
    Smooth lip Old style Lightning seal, wide mouth
    Product jar

1153. GREEN MOUNTAIN C-A-Co (within frame).............. Aqua $12-15
    Smooth lip Old style Lightning seal, wide mouth
    Product jar

                                        #1155

1154. GRIFFEN'S PATENT OCT 7 1862 (on lid)..............Clear $95-110
    Ground lip Glass lid Iron cage-like clamp   Aqua $95-110

1155. GRIFFEN'S PATENT OCT 7 1862 (on lid)........ ....Clear $125-150
    Ground lip Glass lid Iron cage-like clamp   Aqua $125-150
    Illustrated at right, this jar shows a
    variation of the clamp, which is rarely
    found.

1156. FLUID OR DRY SEALING ADJUSTABLE BY ATMOSPHERIC
    PRESSURE GRISWOLD'S PATENT 1862 (all on front)....Clear $400 & up
    Ground lip Closure: cork
    This unusual jar from the Richard Vanderlaan
    collection has a long neck, and the patent
    mentions this is so the sealing cork can be
    drawn down into the neck.

#1150

#1156

1157. H (on base)... Aqua $6-8
      Groove ring wax sealer, pressed laid-on ring   Ball blue $6-8

1158. H & R (on base)... Aqua $8-10
      Groove ring wax sealer, pressed laid-on ring   Light green $8-10

1159. H & C (within circle).. Aqua $12-15
      Smooth lip   Old style Lightning seal

1160. H & C (without circle)... Aqua $12-15
      Smooth lip   Old style Lightning seal

1161. HACKER PAT'd JULY 28 '59 REIS'd APRIL 19 '64 PHILA......... $100-125
      On lid of tin can

1162. H & H... Clear $1-2
      Base: Crystalvac Container U. S. Pat. Off.
      Smooth lip   Mason beaded neck seal
      Product jar

1163. HAHNE & CO. NEWARK N.J. (around star, front)............. Aqua $30-40
      Reverse: MASON'S PATENT 1858
      Smooth lip   Mason shoulder seal

#1165

1164. HAHNE & CO. NEWARK N.J. (around star, front) Reversed J........ Aqua $35-45
      Reverse: MASON'S PATENT 1858
      Base: Star   or   mold number only
      Smooth lip   Mason shoulder seal

1165. HAHNE & CO. NEWARK N.J. (around star, front)......... Aqua $30-40
      Reverse: MASON'S PATENT NOV 30th 58
      Ground lip   Mason shoulder seal

1166. HAHNE & CO. NEWARK N.J. (around star, front)........ Aqua $30-40
      Reverse: MASON'S PATENT NOV 30th 1858
      Ground lip   Mason shoulder seal

1167. PAT'd AUG 13 1867 BY JOEL HAINES
      W. MIDDLEBURG, O. (on shoulder)................... Unpriced
        Tin can with tin lid   Wooden bar to hold
        lid in place

1168. HAINES COMBINATION............................... Aqua $100-125
      Bast: Pt. Pend.
      Jar has a groove on top   Glass lid & wire clamp
      Lid: Haines Combination

#1168

1169. HAINES'S PATENT MARCH 1st 1870................... Aqua $65-75
      Glass lid & wire clamp
      Lid: Patented Mach 1st 1870
      Top of jar has slight grooves to hold the
      gasket.   Bottom of lid has slight grooves,
      & top of lid has spiral ramps.
      An amber lid has been reported, but not an
      amber jar.

1170. HAINES'S 3 PATENT MARCH 1st 1870.............. Aqua $65-75
      Closure as in #1169

#1169

1171. HAINES' 1 IMPROVED MARCH 1st 1870................................ Aqua $65-75
        Closure as in #1169

1172. HAINES'S IMPROVED MARCH 1st 1870.............. .... Aqua $65-75
        Closure as in #1169   ½ pint Aqua   Unpriced

1173. HAINES'S IMPROVED "N E PLUS ULTRA" PATd
        APRIL 21st 1868 MCH 1st 1870
        NOV 2d 1875 (all on front)........................ ......Aqua $175-200
        Base: Putnam Glass Works Zanesville, O.
        Glass lid & wire clamp
        Lid: Patd April 21st 68 Mch 1st 70
            Nov 2d 75 (N in Nov. is sometimes
            reversed)
        Lid has spiral ramps on top & slight
        grooves on underside. Top of jar has
        slight grooves.

1174. HAINES'S IMPROVED "N E PLUS ULTRA" PATd
        APRIL 21st 1868 MCH 1th 1870
        NOV 2d 1875 (all on front)......................Aqua $175-200
        Base: Putnam Glass Works Zanesville, O.
        Closure as in #1173
        Jar is same as #1173 except has MCH 1th
        instead of MCH 1st.   #1173

1175. H & L (on base).. ......Aqua   Unpriced
        Groove ring wax sealer, pressed laid-on ring

1176. C. K. HALLE & CO 121 WATER ST CLEVELAND, O..... .....Aqua $150-175
        Stopper neck finish for Kline stopper

1177. C. K. HALLE & CO 121 WATER ST CLEVELAND, O..... ....Aqua $150-175
        Groove ring wax sealer, pressed laid-on ring

1178. MRS. G. E. HALLER PATD. FEB. 25. 73 (on stopple ..Aqua $100-125
        Blown lugs on inside of jar neck
        Blown stopple with juice hole   #1182

1179. Wm L. HALLER CARLISLE Pa............................ ..Aqua $150-200
        Stopper neck finish for cork or
        Willoughby stopple

1180. Wm L. HALLER CARLISLE Pa. (front)................ ..Aqua $400-450
        Reverse: THE LADIES FAVORITE
                Embossed lady
        Stopper neck finish for Willoughby stopple
        Stopple: Patd. Jan 4 1859 J. D. Willoughby

1181. Wm. L. HALLER CARLISLE Pa. (front).......... ....Aqua $400-450
        Reverse: THE LADIES FAVORITE
                Embossed lady
        Closure as in #1180
        Jar is same as #1180 except lady's skirt
        is pleated

1182. Wm. L. HALLER CARLISLE Pa. (front)........   Aqua $500 & up
        Reverse: THE LADIES FAVORITE
                Embossed lady
        Metal stopper fitting outside of neck
        Stopper: William Haller Patd. Aug 7 1860   #1183

1183. J. D. WILLOUGHBY & CO. NEW YORK (front)..............   Aqua $600 & up
        Reverse: THE LADIES FAVORITE (embossed lady)
        Stopper neck finish for Willoughby stopple
        Stopper: Patd Jan 4 1859 J. D. Willoughby

1184. H & S (in block letters, for Haller & Samuel)............... Aqua $350-400
      Ground lip Metal stopper which fits like   Clear $350-400
      a collar over the outside of the neck
      Stopper: William Haller Patd Aug 7 1860

1185. H & S (in block letters)..................... Aqua $350-400
      Ground lip Rounded shoulders   Clear $350-400
      Closure as in #1184

1186. H & S (in script)....................... Aqua $350-400
      Ground lip Closure as in #1184   Clear $350-400

1187. H & S PHILa............................ Aqua $350-400
      Ground lip Closure as in #1184   Clear $350-400

#1184

1188. HAMILTON.................................... ..Clear $40-50
      Ground lip Glass lid & metal strap clamp
      Lid: Patd Feb 2 1886

1189. HAMILTON GLASS WORKS 1 QUART.................. .. Aqua $225-250
      Neck finish for cork stopper
      Canadian sealer

#1186

1190. HAMILTON GLASS WORKS 1 QUART................................... Aqua $175-200
      Glass lid & iron yoke clamp with thumbscrew
      Lid: Hamilton Glass Works
      Canadian sealer

1191. HAMILTON NO 1 GLASS WORKS...................... ..... Aqua Unpriced
      Neck finish for cork stopper
      Canadian sealer, one known

1192. HAMILTON NO 1 GLASS WORKS...................... ..... Aqua $550 & up
      Glass lid & iron yoke clamp with thumbscrew
      Lid: Hamilton Glass Works
      Canadian sealer

1193. HAMILTON NO 2 GLASS WORKS...................... ..... Aqua $400-450
      Neck finish for cork stopper
      Canadian sealer

#1193

1194. HAMILTON NO 2 GLASS WORKS........................... Aqua $300-350
      Glass lid & iron yoke clamp with thumbscrew
      Lid: Hamilton Glass Works
      Canadian sealer

1195. HAMILTON NO 3 GLASS WORKS........................... ... Aqua $350-400
      Neck finish for cork stopper
      Canadian sealer

1196. HAMILTON NO 3 GLASS WORKS........................... .. Aqua $250-300
      Glass lid & iron yoke clamp with thumbscrew
      Lid: Hamilton Glass Works
      Canadian sealer

1197. HAMILTON NO 4 GLASS WORKS........................ . Aqua Unpriced
      Neck finish for cork stopper
      Canadian sealer, one known

1198. HAMILTON NO 4 GLASS WORKS........................ . Aqua $400-500
      Glass lid & iron yoke clamp with thumbscrew
      Lid: Hamilton Glass Works
      Canadian sealer

      The Hamilton jars are Canada's oldest known sealers. #1198

1199. HAMILTON GLASS WORKS (front)...................................... Aqua $175-200
      Reverse: CLAMP JAR 1/2 GAL.
      Glass lid & iron yoke clamp with thumbscrew
      Lid: Hamilton Glass Works
      Canadian sealer

1200. HAMILTON GLASS WORKS (front).................... .... Aqua $200-225
      Reverse: OLAMP JAR 1/2 GAL. (error)
      Closure as in #1199   #1204

1201. CANADIAN HAMILTON CANNERS LTD. (on base)............. ....Clear $6-8
      Smooth lip Screw cover
      Canadian product jar

1202. FROM JAS. HAMILTON & CO. GREENSBORO PA............. .... $40-50
      Gray stoneware jar with blue stenciling
      Wax seal groove

1203. HAMILTON & JONES GREENSBORO PA.................. .... $40-50
      Gray stoneware jar with blue stenciling
      Wax seal groove

1204. HAMDEN CREAMERY (with circle).................... Aqua $35-40
      Base: Cohansey
      Ground lip Cohansey glass lid & wire clamp
      Pint, product jar   #1205

1205. HANDY JAR..Clear $25-30
      Base: Made By Smalley, Kivlan & Onthank
            Boston, Mass. Patented April 27 1909
      Smooth lip Flat metal lid, with hook on
        each side & carrying handle.
      Lid: To Open Press handle Down And Slide
        Sideways Patented April 27 09

1206. HANSEE'S PALACE HOME JAR.................... ......Clear $40-50
      Base: Pat. Dec. 19 1899
      Ground lip Glass lid Wire clamp & neck
                      tie wire

      Lid: PH monogram   #1206

1207. HAPPER EXTRACT AND PERFUME COMPANY.......................Clear $8-10
      Smooth lip Glass lid & screw band
      1/2 Gallon product jar

      HABIGHT, BROWN & CO. see jar No. 769
      H & R see jar No. 1158

1208. HARRIS... . Aqua $125-150
      Ground lip Metal press-down lid

1209. HARRIS MH IMPROVED................................. . Aqua $175-200
      Ground lip Glass lid, held on by a
        concave hoop with movable arm for
        tightening   #1209

1210. HARRISON BROS & CO. PHILADELPHIA, NEW YORK & CINCINNATI........ Aqua   Unpriced
      Ground lip Metal screw cover
      Possible product jar

1211. HARTELL'S GLASS AIR TIGHT COVER PATENTED
      OCT. 19 1858 (all on lid)................................. Aqua $50-60
      Ground lip Glass lid with internal lugs.   Cobalt blue $500 & up
      Lugs on jar neck to engage lid
      Two cobalt blue pints, and one ½ pint are known.
      Also a green pint with mouth opening of 2" has been reported.

1212. PATENTED OCT. 19 1858 (on lid)................................. Aqua $40-50
       Ground lip Glass lid with internal lugs
       Lugs on neck of jar

1213. HARTELL & LETCHWORTH PATENT MAY 22 1866 (on lid)........... Aqua $70-80
       Ground lip Metal lid with 3 formed lugs on
          inside to engage on lugs on neck of jar
       Lid: Hartell & Letchworth Patent May 22 1866
             (In two straight lines)
          Or: Same marking but in two circles

1214. HARTFORD FRUIT JAR COMPANY (on base)................ ..Clear $30-35
       Ground lip Glass lid & screw band
       Several sizes and variations have been reported.

1215. HARVEST MASON.. ..Clear $6-8
       Smooth lip Mason beaded neck seal 2 pc. lid
       Glass insert: Harvest

#1212

1216. HASEROT COMPANY CLEVELAND MASON PATENT.................... Aqua $12-15
       Smooth lip Mason shoulder seal

1217. HASEROT CONPANY CLEVELAND MASON PATENT (error)............. Aqua $15-18
       Smooth lip Mason shoulder seal

1218. HASEROT COMPANY CLEVELAND MASON PATENT............ .... Aqua $15-18
       In dual line embossing
       Smooth lip Mason shoulder seal

1219. HAWLEY GLASS CO. HAWLEY, PA. (on base)......... .... Aqua $12-15
       Ground lip Mason shoulder seal

1220. E. C. HAZARD & CO. SHREWSBURY, N. J. (on base). .... Aqua $10-12
       Ground lip Glass lid & Safety Valve clamp
       Product jar

1221. E. C. HAZARD & CO. NEW YORK 7 OZ. (on base).... .... Aqua $10-12
       Ground lip Glass lid & Safety Valve clamp
       Product jar

#1224

1222. E. C. HAZARD & CO. SHREWSBURY, N. J.(on base).............Pale green $10-12
       Ground lip Old style Lightning seal
       Product jar

1223. E. C. HAZARD & CO. NEW YORK (around shoulders)................Clear $10-12
       Base: Trademark Lightning
       Ground lip Old style Lightning seal
       Product jar

1224. E. C. HAZARD & CO. NEW YORK (vertically on jar)   Lt. blue $12-15
       Applied lip Cork closure
       Product jar

1225. HAZEL.. ....Clear $12-15
       Smooth lip Old style Lightning seal   Aqua $12-15

1226. THE HAZEL (on lid insert)....................... ....Clear $20-25
       Ground lip Milkglass insert & screw band   Amber $40-50

1227. HAZEL ATLAS E Z SEAL............................ ....Clear $8-10
       Smooth lip Old style Lightning seal   Aqua $8-10

1228. HAZEL ATLAS LIGHTNING SEAL............... ....Clear $8-10
       Smooth lip Old style Lightning seal   Aqua $8-10

#1226

1229. HAZEL ATLAS LIGHTNING SEAL...Clear $6-8
       Smooth lip   Lightning beaded neck seal

1230. HAZEL PRESERVE JAR................................ .. ½ Pint Clear $6-8
       Smooth lip   Lightning dimple neck seal

1231. HAZEL HA PRESERVE JAR...................... . ...o....Clear $4-6
       Smooth lip   Lightning dimple neck seal   #1230

1232. HEALTH OYSTER JAR SEAL (front)...................................Clear $4-6
       Reverse: FULL QUART OYSTERS (in circle)
       Base: Smalley, Kivlan & Onthank Boston Mass.
       Smooth lip   Closure unknown
       Milkbottle shaped product jar

1233. HECA (in script).. Aqua $12-15
       Base: 1 L.
       Ground lip   Glass lid: Heca R. I.   with a
                     moon & stars in shield and circle
       Indentations on shoulders for clamp
       Foreign jar

1234. H. J. HEINZ CO. TRADEMARK KEYSTONE PICKLING &
PRESERVING WORKS PITTSBURG U.S.A................... .. $40-50
       Gray stoneware jar with blue stenciling
       Inside of jar has brown glaze   #1234

1235. HELME'S RAILROAD MILLS.................................Amber $12-15
       Smooth lip   Glass insert & screw band
       Snuff jar

1236. GEO. W. HELME CO. OF NEW JERSEY PATENT JULY 16 1872 (lid).......Amber $10-12
       Base: P. Lorrilard Co.
       Ground lip   Glass lid & circular wire clamp
       Snuff jar

1237. HENDRICKS AD-A-Man-Tor Co. U.S. AND FOREIGN PATENTS
PENDING GRAND RAPIDS, MICH. (all on front of jar)....Clear $6-8
       Smooth lip   Old style Lightning seal
       Pint product jar

1238. C. HERMANN & CO. MILWAUKEE (within oval)................Clear? $15-20
       Incised on brown stoneware jar   Stoneware lid

1239. HERMETIQUE (on lid)...................................Clear   -$1
       Base: Made In Italy 1 L. 12 70
       Smooth lip   Hinged glass lid with locking wire
       Italian jar, circa 1970   #1240

1240. HERO (above cross)......................... Aqua $30-35
       Ground lip   Glass lid & wire bail (differing   Clear $30-35
               from Putnam's wire bail)
       Lid: Cross in center with H F J Co in wings
            Pat Feb 27 94 Jan 29 95
       Jar is found in both regular mouth and wide
         mouth sizes.

1241. THE HERO... Aqua $30-35
       Base: Cunningham & Ihmsen Pittsburgh Pa
       Ground lip   Tin insert & zinc screw band
       Insert: T. G. Ottersons Patent Nov 4 1862 &
            C. G. Imlays Patent Dec 6 1864

                                  #1241

1242. THE HERO.. Aqua $30-35
      Base: Patd Nov. 26 1867   Honey Amber Unpriced
      Ground lip Closure as in #1241
      Only 1 amber jar is known

1243. THE HERO..Aqua $15-20
      Base: unmarked
        Or: Patd Nov 26 1867 Pat'd Dec 17 61 Reis Sep 1 68
      Ground lip Glass insert & screw band
      Insert: Patd Feb 12 56 Dec 17 61 Nov 4 62 Dec 6 64
            June 9 68 Sep 1 68 Dec 22 68 Jan 19 69
      The tin insert & zinc screw band closure could also
      be used on this jar, and would be priced $30-35.

1244. THE HERO..Aqua $30-35
      Base: Patd Nov 26 1867 Pat'd Dec 17 61 Nov 4 62
           Dec 14 69 Reis's Sep 1 68 June 9 69
      Ground lip
      Closure variations:
        (1) Tin insert & zinc screw band as in #1241
        (2) Tin insert over glass insert & zinc screw band
           Tin: Sep 1th & Dec 22d 1868 & Dec 14th 1869
              Patd Feby 12th 1856 Dec 17th 1861
              Nov 4 1862 Dec 6th 1854 June 9th Sep 1st
           Glass: Patd Sept 3 1872 (star in center)
        (3) Glass insert & screw band
           Insert: Patd Feb 12 56 Dec 17 61 Nov 4 62
             Dec 6 64 June 9 68 Sep 1 68
             Dec 22 68 Jan 19 69

THE
HERO
IMPROVED

#1247

1245. THE HERO..Aqua $250-300
      Base: Patd Nov 26th 1867 H. Brooke Mould Maker N.Y.
      Ground lip Glass insert & screw band
      Gallon size

1246. HERO IMPROVED..Aqua $15-20
      Base: Pat. Nov 26 67 Pat Dec 17 61
           Reis Sept 1 68
      Ground lip Glass insert & screw band
      Insert as in (3) under #1244
      The tin over glass insert as in (2) under
      #1244 could also be used, and would be
      priced $30-35 with this closure.

1247. THE HERO IMPROVED...Aqua $15-20
      Base: Patd Nov 26 1867
        Or: Pat Nov 26 67 Pat Dec 17 61 Reis Sept 1 68
        Or: Patd Nov 26 1867 Patd Dec 17 61 Nov 4 62
           Dec 14 69 Reis's Sep 1 68 June 9 69
      Closure as in #1246

1248. THE HEROine..Aqua $25-30
      Base: Unmarked
        Or: Patd Nov 26 1867
      Ground lip Glass insert & screw band
      Insert: Patd Feb 12 56 Dec 17 61 Nov 4 62
          Dec 6 64 June 9 68 Sep 1 68 Dec 22 68
          Jan 19 69

THE
HERO
INE

#1248

1249. THE HEROine..Aqua $25-30
      Base: Cunningham & Ihmsen Pittsburgh Pa. Nov. 26 67
      Ground lip Closure as in #1248

1250. HESTON & TRESSEL'S EUREKA JAR PAT'D FEB. 7th 1888........................Aqua   Unpriced
        Ground lip Glass lid with vent hole
        Wire bail and cast iron lever Neck tie wire
        This rare jar was reported by Barbara & Roy
         Brown and only one jar is presently known.

1251. HEYSER'S OYSTERS CONTENTS 1 PT. NET (vertically)................Clear $6-8
        Reverse: PACKED BY WM. HEYSER BALTO. Md.
        Base: Licensed by P. F. P. Co. Balto. Md.
              Patd January 7 1913
        Smooth lip Metal lid (same as on Thrift jar)
        Product jar

1252. CHAS. M. HIGGINS & CO. 14 OZ BROOKLYN N.Y.................Clear $2-3
        Smooth lip Screw cover Product jar

#1250

1253. THE "HIGH GRADE" M'F'G'D FOR KINNEY & LEVAN CLEVELAND O........Clear $20-25
        Reverse: MASON'S PATENT NOV 30th 1858
        Smooth lip Mason shoulder seal

1254. THE HIGH GRADE M'F'G'D FOR KINNEY & LEVAN CLEVELAND O.........Clear $20-25
        Reverse: MASON'S PATENT NOV 30th 1858
        Smooth lip Mason shoulder seal

1255. HILLSIDE FARM DAIRY WINTERTON SUL. Co. N. Y. (front)........... Aqua   Unpriced
        Reverse: THIS JAR TO BE WASHED AND RETURNED
        Base: Pushed up Closure: cork
        An early milkbottle in Gallon size

1256. HILTON'S PAT. MAR. 10th 1868...................... . Aqua $200-250
        Base: Mass. Glass Co. or Unmarked
        Ground lip Glass lid with ramps
        Metal yoke clamp

        Also see POMONA jar No. 2372

#1256

1257. HIRSCH BROS & CO FOX BRAND (fox/fish in mouth)
     LOUISVILLE KY. & PITTSBURGH PA. (all on front)......   ....Clear $125-150
        Flour & leaf design around jar   Milkglass $500 & up
        Ground lip Milkglass insert & screw band
        Insert: Slightly dome shaped and marked:
         Hirsch Bros & Co. Louisville, Ky. &
         Pittsburg, Pa. Fruit Products (fox head
         with fish in mouth, in center)
        Product jar

1258. HOLLIEANNA MASON................................. ..Clear $4-6
        Base: Root
          Or: Root erased & replaced by OI trademark
        Smooth lip Mason beaded neck seal

1259. HOLZ CLARK & TAYLOR SALEM N. J. ....   Aqua $350 & up
        Base: Pat. Applied For
        Threaded glass stopper Threaded jar neck

        Also see THE SALEM JAR No. 2543 & 2544

#1260

1260. HOME MADE PRESERVES MANUFACTURED BY
      H.A. JOHNSON & CO. BOSTON, MASS. (within square)...................... $15-18
        White stoneware jar with dark blue stenciling
        Stoneward lid, wire carrying bail, wooden handle

1261. THE "HOME" PRESERVING JAR 2...................................Clear $10-12
        Smooth lip Glass insert & screw band
        Made in Great Britain

-92-

1262. HOM-PAK MASON...Clear $2-3
      Base: H within triangle
      Smooth lip Mason beaded neck seal

1263. HONEY C. O. PERRINE...Clear $1-2
      Smooth lip Glass insert & screw band
      Insert: Honey C. O. Perrine
      Product jar

1264. HONEST MASON JAR PAT. 1858.................... Aqua $12-15
      Smooth lip Mason shoulder seal   Clear $12-15

1265. 1 LB. HONEYMOON PEANUT BUTTER DISTRIBUTED
     BY WHITE STORES, INC. (within heart)...........Clear $1-3
      The O's in Honeymoon are heart shaped
      Smooth lip Mason beaded neck seal
      Barrel shaped product jar

#1265

1266. HOOSIER JAR.. Aqua $300-350
      Base: Holwig & Reese Indls. Ind.
      Ground lip Mason shoulder seal
      Glass lid: Patd Sept 12 1882 Hoosier Jar
              Jan 3d 1883

   Also see CADIZ jar No. 548 & ECLIPSE jar No. 885

1267. T. HOPKINS Jr SKIPTON Md...................... Aqua $700 & up
      Base: bare iron pontil scar
      The lip appears to be hand filed and crude.
      Closure was probably a wax dipped cork.
      This rare jar from the Alex Kerr collection is
      believed to date circa 1855. Only 1 known.

#1267

1268. HORMEL FINE FOOD...Clear $1-2
      Smooth lip Mason beaded neck seal
      Product jar

1269. HORMEL FINE FOOD...Clear $1-3
      Smooth lip Lightning beaded neck seal
      Product jar

1270. HORMEL GOOD FOOD (within frame)..................Clear $1-2
      Smooth lip Mason beaded neck seal
      Product jar

1271. HORMEL GOOD FOOD..Clear $1-3
      Base: Kivlan Onthank Patd. June 28 21 HA   ½ Pint Clear $1-3
      Smooth lip Glass lid & twin wire clamps
      Lid: Hormel Good Food   Product jar

1272. HOUSEHOLD W. T. CO. FRUIT JAR...............Clear   Unpriced
      Very shallow groove on top, probably for
      a rubber gasket. Glass lid & metal clamp
      with thumbscrew. Two jars are presently #1272
      known.

1273. J. A. HOWARD PURE HONEY (front)..................Clear $1-3
      Reverse: ROBERT COLE, OAKLAND, CALIFORNIA
      Base: Robert Cole Oakland, California
      Smooth lip Mason beaded neck seal   Product jar

1274. THE HOWE JAR SCRANTON, PA.......................Clear $40-50
      Ground lip Dome shaped glass lid & wire bail   Aqua $40-50
      Indentations in neck for bail ends
      Lid: Pat. Feby 28/88
                                #1274

1275. HUDSON (on base)..Clear $1-2
      Smooth lip Mason beaded neck seal   Product jar

1276. M. B. HUMPHREY PHILA (within circle)........................ Aqua $35-40
      Base: Cohansey
      Ground lip Cohansey lid & wire clamp
      Product jar

1277. HUYETT & FRIDLEY CARLISLE, PA. LADIES CHOICE........ .... Aqua $350-400
      Ground lip Iron rim & gutta percha insert
      Iron rim: Fridley & Cornman's Patented
              Oct. 25th 1859
          Or: Fridley & Cornman's Carlisle, Pa.
              Patd. Oct. 1859
      Small mouth jar

      Also see BURNHAM, jar No. 544
            FRIDLEY & CORNMAN jar No. 1038
            KEYSTONE jar No. 1390

#1277

1278. H W (within shield) ....Clear $12-15
      Smooth lip Mason beaded neck seal

· NOTES ·

1279. I (on front).. Aqua $20-25
      Groove ring wax sealer, pressed laid-on ring

1280. THE IDEAL.. Aqua $15-18
      Ground lip Glass insert & screw band   Midget pint aqua $30-35
      Insert: The Ideal
      Canadian sealer

1281. THE IDEAL IMPERIAL PT.................... .... Aqua $30-35
      Ground lip Closure as in #1280

1282. THE IDEAL IMPERIAL QT.................. .... Aqua $15-18
      Ground lip Closure as in #1280

1283. THE IDEAL IMPERIAL 1/2 GAL............ .... Aqua $15-20
      Ground lip Closure as in #1280

                                    #1282

1284. IDEAL WIDE MOUTH JAR (within shield) MADE IN CANADA............Clear $3-5
      Base: D within diamond
      Smooth lip 2 pc. metal closure

1285. IDEAL (above monogram).. Aqua $10-15
      Base: C. S. & Co. Lt.
      Smooth lip Glass insert & screw band
      English jar

1286. I G Co. (on base).. Aqua $18-20
      Groove ring wax sealer, pressed laid-on ring

1287. I G Co (within diamond, on lid)............   ½ Pint Clear $15-18
      Smooth lip Glass screw cover

1288. C. IHMSEN & SON PITTSBURGH, PA. (on base)....   .... Aqua $20-25
      Groove ring wax sealer, pressed laid-on ring   #1287

1289. C. IHMSEN & SON PITTSBURGH, PA. (on base)...................... Aqua $125-150
      Stopper neck finish for cork or metal stopper

1290. I'M ALL RIGHT. I CAME FROM THE PIONEER STORE
      LYNCH, NEB. J. C. HOFFMAN, PROP. THE BEST
      PLACE TO TRADE. (within square)...............   ...... $18-20
      White stoneware jar with blue stenciling
      Base: January 24 1899
      Zinc screw lid   1/2 Gallon

1291. IMPERIAL TRADEMARK (hand holding a mace)....   . Aqua $200-250
      Ground lip Glass lid & metal clamp
      Lid Thomas Patent July 12 1892

      Also see GEO. D. BROWN jar No. 525 & 526

                                    #1290

1292. IMPERIAL QT. (on heel)....................................... Aqua $2-3
      Ground lip Old style Lightning seal
      Canadian product jar

1293. PATENTED IMPERIAL APR'L 20th 1886............................. Aqua $125-150
      Base: The G. H. Hammond Co. Hammond, Ind.   Clear $125-150
            Imperial Pat. April 20th 1886   Amber $500 & up
      Ground lip Glass lid with outside ramps, wire clamp
      Lid: Patented Imperial April 20th 1886

1294. IMPERIAL PAT. APRIL 20th 1886 (on base)........................Clear $35-40
      Ground lip Glass lid with outside ramps & wire clamp   Aqua $35-40
      Lid variations:
        (1) Patented Imperial April 20th 1886
        (2) THE G. H. Hammond Co. Hammond, Ind.
            Imperial Pat. April 20th 1886
        (3) Patented Imperial April 20th 1886
            Lid is completely flat on top
        (4) Imperial Pat April 20th 1886
            Marked on ramps only

1295. IMPERIAL PAT APRIL 20th 1886 (on base)........   Aqua $45-50
      Ground lip Glass lid with outside ramps
                    & wire clamp
      Lid: Patented Imperial April 20th 1886
      Sides of jar are paneled

#1295

1296. IMPERIAL PAT. APRIL 20th 1886
      COULTER MFG. CO. ST JOSEPH, MO. (base)......................... Aqua $40-45
      Ground lip Glass lid with outside ramps
                    & wire clamp
      This jar has 3 indentations in the bulbous
      neck, while the foregoing Imperial jars
      have only 2.

1297. IMPROVED... Aqua $4-6
      Ground lip Glass insert & screw band   Midget pint aqua $15-18

1298. IMPROVED... Aqua $4-6
      Ground lip Glass insert & screw band
      These jars are found in Canada and are
        probably Canadian made. A quart has
        been listed in amber.

1299. (Keystone) IMPROVED.. Aqua $12-15
      Ground lip Glass insert & screw band
      Insert: Mason Fruit Jar Co. Philada.
              Keystone in center

      IMPROVED CORONA JAR, see No. 656
      IMPROVED CROWN, see No. 697
      IMPROVED EVERLASTING, see No. 954 & 955
      IMPROVED GEM, see No. 1094 thru 1098
      IMPROVED JEWEL, see No. 1332

#1299

1300. IMPROVED JAM (front) L G Co. (reverse)............... . Aqua $50-75
      Ground lip Glass insert & screw band
      Canadian sealer

1301. IMPROVED GEM (front) L G Co. (reverse)........... . Aqua $75-100
      Ground lip Glass insert & screw band
      Canadian sealer

1302. IMPROVED JAM (front) L G Co. (reverse).......... . Aqua $50-75
      Erased word Gem beneath Jam
      Ground lip Glass insert & screw band
      Canadian sealer

#1303

1303 IMPROVED JAR IMPERIAL QT...........................Clear $4-6
      Smooth lip Glass insert & screw band   Light olive green $6-8
      Canadian sealer

1304. IMPROVED JAR IMPERIAL QT. (incomplete Q)....................Clear $4-6
      Smooth lip Glass insert & screw band
      Canadian sealer

1305. IMPROVED MASON JAR..Clear $4-6
        Smooth lip Mason shoulder seal

1306. IMPROVED MERCANTILE FRUIT JAR (front).......................... Aqua $250-300
        Reverse: EARLE'S PATENT DEC. 22 1863
        (around anchor, surrounded by 13 stars)
        Ground lip Glass lid & iron yoke clamp
        with tension spring.

        Also see AMERICAN IMPROVED jar No. 74
                NATIONAL PRESERVE CAN, No. 2237
                NATIONAL BUTTER CAN, No. 2236

1307. IMPROVED STANDARD PATENTED APRIL 17th 1888.................... Aqua $250-275
        Ground lip Tin lid, metal collar to form
        a wax seal groove & a wire clamp
        This jar, first reported to us by William
        Dudley, is known in pint & quart sizes.

1308. INDEPENDENT JAR...Clear $35-40
        Ground lip Glass screw cover   Midget pint clear $50-60
        Lid: Pat. Oct 24 1882
        Note: A midget size lid has been found in
              cobalt blue. A blue jar has not
              been reported.

1309. PAT OCT. 24 1882 (on lid).......................Midget pint clear $40-50
        Jar is unmarked
        Ground lip Glass screw cover

1310. PAT OCT 24 1882 (on lid)...Clear $20-25
        Jar is unmarked
        Ground lip Glass screw cover
        Small jar, made with 3 pc. mold

1311. IGCo monogram (on base)...........................Midget pint clear $45-55
        Ground lip Glass screw cover
        Lid: Pat. Oct. 24 1882

#1306   #1307   #1308   #1311   #1313

1312. MANUFACTURED BY INDPLS. GLASS WORKS INDIANAPOLIS. IND.(base)....Aqua $20-25
        Groove ring wax sealer, pressed laid-on ring

1313. INDICATOR..Aqua $250-300
        Ground lip 2 pc. metal lid, with openings on each side
        of rim to engage on raised glass knobs on neck of jar.
        Metal insert: Patent Applied For

1314. INSTANT SEAL (within circle)...................................Clear $6-8
      Base: Pat. Pend. Made In U.S.A.
      Wide flat top, flared out. Sealed with a green rubber
      lid which is marked: Instant Seal Wet Before Using
      Instant Seal Ltd. Toronto, Can. Patent Pending Made
      In U.S.A.

1315. INSTANT SEAL CONSERVA MFG. FOR PHILCO (within circle).........Clear $6-8
      Base: Pat. Pend. Made In U.S.A.
      Closure as in #1314

1316. I. P. G. Co. 269 5 (on heel of jar)...........................Clear $2-4
      Smooth lip Screw top
      Small product jar

1317. IRIS COFFEE REG. U.S. PAT. OFF. HAAS BARUCH & CO. (base).......Clear   -$1
      Product jar, made after 1940

1318. IVANHOE (on base)..Clear $1-3
      Smooth lip Lightning dimple neck seal
      Product jar

1319. IVANHOE (on base)..Clear $1-3
      Smooth lip Lightning beaded neck seal
      Product jar

1320. J (with keystone) NO. 5 PAIL 6158 8 (on base)..................Clear   -$1
      Smooth lip   Mason beaded neck seal
      1/2 Gallon Product jar

1321. J & B (within octagon) FRUIT JAR PAT'D JUNE 14th 1898.......... Aqua $50-60
      Ground lip   Mason shoulder seal   With regular zinc lid $25-30
      The shoulder is octagon shape & top of   Light green $50-60
       lid is also octagon shape, made to fit   With regular zinc lid $25-30
      two wrenches used to aid in opening the jar.

1322. TRADE (monogram) MARK JANNEY & MONZANI
      CLINTONVILLE, CONN. (on front, within frame)........ .Clear $20-25
        Base: A. G. Smalley & Co. Patented April 7th 1896
           Boston & New York
       Ground lip   Old style Lightning seal
       Lid: A. G. Smalley & Co. Boston & New York
       Product jar

1323. JAR SALT DETROIT SALT Co. MASON'S PAT..............   Aqua $20-25
      Smooth lip   Mason shoulder seal
      Product jar

      Also see ATLAS MASONS PATENT, No. 153

1324. JEANNETTE J (within square) MASON HOME PACKER..................Clear $3-5
      Smooth lip   Mason beaded neck seal   2 Pc. lid
      Glass insert: Jeannette J Mason

#1321

1325. JERSEY.. .. Aqua $200-250
      Ground lip   Threaded glass lid & zinc screw band
      Lid: Patented June 12th 1866   Has two raised
         glass knobs on top
      As per the patent, the zinc band was first
      screwed onto the lid & then onto the jar.
      This is the same closure as on the Whitney,
      jar No. 2967.

1326. JEWEL JAR (within frame)............................. .Clear $50-60
      Smooth lip   Glass insert & screw band
      This variation of the Jewel Jar (illustrated
       at right) is difficult to find.
      Canadian sealer

1327. JEWEL JAR (block letters) within frame....... ..Clear $6-8
      Smooth lip   Glass insert & screw band
      Insert: Jewel

#1326

1328. JEWEL JAR MADE IN CANADA..................................Clear $2-4
      Smooth lip   Glass insert & screw band
      Insert: Jewel

1329. JEWEL JAR MADE IN CANADA................... ....Clear $10-15
       Base: C within triangle
      Smooth lip   Glass lid & metal clamp

1330. Unmarked jar, with closure as in #1329... ....Clear $8-10
       Base: C within triangle
      Pint and 1/2 pint sizes

1331. CANADIAN JEWEL MADE IN CANADA....................... ......Clear $1-2
       Base: Jewel Trademark Reg'd   #1329   ½ pint clear $2-4
      Smooth lip   Glass insert & screw band
      Insert: Jewel Made In Canada

1332. IMPROVED JEWEL MADE IN CANADA.................................Clear $1-2
     Smooth lip   Glass insert & screw band
     Insert: Jewel Made In Canada

1333. J F G PRODUCTS NONE BETTER IN ALL THE WORLD........ ....Clear $2-4
     Smooth lip   Metal screw closure
     Jar is in the shape of the world globe
     & has embossed hemispheres.
     Product jar

1334. J F G PEANUT BUTTER MADE OF NO. 1 PEANUTS
     AND SALT   MANUFACTURED BY JFG COFFEE
     COMPANY KNOXVILLE TENN.................................Clear $2-4
     Smooth lip   Metal screw closure
     Jar is shaped as in #1333   Product jar

#1333

1335. JFNCo (monogram) BOSTON (on lid)..................Amber $25-30
     Base: H 2
     Ground lip   Milkglass insert & screw band
     Product jar   for J. F. Nickerson Coffee Co.

1336. JHF monogram...Aqua $20-25
     Base: Unmarked or Trademark Lightning Putnam
     Ground lip   Old style Lightning seal
     Product jar for J. H. Flickinger Packing Co.

1337. J. H. S. (on base)......................................Clear $1-2
     Smooth lip   Old style Lightning seal
     ½ Gallon product jar for J. Hungerford Smith Co.   #1336

1338. J. H. S. C. (on front).................................Clear $15-20
     Ground lip   Glass insert & screw band
     ½ Gallon product jar

1339. J M & CO (on base)...................................... Aqua $15-18
     Ground lip   Old style Lightning seal
     This product jar as described to us by Randy
      Haviland, has a band of vertical grooves around
      the shoulder & around lower portion of jar, with
      a smooth band in center for paper label.

1340. JOHNSON & JOHNSON NEW BRUNSWICK N.J. USA (vertically)......... Amber $20-25
     Ground lip   Cohansey lid & wire clamp   Cobalt blue   Unpriced
     Jar used for surgical dressings

1341. JOHNSON & JOHNSON NEW BRUNSWICK N.J. USA (vertically)......... Amber $15-18
     Ground lip   Glass insert & screw band   Cobalt blue $35-40
     Jar used for surgical dressings

1342. JOHNSON & JOHNSON NEW BRUNSWICK N.J. USA (vertically)........ Amber $15-18
     Ground lip   Glass lid & Safety Valve clamp   Cobalt blue $35-04
     Jar used for surgical dressings

1343. JOHNSON & JOHNSON NEW BRUNSWICK N.J. USA (vertically)........ Amber $15-18
     Ground lip   Glass lid with spiral ramps, wire clamp   Cobalt blue $35-40
     Lid: Patented Columbia Dec 29th 1896
      Or: Unmarked lid
     Product jar for surgical dressings, found in
      several sizes.

1344. JOHNSON & JOHNSON NEW BRUNSWICK N.J. USA (vertically)........ Amber $20-25
     Ground lip   Glass lid & metal clamping ring
     Jar used for surgical dressings

1345. JOHNSON'S 2 PATENT JAN. 7th 1868.. Aqua $250-300
     Ground lip Zinc screw lid
     The jar has threads which differ
      from the usual mason.

1346. JONES YERKES PHILADA... Aqua $125-150
     Stopper neck finish for cork
     An early New Jersey canning factory. See
     "Fruit Jars" by Creswick for history.

#1346

1347. JUMBO (elephant's head) PEANUT BUTTER
     THE FRANK TEA & SPICE CO. CINCINNATI, O........................Clear $1-2
     Smooth lip Metal screw cover   With correct lid $3-5
     There is a variety of shapes and sizes among the
     Jumbo Peanut Butter Jars. We have listed only
     the pint. Various sayings were used on the bottoms
     of the pints, such as:

          "ACCEPT NO SUBSTITUTE FOR JUMBO"

          "ALL THE CHILDREN LIKE JUMBO"

          "IF YOU LIKE JUMBO TELL YOUR FRIENDS"

          "JUMBO GOOD ENUF FOR ME"

          "JUMBO BEST FOR THE KIDDIES"

          "TRY JUMBO PEANUT BUTTER SANDWICHES"   #1347

          "TRY JUBMO PEANUT BUTTER SANDWICHES"
            (error)

          "WRITE FOR JUMBO PEANUT BUTTER RECIPE"

Collectors Notes

1348. K (on base)... Aqua $10-12
      Groove ring wax sealer, pressed laid-on ring

1349. K (on base)... Aqua $10-12
      Groove ring wax sealer, pressed laid-on ring   Clear $10-12
                            Med. Olive green $50-60

1350. K MONROE CO. OHIO (on base)...............................Green   Unpriced
      Groove ring wax sealer, pressed laid-on ring

1351. P. KABIS FRUIT JAR SHIRLEYSBURG, PA. (on lid)......................   Unpriced
      Unmarked stoneware jar with brown glaze
      Wax seal groove Tin lid

1352. THE "KALAMAZOO" JAY BE RHODES COMPANY KALAMAZOO,
      MICHIGAN FILL TO LINE ABOVE ARROW POINT ONE FULL
      LIQUID QUART (all on front)....................................Clear $4-6
      Smooth lip Metal spout marked Jay B. Rhodes Co.
             Patd Jan 17 1922
      Oil jar

1353. KASTRUP (superimposed on embossed twig of cherries)...........Clear   -$1
      Smooth lip Glass lid & spring metal clamp
      Lid: Kastrup
      Made in Denmark Sizes from ¼ Litre to 2 Litre

1354. K C FINEST QUALITY MASON SQUARE SPACESAVER STYLE...............Clear $1-3
      Reverse: MADE IN AMERICA
      Smooth lip Mason beaded neck seal 2 pc. metal lid
      Lid insert: Safe Seal KC Mason Caps Jaques Mfg. Co. Chicago

1355. KEEFER'S No 1... Aqua $175-200
      Stopper neck finish with inside threads
      Threaded glass stopper: G. M. Keefer Patented
                Dec 20th 1870

1356. KEEFER'S No 2... Aqua $175-200
      Closure as in #1355

1357. KERR "ECONOMY" TRADEMARK.....................................Clear $2-4
      Base: Kerr Glass Mfg. Co. Sand Springs, Okla.
            Patented June 9 1903
      Smooth lip Metal lid & spring metal clamp
      Lid: Gold lacquered, embossed: Kerr Economy Jar Cap
      Or: Gold lacquered, embossed: Kerr Economy

#1355

1358. KERR "ECONOMY" TRADEMARK.....................................Clear $2-4
      Base: Kerr Glass Mfg. Co. Sand Springs, Okla.
            Patented June 9 1903
            (two A's and 1 N incomplete)
      Smooth lip Closure as in #1357

1359. KERR "ECONOMY" TRADEMARK.....................................Clear $2-4
      Base: Kerr Glass Mfg. Co. Patented Sand
            Springs, Okla.
      Smooth lip Closure as in #1357

1360. KERR "ECONOMY" TRADEMARK..Clear $2-4
    Base: Kerr Glass Mfg. Co. Sand Springs, Okla.
    Smooth lip Closure as in #1357

1361. KERR "ECONOMY" TRADEMARK..Clear $2-4
    Base: Kerr Glass Mfg. Co. Sand Springs, Ok.
    Smooth lip Closure as in #1357

1362. KERR "ECONOMY" TRADEMARK..Clear $2-4
    Base: Kerr Glasss Mfg. Co. Patented Sand
        Springs, Okla. (error)
    Smooth lip Closure as in #1357

1363. KERR "ECONOMY" TRADEMARK......................................Clear $2-4
    Base: Kerr Glass Mfg. Co. Patented   Light green $8-10
        Portland, Ore.
    Smooth lip Closure as in #1357

1364. KERR "ECONOMY" TRADEMARK......................................Clear $2-4
    Base: Kerr Glass Mfg. Co. Pat. Chicago, Ill
    Smooth lip Closure as in #1357

1365. KERR "ECONOMY" TRADEMARK......................................Clear $2-4
    Base: Kerr Glass Mfg. Co. Chicago, Ill.
    Smooth lip Closure as in #1357

#1365

1366. KERR ECONOMY TRADEMARK..Light green $8-10
    Base: Kerr Glass Mfg. Co. Pat. Chicago, Ill.
    Smooth lip Closure as in #1357

1367. KERR GLASS MFG. CO. PORTLAND, ORE. (on base).........Clear $2-4
    Jar is marked on base only
    Smooth lip Closure as in #1357

1368. KERR GLASS TOP MASON...Clear   -$1
    Smooth lip Mason beaded neck seal 2 Pc. lid
    Glass insert: Kerr

#1368

1369. KERR "Self Sealing" REG. U.S.PAT.OFF. WIDE MOUTH MASON.........Clear   -25¢
    Base: AHK
    Smooth lip Mason beaded neck seal 2 Pc. lid
    Metal insert: Kerr Wide Mouth Mason

1370. KERR "Self Sealing" REG. U.S.PAT.OFF. MASON...................Clear   -25¢
    Base: AHK   ½ Pint Clear $1-3
    Smooth lip Mason beaded neck seal 2 Pc. lid
    Metal insert: Kerr "Self Sealing" Mason Patented

1371. KERR "Self Sealing" TRADEMARK REG. PATENTED MASON......Pint Sky blue   -$25
    Base: Unmarked   Quart Sky blue   -$20
      Or: Kerr Glass Mfg. Co. Patented   ½ Gallon Sky blue   -$25
        Chicago, Ill.
    Smooth lip Closure as in #1370

1372. KERR "Self Sealing" TRADEMARK REG. PATENTED MASON..............Clear $1-2
    Base: Kerr Glass Mfg. Co. Pat. Aug. 31 1915   Light green $3-5
        Sand Springs, Okla.
    Smooth lip Mason beaded neck seal 2 Pc. lid

1373. KERR "Self Sealing" TRADEMARK REG. PATENTED MASON.............Clear $2-4
    Base: Kerr Glass Mfg. Co. Pat. Aug. 31 1815 (error)
        Sand Springs, Okla.
    Smooth lip Mason beaded neck seal 2 Pc. lid
    1/2 Gallon

1374. KERR "Self Sealing" TRADEMARK REG. MASON.....................Clear $1-2
   Base: Kerr Glass Mfg. Co. Sand Springs, Okla.   Light green $3-5
    Pat. Aug 31 1915   ½ Pint clear $3-5
   Smooth lip Mason beaded neck seal 2 Pc. metal lid

1375. KERR "Self Sealing" TRADEMARK REG. PAT. AUG 31 1915 MASON......Clear $1-2
   Base: Unmarked
   Smooth lip Mason beaded neck seal 2 Pc. metal lid

1376. KERR "Self Sealing" TRADEMARK REG. WIDE MOUTH MASON............Clear $1-2
   Base: Kerr Glass Mfg. Co. Sand Springs, Okla.
    Pat. Aug 31 1915
   Smooth lip Mason beaded neck seal 2 Pc. metal lid
   Lid insert: Kerr Self Sealing Wide Mouth Mason Pat 8-31-15
    Or: Kerr Wide Mouth Mason Pat. 8-31-15

1377. KERR "Self Sealing" TRADEMARK REG. PAT. 8.31.1915
WIDE MOUTH MASON...Clear   -$1
   Base: Kerr Glass Mfg. Co. Sand Springs, Okla.
   Smooth lip Mason beaded neck seal 2 Pc. metal lid

1378. KERR "Self Sealing" TRADEMARK REG. WIDE MOUTH MASUN (error)....Clear $2-3
   Smooth lip Mason beaded neck seal 2 Pc. metal lid

1379. KERR "Self Sealing" TRADEMARK REG. MASON..............Clear   -25¢
   Base: Mold numbers
   Smooth lip Mason beaded neck seal 2 Pc. lid

1380. KERR "Self Sealing" MASON.......................Clear   -25¢
   Base: Unmarked
   Smooth lip Mason beaded neck seal 2 Pc. lid

1381. KERR "Seaf Sealing" TRADEMARK REG. MASON (error).......Clear $2-3
   Base: Kerr Glass Mfg. Co. Sand Springs, Okl.
   Smooth lip Mason beaded neck seal 2 Pc. lid

#1383

1382. KERR "Sell Sealing" TRADEMARK REG. PAT. AUG. 31 1915
MASON (error)..Clear $2-3
   Smooth lip Mason beaded neck seal 2 Pc. metal lid

1383. KERR "Sell Sealing" TRADEMARK REG. MASON (error)..............Clear $2-3
   Smooth lip Mason beaded neck seal 2 Pc. metal lid

1384. KERR "Sele Sealing" TRADEMARK REG. MASON (error)..............Clear $2-3
   Smooth lip Mason beaded neck seal 2 Pc. metal lid

1385. KERR Self Sealing TRADEMARK REG. MASON.................½ Pint Clear $2-3
   Base: Kerr Glass Mfg. Co. Sand Springs,
   Okla. Pat. Aug 31 1915
   Smooth lip Mason beaded neck seal 2 Pc. metal lid

1386. KERR "Self Sealing" MASON....................................Amber $10-12
   Base: AHK
   Smooth lip Mason beaded neck seal 2 Pc. metal lid
   These were produced in 1968 for jar collectors.
   Approximately 2500 were made.

1387. KERR "Self Sealing" MASON (front)..............Streaked Cobalt blue $12-15
   Reverse: 65th ANNIVERSARY 1903-1969   Applied gold $20-25
   Smooth lip Mason beaded neck seal 2 Pc. metal lid
   These were made to celebrate the 65th Anniversary
   of the Kerr Glass Company. Approximately 1500
   blue streaked jars were made and 750 jars with an
   applied gold finish. Some were also made with green
   streaks but these were not released.

1388. KERR (on shoulder) "Self Sealing" MASON (near base)............Clear   -$1
       Reverse: Same
       Smooth lip Mason beaded neck seal
       These were made, starting in 1975, for Sanka
         Brand Decaffeinated Coffee, and were intended
         for reuse as a home canning jar.

1389. KERR "Self Sealing" (front)....................................Ruby Red   -$19.76
       Reverse: UNITED STATES BICENTENNIAL 1776 1976   Colbalt Blue -$19.76
       Base: Not To Be Used For Home Canning   Milkglass   -$19.76
       Handblown, bell shaped jar with threaded
         top, ground lip & a pontil scar on base.
         Approximately 750 of each color were
         produced.

1390. KEYSTONE...Aqua $350-400
       Ground lip Iron rim with gutta percha insert
       Rim: Fridley & Cornman's Patented
            Oct 25th 1859

       Also see BURNHAM jar No. 544
                FRIDLEY & CORNMAN jar No. 1038
                HUYETT & FRIDLEY jar No. 1277   #1390

1391. TRADEMARK KEYSTONE REGISTERED..................................Clear $8-10
       Smooth lip Old style Lightning seal, wide mouth

1392. TRADEMARK KEYSTONE REGISTERED..................................Clear $8-10
       Smooth lip Old style Lightning seal, regular mouth

1393. K-G (within oval, on base).....................................Clear $1-3
       Smooth lip Lightning beaded neck seal
       Made in both round & square shapes
       Product jar

1394. K. H. & G. Z. O. (on base).....................................Aqua $12-15
       Groove ring wax sealer, pressed laid-on ring   Yellow Amber $75-85
                         Yellow amber with dark amber streaks $125-150

1395. KARL KIEFER PAT NOV 25 1913 (on lid)...........................Clear $2-4
       Smooth lip Glass lid with grooves for two wire clamps
       Product jar

1396. KIEFER PATENT PENDING (on lid).............. ....Clear $2-4
       Smooth lip Closure as in #1394
       Product jar

1397. PATENTED KARL KIEFER (on lid)................ ....Clear $2-4
       Smooth lip Closure as in #1395
       Product jar

1398. BARRON KILNER MAKER WAKEFIELD............... .Light green $2-4
       Smooth lip Glass insert & screw band
       English jar

1399. KILNER BROS MAKERS LONDON (lower front)..... .Light green $4-6
       Base: C B K 2667
       Glass stopper: J. Kilner & Sons Wakefield
               Or: KBT monogram for Kilner Bros
                   Thornhill   #1399

1400. C B M (on base)..Light green $4-6
       Glass stopper as in #1399
       English jar

1401. C C B (on base)...................................Light green $4-6
      Glass stopper as in #1399   English jar

1402. C B K 1135 (on base).............................Light green $4-6
      Glass stopper as in #1399   English jar

1403. J. K. & S W 1518 (on base)......................Light green $4-6
      Glass stopper as in #1399   English jar

1404. J. K. & S W 2001 (on base)......................Light green $4-6
      Glass stopper as in #1399   English jar
      Jar is paneled

1405. KILNER BROTHERS DEWSBURY & LONDON (on stopper).........Light green $4-6
      Base: N & C 1258
      Jar has "mellon" ribs   English jar

1406. THE "KILNER" FRUIT JAR..........................Light green $4-6
      Smooth lip Glass insert & screw band
      Insert: English Made

1407. THE "KILNER" JAR REGd...........................Clear $2-4
      Smooth lip Glass insert & screw band
      Insert: Kilner Bros. Ltd. Makers
      English jar

1408. THE "KILNER" JAR MAKERS KILNER BROTHERS LTD
      CONISBORO, DEWSBURY AND LONDON...................Aqua $3-5
      Reverse, on heel: 1920
      Base: K. B. Ld. 406
      Smooth lip Glass insert & screw band
      Insert: Kilner Bros. Ltd. Makers
      English jar

#1408

1409. THE "KILNER" JAR IMPROVED REGd..................Aqua $2-4
      Smooth lip Glass insert & screw band   Clear $2-4
      Insert: Kilner Bros. Ltd. Makers
      English jar

1410. KILNER REGd DUAL PURPOSE JAR....................Clear $1-2
      Smooth lip Mason beaded neck seal 2 Pc. metal lid
      Insert: Sealing Disc Kilner Regd. Dual Purpose Jar
              Use Only Once For Preserving Lever With
              Coin To Break Seal.
      English jar

1411. JOHN KILNER WAKEFIELD (on base)................Light green $4-6
      Glass stopper or cork closure
      English jar

1412. Wm S KIMBALL & CO ROCHESTER N Y...............Aqua $12-15
      Ground lip Paneled jar Metal screw cover   Yellow amber $15-18
      Tobacco humidor

      CANADIAN KING, see jar No. 555

1413. KING PATENTED MAY 13' 1873 (on lid).......Clear $8-10
      Glass lid for jelly tumbler

1414. KING (on stippled banner, below Crown)....   Aqua $10-12
      Base: Smalley, Kivlan & Onthank   Clear $10-12
            Boston, Mass.   ½ Pint clear $12-15
      Smooth lip Old style Lightning seal
      Oval shaped jar

#1414

-106-

1415. KING (on stippled banner, below crown)...................... Clear $12-15
        Base: Smalley, Kivlan & Onthank Boston, Mass.
          Or: Smalley, Kivlan & Onthank Boston, Mass.
               Pat'd Feb 23 09
        Smooth lip Glass lid & twin wire clamps
        Oval shaped jar

1416. KING (on banner, below King's head)..................... Clear $12-15
        Smooth lip Old style Lightning seal   ½ Pint Clear $18-20
        Oval shaped jar

1417. KING (on banner, below King's head)..........   .... Clear $15-18
        Base: Unmarked or Pat'd Feb 23 09
        Smooth lip Glass lid & twin wire clamps
        Oval shaped jar

1418. THE KING PAT. NOV. 2. 1869....................   .... Aqua $100-125
        Ground lip Glass lid & iron yoke clamp

      Also see the CHAMPION JAR No. 583

1419. MANUFACTURED FOR J. T. KINNEY TRENTON N. J.   .... Aqua $175-200
        Neck with inside threads for threaded
          glass stopper
        Stopper: J. T. Kinney, Trenton N. J.

1420. MANUFACTURED FOR J. T. KINNEY TRENTON N. J............. Aqua $125-150
        Stopper neck finish for Kline stopper

1421. KINSELLA 1874 TRUE MASON.............................Clear $6-8
        Smooth lip Mason beaded neck seal
        Metal lid, embossed Kinsella Product jar

1422. KLINE'S PATENT OCT. 27. 63 (on blown glass stopper)   Aqua $100-125
        Jar is unmarked Stopper has juice hole

1423. A. KLINE PAT'D OCT. 27 1863 USE PIN (on stopper)....   Aqua $25-30
        Jar is unmarked

1424. A. KLINE PAT'D OCT. 27 1863 USE A PIN (on stopper).   Aqua $25-30
        Jar is unmarked
        Stopper is found in two sizes

1425. A. KLINE PAT'D OCT. 27 1863 USE PIN (on stopper)........ Aqua $25-30
        Center bar of the stopper is divided
        Jar is unmarked

1426. A. KLINE IMPROVED PAT OCT. 27 1863 USE PIN (on stopper)........ Aqua $25-30
        Stopper has inclined ramps & was held on the jar
          with a simple wire clamp.
        Jar is unmarked

1427. A. KLINE PAT'D OCT. 27 1863 USE PIN (on stopper)....   . Aqua $100-125
        Unmarked jar, has screw threads on top for a zinc
          screw band to hold stopper in place.

1428. A. KLINE PAT'D OCT. 27 1863 USE PIN (on stopper)...   Aqua $125-150
        Stopper has ramps on lower portion
        Unmarked jar has two indented lugs in the neck
          to engage the stopper.

1429. KNIGHT PACKING CO. (IPG in triangle) (on base).....   Clear $1-3
        Smooth lip Mason beaded neck seal
        Product jar

#1419

#1422

#1428

1430. KNIGHT PACKING CO. (OI within diamond, on base)..............Clear $1-3
     Smooth lip Mason beaded neck seal
     Jar is paneled Product jar

1431. D. A. KNOWLTON SARATOGA N.Y.................   Green-black   Unpriced
     A very early embossed jar, with crudely
     flared lip. Sealed with a cloth or
     other material, tied with a string
     around the neck. Very dark olive green
     which appears black unless held to light.
     Only 1 jar is known.

#1431

1432. KNOWLTON VACUUM (star) FRUIT JAR..............   ....Aqua $18-20
     Smooth lip Glass insert & perforated zinc cover
     Cover: Knowlton Vacuum Full Glass Top Patented
           Trademark May 12 03
     Glass insert: Knowlton Vacuum Pat'd May 1903

     Also see MANSFIELD jar No. 1619

1433. KNOX MASON (in script)..........................Clear $3-5
     Smooth lip Mason beaded neck seal

1434. KNOX (within circle) GENUINE MASON...............   ...Clear $3-5
     Smooth lip Mason beaded neck seal

1435. KNOX (K within keystone) MASON..................   ..Clear $2-3
     Smooth lip Mason beaded neck seal 2 Pc. lid
     Glass insert: Knox
     Or metal insert: K (in keystone) Knox Mason
     Known sizes include: tall, square ½ gallon,
     medium tall, square ½ gallon, squatty, square
     ½ gallon with wire bail carrying handle.
     Square quart & pint. Round ½ pint. Also
     miniature salt & pepper shaker jars.

#1435

1436. KNOX (K within keystone) MASON.......................½ Pint Clear $3-5
     Base: J within keystone
     Smooth lip Mason beaded neck seal

1437. XNOX (K within keystone) MASON (error).......................Clear $3-5
     Smooth lip Mason beaded neck seal

1438. B. KOEHLER & CO. DEALER IN GROCERIES DRY GOODS
HARDWARE POMEROY OHIO.....................................   .... $40-50
     Gray stoneware jar with blue stenciling
     Wax seal groove

1439. KOENIG 5¢ (on both front & reverse)............   ...Clear $4-6
     Smooth lip Mason beaded neck seal
     Lid: "Ever Fresh Vacuum Packed Coffee,
         Every Sip Satisfies"
     Product jar

1440. KOHRS DAVENPORT, IA (vertically on jar)........   ..Clear $1-3
     Smooth lip Screw cap
     Diamond shaped product jar

#1442

1441. KOHRS DAVENPORT, IA (within circle) PAT. JULY 14, 1908........Clear $3-5
     Smooth lip Lightning dimple neck seal
     Product jar

1442. KOLD PROSSO (embossed canner) CANNER........................Clear $15-18
     Smooth lip Glass lid & twin wire clamps
     Made for Smalley, Kivlan & Onthank, Boston, Mass.

1443. A. KRAYER FULTON M'K'T N. Y. (within circle)....................Aqua $20-25
      Reverse: Erased Leotric
      Base: Reg. T. M. No. 43288
      Ground lip Old style Lightning seal
      Product jar

1444. K. S. & Co. PATENTED DEC 17th 1872 (on base)...   ....Clear $6-8
      Ground lip Metal press-down lid
      Candy jar

1445. PATENTED DEC 17th 1872 (on base).............   ....Clear $6-8
      Ground lip Metal press-down lid
      Candy jar

#1443

1446. K. Y. G. W. (on base)... Aqua $18-20
      Groove ring wax sealer, pressed laid-on ring   Amber $100-125
                                                            Olive Green $85-100

1447. KY G W Co. (on base)... Aqua $18-20
      Groove ring wax sealer, pressed laid-on ring   Amber $100-125
                                                            Olive Green $85-100
                                                         Deep Aqua Green $20-25

NOTES

1448. LA ABEJA (within circle) PAT'D JULY 14 1908.........   ..Clear $2-3
        Smooth lip   Lightning dimple neck seal
        Product jar

1449. LA ABEJA (within circle, on front)................   .Clear $2-3
        Reverse: PAT'D JULY 14 1908
        Smooth lip   Lightning dimple neck seal
        Product jar

1450. LAFAYETTE (below profile of Lafayette)............   . Aqua $300-350
        Stopper neck finish   3 Pc. glass & metal stopper   Amber   Unpriced
        Lid: Patent Pending
        Only 2 amber jars are known

#1450

1451. THE LAFAYETTE (in block letters)........................... Aqua $250-300
        Closure as in #1450

1452. LAFAYETTE (in script).. Aqua $75-100
        Stopper neck finish   3 Pc. glass & metal stopper   Clear $75-100
        Lid: Patented Sept 2 1884 Aug 4 1885
        Note: A deep green lid has been reported

1452. LA LORRAINE (over thistle blossom)................   .....Aqua $25-30
        Base: 1 Litre
        Glass stopper with attached wire clamp
         The stopper is found in aqua, and also
         in porcelain. Both have an embossed
         thistle blossom on top. An early French
         jar.

1453. LA LORRAINE (over thistle blossom)..............   ...Aqua $25-30
        Base: 1 Litre
        Closure as in #1452
        Jar is "milk bottle" shape

1455. LAMB MASON................................   ..Clear $1-3
        Base: Unmarked or C within circle
        Smooth lip Mason beaded neck seal   2 Pc. lid
        Lid insert: Lamb

#1453

1456. DOULTON & WATTS REGISTERED 1367 LAMBETH POTTERY (within diamond).... $12-15
        Tan stoneware jar
        Lid is stoneware with a heavy metal clamp
         permanently attached to it.

1457. STEPHEN GREEN GLASS LINED INSIDE LAMBETH (within oval).............. $12-15
        Tan stoneware jar. Inside of jar has a white
         glazed finish. Closure as in #1456

1458. STEPHEN GREEN & CO. IMPERIAL POTTERIES LAMBETH (within oval)........ $12-15
        Tan stoneware jar. Closure as in #1456

1459. J. A. LANDSBERGER CO. SAN FRANCISCO U.S.A. PATENTED
        JAN 1 01 JUNE 9 03 JUNE 23 03 (all on base)....................Clear $15-18
        Smooth lip   Metal lid & spring metal clamp
        Product jar

1460. PATENTED JAN 1 01 JUNE 9 03 JUNE 23 03 (on base)..............Clear $10-12
        Smooth lip   Metal lid & spring metal clamp
        Product jar

1461. AND PATENTS PAT JAN 01 APPLIED FOR (on base)...................Clear $10-12
        Smooth lip   Metal lid & spring metal clamp
        Product jar

1462. PATENTED JUNE 9 03 JUNE 29 .03 (on base).......... ....Clear $6-8
        Smooth lip   Metal lid & spring metal clamp
        Jelly tumbler

1463. L. C. Co. (on base).. ...Clear $1-2
        Smooth lip   Metal lid & spring metal clamp
        Product jar

1464. L. B. (on base).. ...Clear $1-2
        Smooth lip   Metal lid & spring metal clamp
        Product jar

                                                            #1465

1465. THE LEADER (one line)...................................... ... Aqua $30-35
        Ground lip   Glass lid & 2 pc. wire clamp   Clear $30-35
        Wire is squarish   Amber $75-85
        Lid: Patented June 28 1892

1466. THE LEADER (two lines).................... ...... Aqua $30-35
        Ground lip   Closure as in #1465   Clear $30-35
                                                                       Amber $75-85
                                                                       Olive Green Unpriced

1467. WM (monogram) TRADEMARK LEADER............. ...... Aqua   Unpriced
        Ground lip   Glass lid & wire bail,
                neck tie wire

1468. LEADER FRUIT JAR IMPROVED TRADEMARK (base).. ....Clear $10-12
        Smooth lip   Old style Lightning seal
        Lid: Leader Fruit Jar TradeMark   #1467

1469. J. ELLWOOD LEE CO. CONSHOHOCKEN, PA. U.S.A. (on lid)..........Amber $25-30
        Ground lip   Amber glass insert & metal
                screw band
        Product jar

1470. J. C. LEFFERTS PATENTED FEB.Y 15th 1859
        MANUFACTURER (all on front)............................. ..... Unpriced
        Cast iron jar & closure, lined with
        vitreous enamel.

1471. Unmarked jar, same shape & closure as #1470........ ..... Unpriced
        Cast iron jar & closure, lined with
        vitreous enamel.

                                                            #1470

1472. LEGRAND IDEAL TRADE (LIJ monogram) MARK....
        PAT'd 7-5-98 VACUUM JAR (all on front)..... ....Aqua $150-175
        Neck: ONE QUART
        Metal lid with center vent hole & rubber
        plug or screw cap plug. Marked: Pat'd
        July 5 1898

1473. LEOTRIC............................ ....Aqua $8-10
        Base: Reg. T. M. No. 43,288
            Or: Unmarked
        Ground lip   Old style Lightning seal

1474. LEOTRIC............................ ....Aqua $8-10
        Base: Salem N. J.   Clear $8-10
        Ground lip   Old style Lightning seal   #1472

1475. LEOTRIC...Aqua $8-10
     Base: Erased H. W. Pettit Salem N. J.
     Ground lip   Old style Lightning seal

1476. LEOTRIC (within circle)......................Clear $6-8
     Base: Reg. T. M. No. 43,288   or Unmarked   Aqua $6-8
     Smooth lip   Old style Lightning seal

1477. LEOTRIC (within circle)......................Clear $8-10
     Base: Reg. T. M. No. 43,288   Aqua $8-10
     Ground lip   Old style Lightning seal

1478. LEOTRIC (below erased, arched TRADEMARK)........... Aqua $8-10
     Made, using a reworked Trademark Electric mold   #1475
     Base: Reg. T. M. No. 43,288   or   Unmarked
     Ground lip   Old style Lightning seal

1479. LEOTRIC (below erased, arched TRADEMARK)........... Aqua $8-10
     Made, using a reworked Trademark Electric mold
     Base: Salem N. J.
     Ground lip   Old style Lightning seal

1480. LEOTRIC (front) Reverse: erased CLARKS PEERLESS... Aqua $8-10
     Ground lip   Old style Lightning seal

1481. LOEB HERMANOS LEOTRIC FRUIT JAR (within circle)... Aqua $15-18
     Smooth lip   Old style Lightning seal
                 #1481

1482. L G Co. (on base).............................Aqua $18-20
     Groove ring wax sealer, pressed laid-on ring   Light yellow Amber $70-80
                     Amber $100-125
                Yellow green $30-40

1483. L. G. Co. F (on base)..........................Aqua $18-20
     Groove ring wax sealer, pressed laid-on ring

1484. L. G. Co. P (on base)......................Lime green $18-20
     Groove ring wax sealer, pressed laid-on ring

1485. L. G. Co. CF (on base).........................Aqua $18-20
     Groove ring wax sealer, pressed laid-on ring   Amber $100-125

1486. L. G. Co. 210 (on base)........................Clear $10-12
     Smooth lip   Mason shoulder seal

1487. LIBBY McNEILL & LIBBY INCORPORATED CHICAGO U.S.A.
     PAT. JULY 11th 1893 (on base)....................Clear $3-5
     Smooth lip   Metal Lid & 3-position wire clamp
     Lid: Pat. July 11 1893
     Product jar

     Also see EASY VACUUM jars, Nos. 878 thru 881

1488. L'IDEALE...Green $15-20
     Smooth lip   Hinged glass lid, with locking wire
     Heavy glass   French jar
                 #1488

1489. TRADEMARK LIGHTNING.............................Aqua $50-60
     Base: Putnam   Cornflower blue $60-70
     Ground lip   Old style Lightning seal
     Jar is about 5" tall, 2½" base dia.

1490. TRADEMARK LIGHTNING.............................Aqua $50-60
     Base: Putnam   Clear $50-60
     Ground lip   Old style Lightning seal   Corn flower blue $60-70
     Jar is 7 3/4" tall, 3¼" base dia.
                 #1489

1491. TRADEMARK LIGHTNING PUTNAM (on base)........ .... Aqua $30-35
    Ground lip Old style Lightning seal
    Jar is about 7 3/4" tall, 3¼" base dia.

1492. PUTNAM (on base)................................... .. Aqua $30-35
    Ground lip Old style Lightning seal
    Jar is about 5" tall, 2½" base dia. #1493

1493. REGISTERED U.S. PATENT OFFICE (on heel of jar).......... ½ Pint Aqua $6-8
    Found with both smooth & ground lip   ½ Pint Clear
    Base: Trade Mark Lightning Putnam

1494. H. W. P. (on base)....................................Aqua $1-3
    Ground lip Old style Lightning seal

1495. PUTNAM (on base).....................................Aqua $1-3
    Ground lip Old style Lightning seal   Amber $20-25

1496. TRADEMARK LIGHTNING PUTNAM (on base)......................Aqua $1-3
    Ground lip Old style Lightning seal   Amber $20-25

1497. TRADEMARK LIGHTNING H. W. P. (on base)..... ....Aqua $1-3
    Ground lip Old style Lightning seal

1498. TRADEMARK LIGHTNING......................... ....Aqua $2-3
    Base: H. W. P.   Amber $25-30
    Ground lip Old style Lightning seal

1499. TRADEMARK LIGHTNING...................... ....Aqua $2-3
    Base: Putnam   Clear $2-3
    Ground lip Old style Lightning seal   Apple green $15-18
                                                  Emerald green $150 & up
                                                  Olive green $150 & up
                                                  Amber $25-30
    #1500   Pint, Cobalt blue   Unpriced

1500. TRADEMARK LIGHTNING (front).................................Aqua $18-20
    Reverse: HWP monogram
    Base: Putnam
    Ground lip Old style Lightning seal

1501. TRADEMARK LIGHTNING REGISTERED U.S. PATENT OFFICE..............Aqua $2-4
    Base: Putnam   Clear $2-4
    Smooth lip Old style Lightning seal, wide   Cornflower blue $20-25
      mouth

1502. TRADEMARK LIGHTNING REGISTERED U.S. PATENT OFFICE............. Aqua $2-4
    Base: Putnam   Clear $2-4
    Ground lip Old style Lightning seal, regular mouth

    Lids for the foregoing Lightning jars are marked:
        Lightning Pat. April 25 82
      Or: Lightning Pat. Apr. 25 82 1875 77 82
      Or: Patd Jan 5 75 Reisd June 5 77 Patd Apr 25 82

1503. TRADEMARK LIGHTNING................. ....   Clear $2-4
    Base: M
    Smooth lip Old style Lightning seal
    Made in Australia

1504. TRADEMARK No. 1 LIGHTNING................... .Aqua $10-15
    Base & lid unmarked
    Ground lip Old style Lightning seal
    Made in Australia

#1504

1505. LIGHTNING FRUIT JAR...Clear $8-10
        Base & lid unmarked
        Smooth lip Old style Lightning seal
        Made in Australia

1506. TRADEMARK V R LIGHTNING (fancy letters)...................... Aqua $30-35
        Base & lid unmarked
        Ground lip Old style Lightning seal
        Made in Australia

1507. THE LIGHTNING N R FRUIT JAR .... Aqua $30-35
        Ground lip Old style Lightning seal
        Made in Australia

#1506

1508. THE LINCOLN JAR.. Aqua $300 & up
        Ground lip Closure unknown
        Only 2 jars are presently known, neither
          were found complete with closure

1509. LINDELL GLASS CO. (on base)................................. Aqua $20-25
        Groove ring wax sealer, pressed laid-on ring   Amber $75-100

1510. THE LIQUID CARBONIC COMPANY (on base)...................Clear $1-2
        Front heel: PATd July 14, 1908
        Smooth lip Lightning dimple neck seal
        ½ Gallon Product jar

1511. THE LIQUID CAPBONIC COMPANY (error) (on base).....................Clear $1-3
        Front heel: PATd JULY 14 1908
        Word BAIL on neck, with reversed B
        Smooth lip Lightning dimple neck seal
        Product jar in quart & ½ gallon sizes.

#1508

1512. LOCKPORT MASON.. Aqua $4-6
        Smooth lip Mason shoulder seal   Clear $4-6

1513. LOCKPORT MASON (superimposed over erased
      Lockport Mason which is reversed)................... Aqua $6-8
        Smooth lip Mason shoulder seal
        An interesting Mold maker's error

1514. LOCKPORT MASON IMPROVED........................... Aqua $4-6
        Smooth lip Glass insert & screw band #1514   Clear $4-6
                                              Light Yellow green $6-8

1515. LONGLIFE MASON (front) Fruit Medallion (reverse)..............Clear   -25¢
        Base: Obear Nester Glass
        Measurements on side
        Smooth lip Mason beaded neck seal
        Made circa 1976 in pints and quarts

1516. LONGLIFE WIDE MOUTH (front) Fruit Medallion (reverse)..Clear   -25¢
        Base: Obear Nester Glass
        Measurements on side
        Smooth lip Mason beaded neck seal
        Made circa 1976 in pints & quarts

1517. LONGLIFE MASON (front) Fruit Medallion (reverse)..Clear   -25¢
        Base: Laurens Quality Since 1910 L 75
        Smooth lip Mason beaded neck seal
        Metal lid insert: Bernardin Standard Mason
                         Snap Lid
        Made circa 1975 in pints & quarts

#1515

1518. F. R. LORENZ MANUFACTURERS PITTS. (on base)...............Light green $150-175
    Base has a pontil scar
    Applied top for waxed cork or metal stopple

1519. F. R. LORENZ MANUFACTURERS IMP. PITTS. (on base)..............Aqua   -$175
    Base has a bare iron pontil scar
    Applied top for waxed cork or metal stopple

1520. L & W (front)...Aqua $25-30
    Groove ring wax sealer, pressed laid-on ring

1521. L & W in ghost, superimposed over ghost PET (front)............Aqua $20-25
    Reverse: Ghost L &
    Groove ring wax sealer, pressed laid-on ring

1522. L & W in ghost, superimposed over ghost PET (front)............Aqua $20-25
    Reverse: Unmarked   Sky blue $40-50
    Groove ring wax sealer, pressed laid-on ring

1523. L & W..Aqua $70-75
    Glass lid & spring wire coiled clamp
    Lid: Patd August 31th 1869 TGO
     Or: Unlined metal cap, gasket & wire clamp
    Also see PET jar No. 2359

1524. L & W (front)   PET (reverse)..................................Aqua $70-75
    Closure as in #1523

1525. L & W (front)   Erased PET (reverse).....................Aqua $70-75
    Closure as in #1523

1526. Erased L & W (front)   PET (reverse)...................Aqua $70-75
    Closure as in #1523

1527. PET superimposed over erased L & W...................Aqua $75-100
    Glass lid & iron yoke clamp
    Lid: Patented Feb 13 1863
    Note: This is the same closure as found on
     the Peerless jar. We cannot be absolutely
     certain this is correct, tho two quarts and
     one pint have been reported with this closure.

#1523

1528. L & W (front)...Aqua $35-40
    Base: L & W
    Stopper neck finish for Kline stopper
    Note: This has been listed in Amber but we
     have not been able to verify this.

1529. L & W (front)...Aqua $125-150
    Reverse: MANUFACTURED FOR RICE & BURNETT
              CLEVELAND, O.
    Base: L & W
    Stopper neck finish for Kline stopper

1530. L & W ' & above erased XL (on front)...................Aqua $25-30
    Groove ring wax sealer, pressed laid-on ring

1531. L & W's X L (on front)..................................Aqua $25-30
    Groove ring wax sealer, pressed laid-on ring

#1530

1532. L & W's X L (all in ghost except W) (front)...................Aqua $25-30
    Groove ring wax sealer, pressed laid-on ring   Med. Citron $65-75

1533. L & W X L (no s) (all in ghost except W) (front)...............Aqua $25-30
    Groove ring wax sealer, pressed laid-on ring

1534. L & W's X L (front)...Aqua $35-45
        Base: Unmarked or 6 pointed star
        Stopper neck finish for Kline stopper & wire clamp
        Stopper: A. Kline Improved Pat. Oct. 27 1863
                Stopper has ramps

1535. W (on slant to right)..Aqua $20-25
        Groove ring wax sealer, pressed laid-on ring   Med. Cobalt blue $300 & up

1536. W (on slant to left)...Aqua $20-25
        Groove ring wax sealer, pressed laid-on ring

1537. W (on slant to left) with ghost L &..........................Aqua $35-45
        Stopper neck finish for Kline stopper
          as in #1534

1538. W (on slant to right) with ghost L &.........................Aqua $20-25
        Groove ring wax sealer, pressed laid-on ring   Med. Cobalt blue $300 & up

1539. W & Co 1 (on base)...Aqua $15-20
        Groove ring wax sealer, pressed laid-on ring   Lt. Cobalt blue $150 & up

1540. W & Co 2 (on base)...Aqua $15-20
        Groove ring wax sealer, pressed laid-on ring   Lt. Cobalt blue $150 & up

1541. W & Co. PITTSBURGH (on base).................................Aqua $15-20
        Groove ring wax sealer, pressed laid-on ring

1542. P. LORILLARD CO. (on base)..................................Amber $10-12
        Ground lip Cohansey lid & wire clamp
        Lid: Cohansey Glass Manuf. Co. Philada. Pa.
              Pat. July 16 1872 Jan 18 1876
        Snuff jar. An original paper label stated
         that the jar could be reused for preserving
         fruit, pickles, etc.

1543. P. LORILLARD CO. (on base)..................................Amber $12-15
        Ground lip Glass lid & wire clamp
        Lid: Geo. W. Helme Co. Of New Jersey
              Patented July 16, 1872
        Snuff jar

1544. F. S. LOVE MFG. CO. FRUIT TABLETS JOHNSTOWN, PA. USA.......... Aqua $6-8
        Glass stopper: F. S. Love Mfg. Co. Johnstown, Pa. USA
         Center of stopper has TradeMark over a heart, pierced
         with an arrow and embossed Love
        Product jar 3-quart size

1545. W. B. LOWRY ROSEVILLE, O.................................. .... $40-45
        Gray stoneware jar with marking incised
        Wax seal groove

1546. LUDLOW'S PATENT JUNE 28 1859 (on lid)............... ..Aqua $100-125
        Ground lip Glass lid & cage-like iron clamp
        Neck of jar has two blown lugs to engage clamp
        Jar is unmarked
        Found in 3-pint size as well as quart &
        ½ gallon

1547. LUDLOW'S PATENT JUNE 28 1859 & AUGUST 6 1861 (lid). .Aqua $100-125
        Ground lip Glass lid & cage-like iron clamp
        Neck of jar has two blown lugs to engage clamp
        Jar is unmarked

#1546

1548. LUDLOW'S PATENT AUG 6 1861 (on lid)................................. Aqua $100-125
    Ground lip Glass lid & clamp as in #1546 & #1547
    Jar is unmarked

1549. LUDLOWS PATENT JUNE 28 59 TEST CAN (on lid)..........Green $450 & up
    Jar is unmarked
    Ground lip Metal band around neck with
    2 soldered metal clamps to hold on lid
    Metal lid with "propeller"

1550. LUDLOWS PATENT JUNE 28 59 TEST CAN (on lid)..... Aqua $350-400+
    Jar is unmarked Shape is different than #1549
    Closure as in #1549

1551. LUDLOW'S INFALLIBLE CAN PATENT FEB.16.1858........ $200-250
    On lid of tin can. Can has two soldered
    prongs on top to engage the metal lid
    Metal lid with "propeller"

1552. LUDLOW'S INFALLIBLE SEALER PATd FEB. 16.58.............. $200-250
    On lid of tin can Closure as in #1551

#1549

#1550

1553. R. E. TONGUE & BROS. CO. INC. LUSTRE
PHILADELPHIA. PA. (within fancy square, front)................. Aqua $8-10
    Base: R. E. Tongue & Bros. Co. Inc.   Yellow green $18-20
        Phila. Pa. Lustre
    Smooth lip Old style Lightning seal, wide mouth

1554. LUSTRE R. E. TONGUE & BROS. CO. INC. PHILA. (within circle).....Aqua $6-8
    Smooth lip Old style Lightning seal   Clear $6-8
    Lid: Tongues Lustre Jar

1555. LUSTRE R. E. TONGUE & BROS. CO. INC. PHILA. (within circle).....Aqua $6-8
    Ground lip Old style Lightning seal
    Lid: Tongues Lustre Jar

1556. LUSTRE R. E. TONGUE & BROS. CO. INC. PHILA.....................Clear $6-8
    Smooth lip Old style Lightning seal
    Lid: Tongues Lustre Jar

1557. LUSTRE R. E. TONGUE & BROS. CO. INC. PHILA (within circle).....Clear $6-8
    Smooth lip Lightning beaded neck seal   Ball blue $6-8

1558. LUSTRE R. E. TONGUE & BROS. PHILADA (within circle)............ Aqua $6-8
    Smooth lip Lightning beaded neck seal   Ball blue $6-8

1559. LUSTRE R. E. TONGUE & BROS. CO. INC. PHILA (within circle)
PAT'd JULY 14, 1908 (all on front of jar)..................Ball blue $6-8
    Smooth lip Lightning dimple neck seal

1560. LUSTRE R. E. TONGUE & BROS. CO. INC. PHILA (within circle).Ball blue $6-8
    Reverse: PAT'd JULY 14, 1908
    Smooth lip Lightning dimple neck seal

1561. JAMES LUTTED BUFFALO N.Y. U.S.A. (on base)........................Aqua $30-35
    Front: J. L. Reverse: large embossed star
    Ground lip Metal screw cover
    Candy jar

1562. L & S (on base)...Clear $1-3
    Lower front: PAT'd JULY 14 1908   Ball blue $1-3
    Smooth lip Lightning dimple neck seal Product jar

1563. L & S (on base)...Clear $1-2
    Smooth lip Lightning dimple neck seal Product jar

1564. LUTZ & SCHRAMM CO (on base)........................Clear $2-4
     Smooth lip Closure unknown
     Paneled jar

1565. PAT'D APPLIED FOR BY LUTZ & SCHRAMM (incised).........$12-15
     Reverse: SHERWOOD BROS. POTTERY NEW
              BRIGHTON, Pa.
     Paneled, beige stoneware jar, glass lid &
     wire & metal clamp
     Clear lid: Sherwood Patent Applied For

1566. PATENTED JULY 19 1909 BY JOS H SCHRAMM (incised)........$12-15
     Paneled, beige stoneware jar, glass lid &
     wire & metal clamp
     Amber lid: Pat. Apld For

#1566

1567. PATd AUG 5th 1862 W. W. LYMAN.........   ......Complete, Aqua $40-50
     Ground lip Metal press-down lid   Incomplete, Aqua $20-25
     with crimped edges
     Lid: N. Whittelsey May 19 1863

1568. PATd AUG 5th 1862 W. W. LYMAN.........   ....Aqua Unpriced
     Ground lip Metal press-down lid
     as in #1567
     Gallon size

1569. PATd AUG 5th 1862 W. W. LYMAN 3......   .....Complete, Aqua $40-50
     Ground lip Metal press-down lid   Incomplete, Aqua $20-25
     as in #1567

1570. PATd AUG 5th 1862 W. W. LYMAN 7......   .....Complete, Aqua $40-50
     Ground lip Metal press-down lid   Incomplete, Aqua $20-25
     as in #1567

#1570

1571. PATd FEB 9th 1864 W. W. LYMAN * ....Complete, Aqua $50-60
     Ground lip Metal press-down lid   Incomplete, Aqua $30-35
     as in #1567

1572. PATd FEB 9th 1864 W. W. LYMAN 5......   ......Complete, Aqua $50-60
     Ground lip Metal press-down lid   Incomplete, Aqua $20-25
     as in #1567

1573. PATd FEB 9th 1864 W. W. LYMAN 11....   ......Complete, Aqua $50-60
     Ground lip Metal press-down lid   Incomplete, Aqua $20-25
     as in #1567

1574. PATd FEB 9th 1864 W. W. LYMAN 12....   ......Complete, Aqua $50-60
     Ground lip Metal press-down lid   Incomplete, Aqua $20-25
     as in #1567

#1571

1575. PATd FEB 9th 1864 W. W. LYMAN 19....................Complete, Aqua $50-60
     Ground lip Metal press-down lid   Incomplete, Aqua $20-25
     as in #1567

1576. PATd FEB 9th 1864 W. W. LYMAN 30....................Complete, Aqua $50-60
     Ground lip Metal press-down lid   Incomplete, Aqua $20-25
     as in #1567

1577. PATd FEB 9th 1864 W. W. LYMAM 30 (error).............Complete, Aqua $55-65
     Ground lip Metal press-down lid   Incomplete, Aqua $25-30
     as in #1567

1578. PATd FEB 9th 1864 W. W. LYMAN 33....................Complete, Aqua $50-60
     Ground lip Metal press-down lid   Incomplete, Aqua $20-25
     as in #1567

1579. PATd AUG 5th 1862 & FEB 9th 1864 W. W. LYMAN.........:....Complete, Aqua $50-60
      Ground lip Metal press-down lid as   Incomplete, Aqua $20-25
      in #1567

1580. PATd AUG 5th 1862 & FEB 9th 1864 W. W. LYMAN.........Complete, Aqua   Unpriced
      Ground lip Metal press-down lid as
      in #1567 Gallon size jar

1581. PATd AUG 5th 1862 & FEB 9th 1864 W. W. LYMAN 11.......Complete, Aqua $50-60
      Ground lip Metal press-down lid as   Incomplete, Aqua $20-25
      in #1567

1582. PATd AUG 5th 1862 & FEB 9th 1864 W. W. LYMAN 21.......Complete, Aqua $50-60
      Ground lip Metal press-down lid as   Incomplete, Aqua $20-25
      in #1567

1583. PATd AUG 5th 1862 & FEB 9th 1864 W. W. LYMAN 23.......Complete, Aqua $50-60
      Ground lip Metal press-down lid as   Incomplete, Aqua $20-25
      in #1567

1584. PATd AUG 5th 1862 & FEB 9th 1864 W. W. LYMAN.........Complete, Aqua $55-65
      The lower date line is upside down & reversed   Incomplete, Aqua $20-25
      Ground lip Metal press-down lid as
      in #1567

1585. PATd AUG 5th 1862 REISd FEB 9th 1864 W. W. LYMAN......Complete, Aqua $50-60
      Ground lip Metal press-down lid as   Incomplete, Aqua $20-25
      in #1567

1586. PATd AUG 5th 1862 REISd FEB 9th 1864 W. W. LYMAN 17...Complete, Aqua $50-60
      Ground lip Metal press-down lid as   Incomplete, Aqua $20-25
      in #1567

1587. PATd AUG 5th 1862 & REISd FEB 9th 1864 W. W. LYMAN....Complete, Aqua $55-65
      The lower date line is upside down & reversed   Incomplete, Aqua $25-30
      Ground lip Metal press-down lid as
      in #1567

1588. PATd FEB 9th 1864 REISd JAN 22nd 1867 W. W. LYMAN.....Complete, Aqua $50-60
      Ground lip Metal press-down lid as   Incomplete, Aqua $20-25
      in #1567

1589. PATd FEB 9th 1864 REISd JAN 22nd 1867 W. W. LYMAN 18..Complete, Aqua $50-60
      Ground lip Metal press-down lid as   Incomplete, Aqua $20-25
      in #1567

1590. PATd FEB 9th 1864 REISd JAN 22nd 867 W. W. LYMAN 19...Complete, Aqua $55-65
      Ground lip Metal press-down lid as   Incomplete, Aqua $25-30
      in #1567

1591. PATd FEB 9th 1864 REISd JAN 22d 1867 W. W. LYMAN 35...Complete, Aqua $50-60
      Ground lip Metal press-down lid as   Incomplete, Aqua $20-25
      in #1567

1592. PATd FEB 9th 1864 REISd JAN 22nd 1867 W. W. LYMAN 48..Complete, Aqua $50-60
      Ground lip Metal press-down lid as   Incomplete, Aqua $20-25
      in #1567

1593. PATd FEB 9th 1864 REISd JAN 22nd 1867 W. W. LYMAN 50..Complete, Aqua $50-60
      Ground lip Metal press-down lid as   Incomplete, Aqua $20-25
      in #1567

1594. LYNCHBURG STANDARD MASON (with various mold numbers)............Aqua $15-18
      Smooth lip Mason beaded neck seal

1595. LYON & BOSSARD'S JAR STROUDSBURG PA.......... .... Aqua $200-250
        Ground lip Glass lid & iron yoke clamp
                    with tightening cam
        Lid: Pat. April 15th 1884
             (often found with reversed 4)
        Clamp: Pat. Apr. 15.84

        Also see ABC jar No. 4

1596. LYON JAR PAT APR. 10 1900 (on lid).......... ....Clear $1-3
        Lids are found in clear & in milkglass
        Product jar

1597. PAT APRIL 10 1900 (on lid)................... ....Clear $1-3
        Lids are found in clear & in milkglass
        Product jar

1598. LYON JAR PATENT ALLOWED (on lid).......... ....Clear $1-3
        Lids are found in clear
        Product jar   #1595
        The Lyon lids all have a groove for a wire
        clamp and fit on various unmarked product jars.

Collectors Notes

1599. MACOMB STONEWARE CO MACOMB ILL (on base)............................ $20-25
     White stoneware jar
     Wax seal groove

1600. MACOMB POTTERY CO PAT APL FOR (on base)........ $10-12
     Bottom is deeply recessed
     White stoneware jar, zinc screw lid

1601. MACOMB POTTERY CO PAT JAN 24 1899 (on base).... $10-12
     White stoneware jar, with brown shoulders
     Zinc screw lid

1602. MACOMB POTTERY CO PAT JAN 24 1899 (on base)...................... $10-12
     All white stoneware jar, zinc screw lid

#1600

1603. MACOMB POTTERY CO. PAT. JAN 24 1899 MACOMB ILL. (on base)............ $10-12
     All white stoneware jar, zinc screw lid

1604. TABLE SYRUP PACKED BY FRANKLIN MACVEACH & CO. CHICAGO...........Aqua $20-25
     Smooth lip   Mason shoulder seal   Product jar

1605. MADE BY THE MEYER FRUIT JAR CO DETROIT, MICH.........   .....Aqua $150-200
     Ground lip   Glass lid & metal clamping ring

1606. THE MAGIC (star) FRUIT JAR.....................   .....Aqua $90-100
     Ground lip   Glass lid   Metal & wire clamp   Amber $450-500
     Lid, insdie: Clamp Pat. March 30th 1886

1607. MAGIC FRUIT JAR Wm McCULLY & CO PITTSBURGH
     Pa SOLE PROPRIETORS (all on front).............   .....Aqua $350-400
       Reverse: PATENTED BY R.M. DALBEY
             JUNE 6th 1866 No 3
     Ground lip   Metal lid & yoke clamp
     Lugs on jar neck with lower sides serrated
       so that the yoke remains securely in place
       when jar is sealed.
     Base of jar has 3 evenly spaced lugs around
       outside diameter which elevates the jar
       about 1/8 inch.

#1608

1608. MAGIC FRUIT JAR Wm McCULLY & CO PITTSBURGH
     Pa SOLE PROPRIETORS No 4 (all on front)..........   ......Aqua $350-400
       Reverse: PATENTED BY R. M. DALBEY
             JUNE 6th 1866
     Ground lip   Closure and base as in #1607

1609. MAGIC FRUIT JAR Wm McCULLY & CO. PITTSBURGH
     Pa SOLE PROPRIETORS 7 (all on front)............   ....Aqua $450-400
       Reverse: PATENTED BY R. M. DALBEY
             JUNE 6th 1866
     Ground lip   Closure and base as in #1607

1610. MAGIC TM MASON JAR (front)   MASON JAR (reverse).   ...Clear -25¢
     Cup & oz. measurements on one side
     Mililiter measurements on other side
     Smooth lip   Mason beaded neck seal   2 Pc. lid
     Metal insert: Magic Button Pops Up When Seal
               Is Broken

#1608

     Circa 1975-76 Quart

1611. MAGIC TM MASON (front) MASON JAR (reverse)..........Clear -25¢
        Description & closure as in #1610
        Circa 1975-76 Pint

1612. MAGNOLIA...Aqua $200-250
        Base: Patd June 19 1883
        Ground lip Glass lid & wire clamp

1613. PAT. JUNE 19 1883 (on base).................Aqua $60-75
        Jar is unmarked
        Ground lip Glass lid & wire clamp

1614. MAINE CONDENSED MILK CO....................Aqua $4-6
        Ground lip Milkglass insert & screw band
        Insert: Baby
        Pint product jar, hexagonal shape

#1612

1615. MALKIN'S BEST (within double circle).......................Clear $3-5
        Ribbed jar with place for paper label on reverse
        Smooth lip Metal screw lid Product jar

1616. MALLINGER..Clear $3-5
        Smooth lip Mason beaded neck seal

1617. PATENTED AUG. 3rd 1858 (on lid)................. $200-250
        Tin can
        The glass lid found on the only known example
        of this can, may not be correct. The patent
        issued to E. Manley calls for a cup-shaped
        stopper made of tin plate.

1618. MANSFIELD GLASS WORKS SOLE MFR'S (around a jar
      embossed) KNOWLTON PATENT MAY 1903 TRADEMARK...... Clear $175-200
        Smooth lip Glass lid & metal screw cap
        Cap: Mansfield Vacuum TradeMark Full Glass Top
            (Cap is not perforated)
        Only 1 jar is presently known

1619. MANSFIELD.. Aqua $40-50
        Base: Mansfield Knowlton May '03 Pat
              Glass W'K'S
        Smooth lip Glass lid & metal screw cap
        Cap: Mansfield Vacuum TradeMark Full Glass Top
            (Cap is not perforated)
        Glass lid: Mansfield Glass Wks. Knowlton
                   Pat May '03 Or Unmarked
        Also see KNOWLTON VACUUM jar No. 1432

#1618

1620. MANSFIELD MASON.....................................Clear $12-15
        Smooth lip Mason shoulder seal Zinc lid

1621. MANSFIELD IMPROVED MASON....................Clear $12-15
        Smooth lip Glass insert & screw band   Pale green $12-15

1622. MANSFIELD WIRE FASTENER..................... Unpriced
        Smooth lip Glass lid & wire bail
        Note: Although this jar was pictured in
         company brochures, an example of the jar
         has not yet been reported.

#1621

1623. J. MARDEN & CO (vertically on jar)..................Clear $1-3
        Smooth lip Metal press-down cover
        Jar has ribbed sides
        Product jar

1624. THE MARION JAR MASON'S PATENT NOV 30th 1858...................... Aqua $10-12
     Ground lip Mason shoulder seal   Light green $10-12
     Zinc lid, outside: Genuine Boyd Cap For
       Mason Jars (around M within diamond)
     Zinc lid, inside: Boyd's Genuine Porcelain
       Lined (around M within diamond)

1625. THE MARION JAR MASON'S PATENT NOV 30th 1858...   ..... Aqua $10-12
     The Marion Jar in fancy lettering
     Ground lip Mason shoulder seal
     Zinc lid as in #1624

1626. MARQUE PALM BRAND FL. 30 OZ...................   .....Clear $1-3
     Base: Habitant Food Products Ltd.
     Smooth lip Screw cap
     Canadian product jar   #1625

1627. MARSTON'S RESTAURANT BOSTON (within circle)...................Clear $8-10
     Base: Smalley Fruit Jar Co. Boston, Mass.
     Ground lip Old style Lightning seal
     Product jar Quart & ½ gallon sizes

1628. MASCOT DISK IMMERSER......................................Clear $175-200
     Ground lip Milkglass disk immerser & screw band
     Immerser, top: TradeMark Disk Immerser "Mascot"
              Pat'd Nov. 30.80 July 20. 86.
     Scalloped bottom of immerser: Patd Nov. 23. 75
              Sept. 12.76 Nov. 30.80 July 20
              1886

1629. THE "MASCOTTE" TRADE MARK PAT'D IMPROVED...........   ..Clear $150-175
     Smooth lip Milkglass disk immerser & screw band
     Immerser: "Mascotte" Trademark Disk Immerser
          Pat'd Nov. 30.80 July 20. 86

1630. "MASCOT" TRADE MARK PAT'D IMPROVED...............   Clear $100-125
     Found with both smooth & ground lips   Amber $350 up
     Closure: Milkglass insert marked: The "Mascot"
     Improved TradeMark Pat'd
     Tudor rose emblem in center of lid
     Zinc screw band..some bands have wire   #1628
     carrying bail.

1631. THE "MASCOT" TRADE MARK PAT'D IMPROVED..........   .Clear $100-125
     Closure as in #1630

1632. MASON (underlined with squared shepherd's crook)............... Aqua $4-6
     Base: Greenfield Fruit Jar Co.   Light Olive green $12-15
         Greenfield, Ind.
     Smooth lip Mason shoulder seal

1633. MASON (underlined with squared shepherd's crook)............... Aqua $4-6
     Base: Mold numbers only   Light Olive green $12-15
     Smooth lip Mason shoulder seal
     Also see jar Nos. 493, 494, & 495
1634. MASON (on slant, not underlined)................................ Aqua $4-6
     Smooth lip Mason shoulder seal

1635. MASON (underline with loop).................................Clear $6-8
     Smooth lip Mason beaded neck seal
     Jar has an octagon shaped neck. Ledge inside
     of mouth for use of a cardboard disc & sealing wax.
     Zinc lid: Sanitary Vacuum Jar Pat. Applied For Mason Improved
     Or Glass lid: Sanitary Mason Jar Glass Cap Pat. Appl'd For

1636. MASON (underline with loop)...Clear $4-6
      Smooth lip Mason shoulder seal   Light Vaseline $6-8

1637. MASON (underlined with rounded shepherd's crook)............. Aqua $4-6
      Smooth lip Mason shoulder seal

1638. MASON (underlined with rounded shepherd's crook
             & marking in upper diagonal corner)........... Aqua $8-10
      Smooth lip Mason shoulder seal

1639. MASON (in script, underlined)................................Clear $4-6
      Smooth lip Mason shoulder seal

1640. MASON (in straight line).. Aqua $2-3
      Smooth lip Mason shoulder seal   Clear $2-3
                                                                 Amber $50-75

#1638

1641. MASON (in straight line)....................................Clear $2-3
      Smooth lip Mason beaded neck seal   Pint Amber $50-75

1642. MASON (in straight line)... Aqua $3-5
      Ground lip Mason shoulder seal

1643. MASON (arched)... Aqua $3-5
      Ground lip Mason shoulder seal   Amber $75-85
                                                                  Citron $30-40
                                                      Midget pint Clear $25-30

1644. MASON (arched).. Aqua $3-5
      Smooth lip Mason shoulder seal

1645. MASON...Clear $4-6
      Base: Gilberd's
      Ground lip Mason shoulder seal

#1645

1646. MASON (in straight line)......................................Clear $2-4
      Smooth lip Mason shoulder seal Canadian sealer

1647. MASON (in straight line)..................................Light blue $2-4
      Smooth lip Mason shoulder seal Canadian sealer

1648. MASON (in straight line, near shoulder).......................Clear   -$1
      Smooth lip Mason beaded neck seal

1649. MASON GC..Clear   -25¢
      Smooth lip Mason beaded neck seal
      Circa 1975-76

1650. MASON (on shoulder) CANADA 16 FL OZ SIZE (on heel).............Clear   -$1
      Smooth lip Mason shoulder seal Canadian sealer

1651. The MASON (word The within initial stroke of M)........... Aqua $4-6
      Smooth lip Mason shoulder seal   Light green $4-6
      Also see jar No. 320

1652. MASON (on slant with "flower" design)................. Aqua $40-50
      Smooth lip Mason shoulder seal
      Only 3 or 4 jars are presently known.

1653. MASON (script, underlined, on front)..............Clear   Unpriced
      Reverse: 1776 (Liberty bell) 1976
      Base: Anchor Hocking Co. trademark
      Smooth lip Mason beaded neck seal
      Modern 2 Pc. closure with insert having
       a printed design of a gleaner.
      From a small sample run, made in 1973-74 by Anchor
       Hocking for their bicentennial jars. The jars can
       be identified by the fact that the bell is crooked
       on the jar, and the base does not carry the year
       date. These jars were not offered for sale. Pints & Quarts

#1652

1654. MASON (script, underlined, on front)...........................Clear   -$1
     Reverse: 1776 (Liberty bell) 1976
     Base: 74 (& Anchor Hocking trademark)
      Or: 75 (& Anchor Hocking trademark)
     Smooth lip Mason beaded neck seal
     Closure as in #1653 Pints & Quarts

1655. MASON QG...Clear $25-30
     Smooth lip Mason shoulder seal

1656. MASON QG with ghost S.................................Clear $25-30
     Smooth lip Mason shoulder seal

1657. QG (without word Mason).............................Clear $25-30
     Smooth lip Mason shoulder seal

1658. MASON SGW..Clear $25-30
     Smooth lip Mason shoulder seal

1659. MASON W G Co.. Aqua $25-30
     Smooth lip Mason shoulder seal

#1655

1660. MASON'S (front shoulder) Reverse shoulder: O.K. PICKLE...Light green $6-8
     Applied lip Glass stopper
     Canadian product jar

1661. MASON'S (in straight line)...........................Aqua $3-5
     Smooth lip Mason shoulder seal   Amber $50-75
     Also see jars Also see jar Nos. 33 & 34

1662. THE MASON AIRTITE......................................Clear $18-20
     Smooth lip Mason beaded neck seal
     Clear heavy glass with hint of yellow
     Made in Australia

1663. "MASON" (immerser) DISK IMMERSER..................Clear $350-400
     Ground lip Milkglass disk immerser & screw band
     Immerser, top: Patd Nov. 23.75 Sep. 12.76
                  Nov. 30.80 July 20.86
     Scalloped base unmarked

1664. MASON FRUIT JAR (on inside liner of zinc cap)......Aqua $8-10
     Jar is unmarked
     Ground lip Mason shoulder seal
     Gallon size

#1663

1665. MASON FRUIT JAR (two lines).........................Aqua $4-6
     Ground lip Mason shoulder seal

1666. MASON'S FRUIT JAR (two lines).......................Aqua $4-6
     Ground lip Mason shoulder seal   Amber $75-85

1667. MASON FRUIT JAR (three lines)..................Clear $4-6
     Smooth lip Mason shoulder seal

1668. MASON'S FRUIT JAR (three lines).........Clear $4-6
     Smooth lip Mason shoulder seal

1669. MASON FRUIT JAR (three lines)............Clear $2-3
     Smooth lip Mason beaded neck seal

#1666

1670. MASON FRUIT JAR (three lines)..................Clear $4-6
     The A in Mason has no crossbar
     Smooth lip Mason beaded neck seal

1671. MASON FRUIT JAR 4 (superimposed over erased
WHITNEY MASON PAT'D 1858)..................................Aqua $6-8
    Smooth lip Mason shoulder seal

1672. MASON FRUIT JAR (2 lines)..................Aqua, Clear $2-3
    Smooth lip Mason beaded neck seal   Amber $50-75

1673. MASON FRUIT JAR (2 lines)..................Aqua, Clear $2-3
    Smooth lip Mason beaded neck seal
    Canadian sealer

1674. MASON FRUIT JAR (2 straight lines)..................Aqua $2-3
    Smooth lip Mason shoulder seal
    Canadian sealer

#1671

1675. MASON FRUIT JAR (2 straight lines)............................Aqua $2-3
    Ground lip Mason shoulder seal
    Canadian sealer

1676. MASON FRUIT JAR (2 lines, front) Reverse: Erased GEM (script)..Aqua $6-8
    Smooth lip Mason beaded neck seal
    Canadian sealer

1677. MASON FRUIT JAR IV......................................Aqua $2-3
    Smooth lip Mason beaded neck seal
    Canadian sealer

1678. MASON FRUIT JAR VII..........................Aqua $2-3
    Smooth lip Mason beaded neck seal   Med. Amber $40-50
    Canadian sealer

1679. MASON FRUIT JAR VII (reversed N in Mason)..........Aqua $4-6
    Smooth lip Mason beaded neck seal
    Canadian sealer

#1679

1680. MASON FRUIT JAR MADE IN CANADA....................Clear $1-3
    Smooth lip Mason beaded neck seal

1681. MASON FRUIT JAR MADE IN CANANA (error)....................Clear $4-6
    Smooth lip Mason beaded neck seal

1682. (Keystone within circle) MASON..........................Aqua $8-10
    Ground lip Mason shoulder seal   Amber $125-150
    Zinc lid, outside: Mason Fruit Jar Co.
    Philada. Pa. (Keystone in center)
    Zinc lid, inside: Mason Fruit Jar Co.
    Boyd's Porcelain Lininig (error)

1683. (Keystone) MASON FRUIT JAR.....................Aqua $8-10
    Ground lip Mason shoulder seal
    Zinc lid as in #1682

1684. (Keystone) MASON FRUIT JAR PATENT NOV 30th 1858..Aqua $10-12
    Ground lip Mason shoulder seal
    Zinc lid as in #1682

1685. MASON'S IMPROVED (wide mouth)...................Aqua $25-30
    Ground lip Glass insert & screw band
    Insert: Mason's Improved
      Or: Mason's Improved May 10 1870

1686. 4 LB. MASON'S IMPROVED BUTTER JAR...............Aqua $50-60
    Ground lip Glass insert & screw band   Clear $50-60
    Insert: Mason's Improved May 10 1870

#1686

1687. MASON'S CFJCO IMPROVED (wide mouth butter jar).................. Aqua $25-30
       Ground lip   Glass insert & screw band   Clear $25-30
       Insert: Mason's Improved May 10 1870

1688. MASON'S CFJCo IMPROVED BUTTER JAR......................... Aqua $45-50
       Ground lip   Closure as in #1687   Clear $45-50

1689. MASON IMPROVED..................................... Aqua $1-3
       Smooth lip   Glass insert & screw band

1690. MASON IMPROVED.................................. Aqua $2-4
       Ground lip   Glass insert & screw band
       Insert: Mason's Improved Patented May 10 1870
         Or: Mason's Improved Pat May 10 70
       Inserts are sometimes found with upside down or
       reversed letters.

1691. MASON IMPROVED (2 dots below word Mason).............. Aqua $2-4
       Ground lip   Glass insert & screw band   **#1692**

1692. MASON IMPROVED (front)............................. Aqua $10-12
       Reverse: Erased KNOWLTON VACUUM (star) FRUIT JAR
       Smooth lip   Glass insert & screw band   Pint

1693. "MASON" IMPROVED................................ Aqua $20-25
       Ground lip   With Disk Immerser, Aqua $40-50
       Closure: Glass insert & screw band
          Or: Milkglass disk immerser & screw band
       Immerser: Patd Nov. 23 75 Sep. 12.76 Nov.30.80
            July 20.86

1694. THE "MASON'S" IMPROVED..............................Clear $20-25
       Ground lip   With Disk Immerser, Clear $40-50
       Closure as in #1693   Amber $70-75
                        With Disk Immerser, Amber $90-100

1695. THE "MASON'S" IMPROVED with erased
       THE "MASCOT" TRADE MARK PAT'D IMPROVED........................Clear $20-25
       Ground lip   With Disk Immerser, Clear $40-50
       Closure as in #1693   Amber $70-75
                        With Disk Immerser, Amber $90-100

1696. THE MASON'S IMPROVED.............................. Aqua $10-12
       Ground lip   Glass insert & screw band

1697. MASON'S IMPROVED..Clear $2-3
       Smooth lip   Glass insert & screw band
       The shoulders are somewhat more squarish
         than on usual Mason's Improved jars.

1698. MASON IMPROVED (without S)................... Aqua $2-3
       Smooth lip   Glass insert & screw band   Clear $2-3
       The shoulders are somewhat squarish as   Light green $2-3
         in #1697

1699. MASON'S IMPROVED............................... Aqua $2-4
       Base: Nov 26 1867
       Ground lip   Glass insert & screw band   **#1698**

1700. MASON'S IMPROVED............................... Aqua $2-4
       Base: Patented May 10, 1870   Clear $2-4
         Or: Patd May 10 1870   Midget Pint, Aqua $10-12
       Ground lip   Glass insert & screw band
       Insert as in #1690

1701. MASON'S IMPROVED................................ Aqua $2-4
       Base: Mold number only   Light Cornflower blue $8-10
       Ground lip   Glass insert & screw band

```
1702. MASON'S IMPROVED.................................................Aqua        $2-4
         Base: Patd Jan 19 1869                        Midget Pint, Aqua        $10-12
         Ground lip  Glass insert & screw band                   Amber        $75-85

1703. MASON'S IMPROVED.................................................Aqua      $250-300
         Base: H. Brooke Mould Maker N. Y.
         Ground lip  Glass insert & screw band
         Insert: Mason's Improved Patented May 10 1870
         Gallon or Gallon plus 1 quart

1704. MASON'S IMPROVED.........................            ...Aqua      $250-300
         Base: H. Brooke Mould Maker N.Y. Pat. Jan. 91 18
                  (meaning Jan. 19, 1869)
         Ground lip  Closure as in #1703

1705. MASON'S IMPROVED (front).......................         ..Aqua      $400-500
         Reverse: MANUFACTURED BY A. R. SAMUEL KEYSTONE
                  GLASS WORKS PHILADA PA.
         Base: Patented May 10th 1870
         Ground lip  Closure as in #1703
         Four Gallon                                                #1706

1706. MASON'S CBCo IMPROVED.............................Light Green       $10-12
         Ground lip  Glass insert & screw band
         Australian jar

1707. MASON'S IMPROVED (front)  Reverse: Shield emblem................Aqua        $6-8
         Base: Patd May 10 1870                        Midget Pint, Aqua       $20-25
         Ground lip  Glass insert & screw band

1708. MASON'S -C- IMPROVED.............................................Aqua       $10-12
         Ground lip  Glass insert & screw band

1709. MASON'S IMPROVED (front)  Reverse: CFJCo.......................Aqua        $3-5
         Ground lip  Glass insert & screw band      Midget Pint, Aqua       $12-15
         Insert: TradeMark Mason's Improved                    Amber      $125-150
                  Registered May 23d 1871           Light Olive Green      $12-15
                  CFJCo in center

1710. MASON'S IMPROVED (front)  Reverse: CFJCo.......................Aqua      $250-300
         Base: H. Brooke Mould Maker N.Y.
         Ground lip  Glass insert & screw band
         Gallon plus 1 quart

1711. MASON'S CFJCo IMPROVED.........................................Aqua        $2-4
         Ground lip  Closure as in #1709            Midget Pint, Aqua       $12-15
                                                              Clear        $2-4
                                                              Amber      $125-150

1712. MASON'S CFJCo IMPROVED (front)  Reverse: CLYDE, N.Y.............Aqua        $3-5
         Ground lip  Glass insert & screw band      Midget Pint, Aqua       $15-18
         Note: Only 1 Cobalt blue jar is                     Clear        $3-5
          known to exist.                                     Amber      $125-150
                                                       Colbalt blue  $3100 & up

1713. MASON'S CFJCo IMPROVED (front)  Reverse: CLYDE, N.Y.
         The E in Clyde has been corrected from D to E .. Midget Pint, Aqua       $20-25
         Ground lip  Glass insert & screw band

1714. MASON'S CFJCo IMPROVED.........................................Aqua      $400-500
         Ground lip  Glass insert & screw band
         Insert: Mason's Improved Patented May 10 1870
         5 Gallon
```

1715. MASON'S IMPROVED CFJCo. (front).. Aqua $400-500
      Reverse: MANUFACTURED AT THE WHITNEY GLASS
              WORKS   GLASSBORO N. J.
      Base: Patented May 10th 1870
      Ground lip Glass insert & screw band
      Insert: Mason's Improved Patented May 10 1870
      4 Gallon

1716. MASON'S IMPROVED CFJCo. (front)...................... . Aqua $400-500
      Reverse: MANUFACTURED AT THE WHITNEY GLASS
              WORKS   GLASSBORO N. J.
      Base & closure as in #1715
      3 Gallon   #1717

1717. TRADE MARK MASON'S IMPROVED (front)   Reverse: CFJCo............. Aqua $10-12
      Ground lip Glass insert & screw band
      Insert: Trademark Mason's Improved Registered
              May 23d 1871 CFJCo in center

1718. MASON'S IMPROVED TRADEMARK (front)   Reverse: CFJCo............. Aqua $4-6
      Ground lip Closure as in #1717   Midget Pint, Aqua $15-18

1719. MASON'S IMPROVED TRADEMARK (front)   Reverse: CFJCo............. Aqua $4-6
      Base: Pat. Jan. 19 1869   Midget Pint, Aqua $15-18
      Ground lip Closure as in #1717

1720. MASON'S IMPROVED TRADEMARK (front)   Reverse: CFJCo............. Aqua $4-6
      Base: Pat. May 10 1870   Midget Pint, Aqua $15-18
      Ground lip Closure as in #1717

1721. TRADEMARK MASON'S CFJCO IMPROVED............................... Aqua $4-6
      Ground lip Closure as in #1717   Midget Pint, Aqua $15-18

1722. TRADEMARKS MASON'S CFJCO IMPROVED.............................. Aqua $4-6
      Base: Pat. Jan. 19 1869 or Mold number only   Midget Pint, Aqua $15-18
      Ground lip Closure as in #1717

1723. MASON'S IMPROVED (cross)....................................... Aqua $2-4
      Base: Pat. Nov 26 67 or Nov. 26 67   Midget Pint, Aqua $12-15
      Ground lip Glass insert & screw band
      Insert: Mason's Improved (cross in center)
              Or: Mason's Improved Hero Glass Works Phila. Pa.

1724. MASON'S IMPROVED (front)   Reverse: cross...................... Aqua $2-4
      Base: Nov. 26 67   Midget Pint, Aqua $12-15
      Ground lip Closure as in #1723

1725. (Cross) MASON'S IMPROVED...................................... Aqua $2-4
      Base: Pat. Nov. 26 67   Midget Pint, Aqua $12-15
      Ground lip Closure as in #1723   Light Olive Green $12-15

1726. (Cross) MASON'S IMPROVED (cross is unlettered)................ Aqua $2-4
      Base: Pat. Nov. 26 67   Clear $2-4
      Ground lip Closure as in #1723

1727. MASON'S (cross) IMPROVED (cross is unlettered)....... Aqua $2-4
      Ground lip Base & closure as in #1723

1728. MASON'S (cross) IMPROVED (cross is lettered H F J C)   Aqua $2-4
      Base: Pat. Nov. 26 67
      Ground lip Closure as in #1723

1729. MASON'S (cross) IMPROVED (cross is lettered H F J Co   Aqua $2-4
      Ground lip Base & closure as in #1723

1730. MASON'S IMPROVED with ghost GEM..................... Aqua $6-8
      Ground lip Glass insert & screw band
      Insert as in #1723

                                    #1729

1731. (Cross) MASON'S IMPROVED with ghost GEM....................... Aqua $6-8
      Base: Pat. Nov. 26 67
      Ground lip Closure as in #1723

1732. (Cross) MASON'S IMPROVED (front) Reverse: Ghost GEM........... Aqua $6-8
      Base: Pat. Nov 26 67
      Ground lip Closure as in #1723

1733. MASON'S (cross) IMPROVED with erased GLASSBORO TRADE MARK...... Aqua $6-8
      Ground lip Closure as in #1723

1734. MASON'S IMPROVED (front) Reverse: HGW................... Aqua $15-18
      Base: Pat. Nov. 26 67   Midget Pint, Aqua $30-35
      Ground lip Glass insert & screw band

1735. MASON'S (keystone)..................... Midget Pint, Aqua $30-35
      Ground lip Mason shoulder seal

1736. MASON'S (keystone) IMPROVED........... .... Aqua $8-10
      Ground lip Glass insert & screw band   Midget Pint, Aqua $20-25
      Insert: Mason Fruit Jar Co. Philada.
         (keystone in center)

#1737

1737. MASON'S (keystone) KEYSTONE........... .... Aqua $15-20
      Base: Patd Jan 19 1869   Midget Pint, Aqua $25-35
      Ground lip Glass or metal insert & screw band

1738. MASON'S LGW IMPROVED.......................................Clear $12-15
      Smooth lip Glass insert & screw band

1739. MASON'S IMPROVED JAR...................... .... Aqua $8-10
      Ground lip Mason shoulder seal   Amber $125-150

1740. MASON IMPROVED PAT'D.................. .... Aqua $6-8
      Smooth lip Glass lid & screw band   Cornflower blue $20-25

1741. MASON JAR (word Mason straight)........ ....Clear $2-4
      Smooth lip Mason beaded neck seal

1742. MASON JAR (word Mason arched)......... .... Aqua $2-4
      Smooth lip Mason shoulder seal

#1738

1743. MASON JAR (word Mason arched)........... ..... Midget Pint, Aqua $25-30
      Ground lip Mason shoulder seal   Midget Pint, Clear $25-30

1744. MASON'S JAR (with S)..Clear $3-5
      Ground lip Mason shoulder seal   Aqua $3-5
                            Midget Pint, Clear $25-30
                            Midget Pint, Aqua $25-30

1745. WIDE MOUTH MASON JAR MADE IN CANADA............................Clear   -$1
      Smooth lip Mason beaded neck seal
      Modern 2 Pc. metal closure

1746. MASON (star) JAR............................ ....Clear   -$1
      Smooth lip Mason beaded neck seal
      Modern 2 Pc. metal closure
      Insert: Star Mason Jar
        Or: Bernardin Standard Mason Snap Lid
      Circa 1965-1976 Pints & Quarts

1747. MASON (star) JAR......................... .Clear   -$1
      Smooth lip   Lightning dimple neck seal
      Pint product jar

#1748

1748. THE MASON JAR OF 1858 TRADEMARK (within circle & square)....... Aqua $40-45
      Base: Patd By Jno. L. Mason Nov 30th 1858
      Ground lip Mason shoulder seal

1749. THE MASON JAR OF 1872.. Aqua $35-40
     Base: Unmarked
     Ground lip Glass insert & screw band
     Insert: Patented September 24th 1872

1750. THE MASON JAR OF 1872.. Aqua $35-40
     Base: Whitney Glass Works, Glassboro N. J.
     Ground lip Closure as in #1749

1751. THE MASON JAR OF 1872 TRADEMARK (within circle & square)....... Aqua $40-45
     Ground lip Mason shoulder seal

1752. THE MASON JAR PAT. SEP 24th 1872................... Aqua $40-45
     Ground lip Glass insert & screw band
     Insert: Patented September 24th 1872

1753. MASON'S JAR OF 1872 with erased IMPROVED......... Aqua $35-40
     Ground lip Closure as in #1751

1754. MASON'S IMPROVED, with erased JAR OF 1872 (front). Aqua $250-300
     Reverse: CFJCo
     Base: H. Brooke Mould Maker N. Y.
     Ground lip Glass insert & screw band
     Insert: Mason's Improved Patented May 10 1870
           CFJCo monogram in center
     Gallon

#1752

1755. MASON'S PATENT....................................Clear $1-3
     Smooth lip Mason beaded neck seal

1756. MASON'S PATENT.................................... Aqua $2-4
     Smooth lip Mason shoulder seal   Ball blue $2-4
                                        Clear $2-4

1757. MASON'S J PATENT.................................. Aqua $3-5
     Smooth lip Mason shoulder seal

1758. MASON'S 1 PATENT.................................. Aqua $3-5
     Smooth lip Mason shoulder seal

1759. MASON'S 3 PATENT.................................. Aqua $3-5
     Smooth lip Mason shoulder seal

1760. MASON'S 4 PATENT.................................. Aqua $3-5
     Smooth lip Mason shoulder seal

1761. MASON'S 5 PATENT.................................. Aqua $3-5
     Smooth lip Mason shoulder seal

1762. MASON'S 6 PATENT.................................. Aqua $4-6
     The 6 is reversed
     Smooth lip Mason shoulder seal

#1764

1763. MASON'S 8 PATENT.................................. Aqua $3-5
     Smooth lip Mason shoulder seal

1764. MASON'S 9 PATENT.................................. Aqua $3-5
     Smooth lip Mason shoulder seal

1765. MASONS PAT. JUNE 2 1857 (on lid)....................Clear $35-40
     Ground lip Mason shoulder seal
     Small jar with squarish shoulders
     Lid is slightly dome shaped, brass, and
      embossed with flowers & leaves along
      with the date.

#1765

1766. MASON'S PATENT 1858..............................Clear $2-4
     Smooth lip Mason shoulder seal   Aqua $2-4

1767. MASON'S PATENT 1858 (front)   Reverse: PORT......................Aqua $4-6
      Smooth lip Mason shoulder seal

1768. MASON'S PATENT 1858 (front)   Reverse: BALL (script).............Aqua $2-4
      Smooth lip Mason shoulder seal

1769. MASON'S PATENT 1858 (front)   Reverse: BALL (script).............Aqua $2-4
      Smooth lip Mason shoulder seal   Yellow-green $12-15

1770. S MASON'S PATENT 1858..Aqua $12-15
      Ground lip Mason shoulder seal   Clear $12-15
                                                              Vaseline $70-80
                                                            Pale Green $12-15
                                                     Deep Olive Green $250-300

1771. MASON'S PATENT NOV 30th 1858...................................Aqua $125-150
      Ground lip Mason shoulder seal   Midget Pint, Aqua $225-250
      Known as the "Crowleytown" Mason, with   Emerald Green   Unpriced
        square shoulders and sharply angled base.
      Lid variations:
        (1) Unlined zinc lid: Masons Pat June 2 1857
        (2) Unlined zinc lid: Trademark SMS Co.
                        Always Reliable
        (3) Brass lid: Masons Pat June 2 1857

1772. MASON'S PATENT NOV 30th 1858....................................Aqua $125-150
      Ground lip Mason shoulder seal   Midget Pint, Aqua $225-250
      Unlined zinc lid: Chases Pat. Oct 27 1857
      Two vertical wrench lugs soldered on top of lid
      A "Crowleytown" Mason

1773. MASON'S PATENT NOV 30th 1858.....................   .Aqua $150-200
      Ground lip Unmarked glass insert & screw band
      A "Crowleytown" Mason   1/2 Gal.

1774. MASON'S PATENT NOV 30th 1858..................   .Aqua $125-150
      Ground lip Unmarked glass insert & screw band
      A "Crowleytown" Mason, wide mouth

1775. MASON'S PATENT NOV 30th 1858..............   .Aqua $125-150
      Ground lip Mason shoulder seal
      Unlined zinc lid: Pat June 2 57
                        Oct. 27 57
      Two horizonal wrench lugs on top of lid

#1777

1776. MASON'S 1 PATENT NOV 30th 1858.................................Aqua $125-150
      Ground lip Mason shoulder seal   Midget Pint, Aqua $225-250
      Unlined zinc lid: Masons Pat June 2 1857
      A "Crowleytown" Mason

1777. MASON'S 2 PATENT NOV 30th 1858.................................Aqua $125-150
      Ground lip Mason shoulder seal
      Unlined zinc lid: Chases Pat. Oct. 27 1857

1778. MASON'S 4 PATENT NOV 30th 1858.................................Aqua $125-150
      Ground lip Mason shoulder seal
      Closure as in #1775
      A "Crowleytown" Mason

1779. MASON'S 7 PATENT NOV 30th 1858.................................Aqua $125-150
      Ground lip Mason shoulder seal   Midget Pint, Aqua $225-250
      Unlined zinc lid: Pat. June 2 57 Oct. 27 57

      The foregoing 9 jars are all "Crowleytown" Masons. The lids
      listed are as found on their jars by various collectors, and
      may or may not be absolutely correct for each particular jar.

1780. MASON'S PATENT NOV 30th 58... Aqua $40-50
    Ground lip Mason shoulder seal   Light Amber Unpriced
    Known as the Christmas Mason because
      of style of lettering Pint only

1781. MASON'S PATENT NOV 30th 58... Aqua $40-50
    Ground lip Glass insert & screw band
    Known as the Christmas Mason Pint only

#1780

1782. MASON'S PATENT NOV 30th 58... Aqua $40-50
    Reverse: THE BALL JAR
    Ground lip Mason shoulder seal
    Known as the Christmas Mason Pint only

1783. MASON'S PATENT NOV 30th 1858 (in circle)........ Midget Pint, Aqua $90-100
    Ground lip Mason shoulder seal
    Known in small mouth pint only

#1783

1784. MASON'S PATENT NOV 30th 1858.. Aqua $6-8
    Ground lip Glass insert & screw band   Amber $75-100
    An Improved type closure on a Mason's Patent jar   Citron $70-80
    Insert: Unmarked   Light Green $6-8
      Or: Ball Bros. Glass Mfg. Co. Buffalo N.Y.   Midget Pint, Aqua $20-25
                                 Midget Pint, Amber $350-400
                                 Midget Pint, Citron $125-150

1785. MASON'S PATENT NOV 30th 1858..Aqua $6-8
    Reverse: embossed circle
    Ground lip Glass insert & screw band

1786. MASON'S PATENT NOV 30th 1858............. Midget Pint, Aqua $40-50
    (Date is all on one line)
    Reverse: HGCo monogram
    Ground lip Mason shoulder seal
    Known in small mouth pint only

#1786

1787. MASON'S PATENT NOV. 30th 1858.................................. Aqua $2-3
    Ground lip Mason shoulder seal   Dark Amber $50-75
    Later 1858's are found with smooth lips   Yellow Amber $50-75
                                        Black $1000 & up
    All of the authentic dark cobalt blue   Cornflower Blue $150 & up
    quarts reported to date have the mold   Med. Cobalt Blue $500 & up
    number P 13 on the base. Only one   Dark Cobalt Blue $1500 & up
    authentic opalescent jar is known..a   Citron $70-80
    quart with aqua swirls. This is   Clear $2-3
    listed as #1788.   Apple Green $6-8
                                 Emerald Green $300 & up
    Known sizes include: Midget pint,   Med. Olive Green $150 & up
    Regular Pint, Quart, ½ gallon,   Dark Olive Green $300 & up
    Gallon, and 3-Gallon.   Vaseline $70-80
                                Midget Pint Aqua $10-12
                                Midget Pint Clear $12-15
                                Midget Pint Amber $350 & up
                    Midget Pint Yellow Amber $350 & up
                            Midget Pint Ball Blue $10-12

#1787

1788. MASON'S PATENT NOV. 30th 1858............................Opalescent Unpriced
    Base: No marking
    Ground lip Mason shoulder seal
    Opalescent with aqua swirls
    Only 1 known Quart size

1789. MASON PATENT NOV 30th 1858 (no S)............................... Aqua $2-4
    Ground lip Mason shoulder seal   Clear $2-4

THE FOLLOWING JARS, THRU #1835, ARE "ERROR" JARS....

1790. MASON'S PATENT NOV 30th (no 1858)..................Aqua $12-15
    Ground lip Mason shoulder seal Pint

1791. MASON'S PATENT NOV 30th 1858 (reversed S).......Aqua $10-12
    Ground lip Mason shoulder seal Quart

1792. MASON'S PATENT NOV 30th 1858 (reversed S).......Aqua $12-15
    Reverse: BALL MASON
    Ground lip Mason shoulder seal ½ Gallon

1793. ASON'S ATENT OV 30th 1858 (missing letters).....Aqua $12-15
    Ground lip Mason shoulder seal Pint

#1790

1794. MASON'S PATENT NOV 30th 1858 (incomplete P)..................Clear $12-15
    Reverse: N.C.L. Co.
    Ground lip Mason shoulder seal
    Zinc lid, outside: Porcelain Lined Cap For Mason Fruit Jars
              Inside: Nail City (around a rosette)
    ½ Gallon

1795. MASON'S PATENT NOV 30th 1858 (incomplete P).........Clear $10-12
    Ground lip Mason shoulder seal ½ Gallon

1796. MASON'S PATENT NOV 30th 1858 (incomplete N in Patent).Aqua $10-12
    Ground lip Mason shoulder seal Quart

1797. MASON'S PATENT NOV 30th 1858 (incomplete N in Nov.)..Aqua $10-12
    Ground lip Mason shoulder seal Quart

#1797

1798. MASON'S PATENT NOV. 30th 1858 (no crossbars on A's)..Aqua $10-12
    Base: Pat. Nov. 26 67 Or Unmarked   Midget Pint Aqua $15-18
    Ground lip Mason shoulder seal
    Quart & Midget pint sizes

1799. MASON'S PATENT NOV 30th 1858 (no crossbar on A in Mason)........Aqua $10-12
    Base: Pat Nov 26 67   Midget Pint Aqua $15-18
    Ground lip Mason shoulder seal
    Quart & Midget pint sizes

1800. MA N'S PATENT NOV 30th 1858 (missing letters)..................Aqua $12-15
    Ground lip Mason shoulder seal Quart

1801. MA ON'S PATENT NOV 30th 1858 (missing letter)..................Aqua $12-15
    Ground lip Mason shoulder seal ½ Gallon

1802. MASONS PATENT NOV 30th 1858 (reversed N's in Patent & Nov)......Aqua $12-15
    Embossed circle on front
    Ground lip Mason shoulder seal Quart

1803. MASONS PATENT NOV 30th 1858 (reversed N's in Patent & Nov)......Aqua $12-15
    Reverse: Ghost circle with design   Clear $12-15
    Ground lip Glass insert & screw band
    Quart

1804. MASON'S PATENT NOV 30th 1858 (reversed N's in Patent & Nov).....Aqua $12-15
    Ground lip Glass insert & screw band
    Quart

1805. MASON'S PATENT NOV 30th 1858 (reversed N's in Patent & Nov)....Clear $12-15
    Reverse: Embossed circle   Light Green $12-15
    Ground lip Glass insert & screw band

1806. MASONS PATENT NOV 30th 1858 (reversed N's in Patent & Nov)......Aqua $12-15
    Reverse: Embossed circle   Clear $12-15
    Ground lip   Mason shoulder seal   Quart

1807. MASON'S PATENT NOV 30th 1858 (reversed N's in Patent & Nov.)....Aqua $12-15
    Embossed circle on front of jar
    Ground lip   Glass insert & screw band   Quart

1808. MASON'S PATENT NOV 30th 1858 (all N's reversed)................Aqua $12-15
    Reverse: CFJCo
    Ground lip   Mason shoulder seal   Quart

1809. MASON'S PATENT NOV 30th 1858 (all N's reversed)................Aqua $10-12
    Ground lip   Mason shoulder seal   Quart

1810. MASON'S PATENT NOV 30th 1858 (reversed N's in Patent & Nov).....Aqua $10-12
    Ground lip   Mason shoulder seal   Quart

1811. MASON'S PATENT NOV 30th 1858 (reversed N in Nov)...............Aqua $10-12
    Ground lip   Mason shoulder seal   Midget Pint, Clear $15-18
    Quart & small mouth pint

1812. MASON'S PATENT NOV 30th 1858 (reversed N in Mason's)...........Aqua $10-12
    Ground lip   Mason shoulder seal   Quart

1813. MASON'S (cross) PATENT NOV 30th 1858...........................Aqua $12-15
    (Reversed E in Patent, Unlettered cross)
    Base: Pat. Nov. 26 67
    Ground lip   Mason shoulder seal   Quart

1814. MASON'S PATENT NOV 30th 1858 (front)   Reverse: cross
    (No crossbar's on the A's) .... Midget Pint, Clear $15-18
    Base: Pat. Nov. 26 67   Midget Pint, Aqua $15-18
    Ground lip   Mason shoulder seal

1815. MASON'S PATENT NOV 30th 1858 (no crossbars on the A's).........Aqua $12-15
    Reverse: BALL (in script)
    Ground lip   Mason shoulder seal   Quart

1816. MASON'S PATENT NOA 30th 1858 (error)..................   ...Aqua $12-15
    Ground lip   Mason shoulder seal   Quart

1817. MASON'S 1 PATENT NOA 30th 1858 (error)............   ..Aqua $12-15
    Ground lip   Mason shoulder seal   Quart

1818. MASON'S PATENT NOV 30 1858 (no th)...............   ..Aqua $4-6
    Smooth lip   Mason shoulder seal   Pint & Quart
    These are probably not error jars.

1819. MASON'S PATENT NOV 30th 1858 (no crossbar on H)...............Aqua $10-12
    Ground lip   Mason shoulder seal   Quart   #1816

1820. MASON'S PATENT NOV 30ht 1858 (reversed th)....................Aqua $12-15
    Ground lip   Mason shoulder seal   ½ Gallon

1821. MASON'S PATENT NOV 30ht 1858 (reversed th & reversed E)........Aqua $12-15
    Ground lip   Mason shoulder seal   ½ Gallon

1822. MASON'S PATENT NOV 30 1858th (misplaced th)...................Aqua $12-15
    Ground lip   Mason shoulder seal   ½ Gallon

1823. MASON'S PATENT NOV 30th 1858 (reversed 3).....................Aqua $12-15
    Ground lip   Mason shoulder seal   Quart

MASON'S PATENT "ERROR" JARS CONTINUED...

1824. MASON'S PATENT NOV 03th 1858 (reversed 30)........ ..... Aqua $12-15
      Ground lip Mason shoulder seal Quart

1825. MASON'S PATENT NOV. 80th 1858 (error).......... .... Aqua $12-15
      Ground lip Mason shoulder seal Quart

1826. MASON PATENT NOV. 80th 1858 (no S & date error). .... Aqua $12-15
      Ground lip Mason shoulder seal Pint

1827. MASON'S PATENT NOV 30th 858 (date error)........ .... Aqua $12-15
      Ground lip Glass insert & screw band Quart   #1825

1828. MASON'S PATENT NOV'30th 1858 (Comma after Nov)............... Aqua $4-6
      Ground lip Mason shoulder seal Quart

1829. MASON'S PATENT NOV 30th 1885 (year date)........... . Aqua $12-15
      Ground lip Mason shoulder seal Quart

1830. MASON'S (keystone) PATENT NOV 30th 1885 (year date). . Aqua $12-15
      Ground lip Mason shoulder seal Pint

1831. MASON (keystone) PATENT NOV 30th 1885 (No S & year). . Aqua $12-15
      Ground lip Mason shoulder seal Pint   #1831

1832. MASON'S 5 PATENT NOV 30th 1858 (no crossbar on A in Patent).... Aqua $10-12
      Ground lip Mason shoulder seal ½ gallon

1833. MASON'S PATENT NOV 30th 58.......................Midget Pint, Aqua $25-30
      (Reversed N's in Patent & Nov)
      Ground lip Glass insert & screw band

1834. MASON'S PATENT NOV 30th 858 (date error).......... . Aqua $12-15
      Ground lip Glass insert & screw band Quart

1835. MASON'S PATENT NOV 30th 1858 (superimposed over
      ghost PATENT NOV 30th L & W...................... . Aqua $12-15
      Base: L & W
      Ground lip Mason shoulder seal Quart

      END OF THE MASON'S PATENT "ERROR" JARS   #1835

1836. MASON'S PATENT NOV 30th 58.............................. Aqua $3-5
      Ground lip Mason shoulder seal   Pint, Yellow Amber $125-150
                                              Midget Pint, Aqua $18-20
                                              Midget Pint, Amber $350 & up
                                              Midget Pint, Light Green $25-30

1837. MASON'S PATENT NOV 30th 58 (front).....................Pint, Aqua $8-10
      Reverse: BALL
      Ground lip Mason shoulder seal

1838. MASON'S PATENT NOV 30th 58.............................. Aqua $6-8
      Ground lip Glass insert & screw band   Amber $125-150
                                         Midget Pint, Aqua $18-20
                                         Midget Pint, Amber $350 & up

1839. MASON'S PATENT NOV 30th 58 (front)......................Aqua $8-10
      Reverse: Shield emblem   Midget Pint, Aqua $25-30
      Ground lip Mason shoulder seal

THE FOLLOWING JARS, Nos. 1840 THRU 1875, ARE EMBOSSED ON FRONT:
    MASON'S PATENT NOV 30th 1858
        Reverse embossings as listed.....

    ACME L. G. Co. see jar #14

1840. Reverse: A within shield.......................................Clear $15-18
        Ground lip Mason shoulder seal Quart

1841. Reverse: BALL (in script).............................. Aqua $3-5
        Ground lip Mason shoulder seal   Light Olive Green $12-15

1842. MASON PATENT NOV 30th 1858 (no S) (front)............... Aqua $3-5
        Reverse: BALL (in script)
        Ground lip Mason shoulder seal

1843. Reverse: BALL (in block letters)......... .... Aqua $3-5
        Ground lip Mason shoulder seal

1844. Reverse: THE BALL JAR (in block letters). .... Aqua $4-6
        Ground lip Mason shoulder seal

1845. Reverse: BALL MASON............................... ... Aqua $15-20
        Smooth lip Mason shoulder seal
        Made by using two front molds
                                                    #1841

1846. Reverse: CRYSTAL.................................... .. Aqua $45-55
        Ground lip Mason shoulder seal

1847. Reverse: Ghost CRYSTAL............................. .. Aqua $15-20
        Ground lip Mason shoulder seal

1848. Reverse: DUPONT (within oval)..................... . Aqua $60-70
        Ground lip Mason shoulder seal   #1848

1849. Reverse, heel: E. H. E............................... Aqua $8-10
        Ground lip Mason shoulder seal   Clear $8-10
                                             Midget Pint, Aqua $25-30
1850. Reverse: F (within shield).......................................Clear $15-18
        Ground lip Mason shoulder seal

1851. Reverse: HGCo monogram .... Aqua $10-12
        Ground lip Mason shoulder seal   Amber $150-200
                                                     Black $1000 & up
                                             Midget Pint, Aqua $30-35

1852. H G Co monogram (on front)........................... Aqua $20-25
        No other embossing on jar
        Ground lip Mason shoulder seal

1853. Reverse: HGCo monogram (different style).................... Aqua $12-15
        Ground lip Mason shoulder seal

1854. Reverse: HGCo monogram (different style)............. Aqua $12-15
        Ground lip Mason shoulder seal

    HAHNE & CO. see jar No. 1165 & 1166

1855. Reverse: HGW monogram................. .... Aqua $10-12
        Ground lip Mason shoulder seal   Amber $200-250
                                             Midget Pint, Aqua $30-35

1856. Reverse HGW (fancy monogram)........... .... Aqua $20-25
        Ground lip Mason shoulder seal   #1856

THE "HIGH GRADE" see jar No. 1253 & 1254

1857. Reverse: Reversed J within shield............................Clear $15-20
      Ground lip Mason shoulder seal

1858. Reverse: MANUFACTURED BY THE HERO GLASS WORKS
              PHILADELPHIA, PA............................Aqua $400-500
      Ground lip Mason shoulder seal
      Lid: Nickle plated brass, unmarked
      This large jar from the Norman Barnett collection
      holds 4 Gallons plus 1 quart.

1859. Reverse: MANUFACTURED AT THE WHITNEY GLASS WORKS
              GLASSBORO N J   CFJCo monogram............Aqua $400-500
      Ground lip Mason shoulder seal
      Lid: Nickle plated brass, unmarked
      4 Gallons plus 1 quart.   #1859

1860. Reverse: Ghost MASON'S JAR.............................. Aqua $18-20
      Base: star emblem
      Ground lip Mason shoulder seal

1861. Reverse, heel: N. C. L............................... Aqua $8-10
      Ground lip Mason shoulder seal   Amber $150-200
      Zinc lid, outside: Porcelain Lined Cap For   Midget Pint, Aqua $25-30
                    Mason Fruit Jars   Midget Pint, Amber $350-400
                Inside: Nail City (around a rosette)

1862. Reverse, heel: N. C. L. Co............................. Aqua $8-10
      Ground lip Mason shoulder seal   Clear $8-10
      Zinc lid as in #1861   Amber $150-200
                                        Midget Pint, Aqua $25-30
                                        Midget Pint, Amber $350-400

1863. Reverse: Ghost PORCELAIN LINED........................ Aqua $6-8
      Ground lip Mason shoulder seal

1864. Reverse: PORT (in script)............................. Aqua $10-12
      Ground lip Mason shoulder seal   Amber $150-200

1865. Reverse: SUN... Aqua $25-35
      Ground lip Mason shoulder seal

1866. Reverse, heel: U. G. Co.............................. Aqua $15-18
      Ground lip Mason shoulder seal   Clear $15-18

1867. Reverse: W within shield.......................... .Clear $15-18
      Ground lip Mason shoulder seal

1868. Reverse: MADE FOR WHEELER & BAYLESS CHICAGO ILL... .. Aqua $60-70
      Ground lip Mason shoulder seal
      Quart Circa 1863-1866   #1868

1869. Reverse: Shield emblem............................... Aqua $6-8
      Ground lip Mason shoulder seal   Midget Pint, Aqua $25-30

1870. Reverse: Shield & rectangle........................... Aqua $8-10
      Ground lip Mason shoulder seal

1871. Reverse: Rectangle & circle........................... Aqua $8-10
      Base: Pat Nov 26 67
      Ground lip Mason shoulder seal   #1870

1872. Reverse: Embossed circle............................... Aqua $8-10
      Ground lip Mason shoulder seal   Midget Pint, Aqua $15-18

1873. Reverse: 2 (within shield)............   ....Clear $15-18
      Ground lip Mason shoulder seal

1874. Reverse: 4 (within shield)............   ....Clear $15-18
      Ground lip Mason shoulder seal

1875. Reverse: "Tudor Rose" emblem..........   .... Aqua $25-30
      Ground lip Mason shoulder seal   Clear $25-30
      Found with zinc lid or Disk Immerser   Amber $350-400
                                              Midget Pints: Aqua $75-100
      Zinc lid, outside: Porcelain Lined Cap #1875   Clear $75-100
       For Mason Jars (Tudor Rose in Center)   Amber $450-500
       The porcelain liner is marked the same.   Apple Green $125-150
      Immerser lid, outside: TradeMark The Mason   Lt. Olive Green $125-150
       Disk Protector Cap Patd Nov. 30 1880
       Bottom of stem: Patd Nov. 23.75 Sept. 12.76
       Nov. 30.80 July 20. 1886

      Note: The prices given are for jars with zinc lids. For jars
             with immerser lids, add $25.

      THE FOLLOWING JARS, Nos. 1876 THRU 1912, ARE EMBOSSED ON FRONT:
         MASON'S PATENT NOV 30th 1858
            Base markings as listed...

1876. Base: B. T. & Co.. Aqua $6-8
      Ground lip Mason shoulder seal

1877. Base: E. H. E. Co... Aqua $6-8
      Ground lip Mason shoulder seal   Midget Pint, Aqua $20-25

1878. Base: EVERETT... Aqua $6-8
      Ground lip Mason shoulder seal

1879. Base: E. H. E..........................Midget Pint, Aqua $20-25
      Ground lip Mason shoulder seal

1880. Base: E. S. & Co.. Aqua $6-8
      Ground lip Mason shoulder seal   Midget Pint, Aqua $20-25

1881. Base: F. H. L. & Co....................................... Aqua $6-8
      Ground lip Mason shoulder seal   Midget Pint, Aqua $20-25

1882. Base: G (within diamond).................................. Aqua $4-6
      Ground lip Mason shoulder seal   Midget Pint, Aqua $15-18

1883. Base: GILBERDS.. Aqua $6-8
      Ground lip Mason shoulder seal

1884. Base: H. G. Co.. Aqua $6-8
      Ground lip Mason shoulder seal

1885. Base: L. A. C... Aqua $6-8
      Ground lip Mason shoulder seal   Midget Pint, Aqua $20-25

1886. Base: L & W.. Aqua $6-8
      Ground lip Mason shoulder seal

1887. Base: JNO. L. MASON....................................... Aqua $10-12
      Ground lip Mason shoulder seal

1888. Base: M. F. J. B. Co... Aqua $6-8
     Ground lip Mason shoulder seal

1889. Base: MOORE BRO'S. GLASS CO. CLAYTON N.J................... Aqua $10-12
     Ground lip Mason shoulder seal

1890. Base: PAT. NOV 26 67... Aqua $2-3
     Ground lip Mason shoulder seal   Med. Cobalt Blue $500 & up
                                        Midget Pint, Aqua $10-12

1891. Base: PAT. FEB. 13 4 (for Feb. 4, 1873)...................... Aqua $2-3
     Ground lip Mason shoulder seal

1892. Base: P. B..Clear $6-8
     Ground lip Mason shoulder seal

1893. Base: PORT... Aqua $6-8
     Ground lip Mason shoulder seal

1894. Base: PORT (in straight line)............................... Aqua $6-8
     Ground lip Mason shoulder seal

1895. Base: S & R... Aqua $6-8
     Ground lip Mason shoulder seal

1896. Base: S. R. & Co.. Aqua $6-8
     Ground lip Mason shoulder seal   Midget Pint, Aqua $20-25

1897. Base: TIGNER & CO. XENIA, IND................................ Aqua $10-12
     Ground lip Mason shoulder seal

1898. Base: TIGNER G. CO. XENIA, IND.............................. Aqua $10-12
     Ground lip Mason shoulder seal

1899. Base: T. W. & CO.. Aqua $6-8
     Ground lip Mason shoulder seal

1900. Base: W. C. D... Aqua $6-8
     Ground lip Mason shoulder seal   Yellow Amber $125-150
                                        Midget Pint, Aqua $20-25

1901. Base: Cross emblem.. Aqua $12-15
     Ground lip Mason shoulder seal

1902. Base: Cross within oval shield.........................Greenish Aqua $18-20
     Ground lip Mason shoulder seal

#1902

1903. Base: Diamond emblem (with or without a letter)............... Aqua $4-6
     Ground lip Mason shoulder seal   Clear $4-6
                                   Midget Pint, Aqua $15-18

1904. Base: Heart emblem.. Aqua $10-15
     Ground lip Mason shoulder seal

1905. Base: Leaf emblem.. Aqua $10-12
     Ground lip Mason shoulder seal   Aqua with Olive green Streaks $18-20
                                        Lime Green $12-15

1906. Base: Shield design... Aqua $10-12
     Ground lip Mason shoulder seal

1907. Base: Small star emblem....................................... Aqua $10-12
     Ground lip Mason shoulder seal

1908. Base: Small star emblem....................................... Aqua   Unpriced
     Ground lip Mason shoulder seal
     Unlined zinc lid: TradeMark M. S. S. Co.
               Always Reliable
     Jar has squarish shoulders like the "Crowleytown" Masons.

1909. Base: Large star emblem.. Aqua $10-12
    Ground lip Mason shoulder seal   Light Green $10-12
                          Midget Pint, Aqua $20-25
                          Midget Pint, Clear $20-25

1910. Base: K within star...............................Midget Pint, Aqua $20-25
    Ground lip Mason shoulder seal

1911. MASON PATENT NOV 30th 1858 (no S, on front).................... Aqua $4-6
    Base: Triangle emblem   Midget Pint, Aqua $15-18
    Ground lip Mason shoulder seal

1912. MASON PATENT NOV 30th 1858 (no S, on front).................... Aqua $4-6
    Base: Small triangle & mold numbers   Midget Pint, Aqua $15-18

    END OF BASE EMBOSSING LISTING
    For illustrations of these & other Mason 1858 jars, see "FRUIT JARS" By Creswick

1913. A (within shield) MASON PATENT NOV 30th 1858..   .... Aqua $15-18
    Ground lip Mason shoulder seal ½ Gallon   Clear $15-18

1914. B (within shield) MASON PATENT NOV 30th 1858.. ......Clear $15-18
    Ground lip Mason shoulder seal ½ Gallon

1915. C (within shield) MASON PATENT NOV 30th 1858.. ......Clear $15-18
    Ground lip Mason shoulder seal ½ Gallon

1916. D (within shield) MASON PATENT NOV 30th 1858.. ..Clear $15-18
    Ground lip Mason shoulder seal ½ Gallon

#1913

1917. E (within shield) MASON PATENT NOV 30th 1858....... Clear $15-18
    Ground lip Mason shoulder seal ½ Gallon

1918. F (within shield) MASON PATENT NOV 30th 1858....... Clear $15-18
    Ground lip Mason shoulder seal ½ Gallon

1919. (Crescent moon & star) MASON'S PATENT NOV 30th 1858 Aqua $60-75
    Reverse: BALL
    Ground lip Mason shoulder seal
    Zinc lid, outside: Genuine Boyd Cap For Mason Jars #1922
          (Crescent moon & star in center)

1920. MASON'S CFJCo PATENT NOV 30th 1858........................... Aqua $2-3
    Ground lip Mason shoulder seal   Amber $60-75
    Zinc lid, outside: Trademark Boyd's Porcelain   Black $1000 & up
    Lined Patd Mar. 30.58 June 9 63 Mar 30.69 Lt. Cobalt Blue $150 & up
    Extd Mar. 30.72   (CFJCo monogram in center) Citron $60-75
    Zinc lid, inside: Consolidated Fruit Jar   Light Green $2-3
    Company New York   (CFJCo monogram in center) Lt. Olive Green $35-40
                    Midget Pint, Aqua $10-12
                    Midget Pint, Amber $350-400
                    Midget Pint Light Green $10-12
                    Gallon, Aqua $250-300

1921. MASON'S CFJCo PATENT NOV 30th 1858 (front).................... Aqua $4-6
    Reverse, heel: CLYDE N.Y.   Midget Pint, Aqua $20-25
    Ground lip Mason shoulder seal

1922. MASON'S CFJCo PATENT NOV 30th 1858........................... Aqua   Unpriced
    Reverse: ROSENTHAL ARONSON & CO. MELBOURNE
    Ground lip Mason shoulder seal Quart

1923. MASON'S CFJCo PATETN NOV 30th 1858 (error)................ Aqua $12-15
      Ground lip Mason shoulder seal
      Zinc lid as in #1920 Quart

1924. MASON'S CFJCo PATENT NOV 30th 185 (error)........ ... Aqua $12-15
      Ground lip Mason shoulder seal
      Zinc lid as in #1920 Quart

1925. MASON'S CFJCo PATENT NOV 30th 1858.............. .. Aqua $400-500
      Ground lip Mason shoulder seal
      Nickel plated lid marked on outside only:
       Trademark Boyd's Porcelain Lined Patd
       Mar. 30.58 June 9 63 Mar 30.69 Extd
       Mar. 30.72 (CFJCo in center)
      4 Gallon size jar

#1923

1926. MASON'S PATENT NOV 30th 1858 (front)........................... Aqua $6-8
      Reverse: CFJCo
      Ground lip Glass insert & screw band

1927. MASON'S PATENT NOV 30th 1858 (front).......................... Aqua $2-4
      Reverse: CFJCo   Med. Cornflower Blue $45-50
      Ground lip Mason shoulder seal   Midget Pint, Aqua $15-18
      Zinc lid as in #1920   Midget, Med. Cornflower Blue $50-75

1928. MASON'S PATENT NOV 30th 7858 (error)......................... Aqua $12-15
      Reverse: CFJCo   Lt. Olive Green $15-18
      Ground lip Mason shoulder seal
      Zinc lid as in #1920

1929. MASON'S PATENT NOV 30th 1858................................... Aqua $15-20
      Reverse: CFJCo
      Base: Made By A. & D. H. Chambers
            Pittsburg
      Ground lip Mason shoulder seal
      Zinc lid as in #1920

1930. MASON'S + PATENT NOV 30th 1858...... .... Aqua $15-20
      Reverse: CFJCo
      Ground lip Mason shoulder seal
      Zinc lid as in #1920

1931. MASON'S (star) PATENT NOV 30th 1858. .... Aqua $15-20
      Reverse: CFJCo   Black $1000 & up
      Ground lip Mason shoulder seal
      Zinc lid as in #1920   #1931

1932. MASON'S PATENT NOV 30th 1858.................... Aqua $400-500
      Reverse: MANUFACTURED AT THE WHITNEY GLASS WORKS
               GLASSBORO N.J. CFJCo
      Ground lip Mason shoulder seal
      Unmarked brass lid
      3 Gallon size

1933. MASON'S GJ PATENT NOV 30th 1858................. ... Aqua $15-18
      Ground lip Mason shoulder seal

1934. MASON'S GCCo PATENT NOV 30th 1858............... ... Aqua $8-10
      Ground lip Mason shoulder seal

1935. MASON'S GCCo PATENT NOV 30t 1858 (no h).......... ...Clear $10-12
      Ground lip Mason shoulder seal Pint

1936. MASON'S CG GC PATENT NOV 30th 1858................ ...Clear $12-15
      Base: D within diamond   #1933
      Ground lip Mason shoulder seal

1937. MASON'S CG GC PATENT NOV 30ht 1858 (error).....................Clear $18-20
       Ground lip Mason shoulder seal ½ Gallon

1938. (Cross) MASON'S PATENT NOV 30th 1858......................... Aqua $2-3
       Base: Pat Nov 26 67   Amber $50-75
       Ground lip Mason shoulder seal   Yellow Amber $50-75
       Zinc lid variations: Citron $50-75
         (1) Outside: TradeMark Boyd's Porcelain Lined   Apple Green $8-10
             Patented July 18 1871 March 30 1869   Midget, Aqua $15-18
             Reissued Oct. 25 1881 (Cross in center)
             Inside: Boyd's Genuine Porcelain Lined
                 (Cross in center)
         (2) Outside: Same as No. 1
             Inside: Boyd's Genuine Porcelain Lined
                 (Without cross in center)
         (3) Outside: TradeMark Rowley's Porcelain Lined
             Patd Dec 31 72 Feb 4 73 July 14 74
             Nov 4 62 Reis June 9 68 (Cross in center)
             Inside: The Hero Fruit Jar Company Phila. Pa.
                 (Cross in center)

1939. MASON'S (cross) PATENT NOV 30th 1858......................... Aqua $2-3
       Base: Pat Nov 26 67 Or Pat. Nov 26 1867   Amber $50-75
       Ground lip Mason shoulder seal   Apple Green $8-10
       Zinc lid as in #1938   Lime Green $8-10
                                                              Olive Green $75-100
                                                       Regular Pint Amber $200-225
                                                         Midget Pint Aqua $12-15

1940. MASON'S (cross) PATENT NOV 30th 1858.................................Aqua $2-3
       (Cross is unlettered)
       Ground lip Mason shoulder seal
       Zinc lid as in #1938

1941. MASON'S PATENT NOV 30th 1858 (front)............... Aqua $4-6
       Reverse: cross   Clear $4-6
       Ground lip Mason shoulder seal   Amber $50-75
       Zinc lid as in #1938   #1939   Apple Green $8-10
                                                     Midget Pint, Aqua $12-15
                                                    Midget Pint, Clear $12-15
                                                    Midget Pint, Amber $350-400
                                              Midget Pint, Apple Green $20-25
                                              Midget Pint, Olive Green   Unpriced

1942. MASON'S (cross) PATENT NOV 30th 1858......................... Aqua $200-300
       Ground lip Mason shoulder seal
       Zinc lid with liner marked: The Hero Fruit Jar Company
                         Philada. Pa. (cross in center)
       Gallon

1943. MASON'S (cross) PATENT NOV 30th 1858 with
       erased THE PEARL just above the cross.................... Aqua $200-300
       Ground lip Mason shoulder seal
       Zinc lid as in #1942
       Gallon

1944. (Cross) MASON'S PATENT NOV 30th 1858 (front)..... Aqua $35-45
       Reverse: FINK & NASSE ST. LOUIS MO.
       Base: Pat. Nov. 26 67
       Ground lip Mason shoulder seal

1945. (Cross) MASON'S PATENT NOV 30th 1858 (front)..... Aqua $6-8
       Reverse: Erased FINK & NASSE ST. LOUIS MO.
       Ground lip Mason shoulder seal

                                                          #1944

       Also see FINK & NASSE jar No. 1002

1946. (Cross) MASONS CFJCo PATENT NOV 30th 1858..................... Aqua $20-25
        Ground lip Mason shoulder seal   Clear $20-25

1947. (Cross) MASONS CFJCo PATENT NOV 30th 1858..................... Aqua $20-25
        Base: I. G. Co.   Clear $20-25
        Ground lip Mason shoulder seal

1948. (Cross) MASONS CFJCo PATENT NOV 30th (no year)................ Aqua $25-30
        Ground lip Mason shoulder seal

1949. (Cross) MASON'S S PATENT 1858................................. Aqua $12-15
        Ground lip Mason shoulder seal

1950. (Cross) MASON'S S PATENT 1858 (front)........................ Aqua $30-35
        Reverse: (Cross) MASON'S PATENT 1858
        Ground lip Mason shoulder seal
        Two front molds were used

1951. + MASON'S S PATENT 1858...................................... Aqua $15-20
        Ground lip Mason shoulder seal

1952. IGCo MASON'S PATENT NOV. 30th 1858........................... Aqua $10-12
        Ground lip Mason shoulder seal

1953. IGCo MASON'S NOV. 30th 1858 (no word Patent)................. Aqua $12-15
        Ground lip Mason shoulder seal

1954. IGCo MASON'S PATENT NOV 30th 1858............................ Aqua $12-15
        Ground lip Mason shoulder seal

1955. MASON'S IGCo PATENT NOV 30th 1858............................ Aqua $12-15
        (This monogram could be IO or OI)   Midget Pint, Aqua $50-60
        Ground lip Mason shoulder seal

1956. MASON'S IGCo PATENT NOV 30th 1858............................ Aqua $15-18
        (This monogram could be IO or OI)
        Ground lip Mason shoulder seal

1957. MASON'S KBGCo PATENT NOV 30th 1858........................... Aqua $12-15
        (Plain monogram)   Clear $12-15
        Ground lip Mason shoulder seal

1958. MASON'S KBGCo PATENT NOV 30th 1858........................... Aqua $12-15
        (Fancy monogram)   Clear $12-15
        Ground lip Mason shoulder seal

#1948   #1952   #1953   #1954   #1955   #1956   #1957   #1958

1959. (Keystone within circle) MASON'S PATENT NOV 30th 1858......... Aqua $6-8
        Ground lip Mason shoulder seal   Amber $175-200
        Zinc lid, outside: Mason Fruit Jar Co. Philada. Pa.
                    (Keystone in center)
        Zinc lid, inside: Mason Fruit Jar Co. Boyd's Porcelain
                    Lining
                Or: Mason Fruit Jar Co.

1960. (Keystone within circle) MASON PATENT NOV 30th 1858............ Aqua $6-8
     No S after Mason, Word Patent offset to the left
     Ground lip Mason shoulder seal Lid as in #1959

1961. (Keystone within circle) MASON'S PATENT NOV 30th 1858......... Aqua $6-8
     Word Patent is offset to the right   Clear $6-8
     Ground lip Mason shoulder seal Lid as in #1959

1962. (Keystone) MASON'S PATENT NOV 30th 1858........................ Aqua $6-8
     Ground lip Mason shoulder seal Lid as in #1959   Amber $175-200

1963. (Keystone) MASON PATENT NOV 30th 1858 (no S after Mason)....... Aqua $6-8
     Ground lip Mason shoulder seal Lid as in #1959

1964. MASON'S (keystone within circle) PATENT NOV 30th 1858.......... Aqua $6-8
     Ground lip Mason shoulder seal Lid as in #1959   Amber $175-200
                                     Midget Pint, Aqua $20-25

1965. MASON'S (keystone) PATENT NOV 30th 1858....................... Aqua $6-8
     Ground lip Mason shoulder seal   Amber $175-200
     Lid as in #1959   Regular Pint, Amber $200-250
                                 Midget Pint, Aqua $20-25

#1961   #1962   #1966   #1968   #1970   #1971   #1973

1966. MASON'S (keystone) PATENT NOV 30th 1858 with ghost PATENT.......Aqua $20-25
     Ground lip Mason shoulder seal Lid as in #1959 Quart

1967. MASON'S PATENT NOV 30th 1858 (front)..............Midget Pint, Aqua $30-35
     Reverse: Keystone emblem
     Ground lip Mason shoulder seal

1968. MASONS (keystone) PATENT NOV 80th 1858 (error)..................Aqua $12-15
     Ground lip Mason shoulder seal Lid as in #1959 Pint

1969. MASONS (keystone) PATENT NOV 30th 1858.........................Aqua $12-15
     Reversed N in Mason
     Ground lip Mason shoulder seal Lid as in #1959 Pint

1970. MASON'S LGCo PATENT NOV 30th 1858..............................Aqua $10-12
     Ground lip Mason shoulder seal   Cornflower Blue $100-150
                               Midget Pint, Aqua $50-60

1971. MASON'S MFJ PATENT NOV 30th 1858 (in dual line letters)........Aqua $18-20
     Ground lip Mason shoulder seal
     Made in Australia

1972. MASON'S PATENT NOV 30th 1858...................................Aqua $15-18
     On threaded neck: M F J Co
     Ground lip Mason shoulder seal ½ Gallon

1973. MASON'S OVGCo PATENT NOV 30th 1858.............................Aqua $20-25
     Ground lip Mason shoulder seal

1974. MASON'S SGCo PATENT NOV 30th 1858........................... Aqua $6-8
      Ground lip Mason shoulder seal   Apple Green $8-10
                                                        Lt. Olive Green $12-15

1975. MASON'S · PATENT NOV 30th 1858.............................. Aqua $8-10
      Ground lip Mason shoulder seal

1976. MASON'S ·· PATENT NOV 30th 1858........   .... Aqua $8-10
      Ground lip Mason shoulder seal

1977. MASON'S ·.· PATENT NOV 30th 1858......   .... Aqua $8-10
      Base: Unmarked or L & W
      Ground lip Mason shoulder seal

1978. MASON'S ···· PATENT NOV 30th 1858.....   .... Aqua $8-10
      Ground lip Mason shoulder seal

1979. MASON'S .·. PATENT NOV 30th 1858......   .... Aqua $8-10
      Base: L & W
      Ground lip Mason shoulder seal

#1976

1980. MASON'S (circle) PATENT NOV 30th 1858....................... Aqua $8-10
      Ground lip Mason shoulder seal

1981. MASON'S (star) PATENT NOV 30th 1858........................... Aqua $15-18
      Base: Pat Nov 26 67
      Ground lip Mason shoulder seal

1982. MASON'S (star) PATENT NOV 30th 1858........................... Aqua $10-12
      Reverse: Embossed Eagle
      Smooth lip Mason beaded neck seal
      Metal screw cover, unmarked, gold lacquered
        or painted white
      Made in 1975 by Owens-Illinois Glass Co.
      4 Gallon size

      THE FOLLOWING JARS, Nos. 1983 THRU 2025, ARE "LETTERED" MASONS
      ALL LETTERS OF THE ALPHABET HAVE BEEN REPORTED

1983. MASON'S A PATENT NOV 30th 1858.......   ....Aqua $10-12
      Base: Unmarked or B. P. & Co.   Midget Pint, Aqua $20-25
      Ground lip Mason shoulder seal

1984. MASON,S A PATENT NOV 30th 1858......   ....Aqua $10-12
      Base: Unmarked
      Ground lip Mason shoulder seal

1985. MASON'S B PATENT NOV 30th 1858.....   ....Aqua $10-12
      Base: Unmarked or B. P. & Co.   Midget Pint, Aqua $20-25
      Ground lip Mason shoulder seal

1986. MASON'S B PATENT NOV 30th 1858......   ....Aqua $10-12
      Base: L & W
      Ground lip Mason shoulder seal   #1983

1987. MASON'S C PATENT NOV 30th 1858   2 ....Clear $10-12
      Ground lip Mason shoulder seal

1988. MASON'S C PATENT NOV 30th 1858.............................. Aqua $10-12
      Base: Unmarked or L & W   Midget Pint, Aqua $20-25
      Ground lip Mason shoulder seal

1989. MASON'S -C- PATENT NOV 30th 1858........................... Aqua $10-12
      Ground lip Mason shoulder seal

1990. MASON'S -C- PATENT NOV 30th 1858.............................Aqua $60-70
    Reverse: DUPONT (within oval)
    Ground lip Mason shoulder seal
    These were used for Dupont paints circa WW 1
    Reported in Pint & ½ Gallon

1991. MASON'S -C- PATENT NOV 30th 1858.........................Aqua $65-75
    Reverse: DUPONT (with reversed N, within oval)
    Ground lip Mason shoulder seal

    Also see jar No. 1848

1992. MASON'S D PATENT NOV 30th 1858..................... ....Aqua $10-12
    Base: B. P. & Co.
    Ground lip Mason shoulder seal

1993. MASON'S E PATENT NOV 30th 1858 ....Aqua $10-12
    Base: B. P. & Co.
    Ground lip Mason shoulder seal

#1989

1994. MASON'S E PATENT NOV 30th 1858.......................Aqua $10-12
    Base: L & W
    Ground lip Mason shoulder seal

1995. MASON'S PATENT NOV 30th 1858 E (within circle).......Clear $10-12
    Ground lip Mason shoulder seal

1996. MASON'S F PATENT NOV 30th 1858.............. ...... Aqua $10-12
    Base: B. P. & Co.
    Ground lip Mason shoulder seal

1997. MASON'S F PATENT NOV 30th 1858.............. ....Aqua $10-12
    Base: B. P. & So. (error)
    Ground lip Mason shoulder seal

#1995

1998. MASON'S F PATENT NOV 30th 1858 (reversed F)....................Aqua $12-15
    Base: L & W
    Ground lip Mason shoulder seal

1999. MASON'S G PATENT NOV 30th 1858...............................Aqua $10-12
    Ground lip Mason shoulder seal

2000. MASON'S H PATENT NOV 30th 1858...............................Aqua $10-12
    Ground lip Mason shoulder seal

2001. MASON'S I PATENT NOV 30th 1858...............................Aqua $10-12
    Base: L & W   Midget Pint, Aqua $20-25
    Ground lip Mason shoulder seal

2002. MASON'S J PATENT NOV 30th 1858.......... ....Aqua $10-12
    Base: L & W
    Ground lip Mason shoulder seal

2003. MASON'S K PATENT NOV 30th 1858.......... ....Aqua $10-12
    Ground lip Mason shoulder seal

2004. MASON'S L PATENT NOV 30th 1858....... ....Aqua $10-12
    Ground lip Mason shoulder seal

2005. MASON.S L PATENT NOV 30th 1858...... ....Aqua $10-12
    Base: L & W
    Ground lip Mason shoulder seal

#2003

2006. MASON'S M PATENT NOV 30th 1858............#2003.............Aqua $10-12
    Ground lip Mason shoulder seal

2007. MASON'S N PATENT NOV 30th 1858...............................Aqua $10-12
    Ground lip Mason shoulder seal

2008. MASON'S N PATENT NOV 30th 1858................................... Aqua $10-12
      Base: L & W
      Ground lip Mason shoulder seal

2009. MASON'S N PATENT NOV 30th 1858................................... Aqua $10-12
      Base: Port
      Ground lip Mason shoulder seal

2010. MASON'S N PATENT NOV 30th 1858................................... Aqua $10-12
      Reverse: THE BALL JAR
      Ground lip Mason shoulder seal

2011. MASON'S O PATENT NOV 30th 1858................................... Aqua $10-12
      Base: L & W
      Ground lip Mason shoulder seal

2012. MASON'S P PATENT NOV 30th 1858................................... Aqua $10-12
      Ground lip Mason shoulder seal

2013. MASON'S Q PATENT NOV 30th 1858................................... Aqua $10-12
      Ground lip Mason shoulder seal

2014. MASON.S R PATENT NOV 30th 1858................................... Aqua $10-12
      Base: L & W
      Ground lip Mason shoulder seal

2015. MASON'S R PATENT NOV 30th 1858 (reversed R)..................... Aqua $12-15
      Base: L & W
      Ground lip Mason shoulder seal

2016. MASON.S S PATENT NOV 30th 1858................................... Aqua $10-12
      Base: L & W
      Ground lip Mason shoulder seal

2017. MASON'S SR PATENT NOV 30th 1858 (reversed R).................... Aqua $12-15
      Base: L & W
      Ground lip Mason shoulder seal

#2014

2018. MASON'S T PATENT NOV 30th 1858................................... Aqua $10-12
      Ground lip Mason shoulder seal

2019. MASON'S U PATENT NOV 30th 1858................................... Aqua $10-12
      Base: L & W
      Ground lip Mason shoulder seal

2020. MASON'S V PATENT NOV 30th 1858................................... Aqua $10-12
      Base: L & W
      Ground lip Mason shoulder seal

2021. MASON'S V PATENT NOV 30th 1858 (Roman numeral).................. Aqua $10-12
      Ground lip Mason shoulder seal

2022. MASON'S W PATENT NOV 30th 1858................................... Aqua $10-12
      Base: L & W
      Ground lip Mason shoulder seal

2023. MASON'S X PATENT NOV 30th 1858................................... Aqua $10-12
      Base: L & W
      Found with both a smooth lip & a ground lip

2024. MASON'S Y PATENT NOV 30th 1858................................... Aqua $10-12
      Base: L & W
      Ground lip Mason shoulder seal

2025. MASON'S Z PATENT NOV 30th 1858................................... Aqua $10-12
      Base: L & W or Unmarked
      Ground lip Mason shoulder seal

#2025

2026. MASON'S 1 PATENT NOV 30th 1858.. Aqua $8-10
    Smooth lip Mason shoulder seal   Clear $8-10

2027. MASON'S 1 PATENT NOV 30th 1858.. Aqua $8-10
    Ground lip Mason shoulder seal   Clear $8-10
                                      Midget Pint, Clear $20-25
                                      Midget Pint, Aqua $20-25

2028. MASON'S 1 PATENT NOV 30th 1858 (1 is reversed)................. Aqua $8-10
    Ground lip Mason shoulder seal

2029. MASON'S 2 PATENT NOV 30th 1858..Clear $8-10
    Smooth lip Mason shoulder seal

2030. MASON'S 2 PATENT NOV 30th 1858............................... Aqua $8-10
    Base: H. C. & T. or Unmarked   Clear $8-10
    Ground lip Mason shoulder seal   Midget Pint, Aqua $20-25

2031. MASON'S 2 PATENT NOV 30th 1858 (2 is reversed)................. Aqua $10-12
    Ground lip Mason shoulder seal   Midget Pint, Aqua $20-25

2032. MASON'S 2 PATENT NOV 30th 1858............................... Aqua $8-10
    Ground lip Mason shoulder seal   Midget Pint, Aqua $20-25

2033. MASON.S 2 PATENT NOV 30th 1858............................... Aqua $8-10
    Ground lip Mason shoulder seal

2034. MASON'S 2 PATENT NOV 30th 1858 (all N's reversed)............. Aqua $12-15
    Ground lip Mason shoulder seal

2035. MASON'S 2 PATENT NOV 30th 1858 (reversed N in Nov)........... Aqua $12-15
    Ground lip Mason shoulder seal

2036. MASON'S II PATENT NOV 30th 1858...... .... Aqua $10-12
    Ground lip Mason shoulder seal   Midget Pint, Aqua $25-30

2037. MASON'S 3 PATENT NOV 30th 1858...... .... Aqua $8-10
    Smooth lip Mason shoulder seal   Clear $8-10

2038. MASON'S 3 PATENT NOV 30th 1858...... .... Aqua $8-10
    Ground lip Mason shoulder seal   Clear $8-10
                                    Lt. Olive Green $10-12
                                    Midget Pint, Aqua $20-25

2039. MASON'S 3 PATENT NOV 30th 1858...... .... Aqua $10-12
    Base: W. F. M.
    Ground lip Mason shoulder seal   #2031

2040. MASON'S 3 PATENT NOV 30th 1858............................... Aqua $10-12
    Base: H. C. & T.
    Ground lip Mason shoulder seal

2041. MASON'S 3 PATENT NOV 30th 1858......... .... Aqua $8-10
    Ground lip Mason shoulder seal

2042. MASON'S III PATENT NOV 30th 1858...... .... Aqua $10-12
    Ground lip Mason shoulder seal   Midget Pint, Aqua $25-30

2043. MASON'S 4 PATENT NOV 30th 1858........ .... Aqua $8-10
    Smooth lip Mason shoulder seal   Clear $8-10

2044. MASON'S 4 PATENT NOV 30th 1858........ .... Aqua $10-12
    Base: E. S. & Co. or Unmarked   Clear $10-12
    Ground lip Mason shoulder seal   Midget Pint, Aqua $20-25
                             #2045

2045. MASON'S 4 PATENT NOV 30th 1858 (4 is reversed)................ Aqua $10-12
    Ground lip Mason shoulder seal

2046. MASON.S 4 PATENT NOV 30th 1858 (reversed S)................... Aqua $10-12
     Ground lip Mason shoulder seal

2047. MASON'S <u>4</u> PATENT NOV 30th 1858...................... Aqua $10-12
     Ground lip Mason shoulder seal   Midget Pint, Aqua $20-25

2048. MASON'S 4 PATENT NOV 30th 1858.....   .... Aqua $8-10
     (Different style 4)
     Ground lip Mason shoulder seal

2049. MASON'S IV PATENT NOV 30th 1858....   .... Aqua $10-12
     Ground lip Mason shoulder seal

2050. MASON'S 5 PATENT NOV 30th 1858.....   .... Aqua $8-10
     Ground lip Mason shoulder seal   Lt. Cobalt Blue $150 & up
                                        Midget Pint, Aqua $20-25

#2048

2051. MASON'S 5 PATENT NOV 30th 1858 (A in Patent without crossbar).. Aqua $10-12
     Ground lip Mason shoulder seal ½ Gallon

2052. MASON'S <u>5</u> PATENT NOV 30th 1858.............................. Aqua $8-10
     Ground lip Mason shoulder seal   Midget Pint, Aqua $20-25

2053. MASON'S 6 PATENT NOV 30th 1858.............................. Aqua $8-10
     Smooth lip Mason shoulder seal

2054. MASON'S 6 PATENT NOV 30th 1858.............................. Aqua $10-12
     Base: H. C. & T. or Unmarked   Med. Olive Green $30-35
     Ground lip Mason shoulder seal   Midget Pint, Aqua $20-25

2055. MASON'S <u>6</u> PATENT NOV 30th 1858.............................. Aqua $8-10
     Ground lip Mason shoulder seal   Midget Pint, Aqua $20-25

2056. MASON'S 6 PATENT NOV 30th 1858 (reversed 6)................... Aqua $10-12
     Ground lip Mason shoulder seal

2057. MASON'S 7 PATENT NOV 30th 1858.............................. Aqua $8-10
     Smooth lip Mason shoulder seal   Clear $8-10

2058. MASON'S 7 PATENT NOV 30th 1858.............................. Aqua $8-10
     Base: W. F. M. or Unmarked   Clear $8-10
     Ground lip Mason shoulder seal   Midget Pint, Aqua $20-25

2059. MASON'S VII PATENT NOV 30th 1858........   .... Aqua $10-12
     Ground lip Mason shoulder seal

2060. MASON'S 8 PATENT NOV 30th 1858 (large 8   .... Aqua $8-10
     Smooth lip Mason shoulder seal

2061. MASON'S 8 PATENT NOV 30th 1858 (large 8   .... Aqua $8-10
     Ground lip Mason shoulder seal

2062. MASON'S 8 PATENT NOV 30th 1858 (small 8   .... Aqua $10-12
     Base: L & W or Unmarked   Midget Pint, Aqua $20-25
     Ground lip Mason shoulder seal

#2063

2063. MASON'S 8 PATENT NOV 30th 1858 (8 within circle).............. Aqua $10-12
     Smooth lip Mason shoulder seal

2064. MASON'S VIII PATENT NOV 30th 1858.............................. Aqua $10-12
     Ground lip Mason shoulder seal

2065. MASON'S 9 PATENT NOV 30th 1858.............................. Aqua $8-10
     Smooth lip Mason shoulder seal

2066. MASON'S 9 PATENT NOV 30th 1858 (large 9)...................... Aqua $8-10
     Ground lip Mason shoulder seal   Med. Olive Green $30-35

2067. MASON'S 9 PATENT NOV 30th 1858 (small 9)................... Aqua $8-10
      Ground lip Mason shoulder seal

2068. MASON'S 9 PATENT NOV 30th 1858 (reversed 9)..... ... Aqua $10-12
      Ground lip Mason shoulder seal

2069. MASON'S IX PATENT NOV 30th 1858................ ... Aqua $10-12
      Ground lip Mason shoulder seal

2070. MASON'S 10 PATENT NOV 30th 1858................ ... Aqua $8-10
      Ground lip Mason shoulder seal   #2069

2071. MASON'S 11 PATENT NOV 30th 1858.................................... Aqua $8-10
      Ground lip Mason shoulder seal   Midget Pint, Aqua $20-25

2072. MASON'S 11 PATENT NOV 30th 1858.................................... Aqua $8-10
      Ground lip Mason shoulder seal

2073. MASON'S 12 PATENT NOV 30th 1858.................................... Aqua $8-10
      Ground lip Mason shoulder seal   Midget Pint, Aqua $20-25

2074. MASON'S 13 PATENT NOV 30th 1858.................................... Aqua $8-10
      Ground lip Mason shoulder seal

2075. MASON'S 13 PATENT NOV 30th 1858.................................... Aqua $8-10
      Ground lip Mason shoulder seal

2076. MASON'S D13 PATENT NOV 30th 1858.................................... Aqua $15-18
      Base: Pat'd By Jno L. Mason Nov 30 1858 D13D
      Ground lip Mason shoulder seal

2077. MASON'S 14 PATENT NOV 30th 1858........ ... Aqua $8-10
      Smooth lip Mason shoulder seal

2078. MASON'S 14 PATENT NOV 30th 1858........ ... Aqua $8-10
      Ground lip Mason shoulder seal

2079. MASON'S 14 PATENT NOV 30th 1858........ ...... Aqua $8-10
      Ground lip Mason shoulder seal

2080. MASON'S 15 PATENT NOV 30th 1858........ ... Aqua $8-10
      Ground lip Mason shoulder seal

2081. MASON'S 15 PATENT NOV 30th 1858........ .... Aqua $8-10
      Ground lip Mason shoulder seal   #2076

2082. MASON'S 16 PATENT NOV 30th 1858.................................... Aqua $8-10
      Ground lip Mason shoulder seal

2083. MASON'S 17 PATENT NOV 30th 1858........ ... Aqua $8-10
      Ground lip Mason shoulder seal

2084. MASON'S 17 PATENT NOV 30th 1858........ ... Aqua $8-10
      Ground lip Mason shoulder seal

2085. MASON'S 18 PATENT NOV 30th 1858....... ... Aqua $8-10
      Ground lip Mason shoulder seal

2086. MASON'S 18 PATENT NOV 30th 1858....... ... Aqua $8-10
      Ground lip Mason shoulder seal

2087. MASON'S 19 PATENT NOV 30th 1858....... ... Aqua $8-10
      Ground lip Mason shoulder seal   #2086

2088. MASON'S 19 PATENT NOV 30th 1858.................................... Aqua $8-10
      Ground lip Mason shoulder seal

2089. MASON'S 20 PATENT NOV 30th 1858.................................... Aqua $8-10
      Ground lip Mason shoulder seal

2090. MASON'S 20 PATENT NOV 30th 1858.................................... Aqua $8-10
      Ground lip Mason shoulder seal

2091. MASON'S 21 PATENT NOV 30th 1858............................... Aqua $8-10
      Ground lip Mason shoulder seal

2092. MASON'S 21 PATENT NOV 30th 1858............................... Aqua $8-10
      Ground lip Mason shoulder seal

2093. MASON'S 22 PATENT NOV 30th 1858........   .... Aqua $8-10
      Ground lip Mason shoulder seal

2094. MASON'S 22 PATENT NOV 30th 1858.......   .... Aqua $8-10
      Ground lip Mason shoulder seal

2095. MASON'S 23 PATENT NOV 30th 1858.......   .... Aqua $8-10
      Ground lip Mason shoulder seal

2096. MASON'S 23 PATENT NOV 30th 1858.......   .... Aqua $8-10
      Ground lip Mason shoulder seal

2097. MASON'S 24 PATENT NOV 30th 1858.......   .... Aqua $8-10
      Ground lip Mason shoulder seal

#2094

2098. MASON'S 24 PATENT NOV 30th 1858............................... Aqua $8-10
      Ground lip Mason shoulder seal

2099. MASON'S 25 PATENT NOV 30th 1858............................... Aqua $8-10
      Ground lip Mason shoulder seal

2100. MASON'S 25 PATENT NOV 30th 1858............................... Aqua $8-10
      Ground lip Mason shoulder seal

2101. MASON'S 26 PATENT NOV 30th 1858............................... Aqua $8-10
      Ground lip Mason shoulder seal

2102. MASON'S 27 PATENT NOV 30th 1858............................... Aqua $8-10
      Ground lip Mason shoulder seal

2103. MASON'S 28 PATENT NOV 30th 1858............................... Aqua $8-10
      Ground lip Mason shoulder seal

2104. MASON'S 28 PATENT NOV 30th 1858............................... Aqua $12-15
      Reverse: CFJCo
      Ground lip Mason shoulder seal

2105. MASON'S 28 PATENT NOV 30th 1858............................... Aqua $8-10
      Ground lip Mason shoulder seal

2106. MASON'S 29 PATENT NOV 30th 1858............................... Aqua $8-10
      Ground lip Mason shoulder seal

2107. MASON'S 29 PATENT NOV 30th 1858............................... Aqua $8-10
      Ground lip Mason shoulder seal

2108. MASON'S 29 PATENT NOV 30th 1858 (reversed 3 & 5)..   .. Aqua $12-15
      Ground lip Mason shoulder seal

2109. MASON'S 29 PATENT NOV 30th 1858 (reversed 30 & 5).   .. Aqua $12-15
      1Ground ip Mason shoulder seal

2110. MASON'S 30 PATENT NOV 30th 1858................... Aqua $8-10
      Ground lip Mason shoulder seal

2111. MASON'S 30 PATENT NOV 30th 1858................... Aqua $8-10
      Ground lip Mason shoulder seal

#2108

2112. MASON'S 31 PATENT NOV 30th 1858............................... Aqua $8-10
      Ground lip Mason shoulder seal

2113. MASON'S 31 PATENT NOV 30th 1858............................... Aqua $8-10
      Ground lip Mason shoulder seal   Midget Pint, Aqua $30-35

2114. MASON'S D39 PATENT NOV 30th 1858..... .... Aqua $15-18
    Reverse: CFJCo
    Ground lip Mason shoulder seal

2115. MASON'S D69 PATENT NOV 30th 1858.... .... Aqua $10-12
    Ground lip Mason shoulder seal

2116. MASON'S D90 PATENT NOV 30th 1858.... .... Aqua $10-12
    Base: D90
    Ground lip Mason shoulder seal

2117. MASON'S 111 PATENT NOV 30th 1858.... .... Aqua $10-12
    Ground lip Mason shoulder seal   Apple Green $12-15
                     Amber $200-250
           Midget Pint, Aqua $30-35

#2115

2118. MASON'S 114 PATENT NOV 30th 1858...................................Aqua $10-12
    Ground lip Mason shoulder seal   Midget Pint, Aqua $30-35

2119. MASON'S 273 PATENT NOV 30th 1858...................................Aqua $15-18
    Reverse: CFJCo
    Ground lip Mason shoulder seal

2120. MASON'S 302 PATENT NOV 30th 1858.............. ......Aqua $15-18
    Reverse: CFJCo
    Ground lip Mason shoulder seal

2121. MASON'S 309 PATENT NOV 30th 1858.............. ......Aqua $10-12
    Ground lip Mason shoulder seal

2122. MASON'S 342 PATENT NOV 30th 1858.............. ......Aqua $10-12
    Ground lip Mason shoulder seal

2123. MASON'S 400 PATENT NOV 30th 1858.............. ......Aqua $10-12
    Ground lip Mason shoulder seal   Midget Pint, Aqua $30-35

2124. MASON'S 401 PATENT NOV 30th 1858...................................Aqua $15-18
    Rev. H. G. W.
    Ground lip Mason shoulder seal

#2121

2125. MASON'S 404 PATENT NOV 30th 1858............................... Aqua $10-12
    Ground lip Mason shoulder seal   Amber $200-250
           Midget Pint, Aqua $40-50
           Midget Pint, Amber $450-500

2126. MASON'S 404 PATENT NOV 30th 1858...................................Aqua $15-18
    Reverse: Shield emblem   Midget Pint, Aqua $40-45
    Ground lip Mason shoulder seal

2127. MASON'S D446 PATENT NOV 30th 1858.... ....Aqua $15-18
    Reverse: CFJCo
    Base: D446
    Ground lip Mason shoulder seal

2128. MASON'S 490 PATENT NOV 30th 1858... ....Aqua $15-18
    Reverse: CFJCo
    Ground lip Mason shoulder seal

    END OF "NUMBERED" MASONS

2129. MASON'S PATENTED JUNE 27th 1876.... ....Aqua $75-90
    Ground lip Mason shoulder seal

#2129

2130. MASON PATENT NOV 30th 1880.................... With zinc lid, Aqua $45-50
    Ground lip Mason shoulder seal   With zinc lid, Clear $45-50
    Closure as in #2131   With immerser lid, Aqua $60-75
           With immerser lid, Clear $60-75

2131. "MASON" PATENT NOV 30th 1880................... With zinc lid, Aqua $45-50
    Ground lip Mason shoulder seal   With zinc lid, Clear $45-50
    Zinc lid, or zinc lid with attached   With immerser lid, Aqua $60-75
     milkglass immerser   With immerser lid, Clear $60-75
    Zinc immerser cap: TradeMark The Mason
     Disk Protector Cap Patd Nov 30 1880
    Milkglass immerser: Patented Nov.30.1880
               Or: Patd. Nov.23.75 Sept.12.76 Nov.30.80
                  July.20.1886
               Or: Patd. Nov.23.75 Sept.12.76 Nov.30.80
                  July.20.1880

2132. MASON PORCELAIN LINED....................................... Aqua $18-20
    Ground lip Mason shoulder seal

2133. MASON'S (shield) UNION............................. Aqua $140-150
    Ground lip
    Zinc lid, with smooth enameled liner, marked on
     outside: Masons Union Pat'd Feb'y 15, 1859
           Always Safe (shield in center)
     Or: unlined zinc lid, two vertical prongs
            soldered on top & marked only
            with a shield in center of lid
    Both lids are illustrated at right.

#2133

2134. MASON VACUUM KNOWLTON PATENT JUNE 9th 1908..... Aqua $40-45
    Smooth lip Glass lid & wire clamp   Lt. cornflower Blue $50-55
    Lid: Knowlton Patent June 9 1908

2135. MASTODON.. Aqua $50-60
    Base: T. A. Evans Pittsburgh, Pa.
    Groove ring wax sealer, pressed laid-on ring

2136. MATTHIAS & HARRISON PATENT (on base)...........................Clear $3-5
    Smooth lip Glass stopper
    English product jar

2137. MATTHIAS & HARRISON LIVERPOOL PATENT (on base).................Clear $3-5
    Smooth lip Glass stopper
    English product jar

2138. MAXAMS PRESERVING HOUSE NEW YORK (within circle).............. Aqua $35-40
    Base: Cohansey Glass Mfg. Co. Philada.
    Ground lip Cohansey lid & wire clamp
    Pint Product jar

2139. D. H. McALPINE & CO. NEW YORK (on base)...........   Amber $35-40
    Ground lip Glass lid & screw band
    8-sided Product jar

2140. G. A. McCARTHEY & BROS. MAYSVILLE, KY.....   ...... $40-50
    Gray stoneware jar with blue stenciling
    Wax seal groove

#2141

2141. THE McCARTY VACUUM FRUIT JAR PAT MAR.7.1899
    THE FRANK. GLASS CO SOLE MFGS WELLSBURG. W. VA.................Clear $100-125
    Stopper neck finish for milkglass stopper
    Stopper: McCarty Pat. Mar 7 1899

2142. McCARTY PAT MAR 7 1899 (on milkglass stopper).................Clear $50-75
    Jar is unmarked

2143. M C Co. 3 (on base).. Aqua $15-18
    Groove ring wax sealer, pressed laid-on ring

2144. W. McC & Co. PITTS- (on base)..........................Aqua $40-50
      Closure: Wax dipped cork
      Jar is made with 4 Pc. mold

2145. Dr. L. McCOLLUM & CO. MANUFACTURERS TIFFIN, OHIO.......Aqua $50-60
      Ground lip Mason shoulder seal   Clear $50-60
      This interesting jar was reported by
      Claude Boone, who mentions that Dr.
      McCollum practicied medicine in Tiffin,
      Ohio during the late 1880's.

2146. THE McCORMICK MANF'G COY LONDON CANADA.................Clear $3-5
      Smooth lip Screw cover
      Canadian product jar

#2145

2147. McDONALD PERFECT SEAL (within circle)...................Ball Blue $4-6
      Smooth lip Lightning dimple neck seal

2148. McDONALD NEW PERFECT SEAL (no circle)...................Ball Blue $4-6
      Smooth lip Lightning beaded neck seal

2149. McDONALD NEW PERFECT SEAL (within circle)
      PATd JULY 14, 1908 (all on front)......................Ball Blue $4-6
      Smooth lip Lightning dimple neck seal

2150. McDONALD PERFECT SEAL (within circle)
      PATd JULY 14, 1908 (all on front)......................Ball Blue $4-6
      Word NEW has been erased
      Smooth lip Lightning dimple neck seal

2151. McDONALD NEW PERFECT SEAL (without circle)
      PATd JULY 14, 1908 (all on front)......................Ball Blue $4-6
      Smooth lip Lightning dimple neck seal

#2152

2152. McDONALD NEW PERFFCT SEAL (within circle, error)
      PATd JULY 14, 1908 (all on front)......................Ball Blue $6-8
      Smooth lip Lightning dimple neck seal

2153. S. McKEE & CO. PITTS PA. (& 7 dots) (on base).........Aqua $18-20
      Groove ring wax sealer, pressed laid-on ring

2154. S. McKEE & CO. PITTS PA. (on base)...................Aqua $18-20
      Groove ring wax sealer, pressed laid-on ring

2155. S. McKEE & CO. (on base)..............................Aqua $18-20
      Groove ring wax sealer, pressed laid-on ring

2156. S. M KEE & CO (on base)...............................Aqua $18-20
      Groove ring wax sealer, pressed laid-on ring
      The tin wax seal lid for the S. McKee jars is
      marked as illustrated at right. Value would
      be higher with correct lid.

#2156

2157. S. McKEE & CO. (on shoulder)..........................Aqua $30-35
      Groove ring wax sealer, pressed laid-on ring

2158. S. McKEE & CO. (on shoulder)..........................Aqua $30-35
      Base: S. McKee & Co. Pitts. Pa.
      Groove ring wax sealer, pressed laid-on ring

2159. PATENT APPLIED FOR (on glass lid)....................Clear $250-300
      Base: Pontil scar Glass stopper
      The jar has a flanged lip which is ground.
      The bottom of the stopper is also ground.

#2159

2160. F & J McKEE PITTSBURGH PA (on glass lid)..............Clear $250-300
      Base has a pontil scar
      The jar has a flanged lip which is ground.
      The bottom of the lid is also ground, and
        the seal was made by wetting the two surfaces
        and joining. The cooling fruit caused a vac-
        uum and aided in sealing.

      #2160

2161. McMECHENS ALWAYS THE BEST OLD VIRGINIA
      WHEELING, W. VA. (within a circle, framing a
      black woman, holding a box lettered "Old
      Virginia Goods")..Clear $125-150
      Flower & leaf design around jar
      Ground lip 1 Pc. screw lid or insert &
        screw band   Product jar

2162. McMECHENS ALWAYS THE BEST OLD VIRGINIA
      WHEELING, W. VA. (within a circle, framing a
      black woman, holding a box lettered "Old
      Virginia Goods")..Clear $100-125
      The jar is square with a ribbed design
        around lower portion. Closure unknown
      A paper label found on the jar reads:
        "McMechens Wine Flavored Mustard, Wheeling,
        W. Va."   Product jar

      #2161

2163. MEDFORD PRESERVED FRUIT BUFFALO N.Y................. Aqua $175-200
      Stopper neck finish for cork

2164. H. H. MELICK ROSEVILLE, O............................. $40-45
      Gray stoneware with marking incised
      Wax seal groove

      #2162

2165. METRO EASI-PAK MASON.................................Clear $1-3
      Smooth lip Mason beaded neck seal
      Glass lid insert: Metro Easi-Pak Mason
      Made circa 1942-1946 only

2166. MFA (on shield having stars & stripes).............Clear $1-3
      Smooth lip Mason beaded neck seal
      Coffee jar used by the Missouri Farmers
        Association

      #2166

2167. M. F. G. Co. (on base).............................Aqua $15-18
      Groove ring wax sealer, pressed laid-on ring   Amber $75-85

2168. M. F. J. Co. 8 (on base)...........................Aqua $15-18
      Groove ring wax sealer, pressed laid-on ring   Amber $75-85
                                              Yellow Amber $75-85
                                                     Green $20-25

2169. M. G. Co. (on base).............................. Aqua $25-30
      Groove ring wax sealer, pressed laid-on ring   Amber $85-100
      Jar is made with 4 Pc. mold   Pushed-up base

2170. M. G. Co. (on base)................................. Aqua $18-20
      Groove ring wax sealer, pressed   Amber $75-85
        laid-on ring   Lt. Amber $70-80
                                                     Citron $60-70
                                                      Green $20-25
                                         Deep Yellow Green $60-70

2171. MGMCo (monogram)...................... Midget Pint, Aqua $40-50
      Ground lip Mason shoulder seal   Midget Pint, Clear $40-50

      #2171

-156-

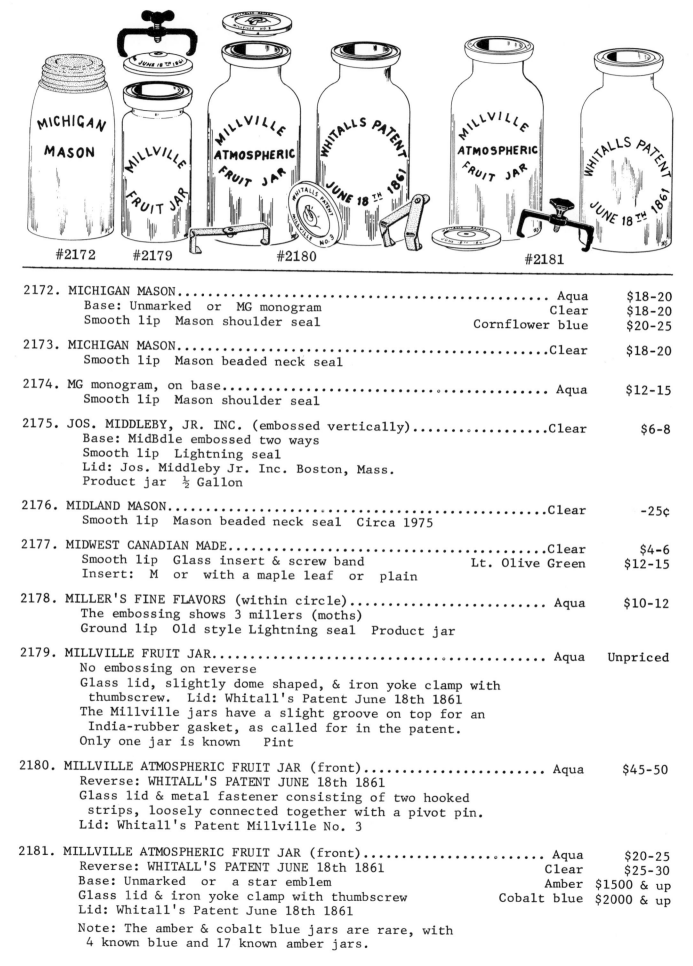

#2172   #2179   #2180   #2181

2172. MICHIGAN MASON.. Aqua $18-20
     Base: Unmarked   or   MG monogram   Clear $18-20
     Smooth lip   Mason shoulder seal   Cornflower blue $20-25

2173. MICHIGAN MASON...Clear $18-20
     Smooth lip   Mason beaded neck seal

2174. MG monogram, on base..................................... Aqua $12-15
     Smooth lip   Mason shoulder seal

2175. JOS. MIDDLEBY, JR. INC. (embossed vertically)................Clear $6-8
     Base: MidBdle embossed two ways
     Smooth lip   Lightning seal
     Lid: Jos. Middleby Jr. Inc. Boston, Mass.
     Product jar   ½ Gallon

2176. MIDLAND MASON...Clear   -25¢
     Smooth lip   Mason beaded neck seal   Circa 1975

2177. MIDWEST CANADIAN MADE...Clear $4-6
     Smooth lip   Glass insert & screw band   Lt. Olive Green $12-15
     Insert: M   or   with a maple leaf   or   plain

2178. MILLER'S FINE FLAVORS (within circle)........................ Aqua $10-12
     The embossing shows 3 millers (moths)
     Ground lip   Old style Lightning seal   Product jar

2179. MILLVILLE FRUIT JAR... Aqua   Unpriced
     No embossing on reverse
     Glass lid, slightly dome shaped, & iron yoke clamp with
       thumbscrew.   Lid: Whitall's Patent June 18th 1861
     The Millville jars have a slight groove on top for an
       India-rubber gasket, as called for in the patent.
     Only one jar is known   Pint

2180. MILLVILLE ATMOSPHERIC FRUIT JAR (front)........................ Aqua $45-50
     Reverse: WHITALL'S PATENT JUNE 18th 1861
     Glass lid & metal fastener consisting of two hooked
       strips, loosely connected together with a pivot pin.
     Lid: Whitall's Patent Millville No. 3

2181. MILLVILLE ATMOSPHERIC FRUIT JAR (front)........................ Aqua $20-25
     Reverse: WHITALL'S PATENT JUNE 18th 1861   Clear $25-30
     Base: Unmarked   or   a star emblem   Amber $1500 & up
     Glass lid & iron yoke clamp with thumbscrew   Cobalt blue $2000 & up
     Lid: Whitall's Patent June 18th 1861

     Note: The amber & cobalt blue jars are rare, with
     4 known blue and 17 known amber jars.

2182. MILLVILLE ATMOSPHERIC FRUIT JAR (front)........................ Aqua $25-30
      Reverse: WHITALL'S PATENT JUNE 18th 1861 (reversed 6)
      Glass lid & iron yoke clamp with thumbscrew
      Lid: Whitall's Patent June 18th 1861
      Pint

2183. MILLVILLE ATMOSPHERIC FRUIT JAR (front)........................ Aqua $75-95
      Reverse: WHITALL'S PATENT JUNE 18th 1861
      Glass lid & iron yoke clamp with thumbscrew
      Lid is slightly dome shaped and marked as in #2182
      The clamp has rounded shoulders, and shoulders of
        the jar are squarish. Quart

2184. Same as #2183, except in size holding 56 ounces..... Aqua $75-100

2185. MILLVILLE (front) Reverse: HITALL'S PATEN.......... Aqua $45-55
      Glass lid & iron yoke clamp with thumbscrew
      Lid: Whitall's Patent June 18th 1861
      This is a ½ Pint, made from a Pint mold which
      was cut down, thereby eliminating some of the
      embossing. Base is unmarked.

#2186

2186. MILLVILLE (front) Reverse: HITALL'S PATEN..... .... Aqua $45-55
      Base: W. T. & Co. U.S.A.
      Closure as in #2185
      ½ Pint

2187. MILLVILLE WTCo IMPROVED..................... ...... Aqua $45-50
      Ground lip Glass insert & screw band   Cobalt Blue Unpriced
      Insert: Whitall's Patent June 18th 1861
          Berries or grape cluster in center
      Note: Shards of a cobalt blue jar have been
      dug. A complete and whole jar has not yet
      been reported.

#2187

2188. MILLVILLE (and upper portion of monogram)............. .. Aqua $100-125
      Ground lip Closure as in #2187
      This is a ½ Pint, made from a Pint mold which
      was cut down, thereby eliminating some of the
      embossing.

#2188

2189. MINNESOTA STONEWARE CO. REDWING (on base).......................... $15-18
      White stoneware jar & lid

2190. MISSION TRADE (bell) MARK MASON JAR
      MADE IN CALIFORNIA (all on front)............................Aqua $8-10
      Base: Mf'd By W. J. Latchford Co.   Clear $8-10
          Los Angeles Calif.   ½ Pint, Aqua $18-20
      Smooth lip Mason beaded neck seal   ½ Pint, Clear $12-15

2191. MISSION TRADE (bell) MARK MASON JAR................. .....Aqua $8-10
      Base: Mf'd By W. J. Latchford Co.   Clear $8-10
          Los Angeles Calif.
      Smooth lip Mason beaded neck seal

2192. MISSION TRADE (bell) MARK MASON JAR
      MADE IN CALIFORINA (error)....................... ....Aqua $12-15
      Base: Mf'd By W. J. Latchford Co.
          Los Angeles, Calif.
      Smooth lip Mason beaded neck seal   #2194

2193. M. J. CO. (on base)................................ ... Aqua $18-20
      Groove ring wax sealer, pressed laid-on ring   Amber $85-100

2194. THE MODEL JAR PATd AUG. 27. 1867........................... Aqua $250-300
      Ground lip   Complete with orig. lid, Aqua $500 & up
      Cardboard lid as in #2195

2195. THE MODEL JAR PATd AUG 27. 1867 ROCHESTER N.Y.................. Aqua $300-325
      Ground lip Cardboard cover   Complete with orig. lid, Aqua $550 & up
      Cover: The Model Jar Patented Aug. 27 1867
         J. J. Van Zandt Proprietor And
         Manufacturer Rochester N. Y.

2196. MODEL MASON...Clear $12-15
      Smooth lip Mason shoulder seal

2197. PATENT NOV 30th 1858 2 (front) Reverse: MOLD PREVENTER........ Aqua $300-350
      Ground lip Mason shoulder seal

2198. MOM'S (mom) MASON JAR...Clear   -50¢
      Base: Home Products Columbus, Ohio
      Smooth lip Mason beaded neck seal
      Circa 1975 Pint & Quart

2199. MONARCH (on shield with stars & stripes).......................Clear $6-8
      Smooth lip Old style Lightning seal Product jar

2200. MONARCH FINER FOODS (around circle with lion's head)..........Clear $2-3
      Smooth lip Mason beaded neck seal Product jar

2201. MOORE BROTHERS (in script)..................................... Aqua $250-300
      Stopper neck finish for cork or Willoughby stopple

2202. MOORE BROTHERS & CO (in script)............................... Aqua $250-300
      Stopper neck finish for cork or Willoughby stopple

#2195   #2198   #2201   #2202   #2203   #2204   #2205

2203. MOORE BROTHERS FISLERVILLE N.J. (in block letters)............. Aqua $250-300
      Stopper neck finish for cork or Willoughby stopple

2204. MOORE'S PATENT DEC 3d 1861..................................... Aqua $70-75
      Glass lid & iron yoke clamp with thumbscrew
      Lid: Patented Dec 3d 1861
      Note: A number of Cobalt blue Moore lids have been found,
        but so far a matching jar has not been reported.

2205. JOHN M MOORE & CO MANUFACTURERS FISLERVILLE N.J.
      PATENTED DEC 3d 1861 (all in script except date line)......... Aqua $125-150
      Glass lid & iron yoke clamp with thumbscrew
      Lid: Patented Dec 3d 1861

2206. JOHN M MOORE & CO MANUFACTURERS FISLERVILLE N.J.
      PATENTED DEC 3d 1861 (all in script except date line)......... Aqua $125-150
      This jar is identical to #2205 except the mouth is smaller,
      using a lid which is 2 1/8 instead of the usual 2 5/8.

2207. JOHN M MOORE & CO MANUFACTURERS FISLERVILLE N.J.
    PATENTED DEC 3d 1861 (all block letters except first line)..... Aqua $125-150
      Glass lid & iron yoke clamp with thumbscrew
      Lid: Patented Dec 3d 1861

2208. JOHN M MOORE & CO MANUFACTURERS FISLERVILLE N. J. (front)...... Aqua $350-400
      Reverse: J.B. WILSON'S AIR TIGHT FRUIT JAR
                PATENTED JUNE 20th 1861
      Glass lid & iron yoke clamp with thumbscrew
      Lid: Patented June 20 1861

2209. MORSE'S CHICAGO...Clear $2-3
      Smooth lip Old style Lightning seal
      Square product jar with arched panels on each side

2210. FINE TABLE SALT FROM J.T. MORTON LEADENHALL
    STREET LONDON..Blue $20-25
      Applied lip with ledge for cork
      Product jar

2211. MOTHERS JAR TRADE MARK R.E.TONGUE & BROS. INC.
    PHILA. PA. (all on front).............................Aqua $25-30
      Smooth lip Mason shoulder seal Wide mouth

#2210

2212. MOUNTAIN MASON..Clear $12-15
      Base: Unmarked
      Smooth lip Mason beaded neck seal

2213. MOUNTAIN MASON..Clear $12-15
      Base: IGCo monogram
      Smooth lip Mason beaded neck seal

2214. M & L (on front)..Aqua $150-175
      Base: Mueller & Lindsay Birmingham Glass Co.
          Pitts Pa.
      Groove ring wax sealer, pressed laid-on ring

2215. H. K. MULFORD CHEMISTS PHILADELPHIA (vertically).......Amber $25-30
      Ground lip Mason shoulder seal
      Unmarked metal screw cap
      A square shaped product jar

2216. MUTUAL GLASS CO. PITT. (on base)........................Aqua $20-25
      Groove ring wax sealer, pressed laid-on ring

#2217

2217. MY CHOICE...Aqua $175-200
      Base: Pat Jan 3rd 1888   Amber $450 & up
      Ground lip Glass lid & wire clamp
      Lid: Pat. Jan 3rd 1888
        Lid is marked on the inside so that it
        reads correctly from outside.
      Only 4 amber jars are presently known.

2218. MYERS TEST JAR..Aqua $75-100
      Ground lip Glass lid & brass clamp
      Clamp: Unmarked
        Or: P. M. Hinman Pat Apl For

#2218

2219. MYERS PAT'D 1868 TEST JAR...............................Aqua $75-100
      Ground lip Metal lid with attached brass clamp
      Clamp marked P. M. Hinman Pat Apl For

#2219

2220. N within star (on base).. Aqua $15-18
     Groove ring wax sealer, pressed laid-on ring   Amber $75-85

2221. N within star, P (on base)..................................... Aqua $15-18
     Groove ring wax sealer, pressed laid-on ring

2222. N within star, P (on base)..................................... Aqua $20-25
     Front: Erased Western Pride Patented June 22 1875
     Groove ring wax sealer, pressed laid-on ring

2223. NABOB (vertically on jar)......................................Clear $1-3
     Smooth lip Mason beaded neck seal
     The Nabob jars are Canadian coffee jars

2224. NABOB BRAND..Clear $1-3
     Smooth lip Mason beaded neck seal

2225. NABOB BRAND KELLY DOUGLAS CO. LIMITED..........................Clear $1-3
     Smooth lip Mason beaded neck seal

2226. NABOB BRAND MADE IN CANADA KELLY DOUGLAS Co. LIMITED...........Clear $1-3
     Smooth lip Mason beaded neck seal

2227. NABOB BRAND KD 32 OZ. NET......................................Clear $1-3
     Smooth lip Mason beaded neck seal

2228. NABOB BRAND KD...Clear $1-3
     Smooth lip Mason beaded neck seal

2229. NAMENLOS (on front).. Aqua $1-3
     Smooth lip Metal cap with glass insert
     Insert: Konservenglas Dose Namenlos Zum Offnen
             Hierein Drucken
     A foreign jar

2230. NATIONAL (on base)...Clear $2-3
     Smooth lip Mason beaded neck seal

2231. NATIONAL (in script, on front)........................Clear $8-10
     Smooth lip Mason beaded neck seal
     Square shape

2232. NATIONAL SUPER MASON..................................Clear $8-10
     Smooth lip Mason beaded neck seal
     Square shape

#2232

2233. NATIONAL JELLY PAT DEC 7 1875 (on lid)................Clear $8-10
     Jelly tumbler, glass lid

2234. NATIONAL 1.. Aqua $50-75
     Stopper neck finish for cork stopper

     Also see UNION 1, jar No. 2838

2235. NATIONAL PATENTED JUNE 27 1876....................... Aqua $150-175
     Ground lip Metal lid
     Lugs on the outside of jar neck, & on
      inside of the lid.

#2235

2236. NATIONAL (shield) BUTTER CAN................................. Aqua $250-300
     Reverse: shield emblem
     Ground lip Glass lid & iron yoke clamp with tension spring

2237. NATIONAL (shield) PRESERVE CAN............................... Aqua $250-300
     Reverse: EARL'S PATENT FEB 2nd 1864 (around anchor)
     Ground lip Glass lid & iron yoke clamp with tension spring

     Also see AMERICAN IMPROVED, jar No. 74
          IMPROVED MERCANTILE, jar No. 1306

2238. CONGRATULATIONS 25th ANNIVERSARY NESTLE FREEHOLD PLANT
     1948-1973 R. SCHUESSLER PLANT MGR. (all on front).............Clear $2-4
     Reverse: D. Andrew Jewski * J. Barkalow E. Boldt *
     F. Bostjancic * J. Bravo E. Chmielewski * T. Cutchall
     P. Deangelis * E. Dorsett * D. Eaves A. Franklin *
     H. Fechner * A. Flora Jr. H. Graham * S. Hulse * J. Jackson
     F. Kravchak * E. McGuigan W. Madden * I. Merola * F. Osborn
     B. Ostergaard * B. Pannkuk L. Perdonia * H. Peterson
     P. Pezold * M. Pydyszewski J. Ratshin* A. Rossi
     R. Schuessler * C. Soini J. Smithson * A. Sotl J. Stans-
     field * J. Surette D. Sucksland * E. Surgent S. Tanay *
     D. Vosburg A. Swanson * A. Zuk * S. Zwolinski * And Local
     #17 Teamster's Union
     Smooth lip Metal lid, press-on and turn Product jar

    NEW GEM see jar No. 1088

2239. NEWMAN'S PURE GOLD BAKING POWDER FAIRPORT N. Y................ Aqua $15-20
     Ground lip Unlined zinc screw cover
     Product jar

#2236   #2237   #2240   #2239   #2241

2240. NEWMAN'S PATENT DEC. 20th 1859................................Aqua $300-350
     Ground lip Metal cover with india-rubber band

2241. NEW MASON VACUUM FRUIT JAR KNOWLTON PATENT JUNE 9th 1908........Aqua $40-45
     Smooth lip Glass lid & wire clamp   Cornflower Blue $50-60
     Lid: Knowlton Patent June 9th 1908

     Also see KNOWLTON VACUUM jar No. 1432 MANSFIELD jar No. 1619
          MASON VACUUM KNOWLTON PATENT jar No. 2134

2242. NEWMARK SPECIAL EXTRA.......................................Clear $8-10
     Base: Mfd. For M. A. Newmark & Co. Los Angeles, Calif.
     Smooth lip Mason beaded neck seal

2243. NEWMARK SPECIAL EXTRA FRUIT JAR......................................Clear $8-10
     Base: Mfd. For M. A. Newmark & Co. Los Angeles, Calif.
     Smooth lip Mason beaded neck seal

2244. NEWMARK SPECIAL EXTRA MASON JAR.................................Clear $8-10
     Base as in #2243   Pale Green $8-10
     Smooth lip Mason beaded neck seal

2245. NEWMARK SPECIAL EXTRA MASON JAR (with fleur-de-lis)............Clear $8-10
     Base as in #2243   Pale Green $8-10
     Smooth lip Mason beaded neck seal

     NEW PARAGON, see jar No. 2289

2246. THE NEW (IGCo monogram) PERFECTION.........   ....Clear $30-35
     Smooth lip Old style Lightning seal
     Note: The correct identification of the
     monogram has not been determined for
     certain. It could be LPRLCo for the
     patentee of the Perfection jars (Lewis
     P.R. LeCompte), or it could be a mono-
     gram for the Illinois Glass Company who
     made some of the Perfection jars.

     N E PLUS ULTRA see jars No. 475 thru 478

#2246

2247. NIAGARA.......................................Light Green $75-100
     Ground lip Old style Lightning seal Wide Mouth
     An Australian jar

2248. THE NIFTY PAT. APPLIED FOR.......................Clear $25-30
     Ground lip Glass lid & spring band clamp

2249. NO. 1..Aqua $35-40
     Groove ring wax sealer, pressed laid-on ring   Amber $125 & up
                                                     Citron $90-100
                                           Olive Green $90-100

2250. NONPAREIL PATENTED JULY 17 1866.............Aqua $200-250
     Ground lip Metal cap   Vaseline $250-275

2251. NORGE (in script)...............................Clear $8-10
     Base: Drammens Glass DG
     Smooth lip Mason beaded neck seal
     Made in Norway

2252. MADE BY NORTON BROS. CHICAGO UNSCREW TO LEFT
     PAT'D MAR. 31. 68 MAR. 4.73 DEC. 7. 1880 (on lid)................... $20-25
     Tin can. Carrying handle soldered to lid
     The author's example of this can has a paper
     label showing it was used for Dunham's
     Cocoanut, from Dunham Mfg. Co., St. Louis, Mo.
     The bottom of the can has a paper label
     giving instructions on how to reuse the can
     for home canning.

#2247

2253. NW ELECTROGLAS MASON...........................Clear $2-3
     Smooth lip Mason beaded neck seal

2254. NW ELECTROGLAS WIDE MOUTH MASON.................Clear $2-3
     Smooth lip Mason beaded neck seal

     NWGCo WHEELING see jar No. 2954

#2253

2255. O. C.. Aqua $45-50
         Fruit bottle with applied lip & cork stopper

2256. OC monogram... Aqua $15-20
         Base: Putnam
         Ground lip Old style Lightning seal
         Tall, slender jar

2257. NO 2 OHIO MADE BY THE OHIO FRUIT JAR Co. OF
      UPPER SANDUSKY, O. (all on front)............... Aqua $350-400
         Reverse: A. W. BRINKERHOFF'S PATENT
                  MARCH 14 1876
         Jar has a groove on top for sealing wax
         Tin lid and 3 pronged wire clamp

2258. NO 2 OHIO MADE BY THE OHIO FRUIT JAR Co. OF
      UPPER SANDUSKY, O. (all on front)............... Aqua $350-400
         Reverse: A. W. BRINKERHOFF'S PATENT
                  MARCH 14 1876
         Jar does not have a groove on top
         Ground lip Glass lid & cast iron & wire
                     clamp
         Lid: dome shaped, & has 3 glass protrusions
              on top to hold wire clamp in place.
              Marked No. 2

2259. THE OHIO NO. 3 1876 MADE BY THE OHIO FRUIT
      JAR CO. OF UPPER SANDUSKY, O. (all on front). ... Aqua $350-400
         Reverse: PATENTED MARCH 14 1876 BY
                  A. W. BRINKERHOFF
         Jar does not have a groove on top
         Ground lip Glass lid & cast iron & wire
                     clamp
         Lid: dome shaped, & has 3 glass protrusions
              on top to hold wire clamp in place.
              Marked No. 3

2260. NO 10 OHIO EUREKA 1876 TRY ME   THE OHIO
      FRUIT JAR COMPANY UPPER SANDUSKY OHIO (front)... Clear $350-400
         Reverse: FOR FRUIT BUTTER HONEY LARD
                  EGGS & C A. W. BRINKERHOFF'S
                  PATENT MARCH 14 1876
         Jar does not have a groove on top
         Closure as in #2259

2261. HONEY JAR 1876 NO. 5 MADE BY THE OHIO FRUIT
      JAR CO. OF UPPER SANDUSKY, O. (all on front).. Clear $250-300
         Reverse: PATENTED MARCH 14 1876 BY
                  A. W. BRINKERHOFF
         Ground lip Glass lid & 3 pronged wire clamp

2262. OHIO QUALITY MASON........................... Clear $10-12
         Smooth lip Mason beaded neck seal

2263. OHIO QUALITY MASON (diff. embossing)......... Clear $10-12
         Smooth lip Mason beaded neck seal

2264. OVGCo JAR 1881............................... Aqua $75-100
         Ground lip Mason shoulder seal   Cornflower blue $125-150

#2257

#2259

#2260

2265. OVGCo JAR 1881 (with erased word ECLIPSE)...................... Aqua $75-100
       Ground lip Mason shoulder seal   Cornflower Blue $125-150

2266. OK... Aqua $200-250
       Top is depressed to form a wax seal groove
       Made with 3 Pc. mold, inner lip is ground

2267. Unmarked jar, same shape as #2266 .... Aqua $75-100

2268. OK encircled by PAT'd FEBy 9th 1864 REISd
       JUNE 22d 1867.............................. .... Aqua $200-250
       Ground lip Press-down glass lid
       Only 1 jar is presently known

2269. OLD CITY MANF Co. REG. QUEBEC. PURE JAMS......... ....Clear $12-15
       Smooth lip Mason beaded neck seal Metal lid #2266   Lt. Green $12-15

2270. OLD CITY MANF Co. LIMITED QUEBEC. PURE JAMS...................Clear $12-15
       Smooth lip Mason beaded neck seal   Lt. Green $12-15
       Canadian product jars

2271. OLD JUDGE COFFEE (around an owl)................................Clear $1-3
       Smooth lip Mason beaded neck seal
       Product jar

2272. OLD STYLE MUSTARD 16 OZ (front) Reverse: fruit medallion......Clear   -25¢
       Base 1975
       Smooth lip Mason beaded neck seal
       Lid: One piece lid, marked Old Style Reusable
            Canner With the Click
       Or: One piece lid, with rim marked, Contains
            Mustard Seed, Distilled Vinegar, Salt,
            Tumeric & Spices, Mfd. By The Olds
            Products Co. Chicago, Ill. 60612
       Pint Product jar

#2272

2273. OPLER BROTHERS, INC. (around OB monogram) COCOA
       AND CHOCOLATE NEW YORK U.S.A.......................................Clear $4-6
       Base: Smalley, Kivlan & Onthank
       Smooth lip Lightning dimple neck seal
       Product jar

2274. OPLER BROTHERS, INC. (around OB monogram) COCOA
       AND CHOCOLATE NEW YORK U.S.A.........................Clear $4-6
       Base: Pat'd July 14, 1908
       Smooth lip Lightning beaded neck seal
       Product jar

2275. OPLER BROTHERS, INC. (around OB monogram) COCOA
       AND CHOCOLATE NEW YORK U.S.A. 32 OZ NEW WEIGHT....Clear $4-6
       Smooth lip Glass lid & twin wire side clamps
       Lid: KantKrack Patd Feb 23 09
       Product jar

#2276

2276. N. OSBURN ROCHESTER N.Y............................. .... Aqua $225-250
       Stopper neck finish for waxed cork

2277. N. OSBORN ROCHESTER N.Y............................. .... Aqua $225-250
       Stopper neck finish for waxed cork

2278. OTTWELL'S PICKLES..................................... .... Aqua $10-12
       Smooth lip Glass lid & screw band
       Canadian product jar

#2277

2279. OSOTITE (within diamond)... Clear $8-10
    Smooth lip Glass lid & spring metal clamp
    Lid: Pat. Pending
    Paraffine was used to seal the jar, along with
      the lid & clamp.

2280. OURS.. Clear $1-3
    Smooth lip Glass lid & screw band
    Lid: Scene with house & palm tree
    Product jar

2281. OUR PURE-FOOD PRODUCTS... Clear $1-3
    Smooth lip Glass lid & screw band
    Product jar

#2279

2282. R.E.T. & BROS. CO. INC. OUR SEAL PHILA PA U.S.A.
    Within double diamonds, within circle, on front.............. Clear $8-10
        Base: R. E. Tongue & Bros. Co. Inc. Phila, Pa.
            Our-Seal Patented Jan. 5 1904
        Smooth lip Old style Lightning seal
    Lid, inside: Our-Seal
    The sealing surface has a slight annular groove
      for a packing ring, & a small thread on the neck,
      as called for in the January 5 1904 patent.

COLLECTORS NOTES

2283. PACIFIC MASON.......................................Clear $8-10
       Base: PC in broken rectangle
       Smooth lip   Mason beaded neck seal

2284. CERTIFIED QUALITY PACIFIC OYSTERS
       ONE PINT (an all four sides of jar)...............Clear $1-2
       Base: Pacific Coast Oyster Growers
            Association NW
       Smooth lip   Product jar   #2285

2285. THE F. H. PALMER MFG. Co. N. Y. PATd NOV 15 '87 (on lid).......Clear $10-12
       Jelly tumbler with metal lid, wire clamp
       welded to the lid
       Base: John Lucas, Philadelphia & New York

2286. PANSY...Clear $125-150
       Ground lip   Unmarked glass insert &   Lt. Green $125-150
       screw band   Wide mouth jar   Amber $450 & up
       Some of the Pansy jars are perfectly
       round.   Others are round with twenty
       panels reaching to the shoulder.
       Canadian sealer

2287. PANSY (superimposed over erased BEST).......Amber $450 & up
       Closure as in #2286
       Canadian sealer

2288. PAPPY (script)..............................Clear   -$1
       Smooth lip   Metal screw cover
       Product jar

                  #2286

2289. NEW PARAGON...Aqua $90-100
       Ground lip   Glass lid & metal band
       Lid: The New Paragon Patented
       The metal band has 3 equally spaced notches
       on the sides, with the metal bent inward
       to form lugs to catch on the glass lugs on
       the neck of the jar. A variation of the
       band has 3 equally spaced metal lugs show-
       on the inside of band only. The notches
       cut into the band to form the lugs, were
       filled with solder, for a smooth outside
       finish.

2290. NEW PARAGON 3...............................Aqua $90-100
       Ground lip   Closure as in #2289

2291. NEW PARAGON 5...............................Aqua $90-100
       Ground lip   Closure as in #2289

2292. THE PARAGON VALVE JAR PATd APRIL 19th 1870........Aqua $125-150
       Base: McE & Co
       Ground lip   Unmarked glass lid with high
       center, & 3 notches on outside rim.
       Metal band as described in #2289
       The jar neck is threaded. 2 Spring wires,
       with one of each fitting into an inden-
       tation in the neck. The lugs on the metal
       band engage on the wire, giving it spring
       valve action.

                #2292

2293. PATENT APPL'D FOR.. Aqua $200-250
        Ground lip Glass lid & metal band clamp
        The clamp has a hole in center to fit
         over a raised hump in center of lid. Also
         found with a metal lid.

2294. PATENT APPLIED FOR... Aqua $45-50
        Base: S. K. & Co. (around N within star)
          Or: Unmarked
        Groove ring wax sealer, pressed laid-on ring

        PATENTED OCT. 19 1858, see jar No. 1212

2295. PATENT SEPT. 18. 1860.. Aqua $75-80
        Wax seal groove formed by downward pressure   Lt. Cobalt Blue Unpriced
         on the blowpipe, while form was still hot
         from the mold.

2296. PATENT SEPT. 18. 1860 (no crossbar on A)....   .... Aqua $75-85
        Wax seal groove as in #2295

2297. Unembossed jar, same shape as #2295 & 2296   .... Aqua $35-40

2298. PATENT SEPT. 18. 1860.....................   .... Aqua $85-100
        Wax seal groove formed as in #2295
        This variation from the William Dudley
         collection is slightly different in
         shape.   #2295

2299. PATd JULY 18 1854 MAY 22d 1860 REISd NOV 24 1863... Aqua $90-100
        Marked on lid only, jar is unmarked
        Metal press-down cover

2300. PATENT JUNE 27 1865... Aqua $200-250
        Ground lip Glass lid & metal band clamp
        The clamp has a hole in the center to fit
         over the raised hump in center of lid.
        Neck of jar has lugs.   #2298

2301. PATENTED JUNE 27 1865.. Aqua $200-250
        Ground lip Closure as in #2300

2302. PATENTED MAR. 22. 1870 (on tin wax seal lid)......... Aqua $30-35
        Jar is unmarked
        Groove ring wax sealer, pressed laid-on ring
        The lid has a series of grooves around the
         outer edge to aid in holding the wire clamp
         in place.

        PATENTED DEC 17th 1872, see jar Nos. 1444 & 1445

2303. PATNd MARCH 2nd 1876 (on tin wax seal lid)...... Aqua $30-35
        Jar is unmarked
        Groove ring wax sealer, pressed laid-on ring #2303

2304. CAP PAT AUG. 15 1876 (on base)............................... Aqua $40-50
        Ground lip Metal cap
        The jar neck has 4 equally spaced lugs.
        Metal cap with flarged bottom edge, with
         4 indentations in the sides to engage
         on the lugs of the jar neck

2305. PAT. OCT. 31 '76 (on tin wax seal lid)....................... Aqua $30-35
        Jar is unmarked
        Groove ring wax sealer, pressed laid-on ring

2306. PAT. APRIL 17th 1877 (on lid).................................Light Green $60-70
      Ground lip Glass lid & wire clamp
      The jar neck has a circular depression
      on each side for the ends of the wire
      clamp.

2307. PATENTED AUG. 8th 1882 (on lid).....................Light Green $60-70
      Ground lip Glass lid & wire clamp
      The jar neck has a notch on the underside
      of the bulge to hold the wire clamp. As
      per the patent issued to F. H. Perry, the
      jar has a double sealing surface.

      PAT. OCT 24 1882, see jar No. 1309
      PAT. JUNE 24, 1884, see jar No. 2620

#2307

2308. PATENTED JULY 27th 1886 (on base)............................. Aqua $50-75
      Ground lip   Clear $50-75
      ½ Gallon with Greek Key design around shoulder   Emerald Green $150-200
        and lower portion of jar
      Closure variations:
      (1) Glass insert marked Patd July 27 1886
          Zinc screw band with carrying bail
      (2) One piece metal screw cover marked
          Patd July 27th 1886, with carrying
          bail
      (3) One piece metal screw cover with four
          protruding knobs on top. Marked Patd
          July 27th 1886

2309. PATENTED JULY 27th 1886 WG (on base).........Clear $50-75
      Ground lip
      ½ Gallon with Greek Key design as in #2308
      Closure as in #2308

2310. PATENTED JULY 27th 1886 (in small oval)(base)........ $75-100
      This is a cobalt blue stoneware jar with
        Greek Key design as in #2308
      Metal cap with bail handle. Marked Gordon
        & Dilworth Table Delicacies, New York
        Patented July 27th 1886

#2308

2311. PATENT APPLIED FOR (in small oval, on base)........................ $75-100
      Cobalt blue stoneware jar with Greek Key
        design & closure as in #2310

2312. Greek Key design around shoulder & lower
        part of jar. No marking on jar front or base.................Aqua $25-30
      Ground lip Metal lid with carrying handle   Clear $25-30

2313. Greek Key design around shoulder & lower
        part of jar. No marking on jar, oval place
        for paper label.....................................Clear $25-30
      Ground lip One piece metal screw lid   Lt. Green $25-30
      Canadian sealer   Amber $75-100

2314. Jar, shaped same as the Greek Key jars but
        without the Greek Key design. No marking....Clear $15-20
      Ground lip One piece metal screw lid
      PATD JANY 11th 1898, see jar Nos. 2625 & 2626
      PATD SEPT. 20th 1898, see jar No. 857
      AND PATENTS PAT. JAN 1 01, see jar No. 1461
      PATENTED JUNE 9 03 JUNE 29 03, see jar No. 1462
      PATENTED IN GREAT BRITAIN, see jar No. 1004

#2313

2315. PAT'D OCT. 24 1905 WARM CAP SLIGHTLY TO SEAL OR UNSEAL (lid)...Clear $15-18
         Smooth lip Glass cover
         Lid: has glass projections on the inner diameter,
             meant to hold the rubber sealing ring in place.
         The top of the jar has screw threads.

2316. P.C.G.Co. (on base)... Aqua $15-18
         Groove ring wax sealer, pressed laid-on ring

2317. P.C.G.W. (on base)... Aqua $15-18
         Groove ring wax sealer, pressed laid-on ring

2318. THE PEARL.. Aqua $25-30
         Base: Patd Dec. 17.61 REIS. SEPT. 1.68
               PATd NOV. 26 1867
         Ground lip Glass insert & screw band
         Insert: Patd. Feb. 12.56 Dec. 17.61 Nov. 4.62
                 Dec 6.64 June 9.68 Dec 22.68 Feb 7.71

2319. THE PEARL.. Aqua $25-30
         Base: Patd Dec. 17.61 Reis Sep 1 68 Patd
               Nov 26 1867 Aug. 23 70 Feb 7 71
         Ground lip Closure as in #2318

2320. THE PEARL (front).. Aqua $30-35
         Reverse: PATd AUG. 23.70 FEB. 7.71
         Base: Patd Dec 17 61 Reis Sep 1 68
               Patd Nov 26 1867
         Ground lip Closure as in #2318
         Size holding 2 3/4 cups   #2318

2321. PEARL FRUIT JAR TRADEMARK (on lid)........................Clear $6-8
         Smooth lip Old style Lightning seal

2322. PEERLESS..Amber   Unpriced
         Glass lid & iron yoke clamp   Aqua $85-100
         Lid: Patented Feb. 13 1863
         Or: Patented Feb. 13 1963 (error)

2323. PEEREESS (error)... Aqua $95-110
         Closure as in #2322

2324. PEERLESS BRAND MOCHA & JAVA COFFEE M. S. AYER
      & CO. WHOLESALE GROCERS BOSTON MASS. U.S.A............Amber $25-30
         Base: Patented Dec 13 1892 April 7th 1896
               Dec 1 1896
         Ground lip Zinc screw lid
         Product jar, intended for reuse as a home
         canning jar.   #2322

2325. PEERLESS BRAND MOCHA & JAVA COFFEE M. S. AYER
      & CO. WHOLESALE GROCERS BOSTON MASS. U.S.A.....................Amber $25-30
         Base: A. G. Smalley & Co. Patented
               Dec. 13 1892 April 7th 1896
               Dec. 1 1896 Boston, Mass.
         Ground lip Zinc screw lid
         Product jar, intended for reuse as a home canning jar.

2326. THE PENN.. Aqua $125-150
         Base: "footed" and marked Beck, Phillips
               & Co. Pitts Pa.
         Groove ring wax sealer, pressed laid-on ring

2327. THE PENN.. Aqua $30-35
         Base: Not footed, marked: Beck Phillips & Co. Pitts. Pa.
         Groove ring wax sealer, pressed laid-on ring

2328. THE PENN (superimposed over erased PET)...................................Aqua $30-35
      Base: Not footed, marked: Beck, Phillips & Co.
                           Pitts. Pa.
      Groove ring wax sealer, pressed laid-on ring

2329. PEORIA POTTERY (incised on base)..................................... $15-18
      Stoneware jar, brown glaze
      Groove ring wax sealer

2330. PERFECTION..Clear $30-35
      Base: Unmarked Jar has sloping shoulders   Aqua $30-35
      Ground lip Glass lid & double wire   Pint, Amber $350-400
        clamps. Metal band around neck of jar
      Lid: Perfection Pat. Mar 29 1887
      Lid has high center fin, which is notched
        for the wires.

2331. PERFECTION.....................................Clear $35-40
      Base: Unmarked or IGCo within diamond
      Jar has squarish shoulders
      Ground lip Closure as in #2330

2332. PERFECTION PAT. MAR. 29 1887 (on lid only).....................Amber $30-35
      No marking on the jar
      Ground lip Closure as in #2330
      Product jar

2333. PERFECT SEAL (within circle)......................................Clear $8-10
      Base: Pat. No. 2,212,804 Made In U.S.A.
      Glass lid marked Perfect Seal
      Or: Metal lid with rubber rim marked
        Perfect Seal West Before Using
        Perfect Seal Inc. Los Angeles, C.
        U.S.A. Patent No. 2,212,804

2334. PERFECT SEAL (in block letters)...............................Clear $8-10
      Base and closure as in #2333

2335. PERFECT SEAL.....................................½ Pint, Clear $4-6
      Smooth lip Old style Lightning seal
    This jar, and the following Perfect Seal jars, thru #2357
    are Canadian sealers.

2336. PERFECT SEAL (in script)..............................Clear $3-5
      Smooth lip Old style Lightning seal
      Square shape

2337. MADE IN CANADA PERFECT SEAL ADJUSTABLE..............Clear $1-2
      Words Perfect Seal within shield
      Neck: To Tighten Spring Move Hinge To Cover Star
      Smooth lip Lightning beaded neck seal
      Tall, slender jar

2338. MADE IN CANADA PERFECT SEAL ADJUSTABLE..............Clear $1-2
      Words Perfect Seal within shield
      Smooth lip Lightning beaded neck seal
      Neck tie wire, wire coils to hold ends of wire bail
      Round jar

2339. MADE IN CANADA PERFECT SEAL WIDE MOUTH ....Clear $1-2
      Words Perfect Seal within shield
      Smooth lip Lightning beaded neck seal
      Neck tie wire, metal pieces to hold ends of wire bail
      Neck: To Tighten Spring Move Hinge To Cover Star
      Round jar

2340. MADE IN CANADA PERFECT SEAE WIDE MOUTH (error)..................Aqua $2-4
     Words Perfect Seae within shield   Clear $2-4
     Smooth lip   Closure as in #2339   Cornflower Blue $20-25

2341. MADE IN CANADA PERFECT SEAL WIDE MOUTH.......................Aqua $2-4
     Words Perfect Seal within stippled shield   Clear $2-4
     Smooth lip   Lightning beaded neck seal   Cornflower Blue $20-25

2342. MADE IN CANADA PERFECT SEAL WIDE MOUTH.......................Clear $1-2
     Words Perfect Seal within shield
     Smooth lip   Lightning dimple neck seal

2343. MADE IN CANADA PERFECT SEAE WIDE MOUTH (error)................ Aqua $2-4
     Words Perfect Seal within shield
     Smooth lip   Lightning dimple neck seal

2344. MADE IN CANADA PERFECT SEAL WIDE MOUTH ADJUSTABLE..............Clear $1-2
     Words Perfect Seal within shield
     Smooth lip   Lightning beaded neck seal   Round jar

2345. MADE IN CANADA PERFECT SEAL WIDE MOUTH ADJUSTABLE..............Clear $1-2
     Words Perfect Seal within shield   Sediment Amber $20-25
     Smooth lip   Lightning beaded neck seal Square jar   Apple Green $6-8
                                                 Emerald Green $30-35

2346. MADE IN CANADA PERFECT SEAL WIDE MOUTH ADJUSTABLE..............Clear $1-2
     Words Perfect Seal within shield
     Smooth lip   Lightning dimple neck seal

2347. MADE IN CANADA PERFECT SEAL WIDE MOUTH ADJUSTABLE..............Clear $1-2
     Words Perfect Seal within shield   Apple Green $6-8
     Smooth lip   Old style Lightning seal   Square jar

2348. THE PERFECT SEAL WIDE MOUTH ADJUSTABLE........................Clear $3-5
     Framed with vines, word The within scroll
     Smooth lip   Old style Lightning seal   Square jar

2349. THE PERFECT SEAL WIDE MOUTH ADJUSTABLE........................Clear $3-5
     Framed with vines
     Smooth lip   Old style Lightning seal   Square jar

2350. THE PERFECT SEAL WIDE MOUTH ADJUSTABLE........................Clear $3-5
     Framed with vines. Two different style E's in
      word Perfect.
     Smooth lip   Old style Lightning seal   Square jar

2351. THE PERFECT SEAL WIDE MOUTH ADJUSTABLE.................. ....Clear $4-6
     Framed with vines. The T in Perfect is uncrossed
     Smooth lip   Old style Lightning seal   Square jar

2352. THE PEREFCT SEAL WIDE MOUTH ADJUSTABLE (error).....   .Clear $4-6
     Framed with vines. Word The within scroll
     Smooth lip   Old style Lightning seal   Square jar

2353. THE PERFECT SEAL WIDE MOUTH ADJUSTABLE............   Clear $3-5
     Without vines Word The within scroll
     Smooth lip   Old style Lightning seal   Square jar

2354. THE PERFECT SEAL WIDE MOUTH ADJUSTABLE............   Clear $4-6
     Without vines Word The in scroll, T uncrossed
     Smooth lip   Old style Lightning seal   Square jar   #2348

2355. THE PERFECT SEA WIDE MOUTH ADJUSTABLE (error)...... ....Clear $4-6
     Without vines Word The within scroll
     Smooth lip   Old style Lightning seal   Square jar

2356. THE PERFEC SE WIDE MOUTH ADJUSTABLE (error).................Clear $4-6
     Without vines Word The within scroll
     Smooth lip   Old style Lightning seal   Square jar

2357. THE PERFECT SE WIDE MOUTH ADJUSTABLE (error)........ ..Clear $4-6
      Without vines Word The in scroll
      Smooth lip Old style Lightning seal Square jar

2358. D. S. PERRIN & CO. LONDON. ONT.................... .Clear $8-10
      Ground lip Metal screw lid
      Canadian product jar

2359. PET.........................°...................... Aqua $70-75
      Glass lid & spring wire clamp, with coil
      Lid: Patd August 31th 1869 T.G.O.
      Or: Patented Aug. 31st T. G. Otterson

2360. THE PET... . Aqua $30-35
      Base: Beck, Phillips & Co. Pitts. Pa.   #2357   Sky Blue $65-75
      Groove ring wax sealer, pressed laid-on ring

2361. PET.. Aqua $30-35
      Base: Beck, Phillips & Co. Pitts. Pa.
      Groove ring wax sealer, pressed laid-on ring

2362. H. W. PETTIT WESTVILLE N.J. (on base)....................... Aqua $8-12
      Ground lip Glass lid & Safety Valve clamp   Cornflower Blue $20-25

2363. H. W. PETTIT SALEM N. J. (on base)....................... Aqua $8-12
      Ground lip Glass lid & Safety Valve clamp

2364. PHOENIX SURGICAL DRESSING CO. MILWAUKEE. WISC.................Amber $35-40
      Ground lip Glass lid & two wire bail clamps
      Metal band around neck of jar
      Lid: Perfection Pat. Mar. 29 1887
      Product jar

2365. PILOT SALAD MUSTARD CONTENTS 12 OZ. GENERAL GROCER
      CO. DISTRIBUTORS ST. LOUIS, MO. (on paper label)...............Clear $2-4
      The smooth top jar is in the shape of a lantern
      & has a wire carrying bail. The metal screw cap
      has an opening in it so the jar could be converted
      into a lamp.

2366. PINE DE LUXE JAR..Clear $4-6
      Smooth lip Lightning beaded neck seal

2367. PINE P (within square) MASON..................... ...Clear $4-5
      Smooth lip Mason beaded neck seal
      Round & square shapes

2368. PINT STANDARD...................................... ... Aqua $50-55
      Groove ring wax sealer, pressed laid-on ring
      Pint size

2369. "PITMAN" PRESERVING JAR......................... ... Aqua $50-55
      Smooth lip Glass insert & screw band   #2366

2370. PLYMOUTH PRESERVING CO. PRESERVES PLYMOUTH, MASS...............Clear $35-40
      All within oval, on shoulder
      Stopper neck finish for cork stopper

2371. WM. POGUE BRIDGETON N. J. (front)......   .... Aqua $2000 & up
      Reverse: FOR PRESERVING FRUIT   Cornflower Blue   Unpriced
      Base: Pushed up & with bare iron
            pontil scar
      Ground lip Wax seal groove, formed
       by depressing the shoulder while
       glass was still hot.
      5 Aqua jars are known & 1 Blue jar.

-173-   #2371

2372. POMONA PATENTED MAR 10th 1868.................................... Aqua $300-350
    Base: Mass. Glass Co.
    Glass lid with ramps & metal yoke clamp
    Lid, underside: March 10th 1868
    Only 1 jar is presently known
    Also see HILTON jar No. 1256

2373. PORCELAIN BBGMCo LINED.................................... Aqua $30-35
    Ground lip Mason shoulder seal   Lt. Green $30-35
    Zinc lid, outside: Porcelain Lined Cap For   Midget Pint, Aqua $75-90
              Mason Fruit Jars
            Inside: Ball Bro's Glass Mfg. Co.
             Buffalo, N. Y.

2374. PORCELAIN LINED... Aqua $15-20
    Base: Pat. Nov 26 67 Pat Feb 4 73   Midget Pint, Aqua $40-50
    Ground lip Mason shoulder seal
    Note: The correct base date is 73 (1873)
     tho it often appears to be 13 on the jar.

2375. PORCELAIN LINLD (error)....................   .... Aqua $20-25
    Base & closure as in #2374 & #2376

2376. PORCELAIN LINED with erased ROWLEYS.........   .... Aqua $20-25
    Base: Pat Nov 26 67 Pat Feb 4 73   Gallon, Aqua $250-300
    Ground lip Mason shoulder seal
    Zinc lid, outside: Trademark Rowley's
     Porcelain Lined Patd Dec.31.72 Feb 4.73
    July 14.74 Nov. 4.62 Reis. June 9.68
          Inside: The Hero Glass Works
            Philadelphia, Pa.   #2376
  Or:
    Zinc lid, outside: Patented Sep't 3d 1872
    Dec 31st 1872 Feby 4th 1873
          Inside: Pat'd Sept 3
            Dec 31 1872

2377. MASON'S PATENT NOV 30th 1858 (front)............   ....Aqua $6-8
    Reverse: erased PORCELAIN LINED
    Base: Pat Nov 26 67 Pat. Feb 4 73
    Ground lip Mason shoulder seal

2378. PORT (on base)...............................   ....Aqua $20-25
    Groove ring wax sealer, pressed laid-on ring

2379. PORT Q (on base)..............................   ....Aqua $20-25
    Groove ring wax sealer, pressed laid-on ring

2380. PORT MASON'S PATENT NOV 30th 1858.............   ....Aqua $15-18
    Base: Port
    Ground lip Mason shoulder seal   #2381

2381. POTTER & BODINE PHILADELPHIA (script)..........   Aqua $85-95
    Ground lip Metal lid with soldered wire clamp
    Lid: J. F. Bodine
    Or: F. & J. Bodine's Patent Feb 12 1867

2382. POTTER & BODINE'S AIR-TIGHT FRUIT JAR PHILADA..... Aqua $250-300
    Reverse: PATENTED APRIL 13th 1858
    Base: Pontil scar
    Groove ring wax sealer

2383. POTTER & BODINE'S AIR-TIGHT FRUIT ʲAR PHILADA..... Aqua $200-250
    Reverse: PATENTED APRIL 13th 18
    Base: Without pontil scar
    Groove ring wax sealer

#2382

2384. POTTER & BODINE'S AIRTIGHT FRUIT JAR PHILADA....... ... Aqua $250-300
    Reverse: PATENTED APRIL 13th 1858
    Wax seal groove formed by depressing the
      blown projection on the neck of the jar,
      while the glass is still in an elastic
      state.

2385. POTTER & BODINE'S AIRTIGHT FRUIT JAR PHILADA.....   Aqua $250-300
    (In straight line instead of arched as in #2384
    Reverse: PATENTED APRIL 13th 1858
    Wax seal groove as in #2384

2386. POTTER & BODINE'S AIR TIGHT FRUIT JAR PHILADA....   Aqua $250-300
    Reverse: PATENTED APRIL 13th 1858
    Wax seal groove as in #2384
    For illustration of this and other Potter & Bodine variations,
      see "FRUIT JARS" By Creswick

#2384

2387. POTTER & BODINE AIRTIGHT FRUIT JAR PHILADA................... Aqua $375-400
    Reverse: PATENTED APRIL 13th 1858 (in 3 lines)
    Base: Pontil scar
    Wax seal groove as in #2384
    Barrel shaped jar

2388. POTTER & BODINE'S AIRTIGHT FRUIT JAR PHILADA..... .. Aqua $375-400
    Reverse: PATENTED APRIL 13th 1858 (in two lines)
    Base: Pontil scar
    Wax seal groove as in #2384
    Barrel shaped jar

2389. POTTER & BODINE'S AIRTIGHT FRUIT JAR PHILADA... . Aqua   -$400
    Reverse: PATENTED APRIL 13th 1858
    Base: Bare Iron pontil scar
    Barrel shaped jar

2390. POTTER & BODINE'S AIRTIGHT FRUIT JAR PHILADA.... . Aqua $375-400
    Reverse: PATENTED APRIL 13th 1858
    Base: Pontil scar
    Wax seal groove as in #2384
    Barrel shaped jar

#2387

2391. Le PRATIQUE (on lid)................................ ..Clear   -$1
    Smooth lip Hinged glass lid
    Modern French jar

2392. PREMIER.. .Clear   -$1
    Smooth lip Mason beaded neck seal
    Product jar

2393. PREMIUM (in straight line)....................... .Clear $15-20
    Smooth lip Glass lid & spring wire clamp
    Lid, inside: Pat. Mar 19th 1901
           Or: Patd March 19th 1901
           Or: Pat Mar 19th 1901 Appn
              Pend On Ipvts (The 9 in
                19th is sometimes reversed)
           Or: Premium Jar Pat'd March 19th 1901
    Advertised in pint, quart, ½ Gal., & Gallon sizes.   #2394

2394. PREMIUM (arched)................................Clear $15-20
    Smooth lip Closure as in #2393

2395. PREMIUM COFFEYVILLE, KAS..........................Clear $15-20
    Smooth lip Closure as in #2393

2396. PREMIUM IMPROVED...Clear $15-20
      Smooth lip Glass lid & spring wire clamp
      Lid: Pat. Mar. 19th 1901 Dec 13th 1910

2397. PREMIUM IMPROVED (front)..................................Clear $15-20
      Reverse: Erased PREMIUM COFFEYVILLE, KAS.
      Smooth lip Closure as in #2396

2398. PRESERVES...   .... Aqua $50-75
      Ground lip Mason beaded neck seal

2399. PRESTO.......................................   .½ Pint, Clear $2-3
      Base: I within diamond
      Smooth lip Lightning dimple neck seal

2400. PRESTO.......................................   .... Clear   -$1
      Smooth lip Mason beaded neck seal
      Closure: Zinc lid
            Or: Aluminum lid marked Presto
           ·Or: Glass insert marked Presto & screw band

                                                    #2398

2401. PRESTO FRUIT JAR................................. Clear   -$1
      Smooth lip Mason beaded neck seal
      Closure as in #2400

2402. PRESTO GLASS TOP (front)................................. Clear   -$1
      Reverse: MANUFACTURED BY ILLINOIS PACIFIC   ½ Pint, Clear $2-4
               GLASS CORP.
      Smooth lip Lightning beaded neck seal

2403. PRESTO GLASS TOP (front)....................   .Clear   -$1
      Reverse: MFG. BY ILLINOIS GLASS CO.
      Smooth lip Lightning beaded neck seal

2404. PRESTO GLASS TOP (front)..........................   Clear   -$1
      Reverse: MANUFACTURED BY ILLINOIS GLASS CO.
      Smooth lip Lightning dimple neck seal

2405. PRESTO GLASS TOP (front)......................   Clear   -$1
      Reverse: MANUFACTURED BY OWENS-ILLINOIS GLASS CO
      Smooth lip Lightning dimple neck seal   #2404

2406. PRESTO GLASS TOP W88X (front)..................... ½ Pint, Clear $2-4
      Reverse: MFG. BY ILLINOIS GLASS CO.
      Smooth lip Lightning dimple neck seal

2407. PRESTO SUPREME MASON (front)...............................Clear   -$1
      Reverse: MANUFACTURED BY OWENS-ILLINOIS GLASS COMPANY
      Smooth lip Mason beaded neck seal

2408. PRESTO SUPREME MASON (front).............................Clear   -$1
      Reverse: MFG. BY OWENS-ILLINOIS GLASS CO.
      Smooth lip Mason beaded neck seal

2409. PRESTO SUPREME MASON (front)..........................Clear $1-2
      Reverse: MANUFACTUPED BY OWENS ILLINOIS GLASS COMPANY (error)
      Smooth lip Mason beaded neck seal

2410. PRESTO SUPREME MASON (front)..........................Clear   -$1
      Reverse: MANUFACTURED BY ILLINOIS PACIFIC GLASS CORP.
      Smooth lip Mason beaded neck seal

2411. PRESTO SUPREME MASON (front)..........................Clear   -$1
      Reverse: MANUFACTURED BY ILLINOIS GLASS CO.
      Smooth lip Mason beaded neck seal Square jar

2412. PRESTO SUPREME MASON DURAGLAS..............................Clear   -25¢
      Base: Owens Illinois Glass Company   ½ Pint, Clear $1-3
      Smooth lip Mason beaded neck seal

2413. PRESTO WIDE MOUTH...Clear   -$1
      Smooth lip Mason beaded neck seal

2414. PRESTO WIDE MOUTH GLASS TOP...........................Clear   -$1
      Smooth lip Lightning beaded neck seal

2415. PRESTO WIDE MOUTH GLASS TOP............................Clear   -$1
      Smooth lip Mason beaded neck seal
      Glass insert & aluminum cover

2416. PRESTO WIDE MOUTH GLASS TOP.......................Clear   -$1
      Reverse: MFG. BY ILLINOIS GLASS CO.
      Smooth lip Mason beaded neck seal
      Glass insert & aluminum cover

2417. PRESTO WIDE MOUTH GLASS TOP DURAGLAS (front)......Clear   -$1
      Reverse: MANUFACTURED BY OWENS-ILLINOIS GLASS CO
      Smooth lip Mason beaded neck seal
      Glass insert & aluminum cover
                                                   #2419

2418. PRINCESS (on shield, within frame).....................Clear $15-18
      Smooth lip Old style Lightning seal

2419. PROSSER PATENT MAY 19, 1863....................... Aqua $250-300
      Neck finish for metal stopple
      Marking on stopple, if any, not known
      Only 3 Prosser jars are presently known

2420. PROTECTOR.. Aqua $35-40
      Ground lip Metal lid with soldered wire clamp
      Lid: F & J Bodine's Patent Feb. 12 1867

2421. PROTECTOR (vertically)............................. Aqua $35-45
      Jar has arched, recessed panels
      Ground lip Closure as in #2420

2422. PROTEOTOR (error, embossed vertically)............ Aqua $45-55
      Jar has arched, recessed panels
      Ground lip Closure as in #2420

2423. PROTECTOR (vertically)............................. Aqua $35-45
      Panels are not recessed
      Ground lip Closure as in #2420   #2421

2424. PUCK (on front & on reverse)......................Clear $2-4
      Base: Puck Worth The Money
      Smooth lip Mason beaded neck seal Product jar

2425. THE PURITAN (front) L S Co (monogram, reverse).. Aqua $150-175
      Ground lip Glass lid, iron ring & wire clamp   Citron $200 & up
      Lid: Patented

2426. THE PURITAN TRADE MARK (sailing ship) FRUIT JAR
      LSCo. (all on front)............................ Aqua $175-200
      Ground lip Closure as in #2425

2427. PUTNAM (on base)................................. Aqua $2-3
      Ground lip Old style Lightning seal   Amber $20-25
      Product jar   #2426

2428. PUTNAM GLASS WORKS ZANESVILLE O. (on base)...... Aqua $20-25
      Groove ring wax sealer, pressed laid-on ring Deep Olive Amber $250 & up
                                                     Deep Yellow Amber $250 & up

2429. PYRAMID...Clear $1-3
      Smooth lip Old style Lightning seal
      Product jar

QG monogram, see jar No. 1657

2430. QUEEN PATENTED MAY 13' 1873 (on glass lid)....................₀₀Clear $8-10
       Clear glass jelly tumbler

2431. QUEEN PATENTED MAY 13 1873 REISSUED JUNE 16 1874 (on lid)......Clear $8-10
       Clear glass jelly tumbler

2432. THE QUEEN encircled by PATd DEC 28th 1858 PATd JUNE 16th 1868.. Aqua $30-35
       Ground lip   Glass lid & screw band   Cornflower Blue $50-60
       Lid: Patd Dec. 28 1858 & June 16 1868

2433. THE QUEEN... ..... Aqua $15-18
       Base: Patd. Nov 2 1869   Clear $15-18
       Ground lip   Glass insert & screw band
       Lid: Queen Jar Patented Nov. 2 1869
       Or: Patented Nov. 2 1869
       Or: Patd Nov. 2 1868 (error)
       Or: Patd Nov. 2nd 1869
       Or: Unmarked lid

2434. THE QUEEN (front)   Reverse: CFJCo monogram..₀₀₀₀ ... Aqua $18-20
       Base: Patd. Nov 2 1869
       Ground lip   Glass insert & screw band
       Lid: Queen Jar Patented Nov. 2 1869   CFJCo in center   #2432

2435. THE QUEEN CFJCo.. Aqua $25-30
       Base: Patd. Nov 2 1869   Midget Pint, Aqua $50-75
       Ground lip   Closure as in #2434

2436. THE CFJCo QUEEN....................................... Aqua $25-30
       Base: Patd. Nov 2 1869   Midget Pint, Aqua $50-75
       Ground lip   Closure as in #2434

2437. SKO QUEEN TRADEMARK WIDE MOUTH ADJUSTABLE....................Clear $2-3
       Word IMPROVED on neck   ½ Pint, Clear $10-12
       Base: Smalley, Kivlan, Onthank Boston, Mass.
       Smooth lip   Glass lid & twin wire clamps
       Lid: KantKrack Patd Feb 23 09

2438. SKO QUEEN TRADEMARK WIDE MOUTH ADJUSTABLE...... ...Clear $2-3
        Word IMPROVED on neck
        Base: Smalley, Kivlan, Onthank Boston, Mass.
            Pat'd Feb. 23.09
        Smooth lip   Closure as in #2437

2439. SKO QUEEN TRADEMARK WIDE MOUTH ADJUSTABLE...... ...Clear $2-3
        Word IMPROVED on neck
        Base: Smalley, Kivlan, Onthank Boston
            Pat'd Feb. 23. 09
        Smooth lip   Closure as in #2437

2440. SKO QUEEN TRADEMARK WIDE MOUTH ADJUSTABLE...... ...Clear $2-3
        Word IMPROVED on neck
        Base: Smalley Kivlan Onthank Boston, Mass.
           I within diamond, trademark
        Smooth lip   Closure as in #2437   #2440

2441. SKO QUEEN TRADEMARK WIDE MOUTH ADJUSTABLE....................Clear $2-3
        Word IMPROVED on neck
        Base: Smalley Kivlan Onthank Boston Mass.
           Pat'd Feb 23 09   I within diamond trademark
          Smooth lip   Closure as in #2437

2442. SKO QUEEN TRADEMARK WIDE MUTH ADJUTABLE (errors)..............Clear $3-5
    Word IMPROVED on neck
    Base: Smalley Kivlan Onthank Boston Pat. Feb 23 09
    Smooth lip Closure as in #2437

2443. SKO QUEEN TRADEMARK WIDE MUOTH ADJUSTABLE (error)......__..Clear $3-5
    Word IMPROVED on neck
    Base: Smalley Kivlan Onthank Boston Pat. Feb 23 09
    Smooth lip Closure as in #2437

2444. SKO QUEEN TRADEMARK WIDE MOUTH ADJUSTABLE..........__.Clear $2-3
    Word TIGHT on neck   Aqua $2-3
    Base: Smalley Kivlan Onthank Boston Union Made
    Smooth lip Old style Lightning seal   #2445

2445. SKO QUEEN TRADEMARK WIDE MOUTH ADJUSTABLE........Tall ½ Pint, Clear $10-12
    Word TIGHT on neck
    Base: Smalley Kivlan Onthank Boston Union Made
    Smooth lip Old style Lightning seal

2446. SKO QUEEN TRADEMARK........................°.....Squatty ½ Pint, Clear $10-12
    Word TIGHT on neck
    Base: Smalley Kivlan Onthank Boston

2447. SKO QUEEN TRADEMARK WIDE MOUTH ADJUSTABLE..................°....Clear $2-3
    Front neck: IMPROVED Reversed neck: MADE IN CANADA
    Base: Smalley Kivlan Onthank Boston, Mass. Pat'd Feb 23 09
    Smooth lip Closure as in #2437

2448. SKO QUEEN TRADEMARK WIDE MOUTH ADJUSTABLE.°..................°....Clear $2-3
    Front neck: IMPROVED Reversed neck: MADE IN CANADA
    Base: Smalley Kivlan Onthank Boston, Mass. Pat'd Feb 23 09
    Smooth lip. Kivlan's 1909 wire side clamps on
    Lightning beaded neck seal. KantKrack lid.

2449. K & O QUEEN TRADEMARK WIDE MOUTH ADJUSTABLE..°......Clear $2-3
    Word IMPROVED on neck
    Base: Kivlan & Onthank Patd. June 28 '21
    Smooth lip Glass lid & twin wire side clamps

    CANADIAN QUEEN see jar No. 557

2450. QUEENSLAND (Q within a pineapple) FRUIT JAR..°...... Lt. Green $75-100
    Ground lip Old style Lightning seal
    Australian jar Wide mouth

2451. QUICK SEAL (within circle)................... Ball Blue $2-4
    Smooth lip Old style Lightning seal

2452. QUICK SEAL (within circle)................°......Clear $2-4
    Smooth lip Lightning dimple neck seal   Ball Blue $2-4

2453. QUICK SEAL (without circle)......................Clear $2-4
    Smooth lip Lightning dimple neck seal   Ball Blue $2-4

2454. QUICK SEAL (within circle) PAT'D JULY 14, 1908......Clear $2-4
    Smooth lip Lightning dimple neck seal   Lt. Green $2-4
                                                   Ball Blue $2-4

2455. QUICK SEAL (within circle) PAT'D JULY 14 1908......Clear $2-4
    Smooth lip Lightning beaded neck seal

2456. QUICK SEAL (within circle) PAT'D JULY 14, 1908......Clear $2-4
    Neck reads: BALE HERE
    Smooth lip Lightning beaded neck seal

#2450

#2454

2457. QUICK SEAL (within circle) PAT'D JULY 14, 1908.................Clear $2-4
      Neck reads: BAIL HERE
      Smooth lip Lightning beaded neck seal

2458. QUICK SEAL (within circle) front.............................Clear $2-4
      Reverse: PAT'D JULY 14, 1908   Ball Blue $2-4
      Smooth lip Lightning beaded neck seal

2459. QUONG HOP & CO. 12 OZ. NET (& Chinese characters)..............Clear $3-5
      Chinese translated: Kown Ho San Francisco, Down Town
      Smooth lip Lightning dimple neck seal
      Pint Product jar

2460. QUONG HOP & CO. 133 WAVERLY PL. S. F. CAL.
      & Chinese characters.......................................Clear $3-5
      Smooth lip Lightning dimple neck seal
      Pint Product jar

2461. BEAN CAKE 12 OZ NET QUONG YUEN, SING & CO. SAN FRANCISCO,
      CALIF..Clear $3-5
      Reverse: Chinese characters
      Smooth lip Lightning dimple neck seal
      Pint Product jar

2462. RACH COCOA CO. WAVERLY, N.Y........................Aqua $2-3
      Ground lip Mason shoulder seal
      Product jar

2463. THE RAMSAY JAR.....................................Aqua $600 & up
      Base: Pat. April 1866 & Nov. 67
      Ground lip Unmarked glass stopper
      Two variations of the stopper are shown   #2463
      The jar has 12 panels, slightly recessed.
      The mouth of the jar and the bottom of the
        stopper are oval shaped rather than round.

2464. DOCTOR RAMSAY'S....................................Aqua $600 & up
      Base: Pat. April 17 1866
      Ground lip Unmarked glass stopper
      The jar has 12 panels, slightly recessed.
      The mouth of the jar and the bottom of the
        stopper are oval shaped.
                           #2464

2465. DOCTOR RAMSAY'S....................................Aqua $600 & up
      Base: Unmarked & pushed-up
      Ground lip Unmarked glass stopper
      The jar has 12 panels, slightly recessed,
        with the panels going to the base of the
        jar.
      The mouth of the jar and the bottom of the
        stopper are oval shaped.   #2465

2466. THE RATH PACKING CO. WATERLOO, IOWA (within circle)
      PAT'D JULY 14, 1908 (all on front of jar)..................Clear $3-5
      Smooth lip Lightning dimple neck seal
      Product jar

2467. THE RATH PACKING CO. WATERLOO, IOWA (within circle)
    PAT'D JULY 14, 1908 (All on front).............................Clear $3-5
      Smooth lip Old style Lightning seal Product jar

2468. RATH'S BLACK HAWK FOOD PRODUCTS THE RATH
    PACKING CO. WATERLOO, IOWA (within circle)....................Clear $1-3
      Smooth lip Mason beaded neck seal Product jar

2469. RAU'S IMPROVED PAT APPLIED FOR GROVE RING JAR.................. Aqua $30-35
      Groove ring wax sealer, pressed laid-on ring   Clear $30-35

2470. RAU'S IMPROVED PAT APPLIED FOR GROOVE RING JAR.................Clear $25-30
      Groove ring wax sealer, pressed laid-on ring

2471. RAVENNA GLASS WORKS (front)......................   .... Aqua $1000 & up
      Reverse: AIR-TIGHT FRUIT JAR
      Base: Bare iron pontil scar
      Tooled wax seal groove, with ground lip
      The ground lip is usually quite rough.
      Barrel shaped Pint

2472. RAVENNA GLASS WORKS OHIO (front)..............   ....Aqua $800 & up
      Reverse: AIR-TIGHT FRUIT JAR   Amber $4000 & up
      Base: Bare iron pontil scar
      Tooled wax seal groove, with ground lip
      Barrel shaped

#2471

2473. R. C. P. Co. AKRON, O. (impressed on base).......................... $8-10
      White stoneware jar & lid
      Pierced ears to hold wire bail handle

2474. RED (superimposed over a key) MASON............... .. Aqua $6-8
      Smooth lip Mason shoulder seal   Clear $8-10

2475. ED (superimposed over a key) MASON (R is ghosted) .. Aqua $10-12
      Smooth lip Mason shoulder seal

2476. RED (over a key) MASON'S PATENT NOV 30th 1858.... .. Aqua $8-10
      Ground lip Mason shoulder seal   Clear $8-10

2477. RED (over a key) MASON'S PATENT NOV 30td 1858.... .. Aqua $10-12
      Ground lip Mason shoulder seal   Clear $10-12

#2477

2478. RED WING STONEWARE CO. (impressed on base)........................ $12-15
      Stoneware jar, brown glaze
      Wax seal groove

2479. RED WING STONEWARE CO. (impressed on base)....... ..... $12-15
      Stoneware jar, brown glaze
      Wax seal groove

2480. RED WING STONEWARE FRUIT JAR MANUFACTURED FOR
    THE RED WING STONEWARE CO. REDWING, MINN.........
      In blue lettering, within shield, on white $15-18
        stoneware jar
      Reverse, within rectangle: "Before Filling,
      Warm Jar By Placing in Hot Water. Then Pour
      Fruit In Boiling Hot. Light cannot Effect
      or Fade The Contents."
      White stoneware jar, mason shoulder seal, zinc lid

#2478

2481. REED'S BUTTER SCOTCH PATTIES.................................Clear $6-8
      Base: Smalley Kivlan Onthank Boston Pat'd June 28, 1921
      Smooth lip Glass lid & twin wire clamps
      Product jar ½ Gallon

2482. REED'S BUTTER SCOTCH PATTIES (vertically)......................Clear $6-8
      Glass stopper   ½ Gallon Product jar

2483. REED'S PATTIES EUGENE O. REED CO. CHICAGO.....................Clear $6-8
      Base: Smalley Kivlan Onthank Boston Patent June 28
      Smooth lip   Glass lid & twin wire side clamps
      ½ Gallon Product jar

2484. REED'S PATTIES REED CANDY COMPANY, CHICAGO.....................Clear $6-8
      Base: Smalley Kivlan Onthank Boston Patent June 28
      Smooth lip   Glass lid & twin wire side clamps
      ½ Gallon Product jar

2485. REED'S PATTIES REED CANDY COMPANY, CHICACO.....................Clear $8-10
      Reversed N in Candy & C instead of G in Chicago
      Base: Smalley Kivlan Onthank Boston Patent June 28
      Smooth lip   Glass lid & twin wire side clamps
      ½ Gallon Product jar

2486. REGAL (within circle)...Clear $2-4
      Smooth lip   Lightning beaded neck seal   Product jar

2487. REID.. Aqua $250-300
      Ground lip   Glass stopper   Pale Aqua $250-300
      Only 3 jars are presently known

2488. REID, MURDOCH & CO CHICAGO........................... .Clear $2-3
      Smooth lip   Mason beaded neck seal   Product jar

2489. RELIABLE HOME CANNING MASON......................... .Clear $2-3
      Base: F within a hexagon
      Smooth lip   Mason beaded neck seal
      Lid insert: Reliable F Mason

2490. RELIANCE BRAND.. .Clear $2-3
      Smooth lip   Mason beaded neck seal

2491. RELIANCE BRAND WIDE MOUTH MASON..................... .Clear $2-3
      Smooth lip   Mason beaded neck seal

#2489

2492. T. F. REPPERT SUCCESSOR TO JAS. HAMILTON & CO.
GREENSBORO, PA.. $40-50
      Gray stoneware jar with blue stenciling
      Wax seal groove

2493. RESE..Clear $4-6
      Base: 1 Lts.
      Ground lip   Closure unknown   German jar

2494. THE RESERVOIR... .. Aqua $150-175
      Base: W. Frank & Son Pitt.
      Jar neck has two blown lugs on the inside
      Glass stopper: Mrs. G. E. Haller
                  Patd Feb 25 73
      The blown stopper has an opening at the
       bottom, and has inclined grooves to engage
      on the blown lugs on the inside of the neck.
      Stoppers are found in Clear & Aqua
      Note: Reservoir jars have reportedly been
       found in amber, but we have not been able
      to verify this.

#2494   #2495

2495. THE RESERVOIR.. Aqua $150-175
      Base: C & I
      Closure as in #2494

2496. THE RESERVOIR (front)... Aqua $200-250
      Reverse: TO OPEN ADMIT AIR BY INSERTING A PENKNIFE
           BLADE BETWEEN THE RUBBER AND GLASS
      Base: A & D H C
      The mouth of this variation is wider and has three
       blown lugs on the inside of the neck.
      Stopper: Mrs. G. E. Haller Patd Feb 25 73

2497. RESERVOIR JAR OF 1876... Aqua Unpriced
      Base: Chas Yockel 235 Bread St. Glass Mould Maker Phila.
      Blown glass stopper: Ella Hallers Patent (star in center)
      This miniature 1¼ oz. size jar, was made as a souvenir of
       the 1876 Centennial Exposition at Philadelphia.

2498. RETENTIVE (vertically on jar)............. Aqua $225-250
      Ground lip Glass lid & wire clamp   Gallon, Aqua $350 & up
      Also found in Gallon size, 2 known

2499. REX...Clear $4-6
      Base: 1 Lts.
      Ground lip Glass lid & metal clamp
      Lid: Original Rex   German jar

2500. REYNOLDS STEEN & CO. (around shoulder)..........Aqua Unpriced
      Groove ring wax sealer, pressed laid-on ring

2501. R. G. W. 1857 (on base)......................Lt. Green Unpriced
      Incised in base, not embossed
      Groove ring wax sealer, pressed laid-on ring

2502. FILL TO THIS LINE ONE FULL LIQUID QUART
      JAY B RHODES KALAMAZOO, MICH (on front)........................Clear $4-6
      Smooth lip Mason beaded neck seal
      This is an oil jar used in gas stations

#2498

2503. RIDGEWAY'S "AD" COFFEE SEE THAT SEAL ON LID IS UNBROKEN........Amber $4-6
      On 3 sides: RIDGEWAY'S "AD" COFFEE
      Canadian Product jar

2504. C RIESSNER & CO. NY PAT. FEB 12.78 (on base)................Complete $25-35
      The jar as originally made is encased in a tin
       jacket, embossed Queen. The tin lid with pouring
       spout was cemented to the jar top. The can was
       advertised as being the best can for Kerosene oil,
       or any other liquid. Also for milk or oysters.

2505. RILLENGLAS GERRIS (on lid)...................................Aqua $2-3
      Smooth lip Glass lid & spring metal clamp
      Made in Denmark

2506. R. I. TEL & ELEC CO. LITTLE GIANT PATENT PROVIDENCE R. I........Aqua $20-25
      Ground lip Mason shoulder seal

2507. ROBINSON (within oval) 3-1065 (or other numbers) on base.......Clear $2-4
      Smooth lip Glass lid & spring metal clamp
      Clamp: Pat. 1939 or U.S. Patent #2281433
       Or: Robinson

    Also see VACU TOP jar No. 2860

2508. ROGERS THE B.C. SUGAR TRADEMARK ROGER REG'D
      REFINING CO. LTD. GOLDEN SYRUP VANCOUVER, B.C.
      PERFFCT SEAL JAR (all on front)...................Clear $20-25
      Smooth lip Lightning beaded neck seal
      Canadian Product jar

#2508

2509. ROLLINS SELF- SEALER.. Clear   Unpriced
      Base: Pat Jan 14 08
      Smooth lip Glass lid
      Lid: To Open Pry Out Rubber At Notch
      The patent called for a waxed cotton cord to
        be used in the groove, and also illustrated
        a jar sealing & vacuum releasing device.

2510. ROOT MASON... Aqua $3-5
      Smooth lip Mason shoulder seal   Honey Amber $40-50
      Zinc lid, outside: Root Glass Company   Olive Green $40-50
        Genuine Zinc Cap For Mason Jars
      Zinc lid, inside: Unmarked

2511. THE ROSE...Clear $35-40
      Smooth lip Glass lid & screw band   Midget Pint, Clear $100-125
      Canadian sealer

2512. E. W. ROTHROCK CO. INC. TYRONE, PA..............Clear $12-15
      Rolled lip Closure unknown
      Product jar

2513. ROYAL...................................... Aqua $50-75
      Base: Pat. Feb 27 1877   Black $1000 & up
      Ground lip Glass insert & screw band
      Insert: Berries & leaf decoration
        Or: Pat'd Feb 27 1877
      Improved type zinc band with two
        vertical, soldered wrench lugs

2514. ROYAL...................................... Aqua $75-100
      Ground lip Unmarked glass lid & zinc collar   Amber $500 & up
      The zinc collar has two soldered wrench lugs.
        In place of screw threads, the band has a
        wire rolled into the bottom edge to engage
        on the jar threads. Pat. June 9 63 is stamped
        into the metal.

2515. ROYAL OF 1876...............................Aqua $75-100
      Ground lip Glass insert & screw band
      Insert: Berries & leaf decoration
      Zinc band as in #2513

2516. ROYAL (below Crown emblem) TRADEMARK FULL MEASURE
      REGISTERED QUART (all on front).........................Aqua $6-8
      Base: A. G. Smalley & Co. Patented April 7th 1896   Clear $6-8
          Boston & New York
      Ground lip Old style Lightning seal
      Lid: A. G. Smalley & Co. Boston & New York
      Known in ½ Pint, Pint, Quart & ½ Gallon sizes

2517. ROYAL (below Crown emblem) TRADEMARK FULL MEASURE
      REGISTERED QUART (all on front)....................Clear $6-8
      Word Royal also superimposed on the crown   Aqua $6-8
      Base: A.G. Smalley & Co. Patented April 7th 1896   Amber $45-50
          Boston & New York
      Ground lip Old style Lightning seal
      Lid: A. G. Smalley & Co. Boston & New York

2518. ROYAL (superimposed on crown emblem) TRADEMARK
      FULL MEASURE REGISTERED QUART (all on front).......Amber $45-50
      Base: A.G. Smalley & Co. Patented April 7th 1896
          Boston & New York
      Ground lip Old style Lighting seal
      Lid: A.G. Smalley & Co. Boston & New York
      The amber jars were made for coffee packers
        and the lids are found in clear only.

#2509

#2514

#2515

#2518

-184-

2519. ROYAL (superimposed on crown emblem) TRADEMARK
FULL MEASURE REGISTERED PINT (all on front)................... Aqua $8-10
   Also word ROYAL on neck of jar   Clear $8-10
     Base: A. G. Smalley & Co. Patented April 7th 1896
       Boston & New York
     Ground lip Old style Lightning seal
     Lid: A.G. Smalley & Co. Boston & New York

2520. ROYAL (superimposed on crown emblem) ROYAL TRADEMARK
FULL MEASURE REGISTERED QUART (all on front)................Clear $6-8
     Base: A. G. Smalley & Co. Patented April 7th 1896
     Smooth lip Old style Lightning seal, wide mouth

2521. ROYAL CUP COFFEE ONE POUND NET (on 3 sides).......   .Clear $1-3
     Smooth lip Mason beaded neck seal
     Product jar

2522. RUBY SPECIAL WIDE MOUTH.........................   Aqua $4-6
     Smooth lip Mason beaded neck seal
     Zinc lid, outside: Ruby
               Inside: Unmarked

#2522

2523. S (on front)...   ... Aqua $20-25
     Groove ring wax sealer, pressed laid-on ring

2524. S (on base)..   ... Aqua $3-5
     Groove ring wax sealer, pressed laid-on ring

2525. SAFE...   ...Clear $8-10
     Base: Made By The Safe Glass Co. Upland,
       Ind. Feb 1903
     Smooth lip Metal lid with sealing gasket

2526. SAFE...   ...Clear $8-10
     Base: Made By The Safe Glass Co. Ind.
       Pat Feb 10 '03 Upland
     Smooth lip Metal lid with sealing gasket

#2525

2527. SAFE SEAL (& names of fruits)on lid......... $2-3
     On lid of tin can

2528. SAFE SEAL (& names of fruits) on lid........ $2-3
     On lid of tin can

    Also see cans Nos. 653, 654 & 2795

2529. SAFE SEAL...   ......Clear $3-5
     Smooth lip Mason beaded neck seal

#2527-28-29

2530. SAFE SEAL (within circle)......................   ...... Clear $4-6
       Smooth lip Lightning beaded neck seal

2531. SAFE SEAL (within circle) PAT'D JULY 14, 1908   ..Ball Blue $4-6
       Smooth lip Lightning dimple neck seal

2532. SAFE SEAL (no circle) PAT'D JULY 14, 1908....   ...Clear $4-6
       Smooth lip Lightning dimple neck seal

2533. SAFE SEAL (within circle)....................   ..Ball Blue $4-6
       Reverse: PAT'D JULY 14, 1908
       Smooth lip Lightning dimple neck seal

#2530

2534. SAFETY..   ... Aqua $35-40
       Ground lip Glass lid & wire clamp   Amber $75-85
       Lid: Patent Applied For

2535. SAFETY..   ... Aqua $150-175
       Base: Cumberland Glass Works Bridgeton N.J.
       Ground lip Glass lid
       Cast iron ring, with wire bail & wire clamp
       Lid, underside: Pat. Nov 27 83

2536. SAFETY SEAL MADE IN CANADA....................   ..Clear $3-5
       Smooth lip Old style Lightning seal
       Lid: Safety Seal or Unmarked
       Canadian sealer

#2535

2537. SAFETY SEAL...................................   ....Clear $3-5
       Smooth lip Old style Lightning seal
       Closure as in #2536   Canadian sealer

2538. SAFETY VALVE PATD MAY 21 1895 HC (over triangle)(on base)...... Aqua $8-10
       Ground lip Glass lid & metal band clamp   Clear $6-8
       Also found with a smooth lip   Amber $125-150
                                                       Kelly Green $75-100
                                                       ½ Pint, Clear $12-15
                                                       ½ Pint, Sky Blue $15-20
                                                       ¼ Pint, Clear $12-15

2539. SAFETY VALVE PATD MAY 21 HC (over triangle) (on base).......... Aqua $25-35
       Greek Key design around shoulder & lower part of jar   Clear $25-30
       Ground lip Glass lid & metal band clamp, with or   Amber $300 & up
                without bail handle   Kelly Green $150-200
       ½ Gallon size

2540. SAFETY VALVE HC (over triangle) PAT'D MAY 21 1895................... $20-25
       Within small rectangle, printed in blue, on white stoneware jar
       Stoneware lid and metal Safety Valve clamp
       Base: Minnesota Stoneware Co. Red Wing,Minn.

2541. SAFETY WIDE MOUTH MASON SALEM GLASS WORKS SALEM N.J   Aqua $12-15
       Smooth lip Mason shoulder seal Wide mouth
       Lid: Gold lacquered with black lettering: SaniCap
         Sanitary Jar Cap For Wide Mouth Mason Jar
         Mfd. By American Can Co. Pat. Applied For
         Salem Glass Works Salem, N. J.

#2542

2542. SAGER..   ....Clear $10-15
       Smooth lip Glass lid & spring metal clamp   Lt. Green $10-15
       Lid: United States Patent No. 1,356,224
            Oct. 19 1920
       The jar was sealed with the aid of a vacuum pump.

2543. THE SALEM JAR..................................   ..... Aqua $225-250
       Base: Pat. Appld For
       Ground lip Threaded glass stopper
       Stopper: Wm. Grange & Son 711 Nth 2nd St. Phila.

2544. THE SALEM JAR (front)...Aqua $250-300
      Reverse: HOLZ CLARK & TAYLOR SALEM N. J.
      Base: Pat. Appld For
      Ground lip   Threaded glass stopper
      Stopper: Wm. Grange & Son 711 Nth 2nd St. Phila.

      Also see HOLZ CLARK & TAYLOR jar No. 1259

2545. SAMCO (within circle) GENUINE MASON........................Clear   -$1
      Smooth lip   Mason beaded neck seal   Pint, Olive Green $18-20
      Closure: Milkglass insert marked Samco & screw band
          Or: 2 Pc. gold lacquered lid marked Samco
            Klick Seal   Genuine Mason Lids
          Or: Zinc lid

2546. Without word Samco in circle GENUINE MASON.........Clear   -$1
      Smooth lip   Mason beaded neck seal
      Closure as in #2545

2547. SAMCO SUPER JAR.................................Clear $1-2
      Smooth lip   Mason beaded neck seal
      Closure: 2 Pc. gold lacquered lid with insert
         marked: Samco Super Seal Trademark Reg.
         U.S. Pat. Off. Mason Fits All Standard Jars #2548

2548. SAMCO SUPER MASON................................Clear $1-2
      Smooth lip   Mason beaded neck seal
      Closure as in #2547

2549. SANETY WIDE MOUTH MASON SALEM GLASS WORKS SALEM N. J......... Aqua $12-15
      Smooth lip   Mason shoulder seal Wide mouth
      Lid as in #2541

2550. Unmarked jar... Aqua $8-10
      Smooth lip   Mason shoulder seal Wide mouth
      Lid as in #2541

2551. SANFORD'S (on base) ONE QUART (on heel).........Clear $10-12
      Smooth lip   Glass lid & metal screw band
      Lid: Sanford Mfg. Co. Chicago & New York
         Patented July 10, 1900

2552. SAN FRANCISCO GLASS WORKS............................... Aqua $250-300
      Groove ring wax sealer, pressed laid-on ring   #2549

2553. SAN FRANCISCO GLASS WORKS............................... Aqua $250-300
      With erased words in arch, above
      Groove ring wax sealer, pressed laid-on ring

2554. SANG YUEN CO. 822 WASHINGTON SAN FRANCISCO, CALIFORNIA.........Clear $3-5
      Side: Chinese characters
      Reverse: NET WEIGHT 12 OZ PACKED IN U.S.A.
      Smooth lip   Lightning dimple neck seal
      Product jar

2555. SANG YUEN CO. 641 JACKSON SAN FRANCISCO, CALIFORNIA.......... Clear $3-5
      Reverse: Chinese characters
      Smooth lip   Metal screw cap Product jar

2556. SANG YUEN CO. 822 WASHINGTON SAN FRANCISCO, CALIF............ Clear $3-5
      Reverse: Chinese characters
      Smooth lip   Metal screw cap Product jar

2557. SANIJAR PAT. NO. 184 2226 (on lid)...................... Clear $1-3
      Smooth lip   Glass lid & rubber sealing rings

2558. SANITARY.. Aqua $12-15
     Base: H. W. Pettit Salem N. J.   Amber $25-30
     Ground lip Old style Lightning seal

2559. SANITARY PACKED BY W. B. THOMAS & SON
    WESTMINSTER, MD..Clear $6-8
     Smooth lip Metal press-down lid
     Product jar

2560. SAN JOSE FRUIT PACKING COMPANY (on base)...............Clear $20-25
     Ground lip Clear or milkglass insert & screw band
     Insert: San Jose Fruit & Packing Co. San Jose, Cal.
          TradeMark California Fruits (around Eagle,
          with outspread wings) over a can of fruit.
          A bear on each side.
     Product jar

2561. THE SCHAFFER JAR ROCHESTER N.Y.................... Aqua $125-150
     Reverse: JCS monogram
     Ground lip Dome shaped lid, wire clamp with
             Spring coil
     Lid: Pat. July 1 79
     The JCS monogram stands for the patentee,
      Jacob C. Schaffer.

                   #2561

2562. THE SCHAFFER JAR ROCHESTER N.Y................... Aqua $125-150
     Reverse: JCS monogram
     Ground lip Unmarked glass lid with raised fins
     Wire bail, neck tie wire

2563. THE J. O. SCHIMMEL PRES'G. CO. PHILADA .... Aqua $35-40
     Base: Cohansey Glass Mfg. Co. Philada
     Ground lip Cohansey lid & wire clamp
     Product jar

                   #2562

2564. C. SCHRACK & CO. PHILADA PAINT WORKS.... Aqua $20-25
     Closure unknown Small product jar

                   #2564

2565. SCHRAM AUTOMATIC SEALER (script)........................... Aqua $8-10
     Smooth lip Metal press-down lid with sealing gasket
     Lid: Schram Auto. Sealer Waterloo Ontario Patd 1901
      Or: Schram Auto. Sealer Co. Waterloo, Ont. Can.
         Patd 1901-03
      Or: Schram Bottle Cap Patd 1901 & 3 Mfg. For Gowans
         Kent Co. Toronto
      Or: Schram Bottle Cap Patd Dec 3 1901 Woodstock
         Ont. Canada
      Or: Schram Bottle Cap Patd 1901 & 3 Woodstock
         Ont. Canada

2566. SCHRAM AUTOMATIC SEALER (script)...............................Clear $8-10
     Base: Schram, St. Louis or Unmarked
     Smooth lip Metal press-down lid with sealing gasket
     Lid: Schram St. Louis Patd 1909
      Or: Schram Automatic Sealer Co. St. Louis
         Mo. Patd 1903

2567. SCHRAM AUTOMATIC SEALER A............................. Clear $8-10
     Smooth lip Closure as in #2566

2568. SCHRAM AUTOMATIC SEALER B............................. Clear $8-10
     Smooth lip Closure as in #2566

2569. SCHRAM AUTOMATIC SEALER B (Automatic Sealer in flag   Aqua $6-8
     Base: Schram St. Louis or Unmarked   Clear $6-8
     Smooth lip Closure as in #2566

                   #2567

2570. SCHRAM AUTOMATIC SEALR (error).................... Clear $8-10
    Base: Schram St. Louis or Unmarked
    Smooth lip Closure as in #2566

2571. SCHRAM AUTOMATIC SEALER B TRADEMARK REGISTERED... Clear $6-8
    Smooth lip Closure as in #2566   Aqua $6-8

2572. SCHRAM FRUIT JAR (Fruit Jar within flag)......... Clear $6-8
    Smooth lip Closure as in #2566
                                            #2573

2573. SCHRAM FRUIT JAR B (Fruit Jar within flag)....... Clear $6-8
    Smooth lip Closure as in #2566   ½ Pint, Clear $15-18

2574. SCHRAM ST. LOUIS (on base)....................½ Pint, Clear $15-18
    Smooth lip Closure as in #2566

    LUTZ & SCHRAMM stoneware jar, see No. 1564 & 1565
    JOS H. SCHRAMM stoneware jar, see No. 1566

2575. SCOTIA TRADEMARK WIDE MOUTH ADJUSTABLE............ Aqua Unpriced
    Ground lip Old style Lightning seal
    This is a Canadian sealer and difficult to find.

2576. THE SCRANTON JAR.................................. Aqua $250-300
    Base: G. H. C. or Unmarked   Citron Unpriced
    Ground lip Glass lid: Sept. 27 1887
    Spring wire clamp, bent over wooden roller,
    hooking under a strap. Wire around neck
    holds clamps in place.
                                            #2576

2577. SEALFAST......................................Clear $1-3
    Base: Foster or Unmarked   ½ Pint, Clear $4-6
    Smooth lip Old style Lightning seal, wide mouth

2578. SEALFAST......................................Clear $1-3
    Base: Unmarked
    Smooth lip Old style Lightning seal, reg. mouth

2579. SEALFAST......................................Clear $2-3
    Base: Unmarked
    Ground lip Old style Lightning seal

2580. FOSTER SEALFAST...............................Clear $1-3
    Base: Foster or Unmarked
    Smooth lip Old style Lightning seal

2581. FOSTER SEALFAST...............................Clear $1-3
    Base: Foster or Unmarked   ½ Pint, Clear $4-6
    Smooth lip Lightning beaded neck seal

2582. TRADE MARK SEALFAST...........................Clear $2-4
    Base: Foster
    Smooth lip Old style Lightning seal
                                            #2580

    The following series of Sealfast jars were made using a "plated" mold. The
    permanent portion of the mold was lettered SEALFAST SOLD BY. The inter-
    changeable circular plates were lettered with the names of the individual cus-
    tomers.

2583. SEALFAST SOLD BY BOLSTER & BARNES GROCERIES
    OLYMPIA, WASH..Clear $20-25
    Smooth lip Old style Lightning seal Quart

2584. SEALFAST SOLD BY J. S. CARVER & SONS GROCERIES
    OGDEN, UTAH..Clear $20-25
    Smooth lip Old style Lightning seal Quart

2585. SEALFAST SOLD BY COBB, BATES & YERXA BOSTON, MASS............. Clear $20-25
      Smooth lip Old style Lightning seal Quart

2586. SEALFAST SOLD BY C. S. & B. CUMMINGS
      NEW BEDFORD, MASS.................................... Clear $20-25
      Smooth lip Old style Lightning seal Quart

2587. SEALFAST SOLD BY CUMMINGS & CUMMINGS
      NEW BEDFORD, MASS.................................... Clear $20-25
      Smooth lip Old style Lightning seal Quart

2588. SEALFAST SOLD BY WM. CUSHARD DRY GOODS CO.
      DECATUR, ILL....................................... Clear $20-25
      Smooth lip Old style Lightning seal Quart

2589. SEALFAST SOLD BY THE EMPORIUM MURRAY, UTAH.......... Clear $20-25
      Smooth lip Old style Lightning seal Quart   #2590

2590. SEASFAST SOLD BY THE EMPORIUM MURRAY, UTAH (error)........... Clear $25-30
      Smooth lip Old style Lightning seal Quart

2591. SEALFAST SOLD BY C. B. HOBBS GROCER PHONE 581 TIPTON, IND..... Clear $20-25
      Smooth lip Old style Lightning seal Quart

2592. SEALFAST SOLD BY McCREW GROCERY CO. PHONES 145 & 180
      WALLA WALLA'S GROCER................................ Clear $20-25
      Smooth lip Old style Lightning seal Pint & Quart

2593. SEALFAST SOLD BY MONARCH HARDWARE CO. SALT LAKE UTAH......... Clear $20-25
      Smooth lip Old style Lightning seal Quart

2594. SEALFAST SOLD BY GEORGE H. MYLKES 46 CHURCH ST.
      BURLINGTON, VT..................................... Clear $20-25
      Smooth lip Old style Lightning seal Quart

2595. SEALFAST SOLD BY P. A. NELSEN & SON GROCERIES, LOGAN, UTAH.... Clear $20-25
      Smooth lip Old style Lightning seal Quart

2596. SEALFAST SOLD BY PACKARD BROS. CO. SPRINGVILLE, UTAH.......... Clear $20-25
      Smooth lip Old style Lightning seal Quart

2597. SEALFAST SOLD BY RADER & LAMPKIN CO. ONTARIO, ORE............. Clear $20-25
      Smooth lip Old style Lightning seal Quart

2598. SEALFAST SOLD BY L. RORDEN & CO. THE DALLES, OREGON.... .... Clear $20-25
      Smooth lip Old style Lightning seal Quart

2599. SEALFAST SOLD BY A. F. SCHERER GROCER CHEHALIS,
      WASH..Clear $20-25
      Smooth lip Old style Lightning seal Quart

2600. SEALFAST SOLD BY SHELLING'S ALLENTOWN, PA........ Clear $20-25
      Smooth lip Old style Lightning seal Quart

2601. SEALFAST SOLD BY TIMOTHY SMITH CO. ROXBURY, MASS. Clear $20-25
      Smooth lip Old style Lightning seal Quart

2602. SEALFAST SOLD BY W. H. VANLEW BAKERY & GROCERIES
      DAYTON, WASH....................................... Clear $20-25
      Smooth lip Old style Lightning seal Pint & Quart #2602

2603. SEAL TITE (in block letters)................................ Clear $8-10
      Base: Pa G. Co.
      Smooth lip Old style Lightning seal

2604. SEALTITE TRADEMARK... Clear $8-10
      Smooth lip Old style Lightning seal

2605. SEAL TITE (script)...Clear $8-10
       Smooth lip Lightning beaded neck seal

2606. SEALTITE WIDE MOUTH MASON.............................Lt. Green $8-10
       Base: I P G Co in diamond
       Smooth lip Mason beaded neck seal

2607. SECURITY (script)....................................... Clear $8-10
       Smooth lip Old style Lightning seal

2608. SECURITY SEAL FGCo (monogram) (within triangles).............. Clear $4-6
       Smooth lip Old style Lightning seal, regular mouth

2609. SECURITY SEAL FGCo (monogram) (within triangles).............. Clear $4-6
       Smooth lip Old style Lightning seal, wide mouth

2610. SELCO SURETY SEAL (within circle)....................... Clear $3-5
       Smooth lip Lightning dimple neck seal   Ball Blue $3-5

2611. SELCO SURETY SEAL PAT'D JULY 14 1908..................... Clear $3-5
       Smooth lip Lightning dimple neck seal   Ball Blue $3-5

2612. SELCO SURETY SEAL (within circle) PAT'D JULY 14 1908.......... Clear $3-5
       Smooth lip Lightning dimple neck seal   Ball Blue $3-5

2613. SELCO SURETY SEAL (within circle, on front).......... ..... Clear $3-5
       Reverse: PAT'D JULY 14 1908   Ball Blue $3-5
       Smooth lip Lightning dimple neck seal

2614. M. SELLER & CO., PORTLAND, O................... .... Aqua $250-300
       Groove ring wax sealer, pressed laid-on ring

2615. M. SELLER & CO., PORTLAND, O. (front)......... ... Aqua $250-300
       Reverse: Erased arch & rectangle
       Words in arch, not discernible
       Words in rectangle were: San Francisco
                             Glass Works
       Groove ring wax sealer, pressed laid-on ring

#2614

      Also see SAN FRANCISCO GLASS WORKS, jar No. 2553

2616. S. G. Co. (on base)................................ ..... Aqua $18-20
       Groove ring wax sealer, pressed laid-on ring

2617. S. G. W. LOU KY (on base)...................... ..... Aqua $18-20
       Groove ring wax sealer, pressed laid-on ring   Lt. Green $18-20
                                                Amber $100-125

2618. SHAKER PRESERVES............................... ..... Aqua $50-75
       Ground lip Mason shoulder seal

2619. J. V. SHARP CANNING CO. WMs TOWN, N.J. (on base)   Clear   Unpriced
       Early fruit bottle, sealed with waxed cork
       Clear with yellowish tinge

#2618

2620. PAT JUNE 24 1884 (on lid)............................. $15-18
       Brown glaze pottery jar with clear glass lid
       Lid has ramps which tighten on a heavy wire
       bar, inserted thru holes on each side of
       the jar neck, and across the lid.

2621. SHERWOOD BROS. POTTERY NEW BRIGHTON, PA (in oval on front). $10-12
       White stoneware jar with unmarked black glass lid
       Wire & metal clamp

2622. Unmarked variation...................................... $8-10
       White stoneware jar with unmarked black glass lid
       Wire & metal clamp

#2621

2623. SHERWOOD PATENT APPLIED FOR (on lid)................................. $10-12
      White stoneware jar with clear glass lid
      Wire & metal clamp

2624. SHERWOOD PATd JUNE 7 1904 (on lid)................................... $12-15
      White stoneware jar with clear glass lid
      Wire & metal clamp Pierced ears on sides
      of jar for wire carrying handle.   Gallon

2625. PATd JANY 11th 1898 (on lid)............................... Clear $1-3
      Jar is unmarked
      Lid has a serpentine groove and is held on
      by a serpentine shaped wire clamp. This
      closure patented by John Schies, is found
      on various product jars.

2626. PATd JANY 11th 1898 (on lid).................... Clear $1-3
      Base: Pat Jany 11 1898 W B C
      Closure as in #2625   Product jar

2627. SIERRA MASON JAR MADE IN CALIFORNIA............. Clear $10-12
      Smooth lip Mason beaded neck seal

#2627

2628. SIGNAL.. Aqua $12-15
      Smooth lip Mason beaded neck seal, wide mouth
      Made in New Zealand

2629. SILICON (within circle)................................... Aqua $10-12
      Smooth lip Old style Lightning seal

2630. SILICON GLASS COMPANY PITTSBURGH, PENNA. (within circle)...... Aqua $12-15
      Base: B within circle or F within circle
      Smooth lip Old style Lightning seal

2631. SILVER MOON COFFEE VACUUM PACKED ONE POUND NET... Clear $1-3
      Base: Oliver Finnie Company, Memphis
      Product jar

2632. SIMPLEX (within diamond) on jar front.......... Clear $10-12
      Smooth lip Glass screw cover
      Lid: Simplex (within diamond)   Small jar

2633. SIMPLEX (within diamond) on lid............... Clear $8-10
      Jar unmarked
      Smooth lip Glass screw cover   Small jar

#2636

2634. SIMPLEX (within diamond) PAT. APLD FOR TRADEMARK REGISTERED... Clear $8-10
      All on lid Jar is unmarked
      Smooth lip Glass screw cover   Small jar

2635. SIMPLEX MASON.. Clear $20-25
      Smooth lip Glass screw cover
      Lid: Simplex Mason Patent Appld For

2636. SIMPLEX MASON.................................... Clear $20-25
      Smooth lip Glass screw cover
      Lid: Simplex Glass Cap For Mason Jars
          Patd Dec. 5. 05

2637. T.M. SINCLAIR & CO. LTD. CEDAR RAPIDS IOWA PORK &
      BEEF PACKERS.................................... Clear $8-10
      Smooth lip Glass lid & metal clamp
      Lid: Patd Jany 11th 1898
      A product jar, using the Shies closure as
      in #2625.

#2637

2638. S. K. & Co. (on base, star in center).......................... Aqua $18-20
       Groove ring wax sealer, pressed laid-on ring

2639. S. K. & Co. (on base, N within star in center)..... ... Aqua $18-20
       Groove ring wax sealer, pressed laid-on ring

2640. E H E Co 7 (on heel)....................................... ... Aqua $20-25
       Base: S. K. & Co Star in center
       Groove ring wax sealer, pressed laid-on ring

2641. SKILTON FOOTE & COS. TRADEMARK BUNKER HILL
       PICKLES (within oval frame)..........................Green $18-20
       Ground lip Glass lid & wire clamp
       Closure is similiar to the Cohansey closure,
         but unmarked. The jar has also been reported
         with the Thomas Patent closure as we have
         illustrated, with the lid marked Thomas Patent
         July 12 1892.

#2641

2642. SKINNER'S SNUFF (within oval, on paneled jar)........Amber $15-18
       Ground lip Glass insert & screw band Snuff jar

2643. A. G. SMALLEY & CO. BOSTON & NEW YORK (on lid).....Amber $25-30
       Base: Pat April 7 1896 Dec 13th 1892
       Ground lip Milkglass insert & screw band

2644. A. G. SMALLEY & CO. BOSTON & NEW YORK (on lid).....Amber $25-30
       Base: A. G. Smalley & Co. Boston & New York
       Ground lip Milkglass insert & screw band

#2642

2645. A. G. SMALLEY & CO. BOSTON, MASS. PATENTED
       APRIL 7th 1896 & DECEMBER 1st 1896 (all on base)..............Amber $25-30
       Ground lip Milkglass insert & screw band
       Insert: A. G. Smalley & Co. Chelsea & New York

2646. A. G. SMALLEY & CO. BOSTON, MASS DEC. 13, 1892
       PATENT APRIL 7 1896 DEC 1 1896 (on base).....................Amber $25-30
       Ground lip Milkglass insert & screw band   ½ Pint, Clear $8-10
       Insert: A. G. Smalley & Co. Boston & New York

2647. SMALLEY FULL MEASURE AGS PINT.................................Clear $8-10
       Base: Patented Dec. 13 1892 April 7 1896   Aqua $8-10
              Dec. 1. 1896
         Or: Patented April 7, 1896
       Ground lip Mason shoulder seal
       Lid variations:
       (1) Unlined Aluminum cap marked Aluminum
              Smalley Cap Purist Metal Known
              AGS monogram in center
       (2) Zinc lid marked TradeMark Full Measure
              For Smalley Fruit Jars. Liner unmarked

2648. SMALLEY FULL MEASURE AGS QUART...................Clear $8-10
       Base & closure as in #2647   Aqua $8-10
                                                      Amber $45-50

2649. SMALLEY FULL MEASURE AGS ½ GALLON..............Clear $8-10
       Base & closure as in #2647   Aqua $8-10

#2648

2650. SMALLEY FULL MEASURE AGS QUART (circle around monogram)........ Aqua $8-10
       Base: Patented April 7 1896
       Ground lip Closure as in #2647

2651. TRADEMARK FULL MEASURE REGISTERED AGS PINT.....................Clear $8-10
       Base: A. G. Smalley & Co. Boston, Mass.
              Dec 1 1892 Patent April 7 1896 Dec 1 1896
       Ground lip Glass insert & screw band

2652. TRADEMARK FULL MEASURE REGISTERED AGS QUART........ .....Clear $8-10
     Base & closure as in #2651

2653. TRADEMARK FULL MEASURE REGISTERED AGS ½ GALLON... ....Clear $8-10
     Base & closure as in #2651

2654. TRADEMARK FULL MEASURE REGISTERED AGS PINT...... ...Clear $8-10
     Ground lip Old style Lightning seal

2655. TRADEMARK FULL MEASURE REGISTERED AGS QUART..... ...Clear $8-10
     Ground lip Old style Lightning seal

2656. TRADEMARK FULL MEASURE REGISTERED AGS ½ GALLON.......... ...Clear $8-10
     Ground lip Old style Lightning seal   #2654

2657. SMALLEY'S NU-SEAL TRADEMARK (within diamonds).................Clear $8-10
     Base: Smalley Fruit Jar Co. Boston, Mass.   ½ Pint, Clear $12-15
        Patented Jan 5, 1904
     Smooth lip Old style Lightning seal

2658. SMALLEY'S NU-SEAL TRADEMARK (within diamonds).. ....Clear $8-10
     Base: A. G. Smalley & Co. Inc. Boston
        Patented Jan 5 1904
     Smooth lip Old style Lightning seal

2659. SMALLEY'S NU-SEAL TRADEMARK (within diamonds).. ....Clear $8-10
     Base: Smalley Fruit Jar Co. Boston, Mass.
        Patented Jan 5 1904
     Smooth lip Lightning beaded neck seal

2660. SMALLEY'S ROYAL (on neck)....................................Clear $2-4
     Smooth lip Lightning beaded neck seal   #2658   ½ Pint, Clear $12-15

2661. SMALLEY'S (crown) ROYAL TRADEMARK NU-SEAL...................Clear $8-10
     Word Royal also superimposed over the crown   ½ Pint, Clear $12-15
     Base: Smalley Fruit Jar Co. Boston, Mass.
        Patented Jan 5 1904
     Smooth lip Old style Lightning seal

2662. A. G. SMALLEY & CO. BOSTON & N.Y. PATENTED
     APRIL 1896 (all on base)........................ ....Clear $4-6
     Ground lip Old style Lightning seal

2663. SMALLEY KIVLAN & ONTHANK BOSTON, MASS. PAT'D
     FEB. 23. 09. (all on base)...................... ....Clear $2-3
     Smooth lip Glass lid & twin wire clamps   #2660
     Lid: KantKrack Patd Feb 23 09
     This oval shaped jar reported by Leo West, has
     a paper label reading Champlain Cocoa, Berry-
     Hall Co., Burlington, Vt.

2664. SMALLEY KIVLAN & ONTHANK, BOSTON (on base).....................Clear $2-3
     Smooth lip Glass lid & twin wire clamps   ½ Pint, Clear $4-6
     Oval shaped jar with lid as in #2663

2665. SMALLEY KIVLAN ONTHANK BOSTON UNION MADE (on base). .Clear $1-3
     Smooth lip Glass lid & twin wire side clamps
     Square jar

2666. TRADEMARK "THE SMALLEY" SELF SEALER............... .Clear $6-8
     Base: Smalley Fruit Jar Co. Trademark,
        Boston & New York
     Ground lip Old style Lightning seal
     Lid: A. G. Smalley & Co. Boston & New York

2667. THE SMALLEY SELF SEALER WIDE MOUTH (within circle)   Clear $6-8
     Base: A. G. Smalley & Co. Inc. Boston, Mass.
     Smooth lip Old style Lightning seal   #2667

2668. THE SMALLEY JAR.. Aqua $150-175

2669. THE SMALLEY FRUIT JAR PAT. SEP. 23 '84........................ Aqua $200-225
      Ground lip High dome shaped lid
      Wire bail & neck tie wire

2670. J. P. SMITH SON & CO. PITTSBURGH (around shoulder)............. Aqua $30-35
      Groove ring wax sealer, pressed laid-on ring   Lt. Cobalt Blue $150 & up

2671. W. D. SMITH N. Y... Aqua $150-175
      Base: bare iron pontil
      Stopper neck finish for cork

2672. SMUCKER APPLE BUTTER ORRVILLE, OHIO (on lid) $8-10
      White stoneware jar & lid
      Wire & metal clamp similiar to the Weir

2673. THE T. A. SNIDER PRESERVE CO. CINCINNATI, O.   .... Aqua $10-12
      Ground lip Glass insert & screw band
      Insert: The T. A. Snider Preserves Co.
              Cincinnati, O.
      Product jar

2674. SOCIETE (on base)..Clear $2-4
      Smooth lip Lightning beaded neck seal
      Product jar

2675. SOCIETE (on base)..Clear $2-4
      Smooth lip Lightning dimple neck seal
      Product jar

2676. SOCIETE SEATTLE (on base)..................................Clear $2-4
      Smooth lip Lightning beaded neck seal
      Product jar

2677. SOCIETTE SEATTLE (on base).................................Clear $2-4
      Smooth lip Lightning dimple neck seal
      Product jar

2678. SOLIDEX (within oval)...................................Deep Green $20-25
      Smooth lip Hinged glass lid
      Deep green, heavy weight glass
      A French jar

2679. SOU G W (on base).. Aqua $18-20
      Groove ring wax sealer, pressed laid-on ring

2680. SOUTHERN DOUBLE SEAL MASON...............................Clear $12-15
      Smooth lip Mason beaded neck seal   ½ Pint, Clear $15-18

2681. SPEAS MFG. CO. U-SAVIT JAR TRADEMARK
      REGISTERED U S PATENT OFFICE (all on base)   ....Clear $1-3
      Smooth lip Mason beaded neck seal
      A product jar with alternating smooth &
       stippled panels, which could be reused
       to make a lamp.

2682. C. F. SPENCER'S PATENT ROCHESTER N.Y.......   .... Aqua $70-75
      Stopper neck finish Metal stopper with   No lid, Aqua $50-55
       finger ring for lifting it from neck.
      Stopper: C. F. Spencers Patent
           Feb. 10 1863

2683. C. F. SPENCER'S PATENT RCOHESTER N.Y. (error)............... Aqua $75-80
      Stopper neck finish   No lid, Aqua $55-60
      Metal stopper as in #2682

#2668

#2669

#2671

#2682

2684. C. F. SPENCER'S PNTENT ROCHESTER N. Y. (error)................ Aqua $75-80
      Stopper neck finish Stopper as in #2682   Minus lid, Aqua $55-60

2685. C F SPENCER'S PAT. 1868 IMPROVED JAR......................... Aqua $150 & up
      Ground lip Unmarked metal lid with
      attached wire loops which fit on
      stepped glass lugs on neck of jar.

2686. SPOTSWOOD...Clear $15-18
      Smooth lip Mason shoulder seal
      Australian jar

2687. SPRATT'S PATENT JULY 18 1854 WELLS & PROVOST
      PROPRIETORS. N. Y. (all on lid)................................   Unpriced
      Lid is made of heavy tin, or lead, & has
      two round raised lugs on top. Lid is
      threaded on inside. Fits on a tin can.

2688. SPRATT'S PATENT JULY 18th '54 IMPROVED WELLS &
      PROVOST PROPRIETORS N.Y. (all on lid)..............   ...   Unpriced
      Lid as in #2687 Fits on a tin can

2689. SPRATT'S PATENT JULY 18 1854 (on lid)..............   ...   Unpriced
      Lid is made of glass, has two oblong raised
      lugs on top, & is threaded on the outside.
      Fits on a tin can. The purpose of the glass
      was so that the contents could be seen.

                                                        #2687

2690. SPRATT'S PATENT JULY 18 1854 PAT'D APRIL 5 1864....................   Unpriced
      Lid is made of glass & described as in #2689
      Fits on a tin can

      Note: For complete illustrations & history of the Spratt's cans,
            see "FRUIT JARS" By Creswick.

2691. SQUARE G MASON..Clear $3-5
      Smooth lip Mason beaded neck seal

2692. SQUARE G WIDE MOUTH MASON.............................   .....Clear $3-5
      Smooth lip Mason beaded neck seal   ½ Pint, Clear $4-6

2693. PATd OCTr 18th 1864 J. J. SQUIRE......   .... Aqua $425-450
      Base: footed, 3 "feet"
      Ground lip Glass lid marked
              Octr. 18th 1864
      The patent calls for two metal
      crossbars, fitting over the
      center hub of the lid.

2694. PATd OCTr 18th 1864 J. J. SQUIRE .... Aqua $425-450
      Base: footed, 4 "feet"
      Ground lip Closure as in #2693
                                          #2693

2695. PATd OCTr 18th 1864 & MARh 7th 1865 J. J. SQUIRE 1.   Aqua $425-450
      Jar has one side opening on lip
      Base: footed, 3 "feet"
      Glass lid marked Patd Octr 18th 1864
      The patent calls for a single locking
      bar, turning on a central hub on lid.

2696. PATd OCTr 18th 1864 & MARh 7th 1865 J. J. SQUIRE 2.   Aqua $425-450
      Jar has two side openings on lip
      Base: footed, 3 "feet"
      Ground lip Glass lid & clamp as in #2695
                                          #2696

2697. PATd OCt 1864 MARCH & SEPt 1865 J. J. SQUIRE........................ Aqua $425-450
       Base: footed, 3 "feet"
       Ground lip Unmarked glass lid with 4 raised
       glass knobs, & vent hole in center.
       The lid was held down by means of an elastic
       band or strap of rubber, as illustrated.

2698. S S CO (& a star) impressed in base............................. $25-30
       Two-tone brown & white stoneware jar
       Wax seal groove

2699. STANDARD (arched)...Amber $450 & up
       Groove ring wax sealer, pressed laid-on ring   Dark Green   Unpriced

#2697

2700. STANDARD (arched)... Aqua $20-25
       Base: Indianapolis Glass Works, Ind.
       Groove ring wax sealer, pressed laid-on ring

2701. STANDARD (front) Reverse, heel: W. McC & Co.................... Aqua $20-25
       Groove ring wax sealer, pressed laid-on ring   Amber $450 & up
                                                         Sky Blue $75 & up
                                               Med. Cobalt Blue $300 & up

2702. STANDARD (front) Reverse, heel: W. McCULLY & CO............... Aqua $20-25
       Groove ring wax sealer, pressed laid-on ring   Lt. Cobalt Blue $150 & up
                                               Med. Cobalt Blue $300 & up

2703. STANDARD (front) Reverse, heel: WM McCULLY & CO............... Aqua $20-25
       Groove ring wax sealer, pressed laid-on ring

2704. W. McCULLY & CO (below erased lettering)....................... Aqua $20-25
       Groove ring wax sealer, pressed laid-on ring   Lt. Cornflower Blue $50-75

2705. STANDARD (front) Reverse: Erased MASTODON..................... Aqua $20-25
       Lower reverse: W. McC & Co   Lt. Cobalt Blue $150 & up
       Groove ring wax sealer, pressed laid-on ring   Green $25-30

2706. STANDARD (over erased MASTODON)................................ Aqua $20-25
       Lower reverse: W. McC & Co   Lt. Cobalt Blue $150 & up
       Groove ring wax sealer, pressed laid-on ring   Med. Cobalt Blue $300 & up
                                                        Deep Green $150 & up

2707. STANDARD FROM FOOTE, BAER & CO CLEVELAND O (front).............Aqua $75-80
       Lower reverse: W. McC & Co.   Med. Cobalt Blue $350 & up
       Groove ring wax sealer, pressed laid-on ring

2708. STANDARD (over erased FROM FOOTE, BAER & CO
       CLEVELAND O).. Aqua $20-25
       Lower reverse: W. Mc C   Med. Cobalt Blue $300 & up
       Groove ring wax sealer, pressed laid-on ring

2709. STANDARD (with looped underline)................................Clear $20-25
       Groove ring wax sealer, pressed laid-on ring

2710. STANDARD (on slant)..Clear $20-25
       Groove ring wax sealer, pressed laid-on ring   Aqua $20-25

2711. STANDARD (underlined with shepherd's crook).................. Aqua $20-25
       Groove ring wax sealer, pressed laid-on ring

2712. STANDARD MASON (word Mason in flag)...........................Lt. Green $6-8
       Smooth lip Mason shoulder seal

2713. Star emblem only (on front)................................Aqua $30-35
       Groove ring wax sealer, pressed laid-on ring   Amber $200 & up
       Tin lid has embossed star emblem   #2713

2714. Star emblem with dot in center (front)........................Aqua $30-35
       Groove ring wax sealer, pressed laid-on ring   Amber $200 & up

-197-

2715. Star emblem only (on base)....................................... Aqua   Unpriced
      Ground lip Closure unknown ½ Gallon

2716. Large Star emblem (on base)...................................... Aqua $18-20
      Erased letters on front, not readable
      Groove ring wax sealer, pressed laid-on ring

2717. Large star emblem (on base)...................................... Aqua $18-20
      Without erased lettering on front
      Groove ring wax sealer, pressed laid-on ring   #2718

2718. STAR (below star emblem) Final stroke of R is straight.........Clear $35-45
      Ground lip Glass insert & screw band   Pale Aqua $35-45
      Canadian sealer   Amber   Unpriced
      Only 1 amber jar is known   Midget Pint, Clear $225-250

2719. STAR (below star emblem) Final stroke of R is curved..........Clear $35-45
      Ground lip Glass insert & screw band   Pale Aqua $35-45
      Canadian sealer   Blue $45-50

2720. STAR (below star emblem)......................................Clear $45-50
      Corrected word Star over erased error)   Pale Aqua $45-50
      Ground lip Glass insert & screw band   Midget Pint, Clear $225-250
      Canadian sealer

2721. STAR (word only).. Aqua $70-75
      Ground lip Glass lid & screw band or
                  Zinc insert & screw band
      Lid variations:
      (1) Glass insert, marked Haller's Patent
              Feb 5th 67
      (2) Unlined zinc insert, embossed star in
              center of lid
      (3) Unlined zinc insert, stamped Haller's
              Patent Feb 5 67
      (4) Unlined zinc insert, stamped Haller's
          Patent Feb 5 67, star in center

2722. STAR (above star emblem)... Aqua $70-75
      Base: Pat'd Feb 5 1867   #2724
      Ground lip Closure as in #2721

2723. STAR (above star emblem, front)................................. Aqua $100-150
      Reverse: A. LIEBENSTEIN & CO. DEALERS IN CROCKERY &
               GLASSWARE 177 RANDOLPH ST. CHICAGO, ILL.
      Ground lip Closure as in #2721

2724. Star emblem, encircled by fruits................................ Aqua $100-125
      Ground lip Closure as in #2721

2725. STAR.. Clear $125-150
      Ground lip Glass lid & wire clamp
      Lid: Patented June 28, 1892

2726. STAR & CRESCENT (moon & star) PAT. MAR. 11th 1890   Aqua $75-100
      Ground lip Glass insert & zinc screw band
      with bail handle. Found with a cup shaped in-
      sert or with a flatish glass insert, unmarked.

2727. PUT RUBBER ON BEFORE FILLING STAR & CRESCENT
      (moon & star) SELF SEALING JAR (erased Mrs. S-T-
      Rorer's).. Aqua $100-125
      Base: Patented Dec'r 10th 1896
      Ground lip Zinc press-down lid with porcelain
                  liner.

2728. PUT RUBBER ON BEFORE FILLING MRS-S-T-RORER'S STAR
      & CRESCENT (moon & star) SELF SEALING JAR............. Clear $100-125
      Ground lip Closure as in #2727   #2728

-198-

2729. STAR GLASS CO. NEW ALBANY IND. (on front).... ...... Aqua $25-30
      Groove ring wax sealer, pressed laid-on ring Amber $500 & up
      Tin lid has an embossed star Lt. Green $25-30

2730. K (within star) STARK JAR PATENTED............. ......Clear $150 & up
      Smooth lip Glass lid, metal clamp & spring
      The jar neck has 4 equally spaced lugs to
      engage the ends of the clamp.

2731. CI - 7641 M831 J 1 GAL L (incised on front)... .... Unpriced
      Stoneware jar, salt glaze 2 lugs on neck
      Stoneware lid with central depression for
      spring & metal clamp as in #2730

2732. STARK QUALITY MASON........................... .....Clear $8-10
      Smooth lip Mason beaded neck seal Pale Green $8-10

2733. 3¢ STATE FAIR FOODS INC. WEST ALLIS, WIS........ .....Clear $1-3
      Smooth lip Mason beaded neck seal Product jar

2734. STEPHENS (front shoulder) GLOUCHESTER (reverse shoulder).......Green $18-20
      Base: B & Co. Ld. K
      Neck finish for glass or cork stopper English jar

2735. STERLING MASON............................... .....Clear $1-2
      Smooth lip Mason beaded neck seal

2736. STERLING MASON............................... ...Clear $1-2
      Smooth lip Mason beaded neck seal
      "Gripper" ribs on sides

2737. STEVENS TIN TOP PATd JULY 27 1875............. ... Aqua $75-85
      Base: S.K. & Co. (around N within star)
      Groove ring wax sealer, pressed laid-on ring
      Top is not "pinched" in.

2738. STEVENS TIN TOP PATd JULY 27 1875............. .. Aqua $75-85
      Base: N within star or Unmarked
      Groove ring wax sealer, pressed laid-on ring
      Top is slightly pinched in on each side to
      engage raised portions on metal lid.

2739. STEVENS TIN TOP PATENTED JULY 27 1875........... Aqua $75-85
      Base: N within star
      Groove ring wax sealer as in #2738

2740. STEVENS TIN TOP PATENTED JULY 27 1875 (front).... Aqua $175-200
      Reverse: MISSOURI GLASS CO. ST. LOUIS MO
      Base: S. K. & Co. (around N within star)
      Groove ring wax sealer as in #2738

2741. STEVENS TIN TOP PATd JULY 27 1875 LEWIS &
      NEBLETT CINCINNATI O. (all on front)............. Aqua $100-125
      Base: S. K. & Co. (around N within star)
      Groove ring wax sealer as in #2738

2742. ST. LOUIS SYRUP & PRESERVING CO. St LOUIS MO...... Aqua $20-25
      Ground lip Mason shoulder seal Product jar

2743. A. STONE & CO PHILADA.......................... Aqua $250-300
      Groove ring wax sealer
      Base: high kick-up & bare iron pontil scar

2744. A. STONE & CO PHILADA.......................... Aqua $200-250
      Groove ring wax sealer
      Base: high kick-up & pontil scar

#2730

#2738

#2740

#2743

2745. A. STONE & CO. -!!- PHILADA................................ Aqua $350 & up
     Base: High kick-up & bare iron pontil scar
     Groove ring wax sealer

2746. A. STONE & CO. -!!- PHILADA................ .... Aqua $300 & up
     Internal threads on jar neck for threaded
      glass stopper
     Stopper: A. Stone & Co. Philada.

2747. A. STONE & CO. PHILADA.................... .... Aqua $300 & up
     Threaded glass stopper as in #2746

2748. A. STONE & CO. PHILADA.................... .. Aqua $300 & up
     Threaded glass stopper as in #2746
     Stopper differs in that the center
     has hallow.

2749. A. STONE & CO. PHILADA................................ Aqua $300 & up
     Threaded glass stopper as in #2746
     Stopper differs in that the center
     has hallow, & is marked: A. Stone
     & Co. Philada E. T. Whitehead

2750. A. STONE & CO. PHILADA................................ Aqua $300 & up
     Base has kick-up
     This jar from the Norman Barnett collection,
     has two projecting lugs on the inside of
     neck, & a glass stopper also with lugs.
     Stopper: A. Stone & Co. Philada

2751. A. STONE & CO. PHILADA (on base only)................ ½ Pint, Aqua $350 & up
     Closure as in #2750

2752. A. STONE & CO. PHILADA MANUFACTURED BY
     CUNNINGHAMS & CO. PITTSBURGH, PA.................... Aqua $400 & up
     Base: High kick-up & bare iron pontil scar
     Groove ring wax sealer

2753. A. STONE & Co PHILADa MANUFACTURED BY
     CUNNINGHAMS & CO PITTSBURGH PA.................... Aqua $400 & up
     Base: High kick-up and bare iron pontil scar
     Groove ring wax sealer

2754. STONE MASON FRUIT JAR UNION STONEWARE CO.
     RED WING, MINN. (within square).................... $15-18
     Base: Pat Jan 24 1899
     White stoneware jar with black stenciling
     Zinc lid

2755. THE STONE MASON PATENT APPLIED FOR (on flat shoulder)................ $10-12
     Base: Kick-up & imprinted Macomb Pottery Co.
     White stoneware jar with brown shoulder
     Zinc lid

2756. STOUT DYER & WICKS X NEW YORK.................... ..... Aqua Unpriced
     Applied lip Waxed cork closure
     Product jar, circa 1865 to 1867 only
     For history of Stout Dyer & Wicks, see
      "Fruit Jars" by Creswick

2757. STRITTMATTERS (bee) PURE HONEY PUT UP BY
     F. J. STRITTMATTER & WIFE R.D. 1 EBENSBURG, PA. Ball Blue $20-25
     Smooth lip Mason beaded neck seal
     Product jar, Pint size

2758. SUEY FUNG YUEN & CO. SAN FRANCISCO, CAL. U.S.A.................Clear $3-5
     Reverse: Chinese characters, BEAN CAKE 12 OZ NET
     Smooth lip Lightning dimple neck seal
     Product jar

2759. SUEY FUNG YUEN & CO. SAN FRANCISCO, CAL. U.S.A. ....Clear $3-5
     Reverse: Chinese characters, BEAN CAKE 12 OZ NET
     Smooth lip   Lightning dimple neck seal   Product jar

2760. SULZBERGER'S PURE HORSE RADISH "AS YOU LIKE IT" $12-15
     White stoneware jar, brown shoulders, blue stenciling
     Lid: Weir Patent 92   Wire & metal clamp   ½ Pint Product jar

2761. SUN (within circle & radiating lines) TRADEMARK ....Lt. Green $50-55
     Base: J. P. Barstow
     Ground lip   Glass lid & metal yoke clamp
     Clamp: Monier's Pat April 1 90 Mar 12 95
       Or: Monier's Pat Apr 1 1890

2762. J. P. BARSTOW TRADEMARK (around sun trademark, on base) ....Lt. Green $30-40
     No marking on jar front
     Ground lip   Closure as in #2761
     Reported in Pint, 1½ Pint & Quart

2763. SUNBURST (just below shoulder) .... .Clear $2-4
     Reverse heel: S within star
     Base: M C Co monogram
     Jar is paneled with 20 small panels
     Smooth lip   Mason beaded neck seal
     Product jar

2764. S within star (on base) .... .Clear   -$1
     Smooth lip   Mason beaded neck seal   Product jar

2765. SUNNY BROOK COFFEE ONE POUND NET (embossed scene
     of trees & brook) all on one side
     "EVERY SWALLOW BRINGS YOU JOY" Reg. U.S. Pat. Off.   #2761 ....Clear $1-3
     One Pound Net (embossed birds) all on two sides
     Smooth lip   Mason beaded neck seal   Product jar

2766. SUNSHINE BRAND COFFEE VACUUM PACKED CONTENTS ONE
  POUND   SPRINGFIELD GROCER CO. ROASTERS AND PACKERS
  SPRINGFIELD, MO ....Clear $1-3
     Smooth lip   Mason beaded neck seal   Product jar

2767. SUNSHINE JAR ....Clear $15-18
     Base: I G Co.   or   Unmarked
     Smooth lip   Glass cover with projections on inside
             to hold sealing gasket in place
     Lid, outside: Sunshine, within stippled diamond
         Inside: I G Co. within diamond

2768. I G Co. (on base) (No front embossing) ....Clear $12-15
     Smooth lip   Closure as in #2767

2769. WARM CAP SLIGHTLY TO SEAL OR UNSEAL PAT'D OCT 24 1905 (lid) ....Clear $15-18
     Jar is unmarked
     Smooth lip   Glass cover with projections on inside
             to hold sealing gasket in place

2770. SUPERIOR A.G.CO. (within circle) .... Aqua $12-15
     Smooth lip   Old style Lightning seal

2771. SURE .... Aqua $200 & up
     Base: Pat'd June 21st 1870
     Ground lip   Glass lid with raised design
     & wire clamp

2772. SURE SEAL (within circle) .... Ball Blue $4-6
     Smooth lip   Old style Lightning seal   Lt. Green $4-6

2773. SURE SEAL (within circle) .... Ball Blue $4-6
     Smooth lip   Lightning beaded neck seal   #2773

2774. WIDEMOUTH SUTCLIFFE 2 LB. PRESERVING JAR..................... Amber   Unpriced
      Smooth lip Metal lid & spring band clamp
      Lid: Sutcliffe 2 Lb. Preserving Jar, Racine, Wisc.

2775. E. SWASEY & CO. PORTLAND ME. U.S.A. .... Clear $12-15
      (Encircling a pine tree within keystone emblem)
      Ground lip Old style Lightning seal
      ½ Gallon Product jar

2776. SWASEY DOUBLE SAFETY (within frame)............................Clear $10-12
      Smooth lip Old style Lightning seal

2777. SWAYZEE MASON....................................... Aqua $6-8
      Ground lip Mason shoulder seal   Ball Blue $6-8

2778. SWAYZEE FRUIT JAR (in two lines)...... .... Aqua $6-8
      Ground lip Mason shoulder seal   Ball Blue $6-8

2779. SWAYZEE FRUIT JAR (in three lines).... .... Aqua $6-8
      Ground lip Mason shoulder seal   Ball Blue $6-8

                                                             Aqua $3-5
2780. SWAYZEE'S IMPROVED MASON....................... Olive Green $20-25
      Smooth lip Mason shoulder seal

2781. SWAYZEE'S IMPPOVED MASON (error)............. .... Aqua $4-6
      Smooth lip Mason shoulder seal

2782. SWAYZEE'S (fleur-de-lis) IMPROVED MASON...... .... Aqua $4-6
      Smooth lip Mason shoulder seal

                                      #2781

2783. SWIFT & COMPANY CHICAGO............................. ...Clear $4-6
      Ground lip Milkglass insert & screw band
      Product jar

2784. SWIFT & COMPANY COPYRIGHT 1905 REG. U.S. PAT.
      OFF. U.S.A. (S in center) (all on lid)......... .Clear $3-5
      Smooth lip Glass lid & twin wire side clamps,
                  neck tie wire
      Product jar

2785. SYDNEY TRADE MARK DINGO FRUIT JAR............... Aqua $100-125
      Ground lip Old style Lightning seal
      An Australian jar. The Dingo is a wild
        dog, native to Australia.

2786. SYKES MACVAY & CO. ALBION GLASS WORKS
      CASTLEFORD (all on glass stopper)............... Green $6-8
      Jar is unmarked Base: T
      An English jar
                                      #2785

#2777

2787. J. E. TAYLOR & CO. PURE FOOD SANTA ANA, CAL.
      (within circle, on front)...................................... Aqua $12-15
      Smooth lip Old style Lightning seal
      Product jar

2788. TAYLOR & HODGETTS' CAN WITH BURNET'S ATTACHMENT
      PATENTED AUG. 21 1855 NEW YORK (all on lid)........................ Unpriced
      Lid is made of zinc or lead and has outside
        threads. Fits on a tin can.

2789. TAYLOR & HODGETTS INFALLIBLE SELF SEALING FRUIT
      CAN WITH BURNET'S ATTACHMENT PATENTED AUG. 21 1855.................. Unpriced
      Marking is all on lid. Made of zinc or lead and
        has outside threads. Fits on a tin can.

2790. THE TELEPHONE JAR TRADEMARK REG. WHITNEY GLASS WORKS............Aqua $8-10
    Ground lip   Old style Lightning seal

2791. THE TELEPHONE JAR TRADEMARK REG. WHITNEY GLASS WORKS............Aqua $6-8
    Within circle on front   Smooth lip
    Old style Lightning seal, regular mouth

2792. THE WIDEMOUTH TELEPHONE JAR TRADEMARK REG. (in circle).........Aqua $6-8
    Smooth lip   Old style Lightning seal

2793. THE WIDEMOUTH TELE HONE JAR TRADEMARK REG. (error)   ....Aqua $10-12
    Within circle on front   Smooth lip
    Old Style Lightning seal, wide mouth

2794. TEMPERED Mo G. Co...   ...Aqua $150-200
    Base: footed, 3 "feet"
    Groove ring wax sealer, pressed laid-on ring

2795. TEMTOR WAX TOP & names of fruits (on lid)........   .... $2-3
    Tin can

2796. TEXAS MASON (with map of Texas)................   ..Clear $8-10
    Base: Made In Texas By Texans
    Smooth lip   Mason beaded neck seal
    Lid: 2 Pc. gold lacquered metal lid with
     insert marked Texas & a map of Texas
    Made in miniature, pint & quart sizes

2797. THOMPSON................................   ....Aqua $100-125
    Base: Patd or Pat'd 1872
    Ground lip   Closure unknown

2798. THOMPSON'S FLAVORS NEW YORK..............   ....Aqua $20-25
    Ground lip   Old style Lightning seal   Amber $75-100
    ½ Gallon   Product jar

2799. THOMPSON & HILLS LTD. AUCKLAND..............................Clear $8-10
    Smooth lip   Mason beaded neck seal
    Made in New Zealand

2800. 3 RIVERS * (on base)..Clear   -$1
2801. 3 RIVERS * HA (on base).....................................Clear   -$1
    Smooth lip   Mason beaded neck seal   Product jars

2802. THRIFT BUCK GLASS CO. BALTIMORE, MD...........................Clear $12-15
    Base: Licensed by P.F.P.Co. Balto. Md. Oct. 7 1913
    Smooth lip   Metal lid marked Pat'd Oct. 7 1913

2803. THRIFT THRIFT JAR CO. BALTIMORE, MD..........................Clear $12-15
    Base: Licensed by P.F.P.Co. Balto. Md. Oct. 7 1913
    Smooth lip   Closure as in #2802

2804. TIGHT SEAL (within circle)...............   ....Clear $2-4
    Smooth lip   Lightning dimple neck seal   Lt Green $2-4
                                     Ball Blue $2-4

2805. TIGHT SEAL (without circle)...............   ....Clear $2-4
    Smooth lip   Lightning beaded neck seal   Lt Green $2-4
                                     Ball Blue $2-4

2806. TIGHT SEAL (within circle, front)..........   ....Clear $2-4
    Reverse: PAT'D JULY 14 1908   Lt Green $2-4
    Neck: BAIL HERE   Ball Blue $2-4
    Smooth lip   Lightning dimple neck seal

2807. TIGHT SEAL (within circle, front)............................Clear $2-4
    Reverse: PAT'D JULY 14 1908   Lt Green $2-4
    Neck: WIRE SIDE (sometimes with reversed d)   Ball Blue $2-4
    Smooth lip   Lightning dimple neck seal

#2794

#2796

#2807

2808. TIGHT SEAL (within circle) PAT'D JULY 14 1908.................Clear $2-4
Smooth lip Lightning dimple neck seal   Lt. Green $2-4
                                                        Ball Blue $2-4

2809. TILLYER.. Aqua $75-100
2810. TILLYER (front) Reverse: Erased WINSLOW JAR..................... Aqua $75-100
Ground lip Glass lid & wire clamp
Lid: Patented Nov. 29th 1870 Patented Feb 25 1873

2811. TORREY'S EGYPTIAN PATENTED MARCH 13th 1866 FRUIT JAR............... Unpriced
Stenciled on stoneware jar Black glaze finish
Stoneware lid & metal clamp

2812. TRADE MILLS COFFEES & SPICES MONTREAL.....................Lt. Green $35-50
Base: Registered
Crude, laid-on ring Waxed cork closure
Overall design of jar resembles a drum
Canadian product jar

2813. TRIOMPHE (on lid)...Clear -$1
Smooth lip Hinged glass lid Modern French jar

2814. TRIUMPH NO. 1.. Aqua $175-200
2815. TRIUMPH NO. 2.. Aqua $175-200
Groove ring wax sealer. Shoulder was pressed
down while hot to form the groove.
Ground lip Made with a 3 Pc. mold

#2814

2816. TOOWOOMBA...Lt. Green $75-100
Ground lip Old style Lightning seal
Made in Australia

2817. TO OPEN PRY OUT RUBBER AT NOTCH (on lid)...........Clear $4-6
Smooth lip Glass lid & metal band clamp

2818. TROPICAL TF (within diamond) CANNERS.............Clear $1-2
Smooth lip Mason beaded neck seal

2819. TROPICAL TF (within diamond) CANNERS (front)......Clear $1-3
Reverse: FLORIDA
Smooth lip Mason beaded neck seal

#2819

2820. TF (on base)................................Clear $1-2
2821. 3 TF (on base)..............................Clear $1-2
2822. 4 TF (on base)..............................Clear $1-2
2823. 5 TF (on base)..............................Clear $1-2
2824. 10 TF HA (trademark) (on base)..............Clear $1-2
Smooth lip Glass lid & wire bail
Lid: J. Hungerford Smith & Co. Rochester NY
Or: Unmarked
½ Gallon product jars. Also reported in Amber   #2819

2825. "TRUE FRUIT" (JHSCo) TRADEMARK REGISTERED (within circles)......Aqua $10-12
Base: The J. H. S. Co.   Clear $10-12
Smooth lip Glass lid & metal Safety Valve Clamp

2826. TRUE FRUIT (HSCo) TRADEMARK REGISTERED CANADA (within circles)..Aqua $10-12
Base: The H.S. Co.   Clear $10-12
Smooth lip Glass lid & metal Safety Valve Clamp

2827. TRUE FRUIT (HSCo) TRADEMARK REGISTERED.....................Clear $4-6
Embossed within circle on shoulder of pint bottle jar
Smooth lip Press-on lid

2828. TRUES IMPERIAL BRAND D.W. TRUE CO. PORTLAND, ME................Clear $6-8
(With draped flags & crown)
Smooth lip Old style Lightning seal
Product jar

2829. U. G. Co. (on base)... Aqua $20-25
      Groove ring wax sealer, pressed laid-on ring

2830. U. G. Co. (on heel)...Green $20-25
      Base: 2
      Groove ring wax sealer, pressed laid-on ring

2831. U. G. Co. (on heel)... Aqua $20-25
      Base: 3
      Groove ring wax sealer, pressed laid-on ring

2832. U. G. Co. (on heel)... Aqua $30-35
      Jar is paneled, 2 round & 4 flat panels
      Groove ring wax sealer, pressed laid-on ring

2833. ULTRE FORM DEPOST (on lid & base)...............................Clear   -$1
      Smooth lip Glass lid & wire clamp Modern French jar

2834. WM. UNDERWOOD & CO. (front) Reverse: BOSTON.................. Aqua   Unpriced
      Base: Kick-up & pontil scar   Deep Cobalt Blue   Unpriced
      Rolled lip, cork closure
      Petaled jar Product jar for ink

2835. WILLIAM UNDERWOOD & CO (on heel) 128 OZ. (below shoulder).......Aqua   Unpriced
      Rolled lip, cork closure Gallon size jar

2836. UNION...Clear   Unpriced
      Base: L & C
      Groove ring wax sealer, pressed laid-on ring

2837. UNION (reversed N).. Aqua   Unpriced
      Groove ring wax sealer, pressed laid-on ring

2838. UNION 1 (superimposed over erased NATIONAL)................... Aqua $50-75
      Applied lip Waxed cork closure

2839. UNION NO 1.. Aqua $200-250
      Wax seal groove, with lugs or ears on each side of neck
      Made with 3 Pc. mold

2840. UNION NO 2.. Aqua $200-250
2841. UNION NO 3.. Aqua $200-250
2842. UNION NO 4.. Aqua $200-250
      Wax seal groove with ears as in #2839
      Made with 3 Pc. mold

2843. UNION.. Aqua $35-40
      Groove ring wax sealer, pressed laid-on ring

2844. UNION N 1.. Aqua $35-40
      Base: Beaver Falls Glass Co. Beaver Falls, Pa.
      Groove ring wax sealer, pressed laid-on ring

2845. UNION NO. 1.. Aqua $35-40
      Groove ring wax sealer, pressed laid-on ring

2846. UNION NO. 1.. Aqua $35-40
      Base: Beaver Falls Glass Co. Beaver Falls, Pa.
      Groove ring wax sealer, pressed laid-on ring

2847. UNION NO. 2.. Aqua $35-40
      Groove ring wax sealer, pressed laid-on ring

2848. UNION NO. 2.. Aqua $35-40
      Base: Beaver Falls Glass Co. Beaver Falls, Pa.
      Groove ring wax sealer, pressed laid-on ring

#2832

#2840

#2848

2849. UNION 2...Clear $35-40
      Groove ring wax sealer, pressed laid-on ring

2850. UNION NO. 3.. Aqua $35-40
      Base: Beaver Falls Glass Co. Beaver Falls, Pa.
      Groove ring wax sealer, pressed laid-on ring

2851. UNION NO. 4.. Aqua $35-40
      Base: Beaver Falls Glass Co. Beaver Falls, Pa.
      Groove ring wax sealer, pressed laid-on ring

2852. UNION 5.. Aqua $35-40
      Groove ring wax sealer, pressed laid-on ring

2853. UNITED DRUG CO. BOSTON MASS. (within frame).......... Clear $6-8
      Smooth lip Old style Lightning seal Product jar #2853

2854. UNITED DRUG CO. BOSTON MASS. (within frame)....................Clear $6-8
      Smooth lip Glass lid & twin wire side clamps
      Product jar

2855. Unmarked jar, advertised as "U-NO-ME" FRUIT JAR................Clear $10-12
      Smooth lip Glass lid & metal spring band clamp

2856. UP-TO-DATE COCOA CO. (on base)..................................Amber $6-8
      Ground lip Metal screw cover Product jar

2857. PATENTED MAY 12 1863, superimposed over large U.S.............. Aqua $175-200
      Groove ring wax sealer, pressed laid-on ring

2858. UNIVERSAL (within frame) L.F. & C. (upside down on jar)........ Blue   Unpriced
      Ground lip jar made for a coffee grinder

2859. V MADE IN BELGIUM...Clear $1-2
      Smooth lip Mason beaded neck seal
      Modern 2 pc. closure with lid insert: V Verlica

2860. VACU-TOP (within oval, on base).................................Clear $2-4
      Smooth lip Inset glass lid & spring metal clamp
      Clamp: U.S.Patent #2281433 or Pat. 1939
        Or: Vacu-top U.S. Patent #2281433

2861. Marked only with the Owens-Illinois trademark on base.........Clear $1-3
      Smooth lip Closure as in #2860

2862. VACUUM (in script)...Clear $10-15
      Smooth lip Glass lid & metal clamp   Lt. Green $10-15
      Lid: Patented In Canada 1924 By Sager Glass
        Corp. Ltd. Toronto
      Jar was sealed with the aid of a vacuum pump device.

2863. VACUUM MADE IN CANADA..Clear $10-15
      Smooth lip Closure as in #2862

2864. VACUUM JAR & FRUIT PACKAGE CO. S.F.PAT. JULY 11 1893 (base)....Clear $18-20
      Ground lip Glass lid & 3 position wire clamp

2865. VACUUM JAR & FRUIT PACKAGE CO. S.F.NO. C2 (on base)............Clear $18-20
      Ground lip Glass lid & 3 position wire clamp

2866. VACUUM SEAL PAT. 1,212,274 PAT'S PEND. (on base)...............Clear $4-6
      Smooth lip Glass lid & metal clamp

2867. PAT. 1,95655 PAT'S PEND. (on base)...Clear $1-3
      Smooth lip Glass lid & metal clamp

2868. VACUUM SEAL JAR PATENTED TO OPEN DO NOT PRY ADMIT AIR BY
      PUSHING PIN DOWN BETWEEN LID AND RUBBER THRU ANY NOTCH (lid)...Clear $4-6
      Smooth lip Glass lid & metal clamp
      The lid has 3 notches around outside edge

2869. VACUUM SEAL JAR COMPANY, INC. NEW YORK PAT'D OCT.10.11
      JAN 12.12 DEC. 12.12 NOV. 15.13 DEC 12 16 JAN. 16.17
      NOV 13.17 (all on base)...Clear $4-6
      Smooth lip Glass lid with notches & metal clamp
      Lid: Vacuum Seal Jar To Open Insert Pin or Any Sharp
           Point Between Lid And Rubber At Any Notch. Allow
           Air To Rush In Fully Before Lifting Lid. Patented
      Or: Unmarked lid

2870. THE VACUUM SEAL FRUIT JAR PATENTED NOV 1st 1904 DETROIT........Clear $50-75
      Closure: hard cardboard disk & sealing wax

2871. VACUUM TITE JAR (on base)..Clear $8-10
      Smooth lip Metal lid
      Lid: Vacuum Tite Co. Pittsburgh, Penna.
           Patented August 19, 1930
      A vacuum pump device was used to aid in sealing
      the jar.

2872. VACUUM TITE JAR (on base).........................Clear $8-10
      Smooth lip Glass lid
      Lid: Vacuum Tite Co. Rapid City, S. D.
           Patented August 19, 1930
      Or: Unmarked
      The complete outfit consisted of jars, lids (which
      were made in 3 sizes), rubber seals, seals & air
      extractor pump.

#2870

2873. THE VALVE JAR CO PHILADELPHIA.................................. Aqua $100-125
      Base: Patd Mar 10th 1868   1½ Pint, Aqua $150-200
      Ground lip Glass or metal lid & wire coil clamp

2874. THE VALVE JAR CO. PHILADELPHIA
      PATENT MARCH 10th 1868 (all on front).............. Aqua $125-150
      Base: Unmarked Ground lip Closure as in #2873

2875. THE VALVE JAR CO. PHILADELPHIA PATENT
      MARCH 10th 1868 W.L. IMLAY (all on front)........ Aqua $150-175
      Ground lip Closure as in #2873

2876. THE VALVE JAR CO. PHILADELPHIA PATD
      MAR 10th 1868 (date in circle) (all on front).... Aqua $150-175
      Ground lip Closure as in #2873

2877. W. R. VAN VLIET'S PAT. APRIL 27th 1880 (circled). Aqua   Unpriced
      Ground lip Glass lid. Wire clamp extending
      vertically around entire jar, a metal plate
      across the top of the lid with thumbscrews on
      each side to tighten the ends of the wire
      clamp.
      Lid: W. R. Van Vliet's Pat. April 27th 1880

#2876

    Note: A priceless item, recently reported by George McConnell, is the
      original (tin) can which was submitted to the United States Patent Office
      along with the patent application, by Warren Van Vliet. A paper label
      attached to the can indicates that it was received by the patent office on
      Feb. 14, 1880. Another label indicates that patent #226,945 was issued
      on April 27th 1880 to Van Vliet of East Stroudsburg, Pennsylvania.

2878. THE VAN VLIET JAR OF 1881......................................Aqua $225-250
      Ground lip Glass lid Metal yoke clamp with   Clear $225-250
         thumbscrew, attached side wire extending   Amber $3000 & up
         vertically around entire jar. The wire goes
         over the face or embossed side of the jar.
         Lid: Pat. May 3d 1881

2879. THE VAN VLIET JAR OF 1881......................... ....Aqua $250-275
      Ground lip Glass lid Closure as in #2878
         except yoke is different shape, and the
         wire does not go over the face or embossed
         side of the jar
         Lid: Pat. May 3d 1881

2880. THE VAN VLIET JAR OF 1881......................... ...Aqua $250-275
      Ground lip Glass lid Closure as in #2878
         except yoke is different shape, and the
         wire does not go over the face of the jar
         Lid: Pat. May 3d 1881   #2878

2881. THE VAN VLIET IMPROVED PATD MAY 3-81.......... .....Aqua $300-350
      Ground lip Glass lid Closure as in #2878   Amber $3000 & up
         with the wire going over the face of the
         jar. Lid: Pat. May 3d 1881

2882. VEAZEY. FORBES. & CO WHEELING. W.V........... .Lt. Green $400-500
      Ground lip Metal rim around neck to form
         a wax seal channel. Tin lid

2883. VEGLA INMAAKGLAS NED. OCTR. AANGEUR (on lid). .....Clear $2-4
      Base: 2 Ltr.
      Glass lid & metal band clamp A Foreign jar   #2879

2884. VETERAN (bust of veteran, within circle, in frame).............Clear $15-20
      Smooth lip Old style Lightning seal   ½ Pint, Clear $20-25

2885. SEAL PAT. FEB. 24 1914 VICTOR JAR CO. DETROIT, MICH. (lid)....Clear $20-25
      Smooth lip Glass lid & 4 spring metal clips
      Jar & lid are square shaped

2886. THE VICTOR PATENTED 1899 (around M within diamond)............ Aqua $35-40
      Smooth lip Glass lid & metal buckle clamp   Clear $35-40

2887. THE VICTOR PAT.FEB. 20 1900 (around M within diamond)......... Aqua $35-40
      Smooth lip Glass lid & metal buckle clamp   Clear $35-40

2888. VICTORY.. Aqua $40-50
      Ground lip Glass cap and zinc screw band
      This jar does not have an indentation in the
         threads as found on the following Victory
         jars, and may be the earliest variation.

2889. VICTORY (encircled by) PATd FEBy 9th 1864
      REISd JUNE 22d 1867.............................. .. Aqua $30-35
      Ground lip Glass cap and zinc screw band
      Indentation in the bulged area of the neck

2890. VICTORY (encircled by) PATd FEBy 9th 1864
      REISd JUNE 22d 1867 (22 date is reversed)....... .. Aqua $35-40
      Ground lip Closure as in #2889

2891. VICTORY 1 (encircled by) PATd FEBy 9th 1864
      REISd JUNE 22d 1867 (all on front)..................... Aqua $30-35
      Ground lip Closure as in #2889   ½ Pint, Aqua $125-150

                              #2890

2892. VICTORY 1 (encircled by) PATd 9th 1864
REISd JUNE 22d 1867 (reversed 9)..............................Aqua $50-55
Ground lip Closure as in #2889 Pint   Clear $50-55

2893. VICTORY 1 (encircled by) PATd FEBy 9th 1864
REISd JUNE 22d 1867 (reversed s).............................Aqua $35-40
Ground lip Closure as in #2889

2894. VICTORY (encircled by) PATd FEBy 9th 1864
REISd JUNE 22d 1867 (all on front)............................Aqua $125-150
Reverse: PACIFIC S. F. GLASS WORKS
Ground lip Closure as in #2889

#2892

2895. VICTORY 1 (encircled by) PATd FEBy 9th 1864
REISd JUNE 22d 1867 (all on front)...........................Aqua $125-150
Reverse: PACIFIC SAN FRANCISCO GLASS WORK   Amber   Unpriced
Ground lip Closure as in #2889

2896. VICTORY 1 (encircled by) PATd FEBy 9th
REISd JUNE 22d 1867 (all on front)...........................Aqua $125-150
Reverse: PACIFIC SAN FRANCISCO GLASS WORK   Lt. Green $125-150
Ground lip Closure as in #2889

2897. VICTORY (within shield) on lid.....................................Clear $8-10
Base: Kivlan & Onthank Boston Victory 3 Patd.
Smooth lip Glass lid & twin wire clamps, &
neck tie wire

2898. VICTORY (within shield) THE VICTORY JAR (on lid)..............Clear $8-10
Base: Kivlan Onthank Pat'd June 28'21 Boston
Smooth lip Glass lid & twin wire clamps, &
neck tie wire

2899. VICTORY (within shield) THE VICTORY JAR (on lid)..............Clear $8-10
Base: Kivlan Onthank Pat'd June 28 '21
Victory Boston
Smooth lip Closure as in #2898

2900. VICTORY (within shield) THE VICTORY JAR (on lid)..............Clear $8-10
Base: Kivlan Onthank Boston   ½ Pint, Clear $10-12
Victory Pat'd April 2, 1929   ¼ Pint, Clear $10-12
Smooth lip Glass lid & twin metal clips, &
neck tie wire
Metal clips: Pat'd Apr 2 1929

2901. VICTORY (within shield) CROWN VICTORY JAR (lid).........Clear $10-12
Base: Crown Cork & Seal Co. Baltimore, Md.
Patented Victory Jar
Smooth lip Milkglass lid, twin metal clips &
neck tie wire
Metal clips: Pat. No. 1,707,439

2902. VICTORY (within shield) THE VICTORY JAR (on lid)   Clear $8-10
Base: Smalley Kivlan & Onthank Boston
Pat'd Feb. 23 09 Victory Jar
Smooth lip Glass lid, twin metal clamps, &
neck tie wire
Metal clamps: Patd Feb. 23.09

#2902

2903. VICTORY REG'D 1925 (on lid)...................................Clear $4-6
Smooth lip Glass lid, twin clamps & neck   ½ Pint, Clear $8-10
tie wire

2904. VICTORY HOM-PAK MASON.......................................Clear $1-3
Smooth lip Mason beaded neck seal

2905. W (on base)... Aqua $3-5
    Groove ring wax sealer, pressed laid-on ring

2906. WALES (on base)... Aqua $15-18
    Ground lip   Metal or glass press-down lid
    Glass lid: Patented Dec. 17 1878

2907. GEO. E. WALES NEWTON CENTRE MASS. PAT. JULY 11 1893
    VJC Co. (all on base)................................. Clear $12-15
    Ground lip   Glass lid & 3 position wire clamp

    WALLACEBURG GEM, see jar No. 1090

2908. WAMPOLE'S MILK FOOD........................... Aqua $3-5
    Ground lip   Metal screw lid   Product jar

2909. WAN-ETA COCOA BOSTON........................ ..Quart, Aqua $4-6
    Smooth lip   Mason beaded neck seal   Quart, Amber $4-6
    Product jar   16 Oz, Amber $6-8
                                   8 Oz, Amber $6-8
           #2909   8 Oz, Clear $6-8

2910. WAN-ETA COCOA ONE POUND (on lid)...........   Unpriced
    Tin can   Screw cover
    This can from the Ed Schwenessen collection, has a
      paper label which reads: Sanitary Notice Fruits and Vegatable Canister.
    Use Rubber Ring And Seal Same as Glass Jar. If wrapped in several sheets of
    thick brown paper, and sealed with rubber ring, this canister will keep hot and
    cold liquids at the same temperature for a considerable time.

2911. THE WARSAW SALT CO. (WGCo) TRADEMARK CHOICE TABLE SALT
    WARSAW, N.Y. (all on front of jar)................................Amber $25-30
    Ground lip   Mason shoulder seal   Product jar

2912. WAUWIL (on lid)..................................Clear   -$1
    Smooth lip   Glass lid & wire clamp   Green   -$1
    Modern Swiss jar

2913. WEARS (on banner, below Crown)....................Clear $12-15
    Base: Smalley, Kivlan & Onthank, Boston,
        Mass. Patd. Feb 23 09
    Smooth lip   Glass lid & twin wire clamps
    Lid: Wears (within shield)
    Oval shaped jar

                                        #2913

2914. WEARS (on banner, below Crown)......................................Clear $12-15
    Base: Smalley, Kivlan & Onthank, Boston,
        Pat'd Feb 23 09 (I within diamond trademark)
    Smooth lip   Closure as in #2913   Oval shaped jar

2915. WEARS (within circle or oval)........................Aqua $10-12
    Smooth lip   Old style Lightning seal

2916. THE WEARS JAR (within circle or oval)............ ..Aqua $10-12
    Smooth lip   Old style Lightning seal

2917. THE WEARS JAR (within circle or oval)............ .Clear $10-12
    Base: Patented Jan. 5 1904
    Smooth lip   Old style Lightning seal
    The sealing surface has a slight annular groove
    & one small thread on the neck, as called for
    in the patent.

                                        #2917

2918. THE WEARS JAR (within stippled frame)........................Clear $10-12
      Smooth lip Old style Lightning seal

2919. THE WEARS JAR (within stippled oval)........................Clear $10-12
      Smooth lip Old style Lightning seal   ½ Pint, Clear $12-15
      Oval shaped jar

2920. THE WEARS JAR (within stippled oval)........................Clear $10-12
      Base: Patented Feb 23 1909   ½ Pint, Clear $12-15
      Smooth lip Glass lid & twin wire clamps
      Oval shaped jar

2921. WEAVER COSTELLO & CO. PITTSBURGH...............   ..Clear $1-2
      Smooth lip Mason beaded neck seal
      Product jar

2922. WEBSTER'S PATENT FEB. 16. 1864................   . Aqua $500 & up
      Ground lip Metal lid. Metal band around   Clear $500 & up
      neck with soldered wire loops. A spring
      steel bar goes thru the wire loops to
      hold on the lid. Rounded shoulders.
      Only about 5 jars are known & these have
      sold considerably higher than book price.   #2922

2923. WEBSTERS PATENT FEB 16 1864................   ....Aqua $500 & up
      Ground lip Closure as in #2922
      Straight sided jar

2924. WEBSTER'S PATENT FEB 16 1864 (front).......   .... Aqua $500 & up
      Reverse: PATENT SEPT 18. 1860   Clear $500 & up
      Ground lip Closure as in #2922
      The jar has a shallow, flat groove around
      the top for a rubber gasket.   #2923

2925. PATENTED WEBSTERS SEPT 18 1860 FEB 16 1864 ...   ..Clear   Unpriced
      (All in ghost lettering)
      Wax seal groove, formed by downward pressure
      on the blowpipe while form was still hot.

2926. WECK (within a strawberry)................   .Clear $4-6
      Base: Weck or Original Weck
      Ground lip Glass lid & metal clamp
      German jar

2927. WECK (within a strawberry)................   .Clear $4-6
      Smooth lip Glass lid & double wire clamp
      Lid: Weck (in strawberry) Massivrand-95
      German jar   #2925

2928. ORIGINAL J. W. WECK 1 LTR. (within heart & banners)...........Clear $4-6
      Base: Original Weck
      Ground lip Glass lid & metal band clamp
      Lid: The Original Weck Weck (in center)
      German jar

2929. SCHUTZMARKE 3 W. FRISCHHALTUNG (heart & banners)..............Clear $4-6
      Base: Weck
      Ground lip Glass lid & metal band clamp
      German jar

2930. WEIDEMAN (above boy with platter in hand) ....Pint, Clear $4-6
      Smooth lip Lightning beaded neck seal
      Product jar

2931. WEIDEMAN BOY BRAND CLEVELAND (boy with platter in hand)........Clear $4-6
      Smooth lip Lightning beaded neck seal
      Product jar

2932. THE WEIR STONE FRUIT JAR 1 PT.. $15-18
    White stoneware jar, black stenciling
    Lid: The Weir Pat'd Mar 1st 1892
    Stoneware lid, wire & metal clamp

2933. THE WEIR PAT'D MAR 1st 1892 (on lid)....... $8-10
    Stoneware jar & lid, wire & metal clamp
    Lid & upper part of jar are brown, body
      of jar white.

2934. THE WEIR PATENTED MARCH 1st 1892 (on lid).............. $12-15
    Amber glass lid on white stoneware jar   #2932
    Wire & metal clamp

2935. PAT. MARCH 1st 92 APRIL 16th 1901 No. 1 (on lid)........ $10-12
    WEIR J MONMOUTH (within circle, on shoulder)
    White stoneware jar & lid
    Wire & metal clamp   Approx 2/3 Pint size

2936. THE WEIR PAT. MARCH 1st 92 APRIL 16, 1901 No. 4 (on lid) $10-12
    White stoneware jar & lid Wire & metal clamp   #2933

2937. WEIR SEAL NO. 4 WESTERN STONEWARE CO. MONMOUTH, ILLINOIS (lid)...... $8-10
    Two-tone brown over-glaze on shoulders, lid &
      body of jar white. Wire & metal clamp

2938. WEIR SEAL NO. 5 WESTERN STONEWARE CO. MONMOUTH, ILLINOIS (lid)...... $8-10
    All white stoneware jar & lid Wire & metal clamp

2939. W. E. WELDING BRANTFORD, ONT... $20-25
    Dark brown stoneware jar, marking incised
    Wax seal groove

2940. WELLMAN PANTRY JAR (on two upper panels).....................Clear $4-6
    Base: Patent Applied For   Lt. Amber $15-18
    Smooth lip Mason beaded neck seal   Smoke $4-6

    WELLS & PROVOST, see jar No. 2687 & 2688
    WENDELL & EPSY, see jar No. 937

2941. MANUFACTURED FOR H. F. WEST CINCINNATI, O......................Aqua $125-150
    Stopper neck finish for Kline stopper

2942. WESTERN PRIDE PATENTED JUNE 22, 1875 (all erased)..............Aqua $20-25
    Reverse, heel: E. H. E. 1
    Base: N within star
    Groove ring wax sealer, pressed laid-on ring

2943. WESTERN PRIDE PATENTED JUNE 22, 1875 (all erased)....Aqua $20-25
    Base: N within star
    Groove ring wax sealer, pressed laid-on ring

2944. WESTERN PRIDE PATENTED JUNE 22, 1875 (all erased)..Aqua $18-20
    Base: Unmarked
    Groove ring wax sealer, pressed laid-on ring

2945. WESTERN PRIDE PATENTED JUNE 22 1875..............Aqua $125-150
    Base: N within star   Clear $125-150
    Smooth lip Glass lid with dual ramps, &
      raised bar in center. Metal clamp
    Lid: Patented June 22 1875

                                                                #2945

2946. WESTERN STONEWARE CO. PAT JAN 24 1899 (on base).................... $10-12
    White stoneware jar, brown shoulders Zinc lid

2947. WESTERN STONEWARE CO. MONMOUTH, ILLINOIS (on lid)................... $8-10
    Stoneware jar & lid Wire & metal clamp
    Found in white stoneware, blue stoneware & reddish brown
      stoneware.

2948. WESTERN STONEWARE CO. MONMOUTH, ILLINOIS (on lid)................... $8-10
    Stoneware jar & lid Wire & metal clamp
    Brown jar & lid

2949. WEYMAN'S COPENHAGEN SNUFF (within frame) ....Amber $85-100
    Groove ring wax sealer, pressed laid-on ring
    Tin lid embossed: Copenhagen Satisfies

2950. WEYMAN'S COPENHAGEN·TRADE MARK SNUFF (framed).........·.....Amber $85-100
    Groove ring wax sealer, pressed laid-on ring
    Glass lid: Weyman's Copenhagen Snuff Pittsburgh, Pa.

2951. W. G. & CO. (on base)..............................Aqua $18-20
    Groove ring wax sealer, pressed laid-on ring

2952. W. G. CO. (on base)..............................Aqua $18-20
    Groove ring wax sealer, pressed laid-on ring

2953. WHEELER FRUIT JAR (on base)......................Aqua $50-75
    Ground lip Glass lid & wire clamp
    Lid: RW (monogram) Pat. Applied For
    Or: Wheeler Fruit Jar Trademark

#2949

2954. WHEELING (on lower front of jar)................................Clear $12-15
    Ground lip Glass lid & screw band
    Design around shoulder of jar
    Lid: N W G Co. within circles Product jar

2955. J. M. Whitall'S PATENT APRIL 11 1865............................Aqua $150-175
    (Marked on underside of glass stopper only)
    Hollow glass stopper, with a ground lip, and
    an opening on top which was plugged with a
    small cork.

2956. WHITALL TATUM & CO. PHILADELPHIA NEW YORK
    PAT JUNE 11th 1895 (all on lid)................Clear $30-40
    Base: pontil scar
    Ground lip Glass lid & metal yoke clamp, with
          thumbscrew
    Lid has a glass fin with hole, on underside
    These were museum specimen jars, and were made
    in 18 sizes, ranging from ½ Pint to 7-Gallon.

#2956

2957. WHITALL TATUM & CO. PHILADELPHIA NEW YORK
    PAT JUNE 11th 1895 (all on lid)................................Clear $30-40
    Base: pontil scar
    Ground lip Glass lid & metal yoke clamp, with
          thumbscrew
    Lid has two glass fins with holes, on underside.

2958. WHITALL TATUM & CO. PHILADELPHIA NEW YORK (on lid)...Clear $30-40
    Base: pontil scar
    Ground lip Glass lid & metal yoke clamp, with
          thumbscrew
    Lid has two glass fins with holes on underside.

2959. WHITALL TATUM & CO. PHILADELPHIA NEW YORK (on lid)...Clear $40-50
    Base: pontil scar
    Ground lip Glass lid, with fins on underside
    Clamp: June 2 1903 Heavy metal clamp with wheel

#2959

2960. WHITE BEAR (bear) DURAND & KASPER CO. CHICAGO ILL..............Clear $10-12
    Smooth lip Old style Lightning seal
    Product jar

2961. WHITE CROWN MASON (within frame)................................Clear $6-8
      Smooth lip Mason beaded neck seal   Aqua $6-8
      Milkglass insert & screw band
      Insert: White Crown Pat 11-22-1910
         Or: White Crown Cap Pat 11-22-10
         Or: White Crown Pat 11-22-1910
             Vacuum Mason Jar Cap

2962. WHITE HOUSE (the White House) VINEGAR.................   ...Clear $10-12
      Smooth lip Glass insert & screw band
      Insert: embossed picture of the White House
      Product jar found in various sizes, as well
        as jugs.

2963. WHITE KING WASHES EVERYTHING (on two sides)........ Green $2-3
      Neck: White King Washes Everything Pat.
         Appld. For Sep. 3-30 No. 5813
      Base: White King
      A soap dispenser jar

2964. WHITMORE'S PATENT ROCHESTER N.Y.................... Aqua $125-150
      Ground lip Glass lid with double fins
      Wire bail with ends hooking into dimples in neck   #2965
      Lid: Patented Jany 14th 68
      Mold numbers are often found on reverse side of jar

2965. WHITMORE'S PATENT ROCHESTER N.Y.................... Aqua $130-155
      Reversed N in Patent
      Ground lip Closure as in #2964

2966. WHITMORE'S PATENT............................... Aqua $150-175
      A plated mold was used to block out other
        marking on the jar.
      Ground lip Glass lid with double fins, slot
         on bottom edge
      Lid: Patented Jany 14th 68 Wire bail as in #2964   #2966

2967. WHITNEY.. Aqua $200-250
      Base: Whitney Glass Works, Glassboro N.J.
      Ground lip Threaded glass lid & zinc screw band
      Lid: 2 raised glass knobs on top, and marked:
        Patented June 12th 1866

2968. THE WHITNEY MASON PAT'D 1858..................... Aqua $15-20
      Smooth lip Mason shoulder seal   Amber $300 & up
      About 12 amber jars are presently known

2969. THE WHITNEY MASON PAT'D 1858..................... Aqua $15-20
      Ground lip Mason shoulder seal
                             #2969

    The following Whitney jars, No. 2970 thru 2999, all have a smooth lip and are Mason
     shoulder seal jars. The "dots" found on some jars are likely vent holes in the mold,
     but nevertheless, create an interesting series. At the request of several collectors,
     we have included all of the variations reported to us.

2970. WHITNEY MASON PAT'D 1858... Aqua $6-8

2971. WHITNEY MASON 1 PAT'D 1858....................................... Aqua $6-8

2972. WHITNEY MASON 1 PAT'D 1858 (6 dots below Whitney)............. Aqua $6-8

2973. WHITNEY MASON 2 PAT'D 1858....................................... Aqua $6-8

2974. WHITNEY MASON 3 PAT'D 1858....................................... Aqua $6-8
                                             Lt. Olive Green $12-15

2975. WHITNEY MASON 3 PAT'D 1858 (3 dots below Mason)... .... Aqua $6-8
      Base: B within circle

2976. WHITNEY MASON 4 PAT'D 1858.......................... ... Aqua $6-8

2977. WHITNEY MASON PAT'D 1858 4 (near base line)..... ... Aqua $6-8

2978. WHITNEY MASON 5 PAT'D 1858.......................... ... Aqua $6-8

2979. WHITNEY MASON 6 PAT'D 1858.......................... ... Aqua $6-8

2980. WHITNEY MASON PAT'D 1858 6 (near base line)...... ... Aqua $6-8

2981. WHITNEY MASON 6 PAT'D 1858 (4 dots above & 5 dots below Mason). Aqua $6-8

2982. WHITNEY MASON 7 PAT'D 1858....................... ... Aqua $6-8

2983. WHITNEY MASON 8 PAT'D 1858 (4 dots below Mason)............... Aqua $6-8

2984. WHITNEY MASON 9 PAT'D 1858 .... Aqua $6-8
     Reversed 9   3 dots below Whitney

#2976

2985. WHITNEY MASON 12 PAT'D 1858............................. Aqua $6-8

2986. WHITNEY MASON 13 PAT'D 1858 (7 dots below Whitney)............ Aqua $6-8

2987. WHITNEY MASON PAT'D 1858 (3 dots below Mason)................. Aqua $6-8

2988. WHITNEY MASON PAT'D 1858 (4 dots below Mason)................. Aqua $6-8

2989. WHITNEY MASON PAT'D 1858 (5 dots below Mason)................. Aqua $6-8

2990. WHITNEY MASON PAT'D 1858 (1 dot above, 5 dots below Mason)..... Aqua $6-8

2991. WHITNEY MASON PAT'D 1858 (2 dots above, 5 dots below Mason).... Aqua $6-8

2992. WHITNEY MASON PAT'D 1858 (4 dots above, 5 dots below Mason).... Aqua $6-8

2993. WHITNEY MASON PAT'D 1858 (5 dots above, 5 dots below &
               1 dot each side of Mason)........... Aqua $6-8

2994. MASON PAT'D 1858 (without word Whitney)....................... Aqua $6-8
     (2 dots above & 5 dots below Mason)

2995. MASON PAT'D 1858 (without word Whitney)....... ... Aqua $6-8
     (3 dots above & 5 dots below Mason)

2996. MASON PAT'D 1858 (without word Whitney)...... ...... Aqua $6-8
     (1 dot above & 5 dots below Mason)

2997. WHITNEY (erased) MASON PAT'D 1858............. ... Aqua $6-8
     (1 dot above & 5 dots below Mason)

2998. WHITNEY (erased) MASON PAT'D 1858............. ...... Aqua $6-8
     (4 dots below Mason)

#2996

2999. WHITNEY MASON PAT'D 185ε (all erased except word MASON........ Aqua $6-8

3000. PATd MARCH 26th 1867 B. B. WILCOX.............................. Aqua $50-60
     Ground lip Glass lid with high center fin
     Wire bail, narrow metal band around neck to
      hold ends of the wire bail
     Lid: with or without "rayed" pattern
     This variation has tapered shoulders, while the
      following Wilcox jars have squarish shoulders.

3001. PATd MARCH 26th 1867 B. B. WILCOX............................. Aqua $50-60
        Ground lip Glass lid with high center fin
        Wire bail, narrow metal band around neck to
          hold the ends of the bail.
        Lid: With or without the "rayed" pattern
        Unmarked lids have been found in milkglass &
          in amber.

3002. PATd MARCH 26th 1867 B. B. WILCOX 1............... Aqua $50-60
        Base: W. J. Co. (for Wilcox Jar Co.)
        Ground lip Closure as in #3001

3003. PATd MARCH 26th 1867 B. B. WILCOX 2............ Aqua $50-60

3004. PATd MARCH 26th 1867 B. B. WILCOX 3............ Aqua $50-60

#3004

3005. PATd MARCH 26th 1867 3 B. B. WILCOX............................ Aqua $50-60

3006. PATd MARCH 26th 1867 7 B. B. WILCOX............................ Aqua $50-60

3007. PATd MARCH 26th 1867 B. B. WILCOX 17............................ Aqua $50-60

3008. PATd MARCH 26th 1867 B. B. WILCOX 18............................ Aqua $50-60

3009. PATd MARCH 26th 1867 B. B. WILCOX 21............................ Aqua $50-60
        All with ground lip Closure as in #3001

3010. A. A. WILCOX PHILA. PAT'D MARCH 19 1872 (on lid)................... $300 & up
        Base: A. A. W.
        Tin can. Metal cover & iron ring, which engages
          on hook shaped lugs on top of the can.

      WILLIAMS & BATTERSON, see jar No. 419

3011. WILLIAMS & REPPERT GREENSBORO, PA................................... $40-50
        Gray stoneware jar with blue stenciling
        Wax seal groove

3012. J. D. WILLOUGHBY 2 3/8 PATENTED JANUARY 4 1859.................Aqua $50-60
        On metal stopper with wingnut Jar is unmarked

3013. J. D. WILLOUGHBY 2¼ PATENTED JANUARY 4 1859......   ..Aqua $50-60
        On metal stopper with wingnut Jar is unmarked

3014. J. D. WILLOUGHBY 2¼ PATENTED JANUARY 4 1859......   ..Aqua $100-125
        On metal stopper with wingnut Jar is unmarked
        Base: 3 "feet"   ½ Gallon size

3015. J. D. WILLOUGHBY PATENTED JANUARY 4 1859..........   .Clear $200-225
        On metal stopper with wingnut Jar is unmarked
        Base: Pontil scar   Size: Gallon+
        Also has been reported in slightly less than Gallon   #3012

3016. J. D. WILLOUGHBY PATENTED JANUARY 4 1859...................Clear $50-60
        On metal stopper with wingnut Jar is unmarked
        Base: High kick-up, no pontil scar

3017. J. D. WILLOUGHBY PATd JAN 4 1859..............................Clear $60-75
        On wingnut of metal stopper Jar is unmarked   Lt. cobalt Blue $200 & up
        Base: High kick-up, with pontil scar

3018. WILSON & WEBB PATENT MARCH 24th 1903..........................Aqua $150-200
        Ground lip Shoulder seal with 3 horizonal
          lugs on the neck instead of threads
        Metal cover with 3 inside lugs, "petal"
          pattern on top of lid

3019. THE WINNER..noted in historical records but a jar with this
      marking has not been reported by collectors

3020. WING WAH SING & CO. (vertically) Chinese characters...........Clear $3-5
      Smooth lip Lightning dimple neck seal Product jar

3021. THE WINSLOW IMPROVED VALVE JAR................................. Aqua $175-200
      Ground lip Glass lid & iron yoke clamp with thumbscrew
      Lid: Pat. April 12th 1870

3022. WINSLOW JAR... Aqua $45-50
      Ground lip Glass lid & wire clamp
      Lid: Patented Nov. 29. 1870

3023. WINSLOW JAR... Aqua $45-50
      Ground lip Glass lid & wire clamp
      Lid: Patented Nov. 29 1870 Patented Feb. 25 1873

3024. WINSLOW PATENTED NOV. 29 1870 PAT. FEB. 25 1873 (on base)...... Aqua $100-125
      Ground lip Unmarked glass lid & wire clamp
      Pint, shaped like the Cohansey jelly jars, but has a
        glass lid, while the Cohansey has a metal lid.

3025. PJR PATENTED NOV. 29 1870 PAT FEB. 25 1873 (on base)........... Aqua $100-125
      Ground lip Closure and shape as in #3024

3026. WO HOP COMPANY 759 CLAY ST. SAN FRANCISCO CALIF USA............Clear $3-5
      Reverse: Chinese characters
      Smooth lip Lightning dimple neck seal Product jar

3027. WOODBURY.. Aqua   -$25
      Base: Woodbury Glass Works Woodbury N.J.   ½ Pint, Aqua $75-100
      Ground lip Glass lid with vent hole, metal band clamp,
                  & mini screw cap
      Lid: Patd Nov 25 1884 Mar 3d 85
      Mini-cap: Pat Nov. 25 84 Mar 3d 85

3028. WOODBURY WGW (monogram)....................................... Aqua   -$25
      Base & closure as in #3027   ½ Pint, Aqua $75-100

3029. WOODBURY IMPROVED WGW (monogram)............................. Aqua   -$25
      Base: Woodbury Glass Works Woodbury N. J.   Amber   Unpriced
      Ground lip Glass lid with vent hole, zinc screw ½ Pint, Aqua $75-100
        cover & mini screw cap
      Lid: Patd Nov 25 84 Mar 3d 85 Mar 16 86 June 29 86
      Zinc cover: Woodbury Improved Patented Nov. 25 84
                  Mar 3 85 June 29 86 Mar 16 86

#3021   #3022   #3024   #3025   #3027   #3028   #3029

3030. WOODBURY WGW IMPROVED...Lt. Aqua   Unpriced
      Reverse: ½ pint, pint & quart measurements,
          ounce graduations
      Ground lip Glass lid with vent hole, zinc screw cover
          & mini screw cap
      Lid: Clear, no marking
      Zinc cover: Woodbury Improved Patented Nov 25 84
          Mar 3 85 June 29 86 Mar 16 86
      Straight sided jar, possibly used for butter, or as
      a sterilizer jar as in #3031

3031. WOODBURY WGW TRADEMARK STERILIZER (within circle)..............Aqua   Unpriced
      Reverse: measurements
      Ground lip Glass lid with vent hole, zinc cover &
          mini screw cap
      The jars are approximately 5½ tall and were used to
      sterilize infant's formula. A set consisted of 4
      jars & a wire rack.

3032. WOODS FRUIT JAR (around shoulder)...............................Aqua $150-175
      Applied lip Waxed cork closure

3033. WOOD & SELICK MANUFACTURING CHEMISTS NEW YORK................Lt Green $12-15
      Reverse: ½ GALLON IMPERIAL BRAND
      Ground lip Old style Lightning seal Product jar

3034. WORCESTER...Aqua $85-100
      Stopper neck finish, glass stopper with high center
      fin, notch in outside edge
      Stopper: Patd June 10 1862 Reisd Mar 28 65
          & Patentd Jan 2. 1866

3035. JOSHUA WRIGHT PHILAD 2 ....Aqua $275-300
      Base: Bare iron pontil scar
      Fruit bottle, somewhat barrel shaped

3036. JOSHUA WRIGHT PHILAD 2..Aqua $150-200
      Base: Without pontil scar
      Fruit bottle, somewhat barrel shaped

3037. W. T. Co (on base)...Aqua $1-3
      Smooth lip Metal screw lid   Amber $2-4
      Product jar

3038. W. W. V. A. S. F. & Co. (on base)..............................Aqua $20-25
      Groove ring wax sealer, pressed laid-on ring

#3035

3039. YEOMAN'S FRUIT BOTTLE (around shoulder)......................Aqua $40-50
      Waxed cork closure

3040. YEOMAN'S FRUIT BOTTLE (front shoulder).......................Aqua $40-50
      Reverse shoulder: PATENT APPLIED FOR
      Waxed cork closure

3041. 1 LB. NET YORK PEANUT BUTTER.................................Clear $1-3
      Reverse: Man milking a peanut cow
      Base: Canada Packers Limited
      Smooth lip Mason beaded neck seal
      Canadian product jar

#3039

3042. FL. 16 OZ. YORK PEANUT BUTTER ....Clear $1-3
      Reverse: Fl. 16 OZ. Man milking a peanut cow
      Base & closure as in #3041 Product jar

3043. YOUNG'S PAT. MAY 27 1902 (on lid)................................... $12-15
     White stoneware jar, brown neck & lid
     Wire & metal clamp

3044. THE ZETLAND AIRTITE...........................Clear $18-20
     Smooth lip Mason beaded neck seal
     An Australian jar

3045. W. ZETTLE J. H. STALLO (on glass lid).......... ... Aqua   Unpriced
     Lid, underside: Patent Entered 1862
     Jar is unmarked Metal clamp

#3045

ADDITIONAL WAX SEALERS & MISCELLANEOUS UNMARKED JARS

3046. Rectangular panel, slightly recessed (front)........ . Aqua $3-5
     Groove ring wax sealer, pressed laid-on ring

3047. 2 (on base)... .Aqua $3-5
     Groove ring wax sealer, pressed laid-on ring

     There are numerous wax sealer jars which are unmarked except
     for a number on the base. The makers of some can be identified
     by the style of the number used, but most are unidentifable as to
     maker.

3048. 3 (on base)... .Aqua $3-5
     Groove ring wax sealer, pressed laid-on ring
     The style of number on this jar identifies the
     maker as Hemingray.

#3046

3049. 4 (on base)...Aqua $3-5
     Groove ring wax sealer, pressed laid-on ring   Black $1000 & up
     The style of number on this jar identifies the
     maker as Hemingray.

     All of the known authentic black glass wax sealers have the mold
     numbers 4, 5, 6, or 7 on the base. The reproductions, which
     were made in Mexico, have a pontil scar on the base, and no
     mold number.

#3050	#3051	#3052	#3053
Aqua $3-5	Aqua $3-5	Aqua $3-5	Aqua $3-5

#3054
Aqua $3-5

#3055
Aqua $3-5

#3056
Aqua $3-5

#3057
Aqua $3-5

#3058

#3059

#3060

#3061

3058. Aqua.......$3-5

3059. Aqua.....$85-95 Vaseline.....Unpriced
       This wax sealer is attributed to Potter & Bodine,
         operating the Bridgeton Glass Works, Bridgeton, NJ

3060. Aqua.....Unpriced Light Cobalt Blue.....Unpriced

3061. Bell-shaped, base unmarked, no pontil scar....Aqua $50-75
       Bell-shaped, base with bare iron pontil scar..Aqua $125-150
       Bell-shaped, base with pontil scar...........Aqua $100-125

#3062

3062. Unmarked jar..Aqua $3-5   Amber $60-70
                     Clear $3-5   Deep Olive Green $50-60

3063. Unmarked jar..Aqua Unpriced

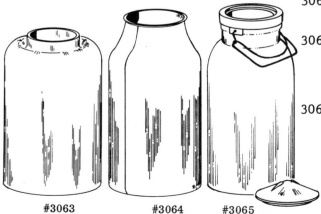

3064. Unmarked jar, in Pint & Quart
       Aqua...Unpriced

3065. Unmarked jar, paper label,
       Climax Peanut Butter, J. W.
       Beardsley's Sons Newark NJ
       USA   Clear...$1-3

3066. Unmarked jar, amber with
       milkglass lid. The milk-
       glass lid on this product
       jar is sometimes wrongly
       attributed to the amber
       Atlas E-Z Seal. $15-20

#3063   #3064   #3065

#3066

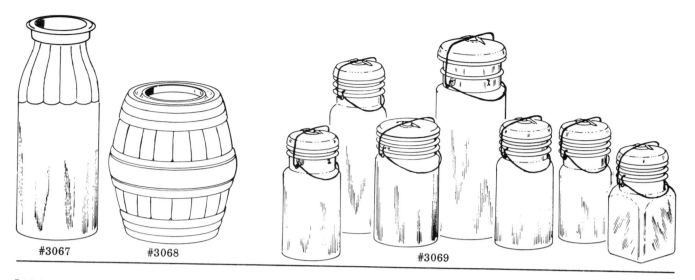

#3067

#3068

#3069

#3067..Petal jar, waxed cork closure. Base: Pontil scar or bare iron pontil scar
   Aqua..$150-175 Deep Green..Unpriced   Med. Cobalt blue..Unpriced

#3068..Unmarked Yellow-ware (pottery), with wax seal groove...$6-8

#3069..A grouping of small, unmarked, clear jars. Some were used to preserve small
   amounts of small seasoning foods, etc. Later type can be found in stores con-
   taining candies, bathsalts, soaps, etc...$1-2

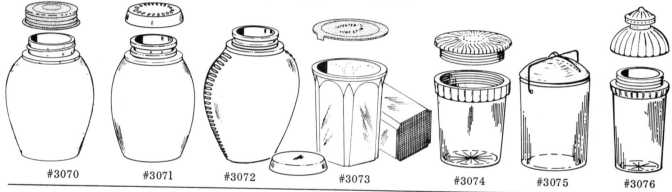

#3070   #3071   #3072   #3073   #3074   #3075   #3076

#3070..Unmarked in blue & white milkglass, tin screw cap...$20-25

#3071..Unmarked in blue & white milkglass, matching press-down lid with rubber gasket
   Some have hand-painted floral designs...$20-25

#3072..Unmarked in white milkglass, matching press-down lid. Oval shaped jar with
   zipper-pattern down sides. Hand-painted roses. $20-25

#3073..Clear jelly jar, tin lid marked: Patented June 27 1871...$8-10

#3074..Clear jar, screw threads on inside of neck, threaded glass lid.
   Lid marked inside: Pat Appd For Also found with threads on the outside of the
   neck. $8-10

#3075..Clear jelly jar, glass lid & wire bail, unmarked...$8-10

#3076..Clear jar, glass screw lid, unmarked...$8-10

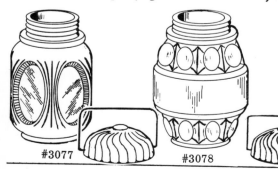

#3077   #3078

#3077..Unmarked jar, ground lip, glass screw cover
   with wire carrying handle. Clear..$25

#3078..Unmarked jar, ground lip, glass screw cover
   with wire carrying handle. Clear..$25
   Also found in amber..$25

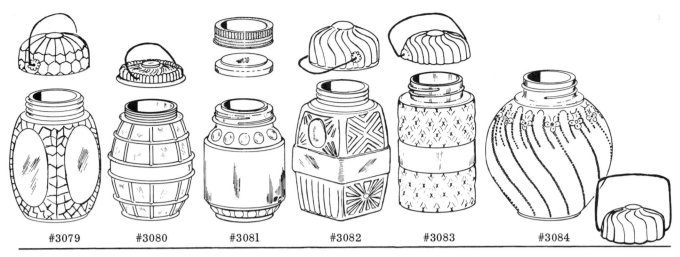

| #3079 | #3080 | #3081 | #3082 | #3083 | #3084 |

#3079..Unmarked jar, ground lip, glass screw lid, wire carrying handle..Clear.....$25

#3080..Unmarked jar, smooth lip, glass screw lid, wire carrying handle..Clear.....$25

#3081..Unmarked jar, smooth lip, glass insert & screw band..............Clear.....$20

#3082..Unmarked jar, ground lip, glass screw lid, wire carrying handle..Clear.....$25

#3083..Unmarked jar, ground lip, glass screw lid, wire carrying handle..Clear.....$25

#3084..Unmarked jar, ground lip, glass screw lid, wire carrying handle..Clear.....$25

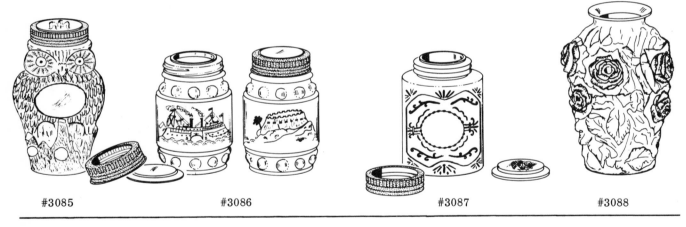

| #3085 | #3086 | #3087 | #3088 |

#3085..White milkglass owl, milkglass insert & screw band. First made by Atterbury,
    later reproduced by Imperial Glass Company in milkglass with yellow glass eyes
    pasted into place...$75-100

#3086..Jar with the Battleship Maine & the Morro Castle embossed. Ground lip, insert
    & screw band closure...Clear...$45-50 Milkglass...$75-100

#3087..Unmarked jar, ground lip, glass insert with Eagle, & screw band closure
    Snuff jar...Clear...$10-12   Amber...$15-18

#3088..Goofus Glass pickle jar in rose pattern. Known in 3 sizes, 5" tall, 7" tall, &
    12" tall. Made in clear & milkglass, and originally covered with a somewhat
    gaudy paint. The paint was not baked on and wore off rather easily. The jars
    were made in clear, milkglass and light green, and in a number of patterns. We
    have illustrated only one. Clear...$7-10 Milkglass...$20-25

3089. BALL (superimposed over erased BOYD) PERFECT MASON........Lt. Green $2-3
       Smooth lip Mason beaded neck seal

3090. BALL (superimposed over erased BOYDS) PERFECT MASON.......Lt. Green $2-3
       Smooth lip Mason beaded neck seal

3091. BALL ECLIPSE (with word Eclipse in slug plate, &
       erased Pat'd July 14, 1908) all on front.................. Clear $1-2
       Smooth lip Lightning beaded neck seal
       Square jar

3092. THE BALL MASON'S PATENT NOV 30th 1858 (no crossbar on E)..... Aqua $6-8
       Ground lip Mason shoulder seal

3093. N. D. BATTERSON CANNED GOODS BUFFALO NY.............   Aqua   Unpriced
       Applied lip, stopper neck finish, cork stopper
       A small jar, holding approximately a ½ pint

3094. DREY IMPROVED EVER SEAL...........................   Clear $1-3
       Smooth lip Lightning dimple neck seal

3095. FAXON BRAND COFFEE NET 1 LB (on base)............   Blue $6-8
       Smooth lip Glass insert & screw band
       Square shaped product jar. Also see No. 986

3096. T & H HALE FRUIT JAR PAT. JANY 27th 1874..........   .....   Unpriced
       At present, only a wooden prototype of this jar
       is known. Patent #146,824 issued to Thomas Hale
       And Henry Hale, Of Wales, N. Y., called for a glass lid and
       screw band. The band had a flat metal band raised over the
       top, with a hole on each side, thru which a metal bar was
       inserted to aid in opening the jar. The shoulder of the jar
       is octagon shape, and the patent called for a jar wrench to
       be used on the shoulder.

3097. HAZEL ATLAS EZ SEAL (with ghost Lightning)................... Aqua $8-10
       Smooth lip Old style Lightning seal   Clear $8-10

3098. HOOSIER JAR PATd SEPT 12th 1882 JAN 3d 1883 (lid)........... Aqua   Unpriced
       Jar is unmarked
       Ground lip Glass screw lid Also see jar No. 1266

3099. PATENTED IMPERIAL APRIL 20th 1886......................... Clear $125-150
       Base: Mold number
       Ground lip Glass lid with outside ramps & wire clamp
       Lid: Patented Imperial April 20th 1886
       Also see jar No. 1293

3100. KERR SELF SEALING WIDE MOUTH MASON (front)................. Clear   Unpriced
       Reverse: LOUIS EATON 42 YEARS OF FAITHFUL SERVICE
                 2-26-35 TO 2-28-77
       Smooth lip Mason beaded neck seal Modern closure
       One of a number of presentation jars which have been
       made by Kerr honoring key personnel. Not offered for sale.

3101. PATENT PENDING (on lid)................................... Aqua   Unpriced
       No marking on jar
       Same shape and closure as on the profile Lafayette
       jar, No. 1450

3102. THE LIQUID CARBONIC COMPANY PAT'd JULY 14, 1908 (on base).... Clear $1-2
       Smooth lip Lightning dimple neck seal
       ½ Gallon product jar. Also see jars No. 1510 & 1511

3103. MASON'S PATENT NOV 30th 1858................................. Aqua $2-4
        Base: X (Roman numeral)
        Ground lip Mason shoulder seal

3104. MASON'S PATENT NOV 30th 1858................................. Aqua $2-4
        Base: XVII (Roman numeral)
        Ground lip Mason shoulder seal
        Note: we have listed only two jars with
        Roman numerals on the base..others exist.

3105. MASON'S O PATENT NOV 30 1858 (no th)......... ..... Aqua $10-12
        Smooth lip Mason shoulder seal
        Also see jar No. 2011

3106. MASON'S PATENT NOV 30th 1858 (front)........ ....Clear $15-18
        Reverse: Y within a shield
        Ground lip Mason shoulder seal

3107. MASON'S 2 PATENT............................. ..... Aqua $3-5
        Smooth lip Mason shoulder seal
        Also see jars Nos. 1758 thru 1764

#3110

3108. MASON'S PATENTED JUNE 27th 1876 (with ghost NATIONAL)......... Aqua $75-100
        Ground lip Mason shoulder seal, regular zinc lid
        Also see jars Nos. 2129 & 2235

3109. PRESTO WIDE MOUTH GLASS TOP (front)...........................Clear   -$1
        Reverse: MANUFACTURED BY OWENS ILLINOIS PACIFIC COAST CO.
        Base: Owens Illinois trademark
        Smooth lip Mason beaded neck seal
        A pint has been reported in light olive green

3110. RAC ....Clear $20-25
        Lid: RAC Marque Deposee
        Smooth lip Glass lid, wire hinge & locking clamp
        Both jar and lid are made of extremely heavy glass
        A French jar

3111. THE SUN FRUIT JAR (on front)................................. Unpriced
        More information is needed on this jar

3112. VICTOR BUTTER SEAL PAT. FEB. 24 1914 PROTECTION JAR (on lid)..Clear $20-25
        Smooth lip Glass lid & 2 spring metal clips
        Jar & lid are square shaped
        Also see jar No. 2885

3113. Tin can, without marking...................................... Unpriced
        This can from the Richard Harris collection, is covered
        by Patent #59,699 issued to G. Williams, Of West Middleburg,
        Ohio on Nov. 13, 1866. Top of can is dome shaped with an
        opening at top. A flattish metal lid & a sealing gasket were
        placed over the opening with one tongue of the lid secured
        under a socket or catch soldered on the top of the can. The
        opposite tongue of the lid was placed over a small screw
        attached to the top of the can, and tightened down by a small
        square shaped nut.

NOTES

NOTES

NOTES